ISRAEL ISIDOR MATTUCK

Israel Isidor Mattuck
Architect of Liberal Judaism

PAM FOX

VALLENTINE MITCHELL
LONDON • PORTLAND, OR

First published in 2014 by Vallentine Mitchell

Middlesex House,
29/45 High Street, Edgware,
Middlesex HA8 7UU, UK

920 NE 58th Avenue, Suite 300
Portland, Oregon,
97213-3786 USA

First published in North America in 2016
www.vmbooks.com

British Library Cataloguing in Publication Data:
An entry can be found on request

ISBN 978 0 85303 878 8 (cloth)
ISBN 978 0 85303 879 5 (paper)
ISBN 978 0 85303 888 7 (ebook)

Library of Congress Cataloging in Publication Data
An entry can be found on request

Printed by TJ International, Padstow, Cornwall

This book is dedicated to Jill Mattuck Tarule in appreciation of all her support and her friendship

Contents

Illustrations

Foreword

Michael A. Meyer

A photograph, taken shortly after the Second World War, shows three principal leaders of Progressive Judaism: Leo Baeck, Lily Montagu and Israel Mattuck. Two of them are well known: Rabbi Leo Baeck, the heroic defender of German Jewry during the Nazi years and president of the World Union for Progressive Judaism; and Lily Montagu, together with Claude Montefiore, a founder of Liberal Judaism in England and a founder, as well, of the World Union. Much has been written about each of them. But the third figure in the photograph has until now remained far less known. And yet Rabbi Israel Isidor Mattuck, the man who firmly established Liberal Judaism in England and enabled it to flourish, is likewise a figure of importance. Fortunately, thanks to the diligent labors of Pam Fox, we now have not only the first full-scale biography of Mattuck, but also one that is likely to prove definitive.

Born in Lithuania, Israel Mattuck quickly erased traces of those origins as he grew up in a Jewish family in Worcester, Massachusetts, a family that, though Orthodox, encouraged his rapid Americanization. From the beginning, the young Mattuck sought to excel and succeed. He studied Semitics at Harvard and soon decided for the Reform rabbinate, believing that Reform Judaism combined the values of the academic world with those of his firmly held faith. At the Hebrew Union College he attached himself especially to its president at that time, the theologian Kaufmann Kohler, adopting both his intellectualism and his opposition to Zionism. Like other Eastern European Jews who became rabbis, including Nelson Glueck, a later president of Hebrew Union College, he married into the German-Jewish aristocracy, which provided him with both social status and financial stability. As Pam Fox stresses, enabled by his natural charisma, Mattuck sought ambitiously to reach the top of his profession.

Given his lofty goals, it is a bit surprising that he agreed to leave the United States – to which he always remained attached – for Great Britain and the leadership of what was then a small 'deviant' branch of English Jewry. Perhaps it was, as our author suggests, the desire to be 'a big fish in a small pond'. In that objective he was certainly successful, playing the central role in an expanding movement while using his rhetorical and organisational talents to take it beyond the narrow bounds set by Claude Montefiore and Lily Montagu. In his personal life Mattuck soon became very British, comfortable and content in the stratified British society. A Classical Reform Jew until his death in 1954, Mattuck consistently rejected political Zionism, the increased use of Hebrew, and the return of abandoned rituals. His Judaism consisted of a rationalistic but firm belief in God and in Prophetic morality. He was decidedly of the opinion that religion could not be separated from the moral issues in society and, though he engaged in dialogue with Christians, was wont to stress the differences between the two faiths. He would not conduct the wedding of a Jew with a Christian.

In this volume, which succeeds admirably in holding the reader's attention, Pam Fox has managed not only to detail Rabbi Mattuck's life based on an extensive array of primary and secondary sources, but to provide an understanding of her subject's motivations, objectives and shortcomings. This is a serious critical biography of a strong-willed, influential Jewish leader who deserves his place within the history not only of Liberal Judaism in Great Britain but also within that of the Reform movement as a whole.

Preface

The idea of writing a biography for Israel Isidor Mattuck, the United Kingdom's first Liberal rabbi, occurred to me towards the end of 2010 as I was finalising my book on the history of the Liberal Jewish Synagogue, the first Liberal synagogue in the UK (*A Place to Call My Jewish Home – Memories of the Liberal Jewish Synagogue 1911–2011*).[1] While compiling this book I had learned a little about Mattuck and was struck by the fact that, although he had occupied a very important position, appeared to have been a highly influential religious leader, and to have had a high public profile, no one had written a full-length account of his career. All that existed were a few short articles about him by Rabbi John Rayner, Senior Rabbi at the Liberal Jewish Synagogue from 1961–89, who had been inspired to become a rabbi by Mattuck.

When a year later I started to look into the possibility further, I discovered that a number of writers and commentators had highlighted the need for a detailed biography of Mattuck, including Rabbi Rayner.[2] I was surprised that no one had taken up the challenge to write the biography because the case for it seemed to be compelling.

In developing the Liberal Jewish Synagogue (LJS) and the Liberal Jewish movement, the Jewish Religious Union (JRU, subsequently the Union of Liberal and Progressive Synagogues, ULPS, and now Liberal Judaism), Mattuck did not work alone, but alongside Dr Claude Montefiore and the Honourable Lily Montagu, for both of whom he developed an immense respect and with whom he had a close and productive relationship. Retrospectively, Mattuck, Montagu and Montefiore became known as the 'Three Ms'. However, of the three, Israel Mattuck appears to have been by far the most influential in developing Liberal Judaism. Given that biographies have been written of both Claude Montefiore and Lily Montagu,[3] it mystified me that Mattuck's contribution had not been explored. I started to think of Mattuck as 'The Missing M'.

At the time of his death in 1954, Mattuck was hailed as a 'Jewish Archbishop of Canterbury'[4] and it was said that, had he been a British citizen rather than an American, he would have been honoured in some way. Sixty years have elapsed since his death and there are very few people alive with first-hand memories of him. As a result, recollections of just how eminent a figure he was in his day have faded. Those who never knew him may suspect that he was over-praised, but the extent of his achievements is undeniable.

I conducted some preliminary research on Mattuck and discovered that within a few years of his arrival from America in 1912 he was regularly speaking to large audiences, was in demand to give lectures and addresses, and frequently wrote or was cited in the Jewish and non-Jewish press. He led the LJS and the Liberal Jewish movement through two world wars and produced prayer books that provided the liturgy for the Liberal Jewish movement for over forty years. He was a man of many talents: he was intellectual and spiritual but also practical, a great organiser, a consummate chairman and eloquent writer. As a preacher and speaker he was said to be mesmerising and as a teacher he knew how to engage both the young and adults. All of this presented a picture of a man who was hugely important in Anglo-Jewish history, but whose career had been largely neglected – it deserved to be systematically explored.

When I started to discuss Mattuck with other people, many seemed to be aware of his role in galvanising the small Liberal Jewish Synagogue to become the largest congregation in England at the centre of a network of Liberal and Progressive communities. Fewer knew about his unique and more specific contributions. These, though documented in archival collections, had not been brought to public attention, especially his achievement in relation to interfaith dialogue. The papers I read showed that, from his early days in England, Mattuck was in contact with Christian clergy. He was one of the prime instigators in the setting up, in 1927, of the London Society of Jews and Christians, which he co-chaired for many years and which provided the model for the Council of Christians and Jews in 1942.

Equally uncharted were Mattuck's religious beliefs. Mattuck, it emerged, was primarily a man of action and not a prolific writer like Claude Montefiore. Many of his writings and sermons had not been analysed and were unpublished. Nevertheless, I came to realise that what he did write is significant and well-crafted, and an exploration of his writings, speeches, lectures, sermons, liturgy and other works reveals a great deal about the man and his theology that would form a substantial element of a biography.

Having become convinced of the case for a biography of Mattuck, I could not ignore it and I set out on the task of researching and writing Mattuck's life story. Although his interesting background immediately captured my attention, I could not have predicted just how riveting the story of Mattuck's life and career would prove to be and just how little his contribution had been understood.

Shortly after I started my research on Mattuck, I was alerted to the fact that Rabbi Danny Rich was also planning to fill the void. Having become aware of each other's intentions, Danny and I originally agreed to work together and set out to do so under the aegis of Liberal Judaism, although we later agreed to publish separately.

Mattuck's life story is an exceptional one not only because of his achievements and his fame, but also because of the twists and turns that it took. It was a life of great contrasts – his insular childhood in an Eastern European *shtetl* compared to the glittering dinners and other events held in high-class venues that were a regular feature of his adult life; his high public profile compared to the closely guarded private time with his beloved family and in scholarly pursuits; the very traditional Orthodox Judaism in which he was steeped as a young man compared to the radical form of Reform Judaism that he adopted in America and imported to the UK. His career was punctuated by controversy, stormy episodes and mystery, and unanswered questions surround some of his opinions and activities. It is the combination of all of these facets that renders his life so fascinating.

Before embarking on *Israel Isidor Mattuck: Architect of Liberal Judaism*, the impression that I had gained from the few articles about him was that Mattuck was something of a paragon – his talents were so outstanding that he was the only person who could possibly have filled the pulpit at the newly established Liberal Jewish Synagogue, he was universally revered by his congregation, he rose to prominence without any major hitches – and that when he died he was still at the height of his career and was surrounded by ardent disciples. The real picture was very different. Mattuck's life was much more complicated and colourful than might have been imagined from the scant biographical details that were available until now. Some of the discoveries that I made, especially about his early career, were spellbinding, and there are some things that he said and did that were extraordinary. Although this biography explodes some of the myths about Mattuck, I believe that at the same time it reveals a more interesting, rounded character and presents a more captivating story.

Chapters One to Three deal with Mattuck's family background, emigration to America, his childhood in Worcester, Massachusetts, and how the family fared in the 'New World'. I battled valiantly to obtain details of Mattuck's early life in Lithuania, returning to the task again and again, but in the end had to be content with snippets of information supplemented by material gleaned from general accounts of life in Lithuania at the time that Mattuck was born there. I was left with burning questions, such as: precisely why did the Mattuck family leave Lithuania when they did? And who was Mattuck's rabbinic grandfather? I was able to obtain more information about the family once they arrived in America, but the information available was not as detailed as I would have wished. Patchy records were helpfully supplemented by the memories of family members, but there remain a few gaps that ideally I would have liked to have been filled, such as the exact nature of Mattuck's relationship with his parents, especially his father. Notwithstanding these limitations, the early chapters provide vital insights into where Mattuck came from and his family environment, which had an indelible influence on the man he became and shaped his worldview.

In Chapters Four to Six we see Mattuck maturing into adulthood, becoming independent from his family and developing ambitious goals and a strong sense of what he wanted to achieve from life both socially and professionally. They cover the period in which he adopted his radical religious views and gained the skills and experience that equipped him to become a foremost Progressive rabbi and prominent religious leader.

Chapters Seven to Thirteen chronicle Mattuck's career once he received the 'call' to England. They describe his involvements, achievements and relationships, and also chart the evolution of his views. Initially my plan was to write a traditional biography, with an emphasis on data and chronology, and to have a separate section on Mattuck's writings, sermons and addresses. However, I soon decided to intersperse extracts from what he wrote and said into the narrative to help bring his story alive. This made the drafting more complicated, but I feel that the additional effort was worthwhile. A much clearer impression of Mattuck is gained from considering factual information alongside his views and opinions. At various points I digress to explore a particular event, a relationship or a certain aspect of Mattuck's career, and where relevant, I have provided contextual information such as geographical or historical details. While I have aimed to keep my personal interventions to a minimum, in a few places I have commented or offered interpretations hoping to enhance the story rather than detract from it.

To avoid interrupting the flow of the narrative, the chapters on Mattuck's career in England contain few details of his personal life, information on which is largely reserved for Chapter Fourteen, when we catch up with how he adapted to life in a country very different from America and with details of his marriage and family. Seemingly, Mattuck was a very private man who rarely wrote or talked about himself. The diary that he kept for three months at the beginning of 1918 is tantalising: it tells us in great detail what he was thinking and feeling at that time. Why didn't he keep a diary for longer? Mattuck's appalling handwriting (he referred to himself as a 'calligraphic sinner') did nothing to help matters – the few personal letters that have survived are virtually illegible.

Nevertheless it has been possible to compile a fairly coherent picture of his private life to accompany the account of his career that forms the main part of the book.

Chapter Fifteen describes Mattuck's final years, then the remaining chapters of the book provide an assessment of the type of man that Mattuck was, his religious outlook, his place in history and his legacy. When John Rayner called for a biography of Mattuck, he identified a number of questions about his life that needed to be addressed: What was the extent of the influence on Mattuck of American Reform Judaism and people such as Kaufmann Kohler? What did Mattuck think of, and to what extent did he go along with, the form of Liberal Judaism established before his arrival? How much did the way in which he developed Liberal Judaism owe to his own original thought rather than to American Reform Judaism or the JRU? What were his views about the relationship between the Liberal and Reform movements in England, and what was the nature of his relationship with Rabbi Harold Reinhart of West London (Reform) Synagogue? What was his attitude towards Zionism and, once it was established, the State of Israel? What was the extent of his impact on Christian attitudes to Judaism in this country? What was the role he played in the World Union for Progressive Judaism?[5] Some answers to these questions, along with a number of others, are to be found in the last chapters of the biography.

I found researching and writing about Mattuck's career immensely satisfying. I visited many different archives in the UK and in America, consulted a plethora of books and journals on a range of topics, read my way through a multitude of correspondence, manuscripts and other documents, spent week after week exploring relevant websites, and spoke to numerous people. These varied sources all produced rich and invaluable information, but special mention must be made of the collection of Mattuck's sermons, lectures and addresses which can be found at the London Metropolitan Archives.[6]

The two thousand or so documents provided excellent insights into Mattuck's views and beliefs, and also shed light on the topical events that formed the backdrop to his long career. In the time available, I was able to read less than half of the collection; I had to concentrate my attention on those most germane to the task of writing a biography.

After over two years of working on this biography of Israel Mattuck (or IIM as I came to know him and how he is referred to in the rest of the book) there will be something of a void in my life, but I am pleased that his life story can now be shared with others. I hope that readers will enjoy the story as much as I have enjoyed writing it.

Pam Fox
January 2014

NOTES

1. Pam Fox, *A Place to Call My Jewish Home, Memories of the Liberal Jewish Synagogue, 1911–2011* (London: Liberal Jewish Synagogue, 2011).
2. Letter from Rabbi John Rayner to Dr Ellen Umanksy, Emory University, 9 December 1982, LJS Archives, Box 1/2.
3. Lucy Cohen, *Some Recollections of Claude Montefiore, 1858–1938* (London: Faber and Faber, 1940); Daniel R. Langton, *Claude Montefiore: His Life and Thought* (London and Portland, OR: Vallentine Mitchell, 2002); Edward Kessler, *An English Jew: the Life and Writings of Claude Montefiore* (London and Portland, OR: Vallentine Mitchell, 2002); Ellen M. Umansky, *Lily Montagu and the Advancement of Liberal Judaism: From Vision to Vocation* (New York: Edwin Mellen, 1984); Eric V. Conrad, *Lily H. Montagu: Prophet of a Living Judaism* (New York, 1953).
4. 'Rabbi Israel I. Mattuck, 'Liberal Judaism in England', *Jewish Newsletter*, 26 April 1954.
5. See letter from Rabbi John Rayner to Dr Ellen Umansky.
6. The collection was temporarily housed at the Montagu Centre, the headquarters of Liberal Judaism, but is being moved to the London Metropolitan Archives.

Acknowledgements

First and foremost I want to thank Liberal Judaism, which commissioned the writing of the book and supported the research process. Rabbi Danny Rich, Chief Executive of Liberal Judaism with whom I collaborated during the research and writing process, made numerous contributions. Without Danny's support the book would not have got off the ground. He helped to plan and accompanied me on a highly successful research trip to America in the spring of 2012 that produced an unexpected amount of new material for me to absorb into the book on our return. Danny also introduced me to many useful contacts including a panel of academics who endorsed the book. He commented on numerous drafts of the manuscript and identified funding to help meet research costs. He provided more direct influence in the writing of Chapter Seventeen on Mattuck's faith. In particular, I benefitted from his ideas on Mattuck's belief in God, his interpretation of the teachings of the Prophets and the 'Mission of Israel' expressed in his unpublished paper, 'The Religious Views of IIM' written in August 2013. Although ultimately we decided to pursue separate publications, I am very grateful for all of Danny's assistance.

I want to extend my deep gratitude to members of IIM's family, who assisted me unstintingly in compiling his biography. Very early on in the process I made contact with Arthur Mattuck (Rabbi Mattuck's nephew) in Boston, USA, Robert Edgar (Mattuck's grandson) in East Sussex and Jill Mattuck Tarule (Mattuck's granddaughter) in Vermont, USA. They gave me access to family archives, shared their memories of Rabbi Mattuck, gave me feedback on drafts of the biography, donated papers and photographs and put me in touch with other family members who were able to provide additional material. I am indebted to them for all of this assistance but also for their unwavering enthusiasm about the project and their openness about Mattuck's foibles as well as his strengths. From them in particular I gained insights into Mattuck's personality. During the course of the research for the book I got to know Arthur, Jill and Rob and Robert and Sarah very well. They are no longer 'Mattuck relatives'; they are firm friends.

One of the additional family members I contacted as a result of introductions from IIM's close relatives was Michael Trapunsky, a distant paternal relation of Mattuck. He deserves a special mention because of his superb genealogical research on the Mattuck family that enhanced the early chapters of the biography. I am also grateful to Dr Mike Starrels, who helpfully gave me access to his family tree.

Although I took the lead on the research and writing for this biography and therefore any faults, mistakes and omissions are my responsibility, I did not work on my own. Numerous others contributed to the 'Mattuck enterprise'. However, I particularly want to thank Rosita Rosenberg, my 'Chief Researcher', for the countless hours she devoted to reading through copies of the *JRU Bulletin*, the *Liberal Jewish Monthly*, *LJS* newsletters and IIM's wartime letters to the armed forces, the meticulous work that she carried out in cataloguing IIM's sermons, lectures and addresses to complete the listings produced by Lionel Lassman, and the interviews she conducted with people who knew Mattuck. I am also grateful for the personal support and encouragement she offered me throughout the project. In preparing the manuscript for publication, Clare Rich's assistance was invaluable.

While gathering material for the book I visited a wide range of archives and was very impressed by the dedication of the people I encountered there. Many archivists went to great lengths to help me locate the documents I was looking for. However, I was particularly impressed by the professionalism, efficiency and helpfulness of the staff at the Jacob Rader Marcus Center of the American Jewish Archives (AJA) in Cincinnati, Ohio. I would like to say a very sincere and heartfelt thank you to Dr Gary Zola, Kevin Proffitt, Dr Dana Herman, Elisa Ho, Jeremy Katz and Michelle Detroit. These wonderfully committed people not only bent over backwards to assist me in Cincinnati, but without demur responded promptly to my numerous follow-up requests for information. Nothing, it seemed, was too much trouble for them.

There are many others who helped in various ways ranging from providing information on particular topics and reading drafts, to putting me in touch with people able to help me in some way, and guiding me to relevant documents and sources of information. I would like to express my gratitude to all of them and to say an especially warm 'thank you' to Rabbi Professor Marc Saperstein, for opening many doors in America and in helping to shape the biography, to Professor Jonathan Sarna, for his superlative advice and guidance, and to Professor Michael A. Meyer and Dr Amy Shevetz, whose encouragement during the early stages of the project was pivotal. I very much appreciated the advice and gentle counsel of my editor, Heather Marchant. Heather was a delight to work with.

Finally, I would like to mention my dear husband Michael Hart, who was forced to live with Mattuck for over two years. I would like to thank him for his patience and tolerance when (all too often!) I was in danger of becoming obsessed with IIM, for his wise advice and guidance on many different aspects of the book, and for keeping me calm when the going got tough.

Abbreviations

AJA: American Jewish Archives, Cincinnati, Ohio

AJA: Anglo-Jewish Association

CCAR: Central Conference of American Rabbis

HUC: Hebrew Union College, Cincinnati

IIM: Israel Isidor Mattuck

JC: *Jewish Chronicle*

JRU: Jewish Religious Union (for the Advancement of Liberal Judaism)

JRU Bulletin: Jewish Religious Union Bulletin

LJM: *Liberal Jewish Monthly*

LJS Archives: Liberal Jewish Synagogue Archives, St John's Wood, London

LJS: Liberal Jewish Synagogue

MCC: Montagu Centre Collection, collection of sermons, addresses and articles temporarily kept at the headquarters of Liberal Judaism, the Montagu Centre, London

UAHC: Union of American Hebrew Congregations

ULPS: Union of Liberal and Progressive Synagogues

Worcester Historical Museum: Archives of Worcester Historical Museum, Worcester, Massachusetts

WUPJ: World Union for Progressive Judaism

CHAPTER ONE

Early Life in Lithuania and Emigration to America

Israel Isidor Mattuck was born in Sirvintos (previously Shirvant) in Lithuania, then part of the Russian Empire. (From now on he will be referred to as 'IIM', which is how friends and colleagues dubbed him during his lifetime and how he signed himself.) Shirvant[1] was a town and an administrative district (*Uyezd*) of the Vilna (now Vilnius) province (or *Gubernia*). Located on the banks of the Sirvinta stream, Sirvintos lies about 50 km to the north-west of Vilnius. It once referred to as 'the Jerusalem of the North' and seen by many Jews as the political, cultural and religious centre of Eastern Europe.

The first Jews settled in Shirvant at the beginning of the eighteenth century. Some of the newcomers rented land from an estate owner called Pesitsky, while others opened inns and pubs along the road between Vilkomir and Vilna. Later, when Pesitsky evicted his Jewish tenants, their main livelihood came from shopkeeping. In 1847 there were 216 Jews in Shirvant. Fifty years later, the government census revealed that Jews made up three-quarters of the population of Shirvant, which then stood at around 2,000.[2]

Conditions in Lithuania in the Late Nineteenth Century

There is some confusion about IIM's exact date of birth, but the one he cited consistently as an adult was 28 December 1883.[3] At the time he was born, conditions for Jewish families were becoming increasingly difficult. For centuries Jews had been plagued and oppressed by successive Tsars.[4] At the end of the eighteenth century, the partitions of Poland brought to Russia an additional Jewish community of around 700,000 people. The Russians responded by establishing what was called the Pale of Settlement ('the Pale'), an area covering the whole of Russian Poland, Lithuania, Belarus, most of the Ukraine, the Crimea and Bessarabia, to which Jewish people were largely confined. Only a limited number of the Jewish population of the Russian Empire was allowed to live outside the Pale.

Within the Pale, Jews were heavily concentrated – often forming a majority – in small towns they referred to by the Yiddish word *shtetl* (little town).

The position of the Jewish community in Russia was dismal under Tsar Alexander I (1801–25), but conditions were immeasurably worse under his brother, Tsar Nicholas I, who was determined to force the Jewish community to relinquish its identity and to become assimilated into the general population. He introduced hundreds of repressive orders and regulations concerning the Jews, of which the most inhumane was the law mustering Jewish boys for up to twenty-five years of military service. Under what was known as the 'cantonist system', a quota was placed on each community, which forced local Jewish leaders to appoint *khapers* (catchers) to kidnap boys from as young as twelve for service. In the army barracks the officers did everything possible to force the boys to adopt Christianity. In addition, the Jewish communal organisation, the *kahal,* was abolished, bringing to an end Jewish autonomy in Poland and Lithuania.

When Nicholas I died in 1855, he was succeeded by Tsar Alexander II, who as a result of his abolition of serfdom, was regarded as being more liberal. The cantonist system was abolished and Jews were granted limited rights in district administration and permitted to practise law. However, these measures did little to improve the wretched lot of Jews living in the Pale. The Polish Revolt of 1863 put an end to the meagre gains when, as a reaction to the uprising, hatred of the Jews resurfaced in government circles and the press agitated against the 'Jewish Peril'.

In 1881 Alexander II was assassinated by a group of Nihilists that included a Jewish woman. Anti-Semitic propagandists exploited this to foment agitation against the Jewish community. The next Tsar, Alexander III, proved to be the Tsar most virulently opposed to the Jews, and in the spring of 1881 a wave of pogroms (physical attacks on the Jews) swept across Russia. Denunciations by Jewish communal leaders in London and New York had no impact, and the pogroms became a regular means for handling what was referred to as 'the Jewish problem'. Jews lived in constant fear of being beaten, robbed and even murdered by their gentile neighbours. A particularly malicious wave of pogroms was in force at the time of IIM's birth.

In 1882, just a year before IIM was born, 'temporary' regulations known as the May Laws were enacted governing the life of Jews in Russia. These remained in force until the 1917 revolution. Jews were now forbidden to live outside the towns, and secondary schools and universities were virtually closed to them. They were also mainly restricted to working as artisans and as a result many were tailors, metalworkers, cobblers and carpenters. Jews lived in increasingly overcrowded conditions and intense competition for jobs forced down wages below the poverty line. Circumstances became even more difficult when Jews living in other parts of Russia were forced to move into the Pale.

Notwithstanding the poverty facing many Jewish families,[5] until the last third of the nineteenth century, the death rate of the Jews in Eastern Europe gradually declined.[6] Particularly striking was the relatively low rate of infant mortality. However, this increased the size of the Jewish population and added to the competition for jobs resulting from governmental restrictions. Because of the worsening economic situation, in 1881 the Lechem Aniyim (Bread for the Poor) society was established in Shirvant, as was a society named Ma'achal Kasher (Kosher Meals), which supplied kosher food for Jewish soldiers stationed in the local garrison.[7]

The spirit of the Jewish community was not broken by either persecution or poverty. Communal life, largely centred on the synagogue and the rabbi, continued. Nor did joy completely disappear. Sabbaths and festivals were often accompanied by singing and dancing.[8] There was a welter of both academic and literary activity and newspapers in Yiddish and Hebrew were widely circulated. However, new ideas such as socialism and Zionism had begun to enter *shtetl* life and were adding to the growing discontent about the economic hardships facing Jews. Shirvant was particularly noted for being a Zionist stronghold and the impact of the *Haskalah* (or Jewish Enlightenment), which often led to the abandonment of traditional Judaism despite the opposition of the rabbis.

The Mattuck Family

Details of IIM's family background are few and difficult to verify. His parents were Benjamin, who was originally known as 'Tsvi Ben Zion'[9] (or Bentsel), and Chaya Batya, whose maiden name was Silver (probably Zilber in Yiddish). We have comparatively little biographical information about Chaya except that she was born in Shirvant in about 1855.[10] Chaya's parents came from two large and prominent Jewish families. Her father was Solomon (Shlioma) Leib Silver, a rabbi who apparently at one time 'had rabbinic charge'[11] of the Kovno (now Kaunas) province of Lithuania. Chaya's mother was Zipah (possibly Tsipa) Katzenellenbogen, a descendent of the eminent fifteenth-century rabbi Meir Ben Isaac of Katzenellenbogen of Hesse, head of the Padua yeshiva.[12]

Chaya and Benjamin were married in Bagaslaviskis near Shirvant on 10 April 1877.[13] At the end of the Middle Ages, Jewish girls were betrothed at a very young age, any time from 12 onwards. However, by the middle of the nineteenth century, the average age of marriage for Jewish women in Eastern Europe had risen to about 20,[14] which means that Chaya was a little older than the average Jewish bride at the time.

More is known about Benjamin Mattuck. He was born in Paberze, a settlement to the north of Kovno, in about 1860.[15] The family was then listed under the name of 'Matuk' (or sometimes 'Mattick'), derived from the name of the village from which they originated.[16] What is now called Matukai, located just to the north of Sirvintos, is likely to have been referred to in Yiddish as Matuk.[17] Benjamin's father, Yacov (Yankel) was born in Shirvant. He is said to have been in the flour business and was comparatively wealthy.[18] At this time, the majority of the factories in the Pale that processed natural produce were Jewish-owned.[19] Benjamin's mother was Yacov's first wife, Malkah. Yacov's father was Shmuel (Hebrew for Samuel). Nothing is known of Yacov's mother, but we know that he had an older sister, Esther.

FAMILY TREE OF BENJAMIN MATTUCK

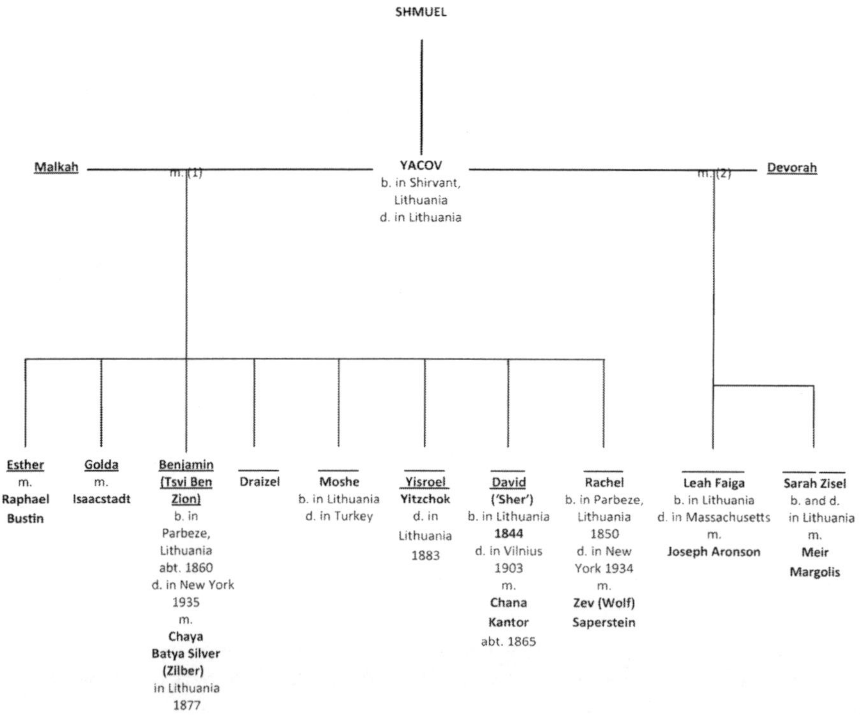

Benjamin Mattuck was one of Yacov and Malkah's eight children. One of their daughters, Esther, married Raphael Bustin, and another daughter, Golda, married a man with the surname Isaacstadt. Both Esther and Golda appear to have remained in Lithuania. However, their younger sister, Rachel (born in Paberze in 1850) married Wolf (Zev) Saperstein and emigrated to America in 1893.[21] The Sapersteins lived for many years in Chelsea, Massachusetts, but Rachel died in Brooklyn, New York in 1934. Benjamin's brother, David (born in Paberze in 1844) changed his surname to Sher, reportedly to avoid conscription into the Russian Army.[22] He married Chana Kantor and died in Vilnius in 1903. Moshe Mattuck emigrated to Turkey, where he died. Nothing is known about Benjamin's two other siblings, Draizel and Yisroel Yitzchok, except that Yisroel Yitzchok died young in 1883.[23] It is possible that when IIM was born later that year, he was named after his uncle, since it is a tradition in Ashkenazi communities to name children after deceased relatives. Yacov married for a second time, and he and his new wife, Devorah, had two daughters, Leah Faiga and Sarah Zisel. Leah Faiga Mattuck married Joseph Aronson and emigrated with him to America in 1887.

Benjamin Mattuck is known to have been a Talmudic Scholar.[24] He may have attended either a yeshiva[25] in one of the main cities of Lithuania or a communal study hall, *bet midrash*, several of which were set up during the nineteenth century in the smaller towns in Lithuania. His learning would have accorded him significant status, since the study of Judaic texts was valued above all other pursuits. Learned men, or the 'Men of the Book', as they were known, often spent their days bowed at the eastern walls of their synagogues, endlessly studying the Talmud, dissecting its exhortations, preparing commentaries on the Holy Word, and commentaries on commentaries.[26] Later, IIM recounted his vivid memory of synagogue life in Lithuania:

> To one who carries about in his memory the picture of the life in a synagogue in a community altogether Jewish in Eastern Europe, a picture, it is true, formed only in the very earliest years of life yet none the less clear for that, the most vivid impressions are not those of people at prayer, but rather of its use as a house of study; of men young in years, yet seeming old because of haggard faces and frail frames, standing in its recesses or along its walls, each with knit brow and intense eye poring over a sacred volume, or of a group of these men earnestly discussing together some knotty problem which is vexing one of them ; or again, of the building filled with the darkness of the night, except in one of its corners where the dim light of

> candles discloses the eager faces and thirsty eyes of old and young men, they are listening to one that is learned expound the law which they so love.[27]

Since scholars were esteemed, they frequently married the daughters of well-to-do families, who often supported the couple during the early years of their marriage while the husband continued his studies, an arrangement known as *kest*.[28] It is therefore possible that Benjamin married well because of his scholarship. There is no evidence to suggest that Benjamin ever received *s'michah* (rabbinic ordination) or practised as a rabbi.[29] Later in life he was referred to as Rev Ben Zion,[30] but this was probably simply a mark of respect for his Talmudic learning. Whatever the origins and nature of his scholarship, at some point in his early years, Benjamin also acquired the tailoring skills that were to lead him and his family to a better life.

IIM was the fourth child of Benjamin and Chaya, who in the first years of their marriage may have lived in Kovno.[31] His older siblings, who then had the Yiddish names of Ette, Jankel[32] and Chanay, were born around 1881, 1882, and the beginning of 1883 respectively.[33] A fifth child, Zadek, was born in 1885.

Mass Migration from Russia

After 1881, the trickle of Jewish emigration from Eastern Europe that had started at the beginning of the nineteenth century turned into a flood. From 1871 until 1880 about 70,000 Jews emigrated from Eastern Europe, including 15,000–20,000 from the Russian Empire. This was a dramatic increase over previous decades, but it was overshadowed by subsequent developments. Between 1881 and 1900 more than 760,000 Jews left Eastern Europe, and in the period from 1901 until 1914 about 1.6 million Jews emigrated, the overwhelming majority of whom were from the Russian Empire.

Of the Jews leaving the Russian Empire, the largest proportion by far settled in America. The numbers entering America might have been higher, but some Jews went to Canada, Australia, Argentina, the UK and South Africa because they could not meet the progressively stringent requirements for admission to the US.[34] Immigration to America from Eastern Europe was brought to an end in 1924 by the Immigration Act (known as the 'Johnson Act') and the National Origins Quota of that year. Under this legislation, the countries where most Jews lived received very low quotas, which meant that Jews were disproportionately affected by the restrictions.

Benjamin's Journey

IIM's family left Lithuania during the very early stages of the period of mass emigration from the Russian Empire. Sometime between 1888 and 1890,[35] Benjamin Mattuck departed in search of a living in America, following in the footsteps of a few Jewish men from Shirvant who had already done so.[36] In the absence of precise information we might speculate on the reasons for Benjamin's early emigration. As a scholar, he would have been aware that America was known to be *treyfe medineh* (the unclean country, a non-Kosher place) and no place for a learned and pious Jew. He must therefore have had pressing reasons for leaving. Benjamin may have known violence or discrimination, but it is more likely that he was propelled towards the New World to seek a better life for his family, which included avoiding the conscription of his three sons.[37] Although the pogroms often involved vicious attacks, it was the restrictions placed on employment and education and increasing overpopulation that were more significant in forcing the Jews out of the Pale.[38] A contemporary scholar, Zvi Falk Widawer, asserted that the Jews settling in America had not endured long journeys 'to slake their thirst for the word of God or to busy themselves in the Torah', they came for one purpose only, namely money.[39]

Benjamin's route to America is unknown, but like most emigrants at the time he probably set out by foot or cart across Lithuania to the German border, where he took a train (possibly at night, when rail travel was cheaper) to one of the two main German seaports of Hamburg and Bremen. This may have been the first time he had seen a train station, a large city, a harbour and an ocean-going vessel. The journey would have been an act of courage; a lonely and difficult passage into an unknown world. The separation of Benjamin from his family was not atypical. Rarely could an entire family afford to leave together and relatives were often temporarily parted as one or more family member departed for America or elsewhere.

As Jews were officially forbidden to travel outside the Pale, Benjamin would probably have had to bribe officials to embark on his journey, and also the soldiers that policed the Russian borders. Only a few Jewish people were able to obtain a passport or a travel permit to leave the area in which they lived. The documentation was not only hard to acquire and could take years to come through, it was also very costly. From the 1880s, the companies that operated the big steamships leaving the German ports advertised passages and sold tickets in Russia. Shipping agents were sometimes able to obtain passports for people who did not have them. Benjamin may have stayed in hostel accommodation at the port from which he embarked while he acquired the necessary documentation, and until the ship on which his passage was booked was ready to set sail.

The speed and comfort of Benjamin's journey would have depended on what he had been able to afford to pay for a ticket.[40] Most Jewish migrants travelled below deck in the third class 'tween decks, where conditions were far from elaborate. Many Orthodox Jews existed during the passage on the herrings, black bread and tea they had brought with them, because they feared that the food on board the ship would not be kosher.[41] For weeks before their departure, Jewish men and women saved money and often walked long distances to toughen their body for the ordeal ahead of them.[42] If Benjamin were amongst the increasing numbers of emigrants who, from the end of the 1880s, boarded ships leaving Baltic ports, such as Riga, the conditions under which he travelled would have been even less salubrious. The vessels departing from Baltic ports were often designed for the shipment of foodstuffs and livestock and took much longer to arrive at their destinations.[43]

Arrival in Boston

Benjamin may have entered America via Castle Garden, New York, as the vast majority of immigrants did at that time.[44] Alternatively, he may have travelled directly to Boston, where employment as a tailor awaited him. Whichever port he sailed to, he may have found the entry as traumatic as the passage itself. Immigrants often had to wait in a large room for hours before they were questioned in a language they did not comprehend. They were then tested for various diseases, including glaucoma and influenza. However, only about 1 per cent of immigrants was rejected for health reasons, since people were vetted in advance of their journeys because steamship companies were required to pay the return passage of those passed as unfit.

It was common for people from the same areas of the Pale of Settlement to follow friends, neighbours and family to a particular city or town in America. The people from each area referred to themselves as *landsleit* (Yiddish for 'fellow Jews', or 'countrymen') and had strong bonds. They welcomed new arrivals and ensured that they had what they needed to start a new life. The Russian Jews travelled to America intending to stay: only 7 per cent returned to Europe compared to up to 30 per cent of other immigrant groups.[45] The sense of mutual responsibility, instilled by Judaism and encouraged by the circumstances in which they found themselves, proved to be one of the greatest assets of Jewish migrants during the adjustment process.

The Russian Jews who arrived in Boston during the latter part of the nineteenth century were, like Benjamin, largely from Lithuania and often literate men with a skilled trade. In contrast to a number of other American cities to which the Eastern European immigrants came, Boston lacked a large, well-established German-Jewish population with a respected place in public and private life.[46] The small number of Jews who had made their way to Boston during the early part of the nineteenth century largely came from Poland. On the one hand this meant that the new wave of immigrants to Boston did not fare as well as those who settled in places such as New York, Cincinnati and San Francisco but, on the other hand, it meant that the tensions between established German-speaking Jews and Eastern European Jews evident elsewhere in America, were less pronounced.[47] Although intra-communal tensions did heighten when the new wave of immigration from Eastern Europe multiplied eightfold in the two decades after 1890, when Benjamin arrived he would have encountered little hostility from earlier Jewish settlers.

There are no records to tell us conclusively where Benjamin lived in Boston, but it is possible that he lodged with or close to his stepsister, Leah Faiga Mattuck (now Leah Aronson) who had emigrated to Boston a few years earlier. Although they later lived in Chelsea (a separate municipality just to the north of Boston), when Leah and her husband first arrived it is likely that they lived in the North End of Boston, the city's most important centre for first-generation immigrants where large numbers of Jewish immigrants settled during the 1880s. Contemporary observers remarked on the 'multi-coloured garb' of the new arrivals and the unmistakeable aroma of 'Old World cooking'.[48] They also remarked on the unappealing conditions prevailing in the North End.[49] However, the city had a growing reputation amongst Jewish people for being a place of employment opportunities and for its freedom from religious persecution.[50]

Benjamin appears to have worked at an enterprise located at 7 Barton Street in Boston.[51] Most Russian-Jewish immigrants at this time found employment in Boston's well-developed textile and shoe industries, including those owned by the few central European Jews who had settled in the city. The new immigrants occupied a niche in the economy that others had overlooked or avoided because of the unpleasantness and low status of the work. Coming from urban settings, as many of them did, and accustomed as they were to an industrialising economy, the Russian Jews fared better than any other immigrant group in Boston's history.[52] They lived cheaply, renting single rooms and receiving free bread, milk and groceries from Jewish dealers in the North End.[53] As a result, they were often soon able to save enough money to pay for the passage of family left behind in the Pale.

The Mattuck Family is Reunited

In September 1891, Benjamin Mattuck was joined by Chaya (who quickly became Ida) and their five children. They travelled from Hamburg to Boston via Glasgow,[54] where they boarded a ship, the SS *Prussian,*[55] bound for Boston. The family was recorded in the ship's manifest under the name of 'Matok'. They were met on the wharf in Boston by Benjamin Mattuck.[56]

We do not have any information on where the family lived in Boston when they were reunited, but we do know that they were there for over a year and that those children who were old enough (including IIM) attended public schools in the city.[57] To a greater extent than other immigrant groups, the Eastern European Jews made use of the American public school system to achieve their aspirations, rather than creating a separate school system to educate their children.

One of IIM's recollections of his early life in America relates to the time when he was at school in Boston. He remembered 'with a vividness as of yesterday':

> a Fourth of July celebration, which, with a broken head [sic], I could not attend. I could barely speak English, and I knew next to nothing what the Fourth of July was about, but I knew that it was going to be a great day, and that there was going to be a great entertainment for school children. And I was looking forward to going when fate interfered by means of a mosquito, and I can still feel the disappointment.[58]

Although the immigration experience may have been traumatic for the young IIM, evidently he embraced life in America with great alacrity.

It is likely that Ida Mattuck either worked alongside her husband or in another occupation as many immigrant women did at this time, owing to financial necessity. This would not have been out of the ordinary, because in Eastern Europe Jewish women were often the main breadwinners, even though they were also expected to carry the main burden of bringing up children and caring for the home. Some later writers overflowed with praise for their hardworking immigrant mothers, recalling them as vigorous, vital women who had been willing to take on difficult and even demeaning work in order to provide for their families and, more specifically, to earn money for their children's education.[59] Whatever their source of income, the Mattuck family were soon able to move on.

NOTES

1. This was its Yiddish name. Its Russian name was Shirvinty.
2. Josef Rosin, *Preserving Our Litvak Heritage: Volume II, A History of 21 Jewish Communities in Lithuania* (League City, TX: JewishGen, 2007), p.166.
3. As a young man IIM was uncertain about his date of birth. See letter from the Recorder of Harvard University, 26 May 1915, in which he states 'He [IIM] does not know the exact date in December 1883 that he was born'. In an application for a scholarship at Harvard in 1902, IIM stated his date of birth as 'Dec. 28 1883 (approximately)'. Harvard University Biographical Files, call number HUG 300. The lack of certainty may be due to the fact that, before emigrating to America, the Mattuck family adhered to the Jewish calendar and the shift to the Gregorian calendar when they settled in America led to confusion. There was a difference of about fourteen days between the two calendars.
4. Masha Greenbaum, The *Jews of Lithuania: a History of a Remarkable Community, 1316–1945* (Jerusalem: Gefen Publishing House, 1999), pp.173–93.
5. Jewish families usually lived in simple, one-storey wooden buildings standing on unpaved streets. There were public bathhouses and pigs walked around the streets. See Norma Feingold and Nancy Sadick, *Water Street: World Within a World* (Worcester, MA: Worcester Historical Museum, 1984), p.14.
6. M. Kupovetsky, 'Population and Migration: Population and Migration before World War 1', YIVO Encyclopedia of Jews in Eastern Europe, 12 October 2010: www.yivoencyclopedia.org.
7. www.jewishgen.org/yizkor/lithuania.
8. Recent writers have stressed that all was not bleak in Eastern Europe at this time. See Antony Polonsky, *Jews in Poland and Russia (Volume 2: 1881–1914)* (Oxford and Portland, OR: Littman Library of Jewish Civilization, 2009).
9. Name given on headstones for his wife and children buried in the family plot at Mount Lebanon cemetery, Glendale, Long Island, New York.
10. This is the date of birth on her death certificate, but other years are given in census records, etc. It is common for Jewish people born in the Russian Empire to be unclear on their exact date of birth. A variety of reasons have been posited for this, including the unwillingness of Jews to keep records that might help them to be identified by their Russian oppressors.
11. See the interview with IIM in the *JC* shortly after his arrival in England, in which he said: 'well I am the grandson of a Russian Rabbi, who had rabbinic charge in the Kovno district', *JC*, 4 March 1912, p.24. Notes made by his daughter, Dorothy Edgar (née Mattuck), tell us that there was also a family anecdote about IIM's connection to the 'Turkish Chief Rabbi'. Mattuck Family Archive kept by Jill Mattuck Tarule (MFAa).
12. See Neil Rosenstein, *The Unbroken Chain: Biographical Sketches and Genealogy of Illustrious Jewish Families from the 15th–20th Century, Volumes 1 and 2* (New York: Computer Centre for Jewish Genealogy, Second Edition, 1990). By the nineteenth century, the Katzenellenborgen family was widely dispersed throughout Eastern and central Europe. There are at least twelve variant Hebrew spellings of the name as well as derivative forms such as Ellenbogen, Elbogen, Bogen, Katz and Katzenelson. The family produced many eminent rabbis.
13. Genealogical research carried out by Michael Trapunsky, the great-great-grandson of Benjamin Mattuck's brother, David Sher.
14. Yaffa Eliach, 'The Shtetl Household': www.rtrfoundation.org.
15. The date that he gave for his birth for his Certificate of Naturalization in 1906 was 1860, but the date given on his death certificate is 1862. Copy of certified death certificate obtained from New York City Council.
16. The origin of the name Mattuck was later confirmed by IIM. He said: 'My Russian ancestors very wisely chose to live in a Russian village which gave them a surname which very few people would recognise as Russian'. Quote from 'Mr Belloc's Book The Jews', sermon given by IIM at the LJS, 20 May 1922, Montagu Centre Collection (MCC). Jews in Tsarist Russia were reluctant to adopt family names because those names enabled oppressive governments to track them more easily and conscript young men into the army.
17. Information provided by Philip Shapiro via JewishGen Litvak Digest network, 19 September 2011. See also Alexander Beider, *A Dictionary of Jewish Surnames from the Russian Empire, Volume 2* (New Jersey: Avotaynu, 2008), p.393, where it is stated that the name Matuk is derived from the village of Matuki, Vilna.

18. See genealogical research carried out by Michael Trapunsky.
19. Dov Levin, *The Litvaks, a Short History of the Jews of Lithuania,* tr. Adam Teller (New York: Berghahn Books, 2001), p.86.
20. The placing of the siblings is indicative. For most of them we do not have birthdates.
21. Letter from George Mattuck to IIM, 29 January 1929, LJS Archives, Box 1/2. The letter states that IIM's parents discovered Rachel living in Chelsea, Massachusetts in 1929 and were reunited with her and her offspring.
22. He may therefore have been the second son, as first sons were spared conscription under Russian law.
23. Death recorded in JewishGen database. It is possible that IIM, born later that year, was named after this brother of Benjamin, as it is a tradition in Jewish communities in Eastern Europe to name children after close relatives who had recently died.
24. Documented in family archives and authenticated by Benjamin's membership of a Talmud study society in Worcester discussed in Chapter Two.
25. An educational institution focusing on the study of traditional religious texts, primarily the Talmud and Torah.
26. Stephen Birmingham, *The Rest of Us, The Rise of America's Eastern European Jews* (New York: Syracuse University Press, 1999), p.14.
27. 'Our Aims', inaugural address delivered by IIM at the LJS at the first of a series of meetings to be held monthly on Sunday afternoons at the LJS, 9 January 1916, MCC.
28. See Eliach, 'The Shtetl Household'.
29. In nineteenth-century Lithuania, many Talmudic scholars studied for interest rather than as a means to an appointment to a rabbinic post. See Levin, *The Litvaks,* p.93.
30. He is referred to as such on the gravestones of his offspring buried in Mount Lebanon Cemetery, Glendale, Long Island, New York.
31. In her marriage certificate, Rose Mattuck stated that she was born in Kovno. Copy of certificated marriage certificate obtained from New York City Council.
32. Jankel (later Jacob) may have been named after his grandfather, Yakov. In Eastern Europe it was customary to name first sons after a dead grandparent. We may therefore surmise that Yakov had died by the time that Jankel was born.
33. These dates are approximate since, as discussed elsewhere, the birth dates of Eastern European Jewish immigrants were not always precise. However, in a later application for a Harvard scholarship, the ages that IIM gives for his siblings correspond with these dates. See application for Scholarship, 10 May 1902, Harvard University Biographical Files, call number HUG 300.
34. Immigration laws were passed in 1891, 1903, 1907 and 1917. They prevented certain categories of people from entering America. Most restrictions involved people with diseases such as tuberculosis and trachoma. Others were aimed at keeping out those who might be an expense to the public purse.
35. These approximate dates are taken from US Census records made available by Ancestry.com.
36. In an 1869–78 list of immigrants to America, eight Shirvint Jews are mentioned: www.jewishgen.org/yizkor/lithuania5/Lit5_166.html.
37. Although the dreaded cantonist system had been abolished, in 1874 a General Draft for all male citizens aged 20 replaced it.
38. Samuel Joseph, 'Jewish Immigration to the United States from 1881 to 1910', *Studies in History, Economics and Public Law,* Vol. LIX, no. 4 (1914), p.62.
39. Quoted in Arthur Hertzberg, *The Jews in America, Four Centuries of an Uneasy Encounter* (New York: Simon and Schuster, 1989), p.156.
40. 'Migration Histories, Jewish Journeys': www.movinghere.org.uk.
41. See Birmingham, *The Rest of Us,* p.42.
42. Ibid., p.41.
43. See 'Migration Histories, Jewish Journeys'.
44. Ellis Island was not opened until 1892.
45. Paula E. Hyman, 'Eastern European Immigrants in the United States', March 2009: www.jwa.org/encyclopedia/article.
46. Jonathan D. Sarna, 'The Jews of Boston in Historical Perspective', in Jonathan D. Sarna, Ellen Smith, Scott-Martin Kosofsky (eds), *The Jews of Boston, Essays on the Occasion of the Centenary of the Combined Jewish Philanthropies of Greater Boston* (New Haven, CT:

Yale University Press in collaboration with the Combined Jewish Philanthropies of Boston, 2005), p.6.

47. Ibid., p.6.
48. Philip Davis, *And Crown Thy Good* (New York: New York Philosophical Library, 1952), p.118.
49. William A. Braverman, 'The Emergence of a Unified Culture, 1880–1917', in Sarna, Smith and Kosofsky (eds), *The Jews of Boston,* p.74.
50. Alexander Woodle, 'Jewish History and Settlement Patterns in Massachusetts', Jewish Genealogical Society of Greater Boston Inc. (2010), p.4: www.jgsgb.org/pdfs/Jewish_Settlement_Patterns_MA.pdf.
51. The manifest for the ship on which Benjamin's wife and family travelled to Boston records that 'the husband' who worked as a tailor at this address met them, but the writing is indistinct. National Archives and Records Administration (NARA); Washington, DC; Crew Lists of Vessels Arriving at Boston, Massachusetts, 1917–1943; Microfilm Serial: T938; Microfilm Roll: 1.
52. See Braverman, 'The Emergence of a Unified Culture', p.81.
53. Ibid., p.77.
54. In his application for an American passport in 1916, IIM stated that he arrived in America from Hamburg via Glasgow, and in his naturalisation papers he confirms the place and date of entry to America as being Boston in September 1891. NARA, Washington DC; Passport Applications, 2 January, 1906 – 31 March, 1925; Collection Number: ARC Identifier 583830 / MLR Number A1 534; NARA Series: M1490; Roll: 321.
55. The SS *Prussian* was built in 1869 by A&J Inglis, Glasgow for Montreal Ocean SS Co. There was passenger accommodation for 90 people first class and 600 third class.
56. See ship's manifest, note 51.
57. According to family sources, a teacher at the school attended by Jacob Mattuck suggested that the spelling of his surname be changed from Matuk to Mattuck, and the name was then adopted by the whole family. Email from Arthur Mattuck, 29 July 2011.
58. 'The Teaching of Civics in American Schools', address given by IIM to the Stepney Teachers' Council, 24 March 1919, MCC.
59. See Eliach, 'The Shtetl Household'.

CHAPTER TWO

Growing up in Worcester

The Move to Worcester

Within a decade from the start of the wave of mass Russian-Jewish immigration most Jewish families had moved from Boston's North End to the less congested neighbourhoods of Roxbury and Chelsea, known as the 'streetcar suburbs'. However, the Mattuck family chose a different location: they moved to Worcester, the second city of Massachusetts, about 40 miles (64 km) to the west of Boston.

Founded in the eighteenth century, Worcester was then one of the most thriving inland cities in America, an important industrial and manufacturing centre with a great diversity of enterprises. In the mid-nineteenth century it had been the centre of the anti-slavery and early American feminist movements. Henry David Thoreau spoke there in defence of John Brown and his raid on Harper's Ferry, and Emma Goldman and Alexander Berkman, the celebrated anarchists, made Worcester their refuge for a number of years. There were also flourishing socialist and trade union movements.[1] Worcester was described by Samuel Nathaniel Behrman, one of its more illustrious residents – who was born in Worcester in 1893 – as 'zippy and exhilarating'.[2]

The Mattuck family settled in the Water Street area on the eastern side of the city. One-third of a mile in length and consisting of just five blocks, over a twenty-year period from 1881 the Water Street became the heart of a large, crowded Jewish community that was marked by its coherence. At the time that IIM was growing up in Worcester, the Jewish population 'lived and worked and played together', had a similar religious outlook and 'no break seemed imminent'.[3]

According to the US Census for 1910, there were 723 people living on Water Street in 35 residential units.[4] The community thrived socially, culturally and economically. Kosher restaurants, bakeries, butcher shops, grocery stores, chicken stores, and fish and fruit markets shared the street with dozens of other little businesses. There were also several manufacturing establishments located at its northern end.[5] The Jewish community had a very low annual death rate – just 5.7 per 1,000 people, compared to 14.9 per 1,000 people for the city as a whole in 1915.[6] The tenements situated above the small stores teemed with young, mainly Jewish immigrants. Of the 123 families living in Water Street in 1910, ninety-three of the household heads stated Russia as their country of origin. The overwhelming majority of these Russian Jews were from Lithuania.[7]

In the same way as Jewish communities in other American cities, the immigrants settling in Worcester struggled to forge a unique transitional way of life fashioned from their Old World values and their New World experiences; they needed to establish a sense of the familiar before they could identify themselves with the unfamiliar. This Yiddish-speaking culture lasted for almost four decades and served to ease the bewilderment and pain of adjustment.[8]

The Russian Jews vastly outnumbered the few German-Jewish families who had settled in Worcester earlier in the century.[9] These families were largely secular and well educated and, because there were so few of them, they had quickly assimilated into American life and had prospered, mainly by establishing textile and garment factories. By the end of the nineteenth century, the earlier Jewish settlers ranked amongst the foremost merchants of the city.[10]

The Mattuck family may have chosen to move to Worcester not only because of the growing garment trade established by the German Jews, which provided a ready source of employment for immigrants with tailoring skills,[11] but also because of Worcester's history of welcoming minority groups. The Jewish immigrants were but one of many groups that had settled there since 1820. The Irish were Worcester's first immigrant group, followed by French Canadians. The Swedes, who came next, were soon joined by Italians, Albanians, Armenians, Finns, Greeks, Lebanese and Syrians.[12] As a Talmudic scholar, religious freedom would have been very important to Benjamin Mattuck and if the family encountered any prejudice in Worcester, it would have seemed mild compared to the virulent anti-Semitism prevalent in the Russian Empire.

Establishing a Living

The Mattuck family were amongst the earliest Russian-Jewish settlers in Worcester,[13] and their life there established a pattern for the many families who came after them. The family arrived in Worcester sometime before 1893,[14] but it was not until 1894 that Benjamin first appeared in the Worcester City Directory as a separate householder.[15] He is listed as a 'stitcher', living at 5 Carpenter Street, a turning off Water Street. By 1898 the family had moved to 5 Harding Street, which ran parallel to Water

Street. Benjamin was still listed as a 'stitcher', but with the additional information that he was employed as a machine operator at David Pobolinski and Sons, underwear manufacturers.[16] This recently opened firm was initially located in Winter Street, which met Water Street at its north-east end.[17] In 1900 Benjamin's occupation changed to 'provisions'. He had now set up a store at 26 Water Street.[18]

In establishing the store, the family may have been able to take advantage of the Jewish-sponsored credit unions, such as the Progressive Credit Union based in Waverley Street, or the Worcester Credit Union located at 135 Water Street, which were a notable feature of the business history of Worcester.[19] Both husbands and wives were able to borrow from the credit unions, and funding from this source was pivotal in encouraging the proliferation of small shops and businesses that opened around the Water Street area.[20]

From the beginning of their life in America, Jewish immigrants exhibited a strong preference for self-employment, which had its roots in the economic conditions prevailing in Eastern Europe and was reinforced by the dictates of their religion, in which freedom was held in high regard. In a sermon he gave some thirty years later, IIM offered a personal insight into this phenomenon, saying that Jews had 'a fondness for small trade above manual labour' and preferred to earn less money running a small shop than working in a factory.[21]

By 1910, two-thirds of Jewish men living in the Water Street area ran their own businesses compared to 12 per cent of the non-Jewish residents of the area, even though the average length of time they had been in America was just seven years.[22] It was later suggested by a close colleague that IIM's successful career owed much to his early exposure to the 'striving for upward mobility' that epitomised the Jewish community of Worcester at the end of the nineteenth century.[23]

According to family members, Benjamin was often deeply engrossed in Talmudic studies, and the running of the provisions store was largely left to Ida. The histories of other Jewish-owned businesses in Worcester at this time reveal the major role played by wives in decision-making and in the day-to-day operation of the various enterprises. In most official documents, these women appear simply as 'housewives' (as Ida did in the 1900 and 1910 US Census), or their occupation was listed as 'none'. However, their labour was often crucial to the family economy. The involvement of offspring, especially young women,[24] in family businesses was also often an economic necessity. One Jewish baker trading in Worcester at the turn of the twentieth century said that 'If a Jewish baker had ten wives and twenty-five kids, there'd be work for all of them'.[25]

Although running their own business may have been preferable to working in a garment factory, the Mattuck family would have had to work very hard to make the store a going concern. The Water Street stores were very small; they were hot in summer but very cold in the winter.[26] The family store, now described as a 'meat market'[27] moved to 57 Water Street at some point between 1906 and 1908 and then to 31 Harrison Street. It appears to have closed by 1912.[28]

In 1905 the family moved home from Harding Street to an apartment at 42 Providence Street in the Union Hill area of Worcester (referred to by the Jewish community as 'The Hill').[29] As the Jewish community increased in size, expansion became imperative and, from around the turn of the century, more prosperous Jews began to move to The Hill, displacing the Irish who had previously lived there. The solid, three-decker, three-family houses that had been built on Providence Street were not particularly attractive, but they were a significant improvement on the houses in the Water Street area, which were 'ugly, vulgar and set extremely close together'.[30] Providence Street was also a desirable location because the area was kept almost purely residential, rather than having a mixed residential and industrial use.[31] The move was therefore an indication of the Mattuck family's increasing prosperity.

Family Life

Once settled in Worcester, Benjamin and Ida completed their family. After a gap of several years due to their separation, Maxwell was born in January 1893,[32] Florence was born in March 1895 and Bernard, the eighth and youngest child, was born in March 1896. It is interesting that Benjamin and Ida selected very typical American names for their younger children and that by now the five children born in Lithuania had anglicised names: Ette had become Rose Edith, Jankel was now Jacob Alexander, Chanay was Anna Judith and Zadek was George Felix. Only Israel retained a name close to his Yiddish one of Yisroel.

Most of the Jewish people moving to Worcester in the 1880s and 1890s came as part of family groups.[33] The Mattuck family may or may not have had relations in Worcester when they moved there, but we do know that shortly after their arrival Ida's sister and her family joined them there.[34] Bessie Silver was married to Raphael Sarasohn and their children were similar in age to the Mattuck siblings. Their offspring included Israel Joshua Sarasohn who later became a Reform rabbi[35] and was described as 'one of the most brilliant Jewish churchmen [sic] in the south'.[36] The Sarasohn family set up a grocery business[37] in Harrison Street that Bessie Sarasohn continued to run after the death of her husband.

Given IIM's future choice of a career and what emerged to be his radical religious views, it is interesting to explore the family's religious involvements in Worcester. The first sign of a Jewish communal presence in the city was when the Sons of Israel Synagogue was erected on Green Street in 1888, the congregation of which is believed to have been formed in 1877[38] when there were probably no more than twenty-five Jewish people living in the city. Worcester's second synagogue, the Sons of Abraham, was built in 1888 in Plymouth Street, close to the first synagogue.

The Mattuck family may have joined one of these two early Worcester synagogues on their arrival in the city. However, they may also have been founding members of one of the new synagogues that sprang up during the 1890s to serve the rapidly expanding Jewish community – the Tower of Truth synagogue (originally Shaarei Zedek) established in 1892, followed by the Agudas Achim in 1893, the Good Brothers in 1897 and the Sons of Jacob in 1900.[39] These synagogues were all Orthodox synagogues, because the new wave of immigrants from Eastern Europe tried to recreate the religious world of the Pale. In 1880 almost 90 per cent of synagogues in America were Reform, but by 1890, when there were 530 Jewish congregations, 60 per cent of synagogues were Orthodox.[40]

As the Jewish community started to move to Providence Street and other parts of Union Hill, they took with them their synagogues so that they remained within easy walking distance. The Sons of Israel moved from Green Street to 24 Providence Street in 1896 and the Sons of Abraham moved from Plymouth to Coral Street, which runs parallel to Providence Street, in 1913. In 1906 a new synagogue was opened in Providence Street. Named Shaarai Torah, it was founded by a group of men who, while wanting to preserve the traditional Orthodoxy of Eastern European synagogues (or 'shuls' as they were called), also wanted to adopt more modern ways in keeping with the American way of life.[41] Many of the founders of Shaarai Torah were younger members of the Sons of Abraham Synagogue, who felt that everything about that synagogue 'was adapted to the needs of the older generation'.[42]

Membership records indicate that Benjamin was not amongst those who joined the new synagogue. It appears that, although he was committed to life in America, Benjamin found security and comfort in the continuation of the religious traditions of the Old World. In 1894 the Society for the Study of The Talmud, the Chevra Gemara, was formed in Worcester. Benjamin was a founding member of the society and participated in its activities. Its extensive rules included mandatory daily study sessions and the regular paying of dues. A surviving journal for the society lists its members, including Benjamin under the name of 'Ben Zion

Son of Yakov Mattick'.[43] The journal also contains a list of women, the wives of the members, which includes Ida.[44] The rabbi involved with the society was Rabbi Silver from the Sons of Israel synagogue in Providence Street, who may have been a relative of Ida. It was this and other study groups established in the city that led to Worcester being regarded as the centre of Talmudic learning in New England at the beginning of the twentieth century.[45] The Chevra Gemara was not affiliated to any of the Worcester synagogues that existed at the time and Benjamin may therefore have chosen to worship more informally in a *shtiebel.*[46]

As Jewish families moved to Providence Street, the Jewish community was starting to become more acculturated, encouraged to do so by Worcester City Council, which established evening classes for immigrant communities, and the availability of newspapers, such as the national Yiddish language newspaper, the *Jewish Daily Forward,* known in Jewish households as the '*Forvertz*'.[47] As well as news, the *Forward* offered explanations of American institutions, translations of American writers and advice on a wide range of topics.[48] At a national level Jewish writers and establishment figures in America were urging immigrants to become American citizens. In Worcester, a Hebrew Political Club was formed in 1891 to 'aid the naturalisation of Jews as American Citizens', which had a membership of about 200 people. Benjamin obviously heeded these messages, because in 1906 he applied for and was granted American citizenship. Just how well the whole Mattuck family had learned their civic lessons and bought into the American dream will be shown in the next chapter.

NOTES

1. Jonah Raskin, *For the Hell of It: The Life and Times of Abbie Hoffman* (Berkeley, CA: University of California Press, 1996).
2. S.N. Behrman, *The Worcester Account* (Worcester, MA: Chandler House Press, 1996).
3. William Harold Somers, 'A Socio-Historical Study of the Jewish Community of Worcester Massachusetts' (Worcester, MA: unpublished MA thesis, Clark University, 1933), p.63.
4. Norma Feingold and Nancy Sadik, *Water Street: World Within a World* (Worcester, MA: Worcester Historical Museum, 1984), p.52.
5. Ibid., p.8.
6. Charles Nutt, *History of Worcester and Its People, Volume 1* (New York: Lewis Historical Publishing Company, 1919), p.340.
7. See Feingold and Sadik, *Water Street*, p.11.
8. Gerald Sorin, *A Time for Building: The Third Migration, 1880–1920 (Vol. 3 The Jewish People in America)* (Baltimore, MD and London: Johns Hopkins University Press, New Edition, 1995), p.xv.
9. See Feingold and Sadik, *Water Street*, p.11. Norma Feingold was a descendant of the first Jew to settle in the city, Abraham Feingold.
10. See Nutt, *History of Worcester,* p.340.
11. Thirty-six per cent of the Jewish immigrants to Worcester from Eastern Europe had tailoring skills. See Nutt, *History of Worcester*, p.340.
12. See Feingold and Sadik, *Water Street*, p.21.

13. At the time that the Mattuck family arrived in Worcester there were only several hundred Jewish people living in the city. By 1910, 8,000 Jews lived in Worcester. Joseph Talamo, 'A Preliminary Social Survey of the Jewish Population of Worcester: A Local Study of Immigration' (Worcester, MA: unpublished MA thesis, Clark University, 1915), p.8.
14. We know that the family arrived in Worcester before 1893 because Maxwell Mattuck was born in Worcester in January 1893. Obituary of Maxwell S. Mattuck, unidentified newspaper cutting, 7 November 1957, Worcester Historical Museum.
15. This may be because the information that furnished the 1894 city directory for Worcester was collected before or just after the family was established in Worcester. See US City Directories, 1821–1989 [database on-line]. Provo, UT, USA: Ancestry.com Operations, Inc., 2011.
16. Ibid.
17. Winter Street had been the centre for Jewish business before the development of Water Street. See Feingold and Sadik, *Water Street*, p.27.
18. In 1900, the US Census lists Benjamin Mattuck as a 'meat dealer'. 1900 US Federal Census for Worcester Ward 3, Worcester, Massachusetts; Roll: 696; Page: 2B, Enumeration District: 1731; FHL microfilm: 1240696, Ancestry.com. 1900 United States Federal Census [database on-line]. Provo, UT, USA: Ancestry.com Operations Inc, 2004. In IIM's application for admission to Hebrew Union College, he stated that his father was a 'meat marketer', American Jewish Archives (AJA), Hebrew Union College Records, MS-5, Box B-7, Folder 11.
19. See Nutt, *History of Worcester*, p.344.
20. See Feingold and Sadik, *Water Street*, p.27.
21. 'The Jew and the World's Work', sermon given by IIM at the LJS, 21 April 1928, Montagu Centre Collection (MCC).
22. See Feingold and Sadik, *Water Street*, p.54.
23. 'The Reminiscences of Dr Maurice L. Perlzweig', Oral History Research Office, Columbia University, 1993, p.220. The desire to succeed was not limited to Worcester; it was a general feature of the Jews who came to America at this time.
24. While young men were encouraged to pursue their studies, girls were expected to support their family and to think in terms of making a good match in the marriage market rather than having a successful career.
25. Quoted in Feingold and Sadik, *Water Street*, p.32.
26. Ibid., p.29.
27. IIM's application for scholarship for the academic year 1902/03, 11 April 1902, Harvard University Biographical Files, call number HUG 300.
28. See city and house directories for Worcester. The 1912 directory shows 31 Harrison Street as being vacant.
29. See Behrman, *The Worcester Account*.
30. See Somers, 'A Socio-Historical Study of the Jewish Community', p.43.
31. Many of the three-decker houses in Providence Street still exist. Seen by the author during a walk of the area, May 2012.
32. In official birth records, Maxwell Mattuck is registered as 'Simon M. Mattuck'. Ancestry.com. Massachusetts, Town and Vital Records, 1620–1988 [database on-line]. Provo, UT, USA: Ancestry.com Operations, Inc., 2011. Original data: Town and City Clerks of Massachusetts. Massachusetts Vital and Town Records. Provo, UT: Holbrook Research Institute (Jay and Delene Holbrook).
33. 'Worcester Jews' by unnamed author, AJA, SC-13228.
34. The death certificate for Israel Joshua Sarasohn states that his parents were Bessie Silver and Raphael Sarasohn. Ancestry.com. North Carolina, Death Certificates, 1909–1975 [database on-line]. Provo, UT, USA: Ancestry.com Operations Inc, 2007. In the 1930 US Census, Israel Sarasohn is listed as having emigrated with his parents from Vilna in 1993. 1900 US Census, Manhattan, New York, New York; Roll: 1088; Page: 12A; Enumeration District: 0167; FHL microfilm: 1241088.
35. Unlike his Mattuck cousins, Israel Sarasohn did not study at an Ivy League university, but at Clark University in Worcester from which he graduated in 1912. See Louis N. Wilson, Librarian (ed.), *List of Degrees Granted at Clark University and Clark College, Vol. 4, 1914–1915* (Worcester, MA: Clark University Press, 1915), p.45. Sarasohn graduated from Hebrew Union College (HUC) in 1915 and became a chaplain in the US Army. He subsequently became a rabbi at a number of synagogues in the American south.

36. 'Jewish New Year Celebrated Here', *Augusta Chronicle*, 27 September 1927, p.7.
37. Raphael Sarasohn worked as a peddler when the family first moved to Worcester but later became a teacher. Ancestry.com. US City Directories, 1821–1989 [database on-line]. Provo, UT, USA: Ancestry.com Operations, Inc., 2011.
38. See Nutt, *History of Worcester*, p.340.
39. Carol Clingen, 'Massachusetts Synagogues and Their Records, Past and Present', Jewish Genealogical Society for Greater Boston, 2010 (CIC 7/6/10 rev.2).
40. Jerry Klinger, 'The Russians Are Coming, the Russians Are Coming': www.jewishmagazine.com.
41. Norma Feingold, *Shaarai Torah, Life Cycle of a Synagogue* (Worcester, MA: Worcester Historical Museum, 1991), p.10.
42. Cited in ibid., p.17.
43. Journal of the Chevra Gemara, Worcester Historical Museum.
44. Ibid.
45. Morris H. Cohen, *Worcester Ethnic Groups, A Bicentennial View* (Worcester MA: Worcester Bicentennial Commission, 1976), p.50.
46. Literally 'little room'. It is a Yiddish term used by Eastern European Jews for their own type of synagogue, combining the functions of a prayer, study, and social centre, usually part of a house or other building.
47. The *Jewish Daily Forward* was founded in New York in 1897. Its famous editor was Abraham Cahan, a Russian immigrant and avowed socialist.
48. See Feingold and Sadik, *Water Street*, p.31.

CHAPTER THREE

The Mattuck Family After Worcester

The Mattuck Siblings

The Mattuck siblings were obviously encouraged by their parents to learn as a means to enter mainstream American life and to take advantage of the best that the country had to offer. This was especially the case for the five Mattuck sons, who were all educated at Ivy League universities. This, more than any other item of information about the Mattuck family, tells us just how resourceful and ambitious they were. Taking over their parents' family grocery shop never seems to have been an option; the Mattuck offspring had much higher aspirations and within barely a generation they achieved middle-class status and a comparatively comfortable existence.

Although immigrant Jewish families tended to keep girls at school longer than other ethnic groups, they usually invested more heavily in the education of their sons.[1] This was definitely the case with the Mattuck family. Rose (referred to by the family as 'Rosie') and Anna ('Annie') both graduated from high school,[2] and Rose in particular is said to have been very intelligent. However, from an early age Rose and Anna went out to work 'at anything they could' in order to raise money to help send their brothers to college.[3]

Rose and Anna may not have had the same level of formal education as their brothers, but they were not without culture and learning. They both belonged to the Maimonides Society,[4] the Hebrew Debating Assembly (of which their brother, George, was at one time the President),[5] a society for the study of the Hebrew language, Jewish history and the Hebrew Bible (Rose Mattuck was its Vice-President),[6] and the Daughters of Zion, which organised regular lectures. These societies met in the Maccabees' Hall at 29 Providence Street, close to the Mattuck family home.[7] The sisters had a high profile in the

MATTUCK FAMILY TREE

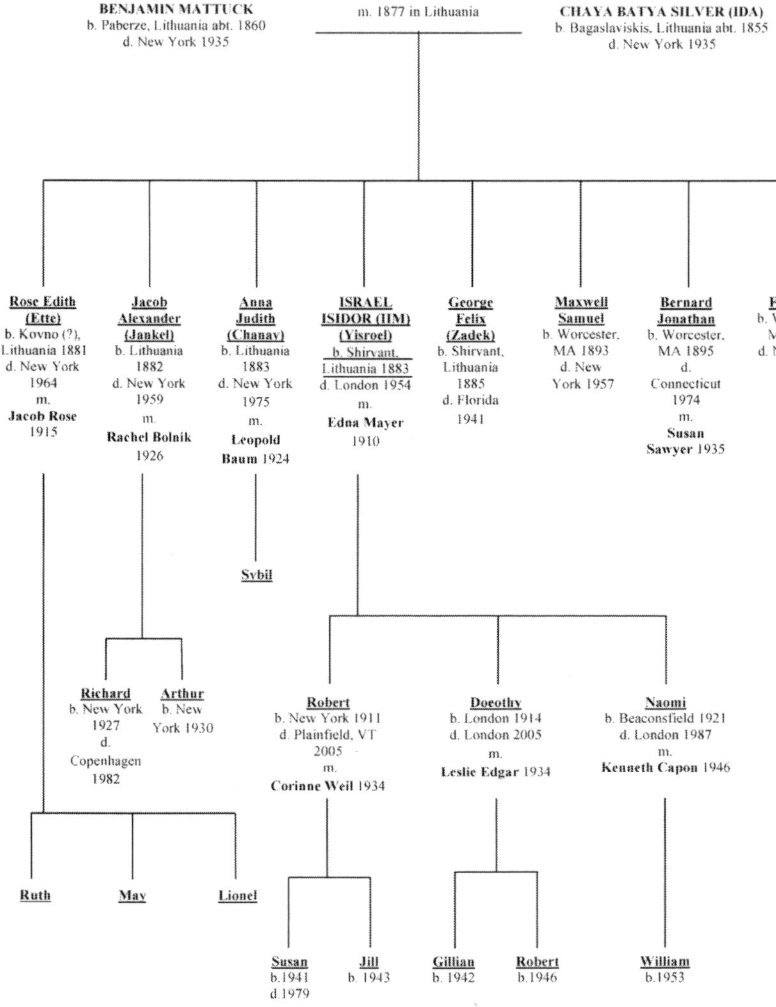

Worcester Jewish community, organising dances and other events for young people including a major event held in 1903 over which George presided, at which Jacob sang a solo and where IIM gave an address on 'Societies', suggesting that at this time the siblings were close.[8]

Rose had a career as an actress on the Yiddish stage.[9] In 1915, when she was 34, Rose married Jacob Edward Rose in New York and became known as Rose E. Rose.[10] Jacob Rose was a real estate lawyer with a 'store-front office', in Pitkin Avenue, Brooklyn. He was looked down upon by her brothers as not being a socially acceptable partner for their sister, because of his 'lower-class manners' and the fact that he did not work in a successful, upmarket law firm.[11] Apparently this view eventually led to the break-up of Rose's marriage.[12]

Rose had three children and, because of her failed marriage, is said to have become 'virtually impoverished'.[13] As they became more prosperous, Rose relied on the financial support of her brothers, which they provided in a rather heavy-handed manner. Reputedly, on several occasions, they announced without warning that it was time for Rose and her children to have a holiday. The children were taken out of school (leading to visits from 'truant officers'), and the family whisked off in a chauffeur-driven car to stay in a rented house in the fashionable resort of Saratoga Springs in upstate New York. Rose and her children never knew when the vacation was going to end until they were told by 'the uncles' to pack for the return to New York City.[14] It is difficult to judge the accuracy of this family anecdote, but it does tell us something about the brothers' attitude to the wielding of money, and perhaps also their attitude towards women.

Rose is said to have had 'spark and wit',[15] and to have pursued a variety of means (such as keeping chickens) for raising money to maintain her home in 528 East 4th Street, a street away from the family home (see below), in the Kensington and Parkville neighbourhood of Brooklyn, where she lived until her death in September 1964.

As a young woman, Anna worked as a bookkeeper in Worcester,[16] an occupation pursued by many young Jewish women at this time, but she later became the de facto housekeeper for the family. She married Leopold (Leo) Baum, a salesman, in New York in 1924 when she was 41,[17] and had one daughter, Sybil, to whom she devoted a lot of attention. Anna's marriage did not last long and she returned to live in the family home. Apparently her estranged husband was not permitted by the family to visit her there and he rented a house nearby so that he could catch glimpses of his daughter.[18]

After the death of her parents, Anna went to live with Sybil, who by then had a busy social life – initially in Queens and then in New Rochelle, a fashionable suburb to the north of the Bronx, where her husband, Edward Lustbader, ran a successful construction firm. Anna, who is said to have been a gentle and caring woman, effectively raised her three grandchildren[19] and remained robust until she died in November 1975 aged 92.

Little is known about the youngest Mattuck daughter, Florence (referred to as 'Flossie' and also by the names 'Tzippy Frieda'), who died in October 1918 at just 22 during the Spanish flu epidemic that hit New York in the autumn of that year. Florence does not appear to have had any schooling and may have had either special educational needs or a disability of some kind.[20]

All five Mattuck sons had successful professional careers. The eldest son, Jacob, known as 'Jack', obtained a scholarship to Brown University in Providence, Rhode Island, where he joined the Sock and Buskin Dramatic Club,[21] and played leading parts in Shakespearean productions. He sang as a First Tenor in the university Glee Club,[22] and was sufficiently accomplished to be considered for the lead role in the opera *Faust*.[23] He was elected to the Phi Beta Kappa Society, to which people were nominated on the basis of scholarly achievement, in 1904,[24] and awarded a Bachelor of Philosophy degree in 1905.[25]

After graduating from Brown University, for the next fifteen years Jacob supported his younger brothers in their education as well as the family still living in Worcester.[26] This responsibility meant that he could not get married or pursue his dream of studying for a PhD in sociology. Instead he became a high school teacher, later specialising in chemistry. He taught for a number of years in Providence, then in several schools in New Jersey. He went on to teach at the Manual Training High School in Brooklyn, before moving with its principal to the newly built Brooklyn Technical High School, where he became the chairman of the large chemistry department, a position he held until retiring at the age of 70.

In August 1926, aged 44, Jacob married Rachel (Rae) Bolnik, who was sixteen years his junior and a public grade school teacher. They had two sons, Richard and Arthur, and lived at various addresses in Brooklyn not far from the Mattuck family home (see below). Richard and Arthur attended public schools in Brooklyn where, encouraged by their parents, they excelled, then they attended Harvard and Swarthmore universities respectively. Richard Mattuck was awarded a PhD in physics from Massachusetts Institute of Technology (MIT) and then moved to Scandinavia to undertake research in theoretical physics. He was a professor of physics at Copenhagen University for twenty years before his death in 1982. Arthur Mattuck gained his PhD in mathematics from Princeton University, and became a mathematics professor at MIT in 1959, where he continues to teach in his 80s.

Although Jacob felt that he had not achieved his full potential because of his family responsibilities, he gained a great deal of pleasure from music. While studying at Brown University, he assembled and conducted his own band, which played at dances. At Brooklyn Technical High School he founded and for a number of years conducted an orchestra. He also conducted and wrote cheer songs for the school

Glee Club, whose concerts were on occasion broadcast on the New York public radio station. Jacob retained his strong tenor voice until late in life. He died in 1959.

The third Mattuck son, George – who closely resembled IIM in looks and stature – had an accident when he was a young man in which he lost a leg, and walked with the aid of a prosthetic leg and a cane.[27] He graduated from Worcester Classical High School in 1903[28] and went on to study at Brown University, where he was considered to be highly intelligent. It was recorded in a Brown yearbook that, 'All the knowledge formerly kept on the curriculum of the Worcester Classical High School slid, without a murmur, into George's greedy brain cells.'[29] Like his brother Jacob, George was musically talented and sang in choirs at school and at university.[30]

For two years after he graduated from Brown University, George worked as a stenographer and as a reporter based in Inman Street, Cambridge, Massachusetts, possibly to enable him to save money to pay for further study.[31] He subsequently studied law at Columbia University Law School,[32] and was admitted to the American Bar, Second Department, in 1912.[33] He set up in practice as a lawyer specialising in theatrical law and represented a number of well-known actors and actresses on New York's Broadway. He initially practised law with Louis Freudenberg[34] and, according to a newspaper columnist, was very successful, reputedly 'winning cases faster than I can drink them'.[35] George was a socially ambitious man, who enjoyed the company of his theatrical clients, was always dressed immaculately,[36] and whose activities were sometimes covered in newspaper gossip columns. He later became a partner in the law firm, Mattuck and Mattuck, with Maxwell and later Bernard (see below).

George did not marry. After leaving university, he lived with his parents before moving to uptown Manhattan to share an apartment with his younger brother, Maxwell.[37] He died unexpectedly in 1941 in Dade, Florida.

Maxwell, known by the family as 'Gaga', 'Max' or 'Mac',[38] became a successful lawyer with a high public profile. Family members describe him as 'very smart'.[39] Because of his prominence, quite a lot is known about him. After graduating from Worcester Classical High School in 1910, where he was considered to be 'as fine a scholar as his brother [IIM]' and as 'one of the most attractive young men of Hebrew extraction',[40] Maxwell studied economics at Harvard, from which he graduated in 1914. He was a member of the college orchestra, sang in the Harvard Choir and a Glee Club,[41] played baseball,[42] 'engaged considerably in track work,[43] and participated in the debating team.[44]

His involvement in these many 'outside activities' detracted from his academic performance.[45] Nevertheless, he went on to Harvard Law School, from which he graduated in 1917.

Maxwell was enlisted in the American Army in June 1917, where he served as a Lieutenant of Artillery in the Quartermaster Corps.[46] He was discharged in January 1919 and entered the law practice Rahmold Schribner, located at 61 Broadway, in Manhattan.[47] In 1920, aged just 27, he was appointed as an Assistant United States District Attorney for the Southern District of New York, and by 1925 he had risen to the role of Chief Assistant United States District Attorney at a time when it was uncommon for Jews to obtain jobs in government agencies.[48] He later headed the Criminal Division and subsequently the Commercial Fraud Bureau of the District Attorney's Office. Under Maxwell's leadership, the Commercial Fraud Bureau successfully prosecuted over 200 people accused of stealing merchandise valued in excess of $1 million.[49] In 1923 he was the chief prosecutor in the controversial trial of Marcus Garvey, a proponent of the Black nationalism and Pan-Africanism movements.[50] He was also instrumental in the conviction of Charles J. Steinberg, a former New York lawyer, for evading income tax and perjury.

Maxwell resigned from the District Attorney's Office in 1925 to join the National Association of Credit Men, where he headed drives against fake bankrupts and stock swindlers. He campaigned for the introduction of more stringent laws against the receiving of stolen goods. Shortly after he joined the National Association of Credit Men, he set up and became a senior partner in the Mattuck and Mattuck law firm located at 165 Broadway in Lower Manhattan, the address from which George had previously practised with his partner, Louis Freudenberg. In 1930 Maxwell served as counsel for the American Watch Importers' Association in the fight against watch smuggling. Six years later he was the defence counsel for Louis Buchalter and Jacob Shapiro, two members of Murder Inc., who were charged with racketeering in the rabbit skin industry, and in 1939 he represented general creditors in the reorganisation of the Hudson River Corporation. [51]

Maxwell remained single, but he had a long-standing, non-Jewish mistress whom he felt unable to marry.[52] Although the Mattuck family knew about Maxwell's mistress, her existence was kept secret from the congregation and the rabbi of the synagogue[53] to which the family belonged.[54] Reputedly Maxwell always 'had a cloud hanging over him', either as the result of the uncomfortable situation with his mistress or because of the Marcus Garvey case.[55] He was a member of several prominent New York clubs such as the Harvard Club of New York and

Long Island, a trustee of Harvard Law School and belonged to the Bar Association of the City of New York.[56] Maxwell died in 1957.

Bernard, known as 'Berk' or 'Bertie', was the youngest Mattuck son. He attended Worcester Classical High School and then Erasmus Hall High School in Brooklyn, where he 'did work of such a quality and was of such character himself that he had the highest appreciation of the faculty'.[57] Bernard went on to study Economics at Harvard in 1914. In 1916 he changed from studying Economics to a course in Government.[58]

Bernard was taller and of a more substantial build than his brothers,[59] but as a young man he suffered from asthma. He had a long period of absence from Harvard during 1916[60] and was forced to leave his studies at Harvard part way through his final year to receive 'prolonged medical treatment'.[61] As a result, he sat his final examinations a year later than scheduled. Nevertheless, he had an excellent academic record and was elected to the Phi Beta Kappa Society in 1917 on the basis of his work during 1916/17[62] and received a Deturs prize.[63] He was musical and played the accordion. While he was at Harvard he was a chorister[64] and was also involved in the Dramatic Club Orchestra for which he played the violin.[65]

Despite his asthma, Bernard served in the US Navy, where he was promoted from Seaman Second Class to Chief Boatswain's Mate before entering the Officer Material School in Cambridge, Massachusetts.[66] After he was demobbed in January 1919, he lectured in Economics and government at the University of Arizona in Tucson.[67] It is said that he found the move to the west away from his family a wrench, but living in the dry atmosphere of the Arizona desert was essential to his health.[68] He was sufficiently cured to return to Massachusetts in 1922 to enrol at Harvard Law School, from which he graduated in 1925. He lived independently in New York, but then moved into the family home (see below) for a number of years.

In May 1935 aged 39, Bernard married (in secret) Susan Davis Sawyer, a non-Jewish woman from a well-to-do family, which again was kept from the family rabbi.[69] The couple set up home in a small apartment in Brooklyn. Later they inherited from Susan's family a holiday home in Roxbury, Connecticut to which they retired in 1965. It is said that Bernard chose not to have children so that he did not, in his view, perpetuate his 'wrongdoing' in marrying a non-Jewish woman.[70]

Bernard entered the Mattuck and Mattuck law practice in 1925. Although he always intended to return to teaching, 'inertia' meant that he continued to practise law for the remainder of his career.[71] He was the last surviving partner in the family law firm, where he practised what is described as 'routine law'.[72] During the Second World War he worked as a Government Appeal Agent for the Local Draft Board. Like his brother, Maxwell, Bernard was a member of several clubs, including the Harvard Club of New York, the Harvard Club of Long Island (where he was Secretary and then Director), and the New York County Law Association. He died in Connecticut in1975.

The Move to New York

As they became more affluent, most Jewish families living in Worcester sought to improve both their living situations and their social standing. From about 1910 onwards, the Jewish community started to move in large numbers from the east to the west of the city and to become involved in public life. However, once again, the Mattuck family did not follow the general trend. Worcester city directories for 1914 indicate that during the previous year the family had moved to New York City. By this time the Mattuck sons (apart from IIM) were living and working there and decided to move their parents to the city. Benjamin and Ida were probably happy with this move not only because it meant they would be close to their sons, but also because a move across Worcester, the obvious next step up for the family, would have meant leaving behind their Orthodoxy. The new Jewish community taking shape in the western side of the city was casting aside the rites and practices of the Orthodox synagogue and centring itself on Worcester's first Reform synagogue.

The lawyer Mattuck brothers initially purchased a house for their parents at 628 East 5th Street, in the Kensington and Parkville neighbourhood of Brooklyn, and then a larger property at 466 Argyle Road, in the Flatbush-Ditmas Park neighbourhood.[73] The two older daughters, Rose and Anna, together with Jacob and Bernard, lived with their parents in Brooklyn until their respective marriages. Anna returned to the family home after her marriage failed.[74] By this time Ida was calling herself Ida Bessie Silber Mattuck and Benjamin was known as Benjamin Harris Mattuck.[75] According to his death certificate, after the move to New York, Benjamin worked as a Hebrew teacher.[76] A number of Mattuck relatives had now emigrated to America and were living in Brooklyn, including Benjamin's cousins, Peter, Tillie and Rachel Karp.[77] Later generations of the Mattuck family were to consider themselves New Yorkers rather than being from Worcester.

Benjamin was a heavy smoker,[78] and relatives who visited the family home in Argyle Road say that, by the 1930s, he was very frail and used a lift converted from a dumb waiter to move around the large house.[79] Benjamin and Ida died within three months of each other; Ida on 21

August 1935 and Benjamin on 1 November 1935.[80] All of the Mattuck offspring, with the exception of IIM, are buried alongside their mother in a family plot purchased in 1933[81] at the Mount Lebanon Cemetery in Glendale, New York. For reasons that are not clear, Benjamin was buried separately at Montefiore Cemetery in Long Island.[82]

Maxwell and George moved into the Argyle Road house following the death of their parents. IIM had a financial interest in this property and, for citizenship purposes, cited it as his American residence.[83]

Reflections on the Mattuck Family

Although he was later to extol (rather sentimentally) the sanctity of the Jewish home and the virtues of family life,[84] IIM did not appear to have had the happiest of home lives or to have remained close to his family. A common motif in early twentieth-century American-Jewish literature is of the family problems and chasms created by the experience of separation and emigration.[85] While it is important to remember that a general rule does not apply to all situations, there are some indications that the Mattuck family were traumatised as a result of their journey to America and by their early life there. For example, family members have commented on how unhappy Ida always appears in photographs. This is not surprising given how hard she must have had to work running the family store and raising eight children.

For many years the whole family of ten lived crowded together in small apartments. Photographs document family events such as the sons' *B'nei Mitzvah* and graduations, but these are largely staged studio portraits with family members wearing obviously borrowed clothes in which they look uncomfortable. As with other immigrant families, these family photographs were possibly intended for relatives back in Lithuania, to demonstrate how well they were doing in America rather than to record moments of happiness and celebration.

Further evidence that the family was possibly dysfunctional is that both of IIM's older sisters had failed marriages, which was very uncommon in the Jewish community at this time. The atmosphere in the Argyle Road house at family events such as *sedarim* (ritual service and ceremonial meal held on the first two nights of *Pesach*) is recalled as being 'joyless' and 'cold',[86] and IIM's offspring were later to ponder on the fact that their father never spoke of his parents, particularly of Benjamin, or about his family background. This they found strange given the 'reams of information' they were given on the maternal side of the family.[87]

Of particular interest is IIM's relationship with his father. Living relatives have spoken about how, especially in his later years, Benjamin played very little part in family life, appearing only at mealtimes.[88] Jewish historians have discussed how some immigrant fathers became estranged from their children and developed feelings of inadequacy because of their inability to provide for them in the New World.[89] As will become evident, the Mattuck family certainly struggled with the costs of educating five sons. IIM was possibly thinking of his own parents in a sermon he gave in 1916 when he said: 'the sacrifices the poor Jewish parents make in order that their children may obtain up to as high a point as is possible, sacrifices which at times seem almost superhuman'.[90] Benjamin's unhappiness may have been compounded by his traditional religion. The impression of relatives who remember him is that he was never fully at home in America, where he found it difficult to maintain the tenets of the religion he held so dear and to reconcile what he had left behind with what he had gained by immigrating from Eastern Europe.

While IIM may have been close to his father as a child, later in life there appears to have been a rift between the two, perhaps as a result of IIM's abandonment of Orthodox Judaism, which will be discussed in detail later.[91] Although IIM never spoke of his father's scholarship, we can assume that the great value he came to place on Jewish learning and acquiring an encyclopaedic range of knowledge resulted, at least in part, from the example provided by his father.

When he first left home to go to university, IIM returned home at regular intervals. However, correspondence suggests that the visits became fewer as time progressed.[92] This may have been because he lived further way from the family home, but his nephew, Arthur Mattuck, believes that he left the family environment at the first opportunity, in fact 'he escaped really'.[93] However, while ardour and ambition may have led IIM to prefer a progressive, if chaotic and uncentred American life, his conscience may not have allowed him to be entirely at peace with the situation or the chasm that opened up between himself and his parents and their ideals.

It was not uncommon for immigrant Jewish families to experience dislocation because of the different outlook of the generation brought up in America.[94] The younger Mattuck sons felt unable to share details of their lives with the family rabbi and joined a Reform synagogue, Temple Beth Emeth, in Flatbush New York.[95] However, perhaps not surprisingly, the gulf between IIM and his parents appears to have become even wider after his move to England. Although the letters he received later from his brothers in America provided him with news on the health of his parents, in his surviving personal correspondence there are no references to his father and mother. On his few return visits to

America, IIM did not visit the family home, but saw relatives in his hotel room.[96]

He seems to have had a mixed relationship with his siblings. As we have seen, when they were growing up together in Worcester, the siblings belonged to the same clubs and socialised together. However, while his siblings remained close and continued to live with or near to each other, IIM apparently had no strong desire to maintain the ties to his brothers and sisters. When he left home for Harvard he had some contact with his sisters Rose and Anna,[97] but there is no evidence that he later corresponded with his two older sisters. There are no clues to IIM's relationship with his youngest sister Florence. While he did correspond with all four of his brothers, it is interesting to note that, despite their growing prosperity, at no point during his life there did IIM's brothers visit him in England.

Surviving letters between them suggest that IIM was closest to his brother George. They were less than two years apart in age and were both born in Lithuania, which possibly separated them culturally from their significantly younger brothers Maxwell and Bernard, who were born and brought up in America. Throughout his lifetime, IIM referred to George affectionately by his Yiddish name, 'Zadek',[98] and felt more able to call on George's services[99] to assist in the recruitment of American rabbis for Progressive congregations in England than he did Jacob, Maxwell or Bernard. According to his son Arthur, Jacob was not close to IIM.[100] After IIM's move to England, Jacob had no contact with his younger brother for many years, apart from once writing to him to seek information on a religious matter.[101] In 1955, just a few years before he died, Jacob and his wife embarked on a world tour, including a trip to England during which Jacob visited IIM's grave. This visit is recorded without comment in the diary that Jacob kept of his travels.[102]

Given the nature of Maxwell's career and the recriminations surrounding his involvement in the trial of Marcus Garvey, it might be surmised that he and IIM did not have much in common, and indeed there is little evidence that they communicated regularly until later in their lives. During the 1940s there are references to assistance that Maxwell provided in connection with IIM's American citizenship, and in one long letter Maxwell commented in detail on an article written by IIM.[103] The tone Maxwell adopted in his letters to his older brother is slightly hectoring.[104]

We know nothing of IIM's relationship with his youngest brother, Bernard, other than that they exchanged letters from time to time and appeared to be on cordial terms. Bernard and Maxwell managed IIM's financial interests in America during his lifetime and were executors of his estate there, perhaps indicating that their relationship was more functional than intimate.[105]

We shall shortly see that IIM shared with his four brothers a burning desire to succeed in life, but he appears to have differed from them in a number of important ways, the most obvious of which were his firm adherence to and love of the Jewish faith, his interest in seeing the world (Jacob was the only Mattuck brother to leave America and that was only towards the end of his life), and his apparent lack of need to remain close to his family.

All in all, this picture of Mattuck family life is rather sad given the potentially bonding experiences they had endured and the many achievements and successes there were to celebrate. However, it does provide helpful insights into the shaping of IIM.

NOTES

1. Paula E. Hyman, 'Eastern European Immigrants in the United States', March 2009: jwa.org/encyclopedia/article.
2. The Mattuck family has in its possession photographs of Rose and Anna's high school graduation, but it is not known which school they attended.
3. Email from Betty Wallach, Rose Mattuck's granddaughter, 4 May 2012.
4. *Worcester Daily Spy*, 20 January 1904, p.2.
5. *Worcester Daily Spy*, 28 August 1903, p.6.
6. *Worcester Daily Spy*, 1 July 1903, p.3.
7. *Worcester Daily Spy*, 2 September 1903, p.1.
8. *Worcester Daily Spy*, 28 August 1903, p.6.
9. This is widely cited by family members, but she is not listed as such in Worcester street directories.
10. For reasons that cannot be explained, two separate marriage certificates were issued for Rose's marriage to Jacob Rose, one dated 11 January 1915 and the second dated 2 May 1915. The first related to a ceremony in a restaurant in Brooklyn, and the second to a ceremony at the family home at 628 East 5th Street. The second wedding may have been a religious wedding that followed a civil wedding, but it does not explain why a second certificate was issued. Certificated copies of marriage certificates obtained from New York City Council.
11. Email from Betty Wallach. In this email she stated that her grandmother was thought of as 'a snob'.
12. Conversation with Arthur Mattuck, 3 October 2012.
13. Email from Betty Wallach.
14. Ibid.
15. Conversation with Arthur Mattuck, 3 October 2012. According to Arthur Mattuck, Rose reported her daughter May to child protection services because she did not think that May was feeding them properly.
16. She was listed as a bookkeeper in Worcester street directories from 1904 onwards, initially at 105 Front Street and later at 181 Commercial Road, Worcester. Ancestry.com. US City Directories, 1821–1989 [database on-line]. Provo, UT, USA: Ancestry.com Operations, Inc., 2011.
17. The fact that both Rose and Anna married late owed something to their role in supporting their brothers financially.
18. Information provided by May (Monie) Salkin, daughter of Rose Mattuck.
19. Ibid.
20. In an application for a scholarship when he was studying at Harvard, IIM said that his youngest sister 'stayed at home', Harvard University Biographical Files, call number HUG 300.

21. *Worcester Daily Spy*, 27 January 1902, p.10.
22. Yearbook for Brown University, 1907, Ancestry.com. US College Student Lists, 1763–1924 [database on-line]. Provo, UT, USA: Ancestry.com Operations, Inc., 2012. Original data: College Student Lists. Worcester, Massachusetts: American Antiquarian Society.
23. Email from Arthur Mattuck, 31 May 2012.
24. Yearbook for Brown University, 1904/05, Ancestry.com, US College Student Lists, 1763–1924.
25. Ibid.
26. Information provided by Arthur Mattuck. This is corroborated by correspondence from Jacob Mattuck to the Dean of Harvard, in which he says that he is having difficulty supporting his brother, Maxwell. For example, in a letter dated 25 September 1915 he said: 'If that were all I had to do with my earnings, I would gladly do it, but as it is there are other demands upon it from my family in Worcester, and that makes it rather hard', Harvard University Biographical Files, call number HUG 300.
27. Arthur Mattuck believes that George lost his leg as the result of a fall in the family store in Worcester when he was a child.
28. *Worcester Daily Spy,* 20 June 1903, p.5.
29. Yearbook for Brown University, 1907, Ancestry.com, US College Student Lists, 1763–1924.
30. *Worcester Daily Spy*, 18 April 1903, pp.1–2.
31. Street directories for Cambridge, Massachusetts, 1908 and 1909. See Ancestry.com, US City Directories, 1821–1989.
32. 'Rabbi Mattuck in Worcester: Head of London LJS to Address Economic Club', *Jewish Advocate*, 28 April 1927, p.2.
33. *New York Times*, 9 May 1912.
34. At this time, Jewish lawyers found it difficult to gain employment in non-Jewish law firms because of prejudice, so they tended to join Jewish firms or to set up in business on their own.
35. 'Mutter and Mumble', *Plain Dealer*, 2 March 1930, p.104.
36. Conversation with Arthur Mattuck, 10 May 2012.
37. The brothers appeared to have lived together for a number of years before they moved into the family home in Argyle Road after the death of their parents. See Ancestry.com, US City Directories, 1821–1989.
38. IIM referred to him as 'Mack'. See letter from IIM to his brother Maxwell, 9 April 1941. In other letters Maxwell signed himself as 'Mac'. See letter to IIM, 27 May 1949. Both letters in the Mattuck Family Archive kept by Jill Mattuck Tarule (MFAa).
39. Meeting with Arthur Mattuck, 10 May 2012.
40. Letter from William Abbot, Worcester Classical High School, to unknown recipient at Harvard College, 22 May 1910, Harvard University Biographical Files, call number HUG 300.
41. *Harvard Crimson,* 20 October 1913.
42. *Harvard Crimson,* 1 May 1916.
43. Letter from Jacob Mattuck to Dean Hurlbut, 7 August 1911, Harvard University Biographical Files, call number HUG 300.
44. *Harvard Crimson*, 29 March 1911.
45. Letter from Lawrence Packard, Maxwell Mattuck's history instructor at Harvard, 1 June 1911, Harvard University Biographical Files, call number HUG 300.
46. He was demobbed in January 1919. US Adjutant General Military Records, 1631–1976, Harvard's Military Record in the World War (Sacramento, CA: California State Library, 1921), Ancestry.com Operations, Inc., 2011.
47. *Class of 1914, Sexennial Report* (Cambridge, MA: University Press, 1920).
48. His appointment was supported by the eminent lawyer Emory Buckner, a friend of Simon Mayer, IIM's father-in-law. Letter from George Mattuck to IIM, 7 March 1925, MFAa.
49. Obituary of M.S. Mattuck, unidentified newspaper, 7 November 1957, Worcester Historical Museum.
50. The trial of Marcus Garvey for defrauding his followers destroyed the Back to Africa movement. Garvey's conviction is said to have resulted more from his unpopular concepts than from the evidence, which, allegedly, was slight. See Bernard Ryan, 'Marcus Mosiah Garvey Trial: 1923', Great American Trials, 2002: www.encyclopedia.com.
51. See obituary of M.S. Mattuck.

52. Conversation with Arthur Mattuck, 10 May 2012.
53. Despite extensive research it has not been possible to identify to which synagogue the Mattuck parents belonged in Brooklyn.
54. See email from Betty Wallach.
55. Information from Jill Mattuck Tarule, 25 August 2013.
56. See obituary of M.S. Mattuck.
57. Letter from the Acting Principal of Erasmus Hall High School to Dean Henry Yeomans, Harvard University, 9 January 1917, Harvard University Biographical Files, call number HUG 300.
58. Letter from unknown author to Bernard Mattuck, 20 April 1916, in ibid.
59. Email from Jill Mattuck Tarule, 3 December 2011.
60. Letter from 'Hay' to Bernard Mattuck, 18 November 1916, Harvard University Biographical Files, call number HUG 300.
61. Letter from L.S. Mayo, Assistant Dean, Harvard to Professor A.B. Hart, 10 January 1918, in ibid.
62. *Harvard Crimson,* 4 December 1917.
63. The Deturs Book Prize is the oldest prize in Harvard and is supported by the charity of Edward Hopkins, founder of the prize. Prizes are awarded to the top 10 per cent of students of the sophomore classes as determined by the grade point average earned in their first year at Harvard.
64. *Harvard Crimson*, 22 January 1918.
65. *Harvard Crimson*, 23 January 1917 and *Harvard Crimson,* 31 March 1917.
66. See US Adjutant General Military Records, 1631–1976, 1921.
67. *Class of 1918 Yearbook* (Cambridge, MA: University Press, 1933), p.131. Bernard Mattuck is reported as being a member of the smart set at the university. See 'Sahauro Club Offers Dinner', *Tucson Daily Citizen*, 15 May 1921, p.4.
68. Conversation with Arthur Mattuck, 11 May 2012.
69. Email from Betty Wallach. Apparently the rabbi only discovered by accident that Bernard was married at a family funeral.
70. Conversation with Jill Mattuck Tarule, 11 May 2012.
71. *Class of 1918, Fiftieth Anniversary Report* (Cambridge, MA: University Press, 1968), p.401.
72. Conversation with Arthur Mattuck, 11 May 2012.
73. The exact date of the move to Argyle Road is not known, but it was sometime after 1917. In that year Bernard Mattuck was still giving his home address as 628 East 5th Street. See papers in the Harvard University Biographical Files, call number HUG 300.
74. Divorce rates for the general population in America at this time were relatively low, but even lower for Jewish couples.
75. See First World War Draft Registration Card for Jacob Mattuck. New York; Registration County: Kings; Roll: 1754595; Draft Board: 67, Ancestry.com. US, World War I Draft Registration Cards, 1917–1918 [database on-line]. Provo, UT, USA: Ancestry.com Operations Inc, 2005..
76. Certified copy of death certificate obtained from New York City Council.
77. Genealogical research carried out by Michael Trapunsky, the great-great-grandson of Benjamin Mattuck's brother, David Sher.
78. Email from Arthur Mattuck, 29 July 2011.
79. Ibid.
80. The inscription on Benjamin's gravestone in the Montefiore Cemetery, Long Island reads, 'Here lies our dear father, Rabbi Ben Zion, Son of Yaacov. You dwelt in God's Torah all your life and so your good name will be remembered forever amongst all those who knew you and it will be engraved in the hearts of your sons and daughters. Died 5 Cheshvan 1935. May his soul be bound up in the bonds of eternal life.' The inscription of Ida Mattuck's gravestone in Mount Lebanon Cemetery, Long Island reads, 'Here lies our beloved mother, Chaya Batya daughter of Rabbi Shlomo Leyb. You did a lot of good deeds here on earth and you will be rewarded for them in the world of souls. Your good deeds will be engraved on your sons' and daughters' hearts. Your soul will be in the chain of life.'
81. This means that Florence Mattuck, who died in 1918, may have been buried elsewhere and a gravestone later added to the family plot.
82. Information taken from the death certificate of Benjamin Mattuck. Certified copy of death certificate obtained from New York City Council. Mattuck relatives have suggested that

Benjamin was buried separately from his wife either because Mount Lebanon was not sufficiently Orthodox or because there had been some sort of marital rift. Neither explanation is satisfactory. It is questionable whether Benjamin would have allowed his wife, who died before him, to be buried in a place of which he did not approve and there is no evidence that Benjamin and Ida were estranged. They died within months of each other and Arthur Mattuck, their grandson, maintains that they were very close.

83. See file of correspondence in London Metropolitan Archive relating to IIM's attempts to retain his American citizenship, ACC/3529/002/2012.
84. See his sermons on 'The Sanctity of the Home' given at Temple Israel, Far Rockaway, New York, 15 January 1910 and 'The Spirit of the Jewish Family', given at the LJS, 6 January 1923, Montagu Centre Collection (MCC).
85. For example, Abraham Cahan, *Yekl, A Tale of the New York Ghetto* (New York: D. Appleton, 1896) and Henry Roth, *Call it Sleep* (London: Picador; reprint edition, 2005).
86. Conversation with Arthur Mattuck 10 May 2012. He described the *sedarim* at which those present would mumble to themselves the story of the Exile. Even during the songs at the end of the meal, there was 'no sense of fun'.
87. Notes made by Dorothy Edgar (née Mattuck), in correspondence with her brother, Robert, MFAa.
88. Notes on the life of IIM made by his daughter, Dorothy Edgar (née Mattuck), Mattuck Family Archives kept by Robert Edgar (MFAb).
89. 'The Jewish American Family': www.jewishvirtuallibrary.org/jsource/judaica.l. 'The many hardships of starting life in a new society put great pressures on the functioning of the family. For example, in the lore of the old country the Jewish father was the natural and unchallenged head of the household, respected and feared by all family members. The Jewish mother was revered for her dedication to her husband and the responsibility she assumed for her young children. Upon reaching America these relationships often changed.'
90. 'Religion and the Children', sermon given by IIM at the Bechstein Hall, morning of the Day of Atonement, 7 October 1916, MCC.
91. See notes made by Dorothy Edgar (née Mattuck) in correspondence with her brother, Robert.
92. See his correspondence with his school friend, Archibald Hillman, cited at length in later chapters, American Jewish Archives (AJA), SC-13649.
93. Email from Arthur Mattuck, 29 July 2011.
94. See 'The Jewish American Family'.
95. Conversation with Arthur Mattuck, 10 October 2012.
96. Email from Arthur Mattuck, 29 July 2011.
97. See later reference in Chapter Five to Rose and IIM attending the theatre together.
98. See, for example, correspondence in which IIM refers to his brother as 'Zad' (abbreviation of Zadek). LJS Archives, Box 1/2.
99. It is likely that George Mattuck had contacts that IIM's other brothers did not have because of the nature of his law practice.
100. Arthur Mattuck, Jacob's son, suggests that the two were not close because Jacob eschewed his Jewish religion.
101. Information provided by Arthur Mattuck. Apparently the brothers had an exchange of correspondence about ethics and the meaning of 'Thou preparest a table before me in the presence of mine enemies', Psalm 23:5.
102. Diary in the possession of Arthur Mattuck.
103. Letter from Maxwell Mattuck to IIM, 26 May 1948, in which he discusses IIM's article in the *Journal of Jewish Studies* on Maritain's essay on Jewish suffering, London Metropolitan Archives, ACC/3529/002/017.
104. For example, a letter from Maxwell Mattuck to IIM, 24 January 1950 contains the sentence: 'If you will read my letter of May 27th, 1949 (I often wonder whether you've kept my letters) it may help you to form a basis of your continued right to citizenship.' MFAa.
105. Conversation with Jill Mattuck Tarule, 25 August 2013.

CHAPTER FOUR

Early Education

Towards the end of the nineteenth century, we start to gain a more detailed and specific picture of IIM's development. No details are known of his earliest school years, either in Lithuania or in Boston. In Lithuania he may have been one of the 10 per cent of Jewish children who managed to gain access to a Russian school, but it is more likely that he attended a *cheder*, where his studies would have been limited to learning the Hebrew alphabet, moving on to reading the Pentateuch with Rashi's basic commentary and selected portions of the Talmud with traditional commentaries.[1] Many years later, IIM was to describe the traditional education of Jewish children in Eastern Europe in such nostalgic detail that suggests he was speaking from first-hand experience:

> When the child has barely learned to lisp 'Father' and 'Mother', his instruction is begun. Hebrew is the subject of that early teaching, he might early learn to pray and understand the prayers, and then he might, when still young, come to know the treasures in the storehouse of the ancient literature. And at an age when other children are beginning their [secular] education, learning perhaps the first rudiments of reading and writing, he begins to seek his way through the difficulties, mazes and logical intricacies of the Talmud.[2]

Although he probably arrived in America with very little secular learning, at some stage, probably in Boston, IIM must have received a sound basic education. By the time that the Mattuck family moved to Worcester, IIM was sufficiently fluent in English and his studies advanced enough to enable him to enrol at the public grammar school in Ledge Street, Worcester.[3] The Supervising Principal of the school, Edgar Thompson, found him to be 'a faithful student and a young man of integrity.'[4]

From the time of his arrival in Boston, IIM lived in a tight-knit, homogenous Jewish community, which strived to recreate the customs and traditions of Eastern Europe on American soil. However, at school he was exposed to the culture and values of America. His time at the Ledge Street School kindled in IIM the American patriotism that was to last a lifetime.

His love of the country was partly a result of the way he was taught American history from the time he was eleven (he later said that the school regarded it as 'a subject of first-class importance'[5]), which made him realise that America stood for high ideals:

> We did think of the Revolutionary war as a fight against dreadful odds for freedom, as an aim, a goal in itself. And so, too, with the Civil war was associated chiefly the freedom of the slaves, I think even more prominently than the freedom of the Union ... The war of 1864, which was a case of land grabbing, was not something we were taught to take pride in.[6]

From the age of 12, IIM was taught Civics and, by the time he was fourteen, he knew by heart all of the articles of the Declaration of Independence and the Constitution of the United States. The lessons not only introduced him to American institutions, but the heated discussions that apparently took place on 'salient constitutional points' were equally important in developing IIM's debating skills. Also seminal was the way in which his school observed public holidays in what he referred to as 'my home town' (Worcester). Thirty years later he recalled the emphasis placed on national holidays: 'explaining them, celebrating them with what we used to call exercises which included the recitation of patriotic poems and bits from patriotic speeches, songs, etc., etc., etc., and the finest way of celebrating, a school holiday'.[7]

He recollected reading at school 'Lincoln's famous speech', Washington's addresses, Webster's 'Oration on Broker Hill' and Patrick Henry's speech on 'Give me liberty or give me death' and also reading poetry such as Emerson's 'Bridge' and Lowell's 'The Crisis'. As a schoolboy, IIM witnessed many holiday parades:

> And what wonderful things those parades were! The uniforms, the horses, the music, all combined to produce one great harmony of effect. Who paraded? Well, first there was a line of policemen – or was there only one? Then came a little man with a terribly high hat doing marvellous things with a stick with a silver ball on the end of it, a stick bigger than himself, then the band. The great men followed, some in carriages, some on horses. There were the mayor, some of his aldermen and councillors, and such other grandees whose presence might be suitable and graceful to the occasion. [The parades] grew smaller and smaller each year, and those who remained tottered more and more and their gait and time grew less steady and their

> uniforms showed great age – this was the Grand Army of the republic, they had fought for the union and its ideals, thirty, forty and fifty years ago.[8]

All of this left an indelible impression on IIM, making him feel that 'there was something lovable about our country, that there was something great in it'.[9]

As important to IIM's development as the instruction that he received was the atmosphere that prevailed in the classroom. Prior to the family's emigration, IIM had been told that America was a 'land of opportunity and equality, where the native and immigrant were treated alike', and he found that these principles were practised in the classroom. 'Rich and poor' and 'native and immigrant' sat and learned side by side, which inspired in him an allegiance to the 'land of the free'.[10]

IIM graduated from the Ledge Street School in 1897[11] and transferred, at the age of 14, to the Worcester Classical High School, which prepared boys for higher education, where he was enrolled until 1901. The Classical High School was located on the corner of Maple Street and Walnut Street in Worcester, about half an hour's walk from where the Mattuck family lived. Founded in 1872, the school became a powerful influence in the educational world and gave rise to the founding of a sister school, the English High School. The Classical High School's first Principal was John Adams, who became President of the United States, and amongst its students were several who went on to have high-profile careers, including the author and playwright S.N. Berhman and Abbie Hoffman, a political and social activist who co-founded the Youth International Party.

IIM excelled in his studies. He was included in the Honor List for the Classical High School having graduated with a 'Second Grade Honor', which meant that he had obtained an A mark in at least three-quarters of the required subjects during the four years he was at the school.[12] Although he did not graduate with the highest honours, his achievement was outstanding for a young man who had emigrated from Lithuania less than ten years previously. IIM later paid tribute to his teachers,[13] but he was not uncritical of some of the teaching methods adopted by the Classical High School:

> I have some unpleasant recollections of hours of boredom connected with that subject [geography]. It is really a rich subject and teaches human life at many points … I recall having been taught something about many countries, their rivers, their mountains and their industries. And I remember the dull and difficult work of memorising

> the product of these countries. I don't know whether school children are now taught these things; but if not they ought to be, in a different way, however; that is by being brought into relation with the child's life, with the food he eats, with the clothes he wears, with the house he lives in, with all the things he uses. If my geography teacher had begun by asking me what I had for breakfast, and then told me that coffee came from the Dutch Indies, and what are the conditions that make the coffee grow there, and how the man that grows it lives, and what countries or seas the coffee travelled thorough before it came to me, I should have been much more interested in my geography.[14]

In addition to his academic studies, IIM participated in the Classical High School's Debating Society, Eucleia, which, according to one commentator 'left its mark upon the school and upon the large number of men and women who received their first training in public speaking in the weekly meetings of the society'.[15] During his school holidays IIM also took part in the activities of the Sumner Club Debating Society, which organised inter-school debates between the Classical, and the English High School. In 1901 he sustained the motion that 'The democratic principles underlying the United States Government are in danger of subversion'.[16]

IIM's schooling was supplemented by attendance at some of the many cultural and educational activities established by the ambitious Jewish community in Worcester.[17] IIM was a member of the Hebrew Debating Assembly (HDA) set up in 1898, which met in rooms in Green Street near the family home at that time. The president of this body was Archibald (Archie) Hillman, who was to become IIM's long-standing friend and confidant.[18] In 1899 IIM spoke against a motion that capital punishment for wilful murder should be retained. His brother, Jacob, was one of the judges.[19] IIM became the President of the HDA in 1901. He was also a member of a drama group, the Thespian Club, which when it was set up encountered opposition from the traditional community in which IIM lived because its members included both young men and women – showing that outside his very Orthodox home relaxations were already beginning to occur.[20] IIM remained in touch with his friends from the Thespian Club for several years after he left home.

IIM was supported in his studies by his scholarly father, who appears to have encouraged him to take an interest in current affairs, such as the Presidential election between McKinley and Byron that took place in 1893 when IIM was thirteen and which provided him with a practical lesson in American civic life.[21] We know that, from a very early age, IIM showed exceptional ability in respect of Jewish learning. His father instructed him on the Talmud,[22] but IIM was also taught privately by a Jewish teacher,[23] and probably attended the supplementary Hebrew School located in Green Street at the heart of the Jewish community which, at the time, formed part of almost every Jewish child's educative experience.[24] According to a contemporary commentator, the Hebrew School was led by a 'rebbe', 'steeped in Talmudic lore and unalterably stern in his teaching methods'.[25] The educational institution that IIM entered following his time at Worcester Classical High School was to be a world apart from this religion school.

NOTES

1. Dov Levin, *The Litvaks, a Short History of the Jews of Lithuania,* tr. Adam Teller (New York: Berghahn Books, 2001), p.99.
2. 'Religion and the Children', sermon given by IIM at the Bechstein Hall at the LJS at the morning service on the Day of Atonement, 7 October 1916, Montagu Centre Collection (MCC).
3. Undated newspaper cutting in Mattuck Family Archive kept by Robert Edgar (MFAb). At least one of IIM's brothers (Bernard) also attended this school. See *Boston Herald,* 14 March 1905, p.2.
4. Letter from Edgar E. Thompson to Richard Cobb, 25 June 1901, Harvard University Biographical Files, call number HUG 300.
5. 'The Teaching of Civics in American Schools', address given by IIM to the Stepney Teachers' Council, 24 March 1919, MCC.
6. Ibid.
7. Ibid.
8. Ibid.
9. Ibid.
10. Ibid.
11. 'Rabbi Mattuck in Worcester: Head of London LJS to Address Economic Club', *Jewish Advocate*, 28 April 1927, p.2.
12. *Worcester Daily Spy*, 16 July 1901.
13. *JRU Bulletin,* Vol. XII, no. 56, November 1927, p.10.
14. 'Religion and Education', sermon given by IIM at the LJS, 31 March 1918, MCC. It is interesting to note that from his report card prepared during his final year at Worcester Classical High School, IIM appears to have dropped Geography as a course of study, Harvard University Biographical Files, call number HUG 300.
15. Charles Nutt, *History of Worcester and Its People, Volume 1* (New York: Lewis Historical Publishing Company, 1919), p.717.
16. *Worcester Daily Spy*, 2 May 1901.
17. Norma Feingold and Nancy Sadik, *Water Street: World Within a World* (Worcester, MA: Worcester Historical Museum, 1984), p.46.
18. Archibald (Archie) Hillman was born in Montreal in August 1882. He was the son of Alexander Hillman (one of the members of the Talmud study group to which Benjamin Mattuck belonged in Worcester). He graduated from the Ledge Street Grammar School at the same time as IIM in 1897 and transferred with him to the Classical High School. However, Hillman was forced to leave because of family finances and worked for five years for a Worcester dress manufacturer. During this time he studied bookkeeping at night school and became the company bookkeeper. He returned to the High School and completed the balance of his course in just seven months. He enrolled at Clark University in Worcester in 1904, where he was a member of the debating team that defeated Tufts in 1908. After leaving Clark, Hillman went on to Harvard Law School in 1907, paying his own way through the three-year course. He became the solicitor for Worcester City Council. See *Worcester Telegraph*, 19 December 1954.
19. *Worcester Evening Gazette*, 10 April 1899, typed copy of the article, American Jewish Archives (AJA), SC-13649.

20. See letter from IIM to Archie Hillman, 30 November 1902, in which he mentions the early opposition to the club but says that 'Worcester is now reconciled to its existence', in ibid.
21. See 'The Teaching of Civics in American Schools'.
22. Rabbi Leslie I. Edgar, 'A Personal Appreciation', in *LJM, In Memoriam of Israel I. Mattuck*, 6 June 1954, p.5. According to Edgar he used to mention this with 'quizzical amusement'.
23. Stated in IIM's application to Hebrew Union College, AJA, SC-13649.
24. William Harold Somers, 'A Socio-Historical Study of the Jewish Community of Worcester Massachusetts' (unpublished MA thesis, Clark University, Worcester, MA, 1933), p.81.
25. Ibid., p.98.

CHAPTER FIVE

Harvard

IIM's Experience of Harvard

In September 1901 IIM entered Harvard College (later Harvard University), in Cambridge, Massachusetts. During his last year at Worcester Classical High School, he is said to have evinced a strong desire to attend Harvard to study Semitics, believing he could do so 'most advantageously' there.[1] He enrolled to read Greek, English, German, Semitics, Economics, and Philosophy and the History of Religion, specialising in Semitics. His teachers included Crawford H. Toy, the eminent Old Testament scholar, and George Foot Moore, the outstanding non-Jewish authority on Rabbinic Judaism.

In applying to Harvard, IIM may have been motivated by a desire to establish himself socially as well as to extend his education. At that time it was the place where the sons of the rich and famous received their higher education and its intake was almost exclusively Protestant. However, thanks to the educational innovations introduced by the liberal president of Harvard, Charles Eliot, Jews were beginning to enter Harvard in increasing numbers. Eliot, who was America's leading college president of the day, relaxed Harvard's entrance requirements and admitted all comers who were able to pass a not very challenging entrance exam,[2] and who were able to 'stand before the president' (make a presentation).[3] In his inaugural address Eliot said that poor and rich students were equally welcome 'provided that with their poverty or their wealth they bring capacity, ambition and purity'.[4] Eliot placed a reliance on urban high schools, including Worcester Classical High School, to send their best students to Harvard.[5]

Eliot appears to have genuinely welcomed Jewish students.[6] At the turn of the century, Jewish students at Harvard were few and far between.[7] IIM's year group consisted of around 400 full-time students, of whom twelve declared themselves to be Jewish.[8] By comparison, in 1922 more than a fifth of Harvard's student body was Jewish.[9] The Jewish students became a challenge to the white Anglo-Saxon Protestant ('WASP') hegemony of Harvard not just by their sheer numbers, but also by raising academic standards and winning a disproportionate share of the scholarships.[10] The success of those Jews who made it out of the tenements was particularly resented.[11] A. Lawrence Lowell, Eliot's anti-Semitic successor, like other Ivy League presidents, began to devise quota systems to prevent Harvard becoming 'too Jewish'.[12]

Although Eliot's innovations were very successful in diversifying Harvard, they created a problem. There was now a 'vast social chasm' between rich and poor students that would not have existed in a more homogenous institution.[13] The lifestyle that IIM led at Harvard would have been very different from that of the patrician undergraduates of the day, one of whom was the young F.D. Roosevelt.[14] The wealthy students lived in the 'Gold Coast' of the Mount Auburn Street area of Cambridge, and dined sumptuously with those who had attended the same exclusive private schools (Groton, St Paul's Andover, Exeter and Pomfret), rather than eating, as IIM probably did,[15] at Memorial Hall on Quincy Street, which served cheap but disagreeable food to the less well off.[16]

During his first term at Harvard, IIM lived with his cousin, Golda Davidson, in Roxbury, Boston. IIM was not very enthusiastic about the arrangement and did not expect to make his cousin's house his permanent home while at Harvard.[17] He subsequently lived in Chelsea – an industrial municipality just to the north of Boston – possibly with his father's stepsister, Leah Faiga Mattuck, now Leah Aronson, and for over a year roomed with a third-year Jewish student, Jacob Krokyn,[18] in Wendell Street in Cambridge. Wendell Street was a 'pleasant location', and only a short walk from both Harvard Yard and the Semitic Museum where some of his lectures were held.[19]

IIM was evidently keen to escape the Jewish working-class enclaves of Boston and was pleased when he managed to obtain a room in a Harvard dormitory, College House just off Harvard Square, and eventually in Stoughton Hall in the Yard itself.[20] Although IIM had aspired to live in the Yard, his accommodation there would not have been luxurious. In those days many dormitory rooms above the ground floor lacked heating and plumbing.[21]

Despite the fact that President Eliot claimed in 1901 (the year that IIM entered the College), that Jews were 'better off at Harvard than at any other American college'[22] there was an increasing segregation between Jewish and non-Jewish students. Many Jewish students were forced to commute because they were not able to afford dormitory costs, which made it difficult for them to participate in extra-curricular activities. However, from the end of the nineteenth century, Jews also began to be spurned by the wealthy non-Jewish fraternities and societies and by the hostility of non-Jewish students. Not a single Jew was elected to Harvard's most prestigious clubs (Fly, Delphic and Porcellian), and their involvement in other activities was only tolerated when their presence was seen to be an asset, such as membership of the Harvard debating clubs, where intellectual attainment mattered more than social pedigree.[23] The Jewish students able to afford to live on campus tended to be concentrated in particular dormitories, especially the Walter Hastings Hall, which was nicknamed 'Little Jerusalem'. This situation has led Jerome Karabel to conclude that, at the beginning of the twentieth century, being Jewish was 'a serious social handicap at Harvard'.[24]

As well as experiencing the 'courteous indifference' of Harvard's elite, IIM may have also experienced difficulties, initially at least, in relating to some of the other Jewish students at Harvard. Prior to the 1900s, most Jewish students at Harvard had a German background and practised Reform Judaism. In general, they had mixed well with other students. When IIM entered Harvard, the ranks of German Jews were only just beginning to be swelled by Jews from Eastern Europe. Daniel Greene has suggested that the presence of Eastern European Jews – who sometimes lacked the refined manners of the German Jews, and spoke poor English – would have been quite shocking to the general student body of Harvard.[25] However, at a time when many Americans were beginning to challenge mass immigration from Eastern Europe, there were also tensions between the German-Jewish students and the newcomers as they were seen as undermining the social position that the earlier settlers had gained.[26] Although welcoming of Jewish students, President Eliot was not particularly sensitive to the cultural and religious differences between them. He may have been unaware that, while the German Jews had easily been absorbed into the dominant social pattern, the Eastern European Jews, who were generally poorer and more culturally exclusive, rarely received a cordial welcome from either non-Jews or their co-religionists.

Life in Boston

From his correspondence with his Worcester school friend, Archibald (Archie) Hillman, we have a detailed account of how IIM spent his time at Harvard. Although he sometimes claimed that he was neglecting his studies, it is clear from his letters that he was thoroughly engaged with his work. Professor Toy, who taught IIM Advanced Hebrew, said that throughout his Harvard career IIM was 'uniformly diligent and conscientious'.[27] In comparison to other students at the time, this was probably the case. Under the liberal elective system established by Eliot, there was a tendency amongst undergraduates to elect for 'snap' and 'cinch' courses (i.e. those that were easy to study and pass). He seems to have hung on to every word uttered by his professors, some of whom were very well known. He was particularly admiring of his English professor, Charles Townsend Copeland, who was also a poet, writer and theatre critic, looking forward to Copeland's weekly lectures.[28] Copeland's stories and anecdotes based on his 'Green Room' experiences were duly reported to Archie.

At the turn of the century, academic life at Harvard was not very demanding and IIM had plenty of time available for pastimes other than his formal studies. Even the more conscientious students such as IIM were then devoting no more than twenty-five hours a week to academic work.[29] In his spare time, IIM visited the Boston Public Library to read Jewish and non-Jewish newspapers, taking a particular interest in both local and national politics. He commented at length on the Boston elections of 1902 to his friend Archie, expressing forcefully his view that party politics should not play a part in municipal elections.[30] While he was scathing about the unprincipled motivations of some voters (he felt that they simply followed the voting habits of their fathers),[31] he was quite clear on his own views saying that on most issues 'one cannot fail to get the impression that the Democratic side of every question is the just side'.[32]

IIM was apparently keen to take advantage of any additional opportunities for learning. He obtained tickets for addresses by prominent people invited to speak at Harvard, such as William Jennings Bryan,[33] the 1900 presidential candidate, Richard Gottheil, the American Semitic scholar and Zionist,[34] and Sidney Lee, 'one of the greatest [Jewish] literary scholars of to-day', who spoke on 'Shakespeare's foreign influence'.[35] The speakers he heard not only shaped his views, they also helped in developing skills he would draw on in his career. He observed that Bryan's power as a speaker was in the use of climaxes that 'so increased the tension on the nerves of his hearers that when the end of the climax was reached, the people exploded as it were, with an uproar of applause'. He noted also that Bryan coupled 'lofty and noble sentiments' and 'wide sweeping generalisations'.[36] IIM was to use this learning to good effect in his later sermons and addresses.

While he was not impervious to the cultural life of Boston, IIM appears to have developed an aversion to theatregoing, which he referred to as 'a piece of folly'[37] and expounded at length on the harm that it could do, especially to young people. He was nevertheless willing to accompany his sister, Rose, to see Mrs Leslie Carter play *Madame Du Barry*, in a production which he pronounced 'wholly ineffective' despite Mrs Carter's good acting.[38]

IIM was impressed by the dignitaries he encountered in and around Harvard, such as Prince Henry, Kaiser Wilhelm's brother, when he came to receive his honorary doctorate,[39] and the Prince of Siam whom he saw walking in Cambridge. Initially he found Boston noisy compared to Worcester,[40] but he was soon walking far and wide or riding on an 'elevated car', taking in the sights of the city and witnessing many events. Although he took more than a passing interest in sporting activities and ushered at major baseball fixtures,[41] he participated only in 'a little light gymnastics'.[42] He was far more interested in intellectual pursuits. He read copiously and widely, including the novels of Dickens and Thackeray, and Shakespeare's plays, relaying his thoughts in detail to Archie.

Given his previous pursuits in Worcester, IIM was particularly interested in the activities of the Harvard Debating Club, even when, as he put it, the club 'met its Waterloo' against Princeton in December 1902.[43] In his early days at Harvard, he endeavoured to be included in the sophomore debating team and attended coaching sessions to help him achieve his goal. He was successful, and from then onwards he regularly participated in both inter-class debates and debates with class teams from other universities,[44] for which he was awarded distinctions.[45] IIM debated on topics as diverse as the Monroe Doctrine and the abolition of customs duties on the import of raw materials to America.[46]

However, IIM was not satisfied with his involvement in class debating teams: his ultimate objective was to belong to the Varsity Debating Club and he prepared in earnest to obtain a place in the team that was to compete against Yale in the latter part of 1903.[47] Although he failed to make that particular team, in 1904 he did become a Debating Club member and, eventually, the club's Vice President.[48] IIM was struck by the high proportion of Jewish students involved in Harvard debating clubs, noting (without comment) that they were mainly German rather than Russian Jews.[49]

Although he was obviously enjoying his new life, IIM made a point of keeping in touch with his friends in Worcester whom, even after eighteen months at Harvard, he still seemed to miss. He wrote to his friend Archie:

> This letter will undoubtedly reach you before you go to the HDA [Hebrew Debating Assembly] affair. So kindly don't forget to take two partners for each dance and dance each dance twice, one partner and one dance being for me; and when you applaud the play, do so twice as loud and twice as long as anybody else, all for my sake ... You mustn't forget to write to me all about the dance.[50]

Perhaps his request was based on a feeling that the world of his childhood was slipping away from him. At this point, IIM was returning home at regular intervals and, when he was able to, for Jewish festivals and to participate in the activities of the Thespian Club and the Hebrew Debating Assembly. He was visited at Harvard by his Worcester friends and by his sisters, Rose and Anna. He remained especially close to Archie, now working in a garment factory and attending evening classes. He sometimes devoted his letters to Archie to passing on knowledge he had acquired and commenting on Archie's exercise to assist him in his studies. His comments were often quite forthright:

> In general I think the exercises have been done well, though you have been careless in many respects ... Be sure you get the case endings on your pronouns and adjectives correct and do not forget the E which is affixed to the datives of monosyllables.[51]

IIM was also solicitous for Archie's welfare and concerned that, between his work and evening classes, he was not finding time to enjoy life as much as IIM was at Harvard.[52]

Strangely absent from IIM's correspondence during his Harvard years is any mention of the influx of Eastern European Jews to Boston at this time. IIM must have been aware of this immigration, the result of the pogroms taking place in Eastern Europe. A large proportion of the newcomers arrived poverty-stricken or destitute and some were forced to send their children to beg on the streets of Boston. Jewish charities and immigrant aid movements, which struggled to provide the immigrants with the support they needed to rebuild their shattered lives, sent out regular appeals. Prominent rabbis encouraged Jews already settled in the city to give what they could to address the crises of these years, and mass meetings were held in centres of immigrant life to spread understanding of the federation of charities that was being established. The situation of the immigrants was discussed in both the Jewish and the non-Jewish press.[53]

There are a number of possible explanations for IIM's silence on Jewish immigration to Boston. Perhaps he still felt too acutely the trauma of his own emigration to discuss the situation of those arriving in the city more recently. Alternatively, already on his way to success, IIM may have been discomfited by the condition of those yet to gain a foot on the ladder, or perhaps even a little disdainful of them. Some American Jewish historians have pointed out that first generation immigrants often felt ambivalent towards more recent immigrants from similar backgrounds.[54]

IIM's Financial Situation

During his presidency, Eliot established a generous programme of scholarships and kept tuition fees low to ensure that able students were not turned away from Harvard due to lack of money. However, throughout his undergraduate years, IIM faced severe financial problems, which at times threatened to curtail his studies. When he applied for a place at Harvard, IIM also submitted an application for financial aid to the Price Greenleaf Fund,[55] which was unsuccessful despite the backing of his teachers who pointed out that he was 'poor', 'without aid' and had to 'make his own way in life'.[56] IIM worked over the summer holiday preceding his entry to Harvard,[57] which enabled him to save money to pay for the first instalment of his tuition fees. However, when he arrived in Boston he was living in the 'most discouraging of circumstances'[58] and it was unclear on how he was going to be able to support himself beyond his first term at Harvard. He was able to supplement his meagre savings by working temporarily as an agent selling insurance for the Mutual Life Insurance Company of New York. He quipped to his friend Archie, 'so if you want to get insured, just let me know'.[59] He occasionally received a 'box of refreshments' from his friends in Worcester to help him 'get by'.[60]

In December 1901 IIM again applied for Price Greenleaf aid saying that, unless he was able to obtain support, he did not know how he would be able to remain at Harvard.[61] It is unclear whether he was successful or not, but by March 1902 his debts were mounting and he applied for emergency financial aid. He explained that he had initially been able to live rent-free, but now had to pay for his board and lodgings. He said that his family were not in a position to help him given that only one of his siblings, his oldest sister, was working and the income from the family business was just $12–14 per week.

Dean Hurlbut arranged for IIM to be given $40 from the Harvard Beneficiary Fund to allow him to finish his first year at Harvard. IIM again worked through his summer holiday to build up his savings,[62] and was awarded a Sewall Scholarship for the academic year 1902/03 and a C.L. Jones Scholarship for 1903/04.[63] However, the scholarships and the money he earned from teaching one evening per week[64] did not meet even his basic costs and, in both 1903 and 1904, IIM was forced to apply to the Dean for further emergency aid.[65] He was awarded a Class of 1856 Scholarship[66] for his final year at Harvard, which he hoped would mean that he would not have to take a job and would therefore be able to concentrate on his studies. His success in obtaining this scholarship was due to his increasing academic progress, but also the backing of the professors who taught him and the testimonial provided by D.G. Lyon, the Curator of the Semitic Museum and Professor of Divinity.[67] He appears to have managed to exist on his scholarship for the first part of the academic year, but in 1905 was once again struggling to pay his tuition fees.[68] It is interesting that he seems to have submitted these applications without any hint of embarrassment. His desire to succeed seemingly helped him overcome any inhibitions he might have had about asking for financial assistance.

Jewish Identity and Religious Beliefs

Over the course of his Harvard career IIM both affirmed his Jewish identity and adopted a new form of Judaism. When he arrived at Harvard, he was still traditionally observant. In one of his letters to Archie he mentions his regular morning prayers.[69] Even more telling, however, is the way in which he wrote about his first visit to the Reform synagogue, Adath Israel.[70] The synagogue was then situated in Columbus Avenue, Boston, within easy walking distance of IIM's cousin's house in Roxbury where he was living.[71] At the time, it was the only Reform synagogue in Boston, and the wealthiest and most socially prominent in New England. After a period of radicalism under the leadership of Rabbi Solomon Schindler, who introduced Reform Judaism to New England,[72] it was in the process of becoming more traditional. It eventually parted company with Schindler's successor, Charles Fleischer, because of his sectarian beliefs.[73]

IIM was surprised to see the number of women attending the Adath Israel service ('there were but three or four men' he told his friend, Archie), the arrangement of men and women sitting together, singing accompanied by an organ (which, he thought, 'adds to the praying in one way, and detracts in another'), the lack of talking during the service and the conduct of prayers in English. IIM also commented on the fact that the service was led by Rabbi Fleischer, rather than by men from the congregation, and on the rabbi's style of address. He noted that the Torah was taken out of the Ark at 'the proper time', but was unsure about Fleischer reading from Deuteronomy in Hebrew and then translating each verse in turn. He was clearly unused to a rabbi who spoke about politics and mentioned social issues of the day. The rabbi sounded to IIM like a 'Catholic priest' and with 'every statement made his anti-Jewish spirit was more evident'. He concluded: 'All in all, I did not like him speaking. He is a young man and "a handsome young fellow", but apparently a very small Jew religiously and politically.'[74] Although IIM would not have been aware of it then, Fleischer was the epitome of the Reform rabbi of the time. It was a style that IIM was to make his own. The importance of IIM's experience at Adath Israel cannot be overestimated.

IIM also wrote to Archie about witnessing mass meetings organised by Zionists. At this time Boston was one of the most prominent American cities for Zionism, and organisations such as the Sons of Zion spread out in a network across the areas of Jewish settlement in the city. In 1902 *The*

Boston Herald reported that 'The Zionists are in dead earnest ... They argue zealously in scenes of wild confusion during the debates on powers of the Zionist Federation.'[75] IIM deplored the haranguing of the speakers and felt that the meetings were 'dominated by a spirit of pugnacity'.[76] The Zionist organisations were largely made up of people from Eastern European backgrounds similar to IIM's. His derogatory comments are therefore very interesting and suggest either an aversion to Zionism dating back to his childhood in Lithuania, or perhaps a dislike of the loudness and brashness of recent immigrants from whom he wanted to distance himself.

IIM was deeply moved by the opening of the new Semitic Museum[77] at Harvard, an event he attended as an usher in February 1903. He reported the occasion in detail to Archie and enthused about his sightings of a number of Jewish dignitaries, including the railroad financier and philanthropist Jacob Schiff (who had presented to Harvard his Semitics collection together with the money for the new museum), Cyrus Adler, founder of the Jewish Welfare Board and editor of the *Jewish Encyclopaedia,* Dr Solomon Schechter of the Jewish Theological Seminary in New York and Joseph Strauss, co-owner of Macy's department store and President of the Jewish Educational Alliance. According to IIM, at this event 'Plaudits for the Jewish race were showered in heaps'.[78]

While IIM may have been socially ambitious and keen to grasp the opportunities offered by life in America, he clearly had no desire to become totally assimilated. To him it would probably have seemed contrary to the spirit of democracy for which he had come to believe that America stood – democracy meant freedom to make choices, freedom to be oneself. The wiping out of his culture seems to have been too high a price to pay for becoming an American. Although this outlook may not yet have been fully articulated, it was to become a theme of his later sermons.

Whether from choice or necessity, he largely associated with Jewish students and thought a lot about Jewish issues. In one of his letters to Archie, he told his friend that a fellow Jewish student had come to his room at 8.00 one evening, and they had spoken until 1.30 in the morning about the duty of Jewish students to the Jewish people.[79] He appears to have been quite excited when an informal Jewish group was set up in 1903 by Leo Mayer,[80] who was in the same year group as IIM and had a deep interest in Jewish issues.[81] IIM promptly joined the group, the aim of which was to enable Jewish undergraduates to 'discuss things Jewish' for 'pleasure and enlightenment'.[82]

Initially the unnamed Jewish group met irregularly in the room of one of its members and its meetings were led in turn by those participating in its activities. Early discussions included one on the causes of anti-Semitism and at another meeting there was a presentation on the recent travels of one of the 'fellows' through Eastern Europe, which IIM enjoyed even though there was 'comparatively little new that came out of the discussion'.

Although the Jewish group was never recognised as an official campus body and it continued to maintain a fairly low profile, its existence did not go unnoticed and it began to attract hostile criticism. Until this point Jewish students at Harvard had generally sought to avoid friction by going about their business quietly and unobtrusively and adopting a policy of either ignoring or denying any anti-Semitism they encountered.[83] The group responded to the hostility by saying that while reticence was important in helping to reduce prejudice, 'the study of his religion and its ideals must brighten the Jew's mounting self-esteem'.[84] The group may have been very helpful in allowing IIM to maintain his Jewish identity in a citadel of 'WASP' culture.

By 1905 the unofficial group was sufficiently well organised to attract prominent speakers to address its meetings. The speakers included Julia Richman, a prominent educationalist in New York's East Side and a leading member of the Council of Jewish Women, who spoke on 'The East Side'; Charles Fletcher Dole, an influential Minister who spoke on 'The Twentieth Century Religion'; Simon Julius Lubin, who graduated from Harvard in 1903 and became a settlement worker in Boston's South End. Le Baron Russell Briggs, the first Dean of Men at Harvard University, where he also served as Dean of the Faculty, spoke about 'Jewish Prejudice at Harvard'; and Professor George Herbert Palmer, Alford Professor of Natural Religion, Moral Philosophy and Civil Polity at Harvard, spoke on 'The Education of the Jewish Immigrant'.[85]

IIM was present at a meeting of the Jewish group held in the Perkins Hall at Harvard on 6 January 1905, when Solomon Schindler[86] led a 'spirited and interesting discussion' on 'inter-marriage between Jew and non-Jew'.[87] Schindler (see above) was an anti-Zionist and the author of *Dissolving Views of the History of Judaism*,[88] a compilation of his lectures delivered at Adath Israel between 1887 and 1888. Rabbi Fleischer, whom IIM had witnessed preaching in 1901, also spoke on the subject of intermarriage.[89] Given the combination of the membership of the group, which was largely made up of American-born German Jews, and the progressive views of some of the visiting speakers, this group must have been a strong influence on IIM's developing outlook. It may also have been the genesis of his lifelong esteem for all things German. Some years later he was to declare that the Germans were 'a very clever people, so clever that the world, even when reprobating them, had to admire their ingenuity'.[90] While he appears to have been somewhat in awe of the German Jews in his early days at Harvard, by the end of his time there, some of his closest friends were German Jews including 'Dietz' (Richard Priest Dietzman), a co-member of the Harvard debating teams.[91]

We are able to say with some authority that IIM's remarkable shift away from Jewish orthodoxy took place while he was at Harvard. He may have been questioning Jewish traditions while still at school in Worcester, but it is clear that gaining access to one of America's elite institutions was the main catalyst for IIM to reconsider his self-definition as a Jew in a liberal society and his religious beliefs. We have seen that on his arrival in Cambridge he was traditionally observant and critical of a Reform service, but within a few years he had turned his back on the restrictions of religious orthodoxy and had taken the decision to enter a Reform seminary. In the absence of any memoirs and the availability of only a handful of personal reminiscences, it is not possible to reconstruct this transition in great detail. However, we are able to gain some insight from a moving statement IIM made seven years after leaving Harvard:

> In my own case ... real faith began at a time when I was really denying all the dogmas I had been taught, and refusing belief to anything supernatural or out of the normal. It was not until I had thrown overboard the mass of doctrines and practices that I adhered to in my state of orthodoxy that I could feel the quickening of faith within me. Before that time, it is true I was afraid of God and shuddered at the very thought of violating the least of His commands, thinking of the dire consequence that would follow in the form of very hot fires. Yet, after I had thrown these all over, there remained a certain indefinable longing for something that would explain the universe, rationally it is true, but above all, satisfactorily to the desires of the heart; a groping about for a star to which I might link my humble cart to be led and guided through the unmeasured immensities of life.[92]

In the latter part of the nineteenth century, Eastern European Jews had been shunned by the acculturated German Jews because of the rigidity of their beliefs and for being 'lower class'. However, as the newcomers began to assimilate and prosper, the 'Ostjuden' came to be regarded as a new source for bolstering and ensuring the future vitality of Reform communities.[93] The interest was sometimes mutual. For the upwardly mobile Eastern European Jews, the Reform synagogue represented social status.[94] Therefore, just as IIM may have been attracted to Harvard partly as a means for self-advancement, he may not have been immune to the institutional prominence of and kudos attached to Reform Judaism, seeing its adoption not only as a mark of independence from his upbringing, but also a move to a higher social class.

In shifting away from the strict orthodoxy of his early years to the then radical theology of Reform Judaism, we might suspect that a specific individual influenced IIM. While there is no firm evidence to confirm this, a possible candidate is Rabbi Charles Fleischer of Adath Israel. Although he later parted company with the synagogue because of his sectarian views, during IIM's Harvard days Fleischer was one of the foremost ambassadors for Reform Judaism. Fleischer was a close friend of Charles Eliot, and advertised services in the *Harvard Crimson* encouraging Jewish students to attend.[95] He gave many lectures and addresses at Harvard, and advised the college on matters of Jewish faith. Fleischer would therefore have been well known to IIM, who may have been amongst the sons of Eastern European Jews (along with many non-Jews) who are said to have flocked to his Sunday services.[96] Fleischer appealed particularly to those who, like IIM, were of a scholarly disposition. In 1905 a Boston newspaper wrote of Fleischer that 'no man in Boston ... [has] a greater following amongst young intellectuals'.[97] At around this time, the Central Council of American Rabbis, the governing body for Reform rabbis in America, began to encourage rabbis to reach out to Jewish university students to retain their loyalty while they studied in Christian environments.[98]

In addition, many of Fleischer's views closely resembled those for which Mattuck was later renowned. Fleischer was noted for speaking out on myriad ideas, causes and issues of the day, bringing together Jews and Christians, his support of women's suffrage and the participation of women in synagogue life, his anti-Zionism (he derided Zionists as 'not Americans' and insisted that Zionism had died two thousand years previously),[99] his advocacy of labour rights, and his commitment to social justice. He made his synagogue into a civic forum, and organised talks, discussion groups and lectures by and involving like-minded reformers.[100] Fleischer was proud of the fact that he had not been born in America, but had managed to fashion for himself a strong American identity.[101] A cultural pluralist before the term was coined, Fleischer's main platform that Jews could be both Jews and good citizens of the countries in which they lived was to become one of IIM's most abiding beliefs.

Whether or not Fleischer was a seminal influence, it is noteworthy that IIM made the dramatic shift towards Reform Judaism and evinced a deep antagonism towards Zionism in a city that had one of the least progressive Jewish communities and was known as a centre of Zionism. Interestingly, one of the lengthy essays that he wrote as part of his Harvard studies included a very detailed discourse on the rise of Zionism and arguments against it.[102]

When IIM entered Harvard he was undecided on his future career. In his scholarship applications he indicated that he might become either a Semitics teacher or study for the rabbinate, with a leaning towards the former.[103] In his letters to Archie he appears on occasion to be testing out some of the skills that he might need in either of these professions – his sermon-like discourses, his ponderings on ethical issues, his semi-lectures on various topics. Eventually in his final year as an undergraduate he decided that he would study for the rabbinate. A few years hence IIM was to reveal that his father had always hoped he would become a rabbi.[104] However, his father's shock may have been quite profound when IIM announced that he intended to become a Reform rabbi.

Having reached his decision, IIM set out with characteristic determination to ensure he gained the relevant experience to give him a good start in his chosen career. Over the summer preceding his final year at Harvard he spent some time travelling before serving for three months as the temporary rabbi at the Reform congregation, Sons of Israel and David (later Temple Beth-El), in Providence, Rhode Island (perhaps lodging with his brother Jacob, who was now teaching in the city). At the end of this appointment, IIM was commended by the lay leadership of the synagogue for the capable way in which he had assisted both in taking services and instructing the confirmation class.[105]

This experience was probably pivotal in his successful application to study at Hebrew Union College (HUC) in Cincinnati. IIM may have been attracted to HUC because of its progressive reputation, but perhaps also by the availability of tuition-free education and scholarships[106] and the increasingly high salaries that Reform rabbis were able to command as their status rose commensurate with the social status of the laity they served.[107] Even small congregations, many of them burdened with building debt, were willing to strain their meagre resources to place their rabbi in a position of relative comfort and independence.[108] IIM's career at HUC will be discussed in detail in the next chapter.

Academic Achievement

From the outset of his Harvard career, IIM obtained good grades in each of his courses, and his performance improved to excellent as his studies progressed.[109] By the end of his third year at Harvard, he had accrued sufficient credits to receive the degree of Bachelor of Arts (AB) *magna cum laude*,[110] which would normally have taken four years to obtain. Having achieved the highest possible distinctions, he was placed in the 'First Group', which included those whose work 'entitles them to very high academic distinction'.[111] Just fifty out of 2,000 students at Harvard attained this rank annually. He was also awarded a Deturs Prize for a paper he wrote on Bacon's essays,[112] and was elected to the prestigious national undergraduate honour society, Phi Beta Kappa, the pin for which he subsequently wore on formal occasions.[113]

In his junior year at Harvard (1903–04) IIM dropped courses in Economics and Philosophy in favour of Semitics modules and became involved in the activities of the Semitic Conference that met in the new Semitic Museum. IIM sometimes spoke at Semitic Conference meetings, such as at the meeting held in June 1904 when he gave an address on 'Job and Plato'.[114] In his final year at Harvard (1904–05), IIM concentrated exclusively on Semitics. According to Harvard records, IIM excelled in this but, for reasons that are not apparent, the awarding of his Master of Arts Degree (AM) was postponed until 1907.[115] During his time at Harvard, IIM received two 'honorable mentions' for Semitic languages and one for German.[116] He was also commended for his ability and tact as a teacher.[117]

When IIM left Harvard, its Dean remarked that he had been 'a brilliant student' and that his 'connection with College has been in every way creditable'.[118] Professor Toy described IIM as 'an exceptionally promising man, both in scholarship and character', and said, 'I expect great things from him both as a Minister and as a scholar'.[119] Professor Moore was equally fulsome, saying, 'I have the impression that he is a man of much more than ordinary promise'.[120]

After Harvard

Over the summer of 1905 IIM travelled through America, ending up in Louisville, Kentucky to stay with his friend 'Dietz' at his home 'half out in the country'. After his friend returned to Cambridge to attend Harvard Law School, IIM remained as a guest of Dietzman's parents.[121] The Dietzmans made things 'very pleasant' for IIM, taking him around the town in one of their horse-drawn carriages to meet some of the prominent Jewish people in the area, including the proprietors of the Kaufman-Straus & Co department store (Henry Kaufman and Benjamin Straus) and its treasurer, 'a man named Dreyfuss', who was also president of the Young Men's Hebrew Association.[122] IIM clearly relished meeting people with wealth and status.

His letters to Archie suggest that IIM may have been attracted to one of the young women in their close group of friends but that the relationship did not work out.[123] This is confirmed by Mattuck family members who understand that a relationship he formed in Worcester was broken off because, at that stage, 'he had no prospects'. [124] However, by the time he reached Louisville, Mattuck had plainly embarked on the quest for a marriage partner and was looking far beyond the Worcester community for a potential wife. In his eyes, marriage, like education, was a potential means for advancement. Writing to Archie, he described the young women of Louisville as 'beauties', and 'a treat just to look at'.[125] He revealed to Archie that Mr Dreyfuss had promised to introduce him to his daughter, whom IIM had already noticed when out driving with Dietz's parents. This introduction failed to happen, but IIM was seemingly more upset that he had not been able to keep 'the dates' that had been arranged for him the previous week.[126] It is possible that the family back in Worcester may have identified a suitable partner for IIM in the Jewish community there, but he clearly was set on making his own decision. However, it was to be several years before he was to find a woman whom he regarded as being a suitable partner.

From Louisville IIM moved on to Mount Vernon, Indiana where he preached on a Friday night and a Saturday morning of the High Holydays. His preaching 'went off fairly well' and he 'wasn't kicked from the pulpit'. However, he was much less enamoured with the town than he had been with Louisville. It had a small Jewish community of just thirty families supporting a small temple. Some of his 'parishioners' had pretty daughters, which was its only redeeming feature.[127] He was now starting to look forward to embarking on his course at Hebrew Union College and had already found accommodation in Cincinnati.

NOTES

1. Letter from William Abbot (IIM's Homer instructor at Worcester Classical High School) to 'Whom it may concern', 15 April 1901, Harvard University Biographical Files, call number HUG 300.
2. Jerome Karabel, *The Chosen: The Hidden History of Admission and Exclusion at Harvard, Yale and Princeton* (Boston, MA and New York: Houghton Mifflin Company, 2005), p.22.
3. Daniel Greene, *The Jewish Origins of Cultural Pluralism, The Menorah Association and American Diversity* (Bloomington, IN: Indiana University Press, 2011), p.20.
4. Quoted in Karabel, *The Chosen*, p.40.
5. Jenna Weissman Joselit, 'Without Ghettoism: A History of the Intercollegiate Menorah Association, 1906–1930', *American Jewish Archives Journal*, 30, no.2 (1978), p.133.
6. Jonathan D. Sarna, 'The Jews of Boston in Historical Perspective', in Jonathan D. Sarna, Ellen Smith and Scott-Martin Kosofsky (eds), *The Jews of Boston, Essays on the Occasion of the Centenary of the Combined Jewish Philanthropies of Greater Boston* (New Haven, CT: Yale University Press in collaboration with the Combined Jewish Philanthropies of Boston, 2005), p.15.
7. William A. Braverman, 'The Emergence of a Unified Culture, 1880–1917', in ibid., p.81.
8. *Harvard College, Class of 1905, Secretary's First Report* (Cambridge, MA: Harvard University Press, 1906), p.17.
9. See Braverman, 'The Emergence of a Unified Culture', p.80.
10. Marcia Graham Synnott, *The Half-Opened Door: Discrimination and Admissions at Harvard, Yale and Princeton, 1900–1970* (New Brunswick, NJ: Transaction Publishers, 2010), back cover.
11. Nitza Rosovsky, *The Jewish Experience at Harvard and Radcliffe* (Cambridge, MA: Harvard Semitic Museum, 1986), p.6.
12. Hasia Diner, *A New Promised Land: A History of Jews in America* (New York: Oxford University Press, 2003).
13. See Karabel, *The Chosen,* p.45.
14. F.D. Roosevelt was in the year ahead IIM, having entered Harvard in 1900. Although he had a Jewish background he does not appear to have associated with the Jewish students.
15. It is not known whether at this time kosher meals would have been available at Harvard.
16. See Karabel, *The Chosen*, p.14.

17. Letter from IIM to Archie Hillman, 3 October 1901, American Jewish Archives (AJA), SC-13649.
18. Krokyn graduated from Harvard with a degree in architecture in 1905. He was one of the first Jews to be registered as an architect in Boston. Krokyn was born in Boston but his parents immigrated to America from Eastern Europe. IIM referred to Krokyn unflatteringly as a 'Boston Kike'. Letter from IIM to Archie Hillman, 28 September 1902, in ibid.
19. Ibid.
20. During his Harvard days IIM lived at 4 Sherwin Street, Roxbury (the home of his cousin); 186 Arlington Street in Chelsea, Massachusetts (Arlington Street lay at the heart of a poor, predominantly Jewish area of Chelsea, which became known as 'Yerushalayim D'America'); 57 Wendell Street; Room 61 College House and then Room 3 Stoughton Hall, where he lived during his fourth year at Harvard. Information in IIM's letters to Archie Hillman, in ibid.
21. See Karabel, *The Chosen,* p.14.
22. See Synnott, *The Half-Opened Door*, p.45.
23. See Joselit, 'Without Ghettoism', p.135.
24. See Karabel, *The Chosen,* p.98.
25. See Greene, *The Jewish Origins of Cultural Pluralism,* p.18.
26. See Synnott, *The Half-Opened Door,* p.45.
27. Letter from C.H. Toy to unknown recipient, 12 April 1904, Harvard University Biographical Files, call number HUG 300.
28. Letter from IIM to Archie Hillman, 13 December 1902, AJA, SC-13649.
29. See Karabel, *The Chosen,* p.21.
30. Letter from IIM to Archie Hillman, 13 December 1902, AJA, SC-13649.
31. Ibid.
32. Letter from IIM to Archie Hillman, 12 January 1902, in ibid.
33. Letter from IIM to Archie Hillman, 12 January 1902, in ibid.
34. Letter from IIM to Archie Hillman, 3 April 1902, in ibid.
35. Letter from IIM to Archie Hillman, 18 February 1903, in ibid. Sir Sidney Lee (1859–1926) was an English biographer and critic. He was born Solomon Lazarus and became editor of the *Dictionary of National Biography*.
36. Letter from IIM to Archie Hillman, 12 January 1902, in ibid.
37. Letter from IIM to Archie Hillman, 20 May 1902, in ibid. He made this pronouncement on hearing that his sister (it is unclear which one) had been badly frightened by a theatre performance.
38. Letter from IIM to Archie Hillman, 18 February 1903, in ibid.
39. Letter from IIM to Archie Hillman, 9 March 1902, in ibid.
40. Letter from IIM to Archie Hillman, 3 October 1901, in ibid.
41. *Harvard Crimson*, 20 November 1903.
42. Letter from IIM to Archie Hillman, 30 November 1902, AJA, SC-13649.
43. Letter from IIM to Archie Hillman, 3 December 1902, in ibid.
44. *Harvard Crimson*, 8 May 1903. IIM was a member of the class debating team that debated against a team at Williams College, the private liberal arts college in Williamstown, MA.
45. *Harvard College, Secretary's First Report, Class of 1905* (Cambridge, MA: Cambridge University Press, 1906).
46. *Harvard Crimson*, 21 December 1902.
47. Letter from IIM to Archie Hillman, 13 December 1902, AJA, SC-13649.
48. *Harvard Crimson*, 27 May 1904.
49. Letter from IIM to Archie Hillman, 13 December 1902, AJA, SC-13649.
50. Letter from IIM to Archie Hillman, 8 February 1903, in ibid.
51. See for example letter from IIM to Archie Hillman, 16 December 1903, in ibid.
52. For example, letter from IIM to Archie Hillman, 13 November 1901, in ibid.
53. Account taken from J. Jacob Neusner, 'The Rise of the Jewish Community in Boston, 1880–1914' (unpublished BA thesis, Harvard University, 1953), AJA, SC-1240.
54. See for example: Jonathan D. Sarna and Jonathan Golden, 'The American Jewish Experience Through the Nineteenth Century: Immigration and Acculturation', Brandeis University, National Humanities Centre: nationalhumanitiescenter.org/tserve/nineteen/nkeyinfo/judaism.htm
55. Letter from IIM to Richard Cobb, 24 April 1901, Harvard University Biographical Files, call number HUG 300.

56. Letter from William Abbot, 15 April 1901, and from Edgar E. Thompson, 25 June 1901, in ibid.
57. Mentioned in his letters seeking financial aid, in ibid. Where he worked is not specified.
58. Letter from IIM to Richard Cobb, Harvard College, 13 December 1901, in ibid.
59. Letter from IIM to Archie Hillman, 3 November 1902, AJA, SC-13649.
60. Letter from IIM to Archie Hillman, 13 December 1902, in ibid.
61. See letter from IIM to Richard Cobb, 13 December 1901.
62. Again we do not know where he worked.
63. See Harvard College, Secretary's First Report.
64. Letter from IIM to Dean Hurlbut, 28 March 1903, Harvard University Biographical Files, call number HUG 300. We do not know where he taught.
65. See letters from IIM to Professor Hurlbut, 1 April 1903 and 3 June 1904, in ibid. In 1903 IIM received aid of $40, and in 1904 he received aid of $20. The Dean asked him to regard this aid as a loan to be repaid in due course. When, seven years later, IIM's brother Maxwell Mattuck found himself struggling in the same way as IIM, the Dean of the College in response to a request for aid from Maxwell, suggested that he should now look to IIM for support. See letter from Dean Hurlbut, 21 September 1911.
66. 'Application for Fellowship 1904/5', in ibid.
67. Letter from D.G. Lyon to Dean Hurlbut, 11 May 1904, in ibid.
68. Letter from IIM to Dean Hurlbut, 3 February 1905, in ibid.
69. Letter from IIM to Archie Hillman, 20 May 1902, AJA, SC-13649.
70. The synagogue started out as an Orthodox temple but became more radical.
71. Letter from IIM to Archie Hillman, 3 November 1901, AJA, SC-13649.
72. Solomon Schindler (1842–1915) was born in Neisse, Germany. After emigrating to America in 1871, he became the minister of the congregations at Hoboken, New Jersey before becoming the rabbi at Adath Israel. He left Judaism declaring himself to be a socialist and an agnostic, but later returned to Judaism.
73. After serving as an assistant rabbi in Philadelphia, Fleischer (1871–1942) was appointed to Adath Israel in 1894 and left in 1911. Having emigrated from Breslau in 1880, Fleischer graduated from the College of the City of New York in 1888 and from the University of Cincinnati in 1893. He studied for the rabbinate at HUC. After he left Adath Israel he founded a Progressive, non-denominational religious institution, the Sunday Commons of Boston.
74. Letter from IIM to Archie Hillman, 3 November 1901, AJA, SC-13649. Fleischer was known as Back Bay's 'most eligible bachelor' or the 'Beau Brummel of the Back Bay'.
75. Quoted in Neusner, 'The Rise of the Jewish Community in Boston'.
76. Letter from IIM to Archie Hillman, 21 June 1902, AJA, SC-13649.
77. The Semitic Museum was founded in 1889, and moved into its present site at 6 Divinity Avenue in 1903. It was opened by President Eliot and speeches were given by Professor D.G. Lyon, Curator of the Museum, as well as by Schiff.
78. Letter from IIM to Archie Hillman, 5 February 1903, AJA, SC-13649.
79. Letter from IIM to Archie Hillman, 15 January 1903, in ibid.
80. Leo Mayer went on to become a prominent orthopaedic surgeon.
81. *American Hebrew and Jewish Messenger*, 3 February 1905, p.341.
82. Ibid.
83. For example, see letter written by Alfred Benesch, in Rosovsky, *The Jewish Experience at Harvard and Radcliffe*, pp.70–1.
84. Letter written by A.W. Goldsmith, 'Jewish Societies at Harvard', *The American Israelite*, 30 March 1905, p.4.
85. *American Hebrew and Jewish Messenger*, 3 February 1905, p.341. List of names taken from this newspaper article, but information on the speakers derived from information available on the Internet.
86. See note 72 on Schindler.
87. *American Hebrew and Jewish Messenger*, 3 February 1905, p.341.
88. Solomon Schindler, *Dissolving Views in the History of Judaism* (Cambridge, MA: Lee and Shepard, 1888).
89. *American Hebrew and Jewish Messenger*, 3 February 1905, p.341.
90. 'Religion and the Children', sermon given by IIM at the Bechstein Hall at the LJS morning service of the Day of Atonement, 7 October 1916, Montagu Centre Collection (MCC).
91. Harvard University, Class Album for the Class of 1905, Harvard University Archives.

92. 'The Aims of Our Religion School', address given by IIM at a meeting of the LJS congregation held in the Wharncliffe Rooms at the Hotel Great Central, 7 March 1912, MCC.
93. Alan Silverstein, *Alternatives to Assimilation, The Response of Reform Judaism to American Culture, 1840–1930* (Boston, MA: Brandeis University Press, 1994), p.149.
94. Herbert Parzen, *Architects of Conservative Judaism* (New York: Jonathan David, 1964), pp.63–6.
95. *Harvard Crimson,* 3 October 1902.
96. Abraham J. Karp, 'A Century of Conservative Judaism in the United States', *American Jewish Year Book 1986* (Philadelphia, PA: Jewish Publication Society of America, 1986), p.18.
97. Quoted in Arthur Mann, 'Charles Fleischer's Religion of Democracy, An Experiment in American Faith, *Commentary* (June 1954), p.558.
98. See 'Report of the Committee on Religious Works in Universities', *CCAR Yearbook* XVI (1906), pp.188–9.
99. See Mann, 'Charles Fleischer's Religion of Democracy', p.560.
100. David Carl Olson, 'On Trees and Trimming: Thoughts on the Turning of the Year', 30 December 2001: www.commchurch.org/ontrees.doc.
101. See Mann, 'Charles Fleischer's Religion of Democracy', p.560.
102. London Metropolitan Archives, ACC/3529/002/065.
103. See scholarship application for the academic year 1902/03 dated 11 April 1902, Harvard University Biographical Files, call number HUG 300.
104. 'Liberal Judaism, Interview for the *Jewish Chronicle* with the Rev. I.I. Mattuck', *JC*, 4 March 1912, p.24.
105. Letter from the two Presidents and Secretary of the Congregation, Sons of Israel and David to Israel Mattuck, 30 June 1905, London Metropolitan Archives, ACC/3529/002/018.
106. IIM was awarded the Louis J. Goldman Scholarship of $300 per annum, paid in monthly instalments of $25. Minute Book of the HUC Board, 1905, p.52, AJA, Hebrew Union College Records, MS-5, Box D-22.
107. See Silverstein, *Alternatives to Assimilation,* p.28.
108. *New Orleans Jewish Ledger,* 3 June 1910, cited in ibid., p.141.
109. IIM's academic record at Harvard shows that while in his first two years he was awarded a mixture of As and Bs, in his Junior and Senior years (third and fourth years) he was achieving straight As. Harvard University Biographical Files, call number HUG 300.
110. An academic level of distinction signifying a degree that was received 'with great honor'.
111. Letter from George Moore to Kaufmann Kohler, 10 May 1905, LJS Archives, Box 1/2.
112. The subject IIM chose for his submission for the prize was given in his letter to Professor Hurlbut, 2 February 1905, Harvard University Biographical Files, call number HUG 300.
113. The Phi Beta Kappa society's mission is to 'celebrate and advocate excellence in liberal arts and sciences' and induct 'the most outstanding students of arts and sciences at America's leading colleges and universities'. It is the oldest honour society in America.
114. *Harvard Crimson*, 1 June 1904.
115. See correspondence between IIM and David Bailey relating to IIM's entry in the Harvard University Quinquennial Catalogue for 1930, Harvard University Biographical Files, call number HUG 300. The note from IIM reads 'Work for AM completed in 1905; degree should have been taken in 06 but was actually taken in 07'.
116. See *Harvard College, Secretary's First Report.*
117. Letter from Henry Haynes, 4 May 1905, LJS Archives, Box 1/2.
118. Letter from B.S. Hurlbut to Kaufmann Kohler, 25 May 1905, in ibid.
119. Letter from C.H. Toy to Kaufmann Kohler, 5 May 1905, in ibid.
120. Letter from George Moore to Kaufmann Kohler, 10 May 1905, in ibid.
121. Letter from IIM to Archie Hillman, 2 October 1905, AJA, SC-13649.
122. Ibid.
123. Letter from IIM to Archie Hillman, 14 January 1903. IIM talks about being 'intoxicated but not with liquor' after a trip home, but in his letter dated 2 October he says that he felt 'funny' after leaving Worcester. Letters in ibid.
124. Information from May (Monie) Salkin, daughter of Rose Mattuck.
125. Letter from IIM to Archie Hillman, 2 October 1905, AJA, SC-13649.
126. Ibid.
127. Ibid.

CHAPTER SIX

Professional Training and Early Career

Hebrew Union College

Hebrew Union College (HUC) was established in 1875 by Rabbi Isaac Mayer Wise,[1] a native of Bohemia, founder and editor of the newspaper *American Israelite* and leader of the unified Jewish Reform movement, the Union of American Hebrew Congregations (UAHC), founded two years prior to HUC. The college was the first permanent Jewish institution of higher learning in the New World.[2] At a time when Christian denominational colleges were springing up by the score, Wise hoped that the seminary would help to guarantee Jewish survival in America. He saw it as a cross between a German university and a theological college that would accommodate the full range of ideological and geographical sectors in American Jewry.[3] Cincinnati was chosen as the location for the new institution because of its increasing recognition as the centre of American Reform Jewry, mainly as a result of Wise's endeavours. The officers and main supporters of the UAHC all had their homes in the city. While continuing to serve as the rabbi of Bene Yeshurun (often referred to as the Plum Street Temple, and now known as the Isaac Wise Temple), Wise became the unpaid President of the HUC faculty.

Although Wise remained influential, in the decade following its establishment, the Reform movement became dominated by a younger generation of rabbis led by Kaufmann Kohler.[4] Kohler was the son-in-law and spiritual heir of David Einhorn, a pioneer of Reform Judaism in Germany, who emigrated to America from Bavaria in the mid-nineteenth century. Einhorn developed and promulgated a very radical form of Judaism, challenging the more moderate Wise. Einhorn's prayer book, *Olat Tamid*, appeared in 1858. Although Wise's own prayer book, *Minhag Amerika*, became popular with congregations in the Midwest and the south,[5] *Olat Tamid* remained the preferred liturgy of many congregations and had a more significant influence on the UAHC prayer book, *Seder Tefilot Yisrael*, which appeared in 1895.[6]

At a rabbinic conference held in Pittsburgh in 1885, Kohler and others drew up a constitution for Reform Judaism (the 'Pittsburgh Platform'), designed to distinguish it both from Orthodox Judaism and the radical universalism being advocated by the New York Society for Ethical Culture founded by Felix Adler in 1876. Kohler and his colleagues rejected the Mosaic and Rabbinical laws regulating diet, priestly purity and dress as well as the concept of heaven and hell, but maintained that the moral laws of Judaism continued to represent 'the highest conception of the God-idea'. Unlike Adler, they emphasised the distinctiveness of the Jewish people. The reformers saw themselves as a modern, progressive religious community and not a people expecting a return to Palestine.[7] Although the Reform movement never officially adopted the Pittsburgh Platform,[8] it served as the theological basis of what became known as 'classical' Reform Judaism, which reached its heights during the last decade of the nineteenth century and early years of the twentieth century.[9] The platform caused a number of more traditional congregations to leave the UAHC.

In an attempt to gain the support of all branches of American Jewry, Wise initially stressed that the HUC faculty taught only from the sacred texts of Judaism and expounded only the views of the ancient rabbis. No attention was given to biblical criticism and doctrinal issues were purposely avoided.[10] Wise also appointed a broad range of prominent rabbis, including some of his bitter enemies, as members of the Board of Examiners.[11] However, he found it difficult to maintain this pluralist position. At the very first ordination ceremony in 1883, the more traditional guests were scandalised by the serving of shellfish. The event, which became known as the 'Trefa Banquet', marked a parting of the ways between the radical and conservative congregations of UAHC. Wise cast his lot with the more progressive reformers, and HUC gradually became an institution specifically for the Reform movement. In 1886 the Jewish Theological Seminary was set up in New York to train rabbis for more conservative congregations. This reinforced the divergence, but did not halt the progress of HUC, which went on expanding during the 1880s and 1890s. By 1889 Wise and his followers were able to organise the alumni of HUC into the Central Conference of American Rabbis (CCAR), which became 'the weathervane for shifting rabbinical view'.[12] The institutional framework for American Reform Judaism was now complete. IIM was later to say of Wise:

> There were men about the middle of the 19th century in America who were greater than Wise, but they did not exceed him in fervour, in the genuine love of Judaism, and a sincere desire to perpetuate the best of it. He left his greatest mark, however, on Jewish life through

> his organized [sic] ability. He was the organizer 'par excellence' of Liberal Judaism in America.[13]

Twenty-five years of steady progress at HUC was brought to an abrupt halt by Wise's death in March 1900. According to Michael A. Meyer, HUC was now thrown into 'a situation of vacillation and decline from which it did not speedily recover'.[14] It took HUC three years to appoint a successor to Wise. During this time major debates took place on the future direction of the college creating a pervading atmosphere of uncertainty and leading to a significant reduction in enrolments to the college.[15] The person eventually selected as the new president was Kaufmann Kohler. He was appointed partly for his reputation as a theologian and preacher and because of his progressive outlook, but also for more pragmatic reasons. As former rabbi of Temple Beth El in New York and the long-standing president of the New York Board of Ministers, he was known in the New York Jewish community. The thinking behind the appointment was that his leadership would enable HUC both to compete with and differentiate itself from the Jewish Theological Seminary.

Kohler had little time for those who disagreed with his views, and he immediately set about imposing his way of thinking on the faculty. He did not regard HUC as equivalent to a Semitics faculty at a university, where different points of view were given a fair hearing; for him the prime role of the college was indoctrination to Reform Judaism.[16] Symbols of traditionalism were banned from the college chapel, and an understanding of Judaism as involving observance of ritual commandments was expunged from the teaching syllabus. However, Kohler was intent on creating a religious atmosphere at the college. Students and faculty members were required to attend daily worship in the chapel as well as Shabbat afternoon services, at which Kohler frequently spoke about issues of the day. Lessons began with religious exercises and on Saturday mornings students attended services at the local Reform synagogues.[17]

Kohler was an ardent anti-Zionist, as most Reform rabbis in America were at this time, believing that the Diaspora was necessary for Jews to 'bring light unto the nations'. Although he tolerated teachers and students who were Zionists, he tried to prevent them from advocating their ideas in the college chapel and the classroom.[18]

Even before he took up his role, Kohler indicated to the HUC Board of Governors that he intended to alter radically the HUC curriculum, and the first college catalogue[19] that appeared after his appointment contained some marked changes from previous catalogues. The most obvious change was the elimination of instruction in Modern Hebrew; to Kohler it was essential that the college should have a thoroughly American character and that students should be imbued with the American spirit. In his first address to students in 1903 he said: 'Neo-Hebraic Literature may be a necessity for Russian Jews who have no genuine national literature from which to derive culture and idealism. For us the English literature is a source of culture and enlightenment.'[20] Semitic languages were also excluded from the curriculum, because he saw them as being of little relevance to a Reform rabbi. As a substitute, the new president introduced Midrash, which he deemed more useful, enabling the students to 'discern the living ethical and spiritual truth behind the stagnant form of the Halakah and the inane discussion that fill so many pages of the Babylonian Gemarah'.[21]

Regular courses in liturgy made their appearance for the first time, as did elocution and pedagogics. Also added was a course in Applied Sociology (Jewish philanthropic activities) taught by Dr Boris Bogen, who had recently arrived in Cincinnati to serve as the Director of the United Jewish Charities.[22]

An Uneasy First Year at HUC

Given Kohler's intolerance of opposing perspectives and the sweeping nature of the changes he was making, it is not surprising that when IIM enrolled in 1905, HUC was in a state of turmoil. This dominated IIM's experience at the college and he appears to have become caught in the crossfire between Kohler and those faculty members who openly challenged his leadership.

Prior to IIM's arrival in Cincinnati, the average age of incoming HUC students was 19. Most were still at high school or about to enter sophomore class at Cincinnati University and therefore receiving only part time instruction at HUC. Very few were rated as being above average intellectually, and only a small number had been awarded a degree. IIM was one of the first Ivy League graduates to enter the college and he was the embodiment of the type of student that Kohler hoped to attract to HUC in his bid to raise academic standards and to convert it from a denominational college into a postgraduate professional institution in keeping with general American trends in job training.

The student intake to HUC in 1905 included Samuel Thurman, who had graduated from Harvard in 1903. Joseph Gorfinkle, another Harvard graduate, had entered the college a year earlier.[23] Wise had been happy to encourage the sons of less well-off German Jews to take up places at HUC, but he had not been as welcoming of applicants from Polish or other Eastern European backgrounds, who were politely made aware of the existence of an Orthodox seminary in New York.[24] In contrast, Kohler was keen to conduct 'meaningful outreach' to the offspring of Eastern European Jews[25] and from this time onwards the college was recognised as an excellent vehicle of upward mobility for the 'Jewishly committed sons of the ghetto'.[26]

Despite his high expectations and the warm welcome he is likely to have received from Kohler, within a few weeks of his arrival in Cincinnati, IIM was expressing his dissatisfaction with the college. He resented being subjected to an intensive oral examination to assess his Jewish learning, and being placed in the 'Third Collegiate' class, which meant that he would have to stay at the college for three years. He also objected to the lack of flexibility in the course, and that in his first year he had to study twelve different subjects. He complained to his friend, Archie:

> The college did not strike me favourably at all. The programme was at first changed every day and it is still being changed ... Things are altogether different than what I have become accustomed to. The atmosphere is much narrower-thinking than I expected. The fellows are for the most part rude and ill-mannered and one or two possess the additional quality of 'swollen headedness'. But I'll have to get used to it all.[27]

IIM was more satisfied with life outside HUC. Cincinnati was then the centre of large acculturated American-German Jewry, 'a sort of paradise for Hebrews'.[28] He found lodgings in Avondale,[29] 'the swellest part of the city', where all the wealthy Jews and prominent people lived, such as the Mayor of Cincinnati. While many HUC students at the time lived in dingy and inhospitable rooms in boarding houses,[30] IIM reported that the people with whom he was living were 'mighty pleasant'. They made him feel at home and ensured that he did not 'have a chance to become lonesome'.[31] He was invited to Kohler's house every Friday evening and also on other evenings,[32] despite the fact that Kohler is said to have rarely entertained students at his home.[33]

IIM found living among the Jewish aristocracy of Cincinnati, who prided themselves on their culture, philanthropy and devotion to civic responsibilities,[34] a stark contrast to the college – a decaying mansion situated in an increasingly run down area in West Sixth Street (described by IIM as a 'fairly dirty district'), in the centre of the city.[35] It was surrounded by cabbage markets, stockyards and communities unrelated and unfavourable to Reform Judaism, including an increasing number of Orthodox Jews from Eastern Europe and poor African-Americans.[36] It was clear that this neighbourhood had little appeal to a young man keen to rise above the hardships of his early years. However, his negativity may have been partly assuaged by a local establishment close to the college, which at this time offered rabbinic students free lunches, thus making their long commute from their Avondale boarding houses more bearable.[37]

HUC was at this time encouraging its students to serve in weekend pulpits or within the Cincinnati Jewish Sabbath school programme, which had the double benefit of providing the trainee rabbis with practical experience as well as helping to strengthen UAHC congregations. IIM was able to supplement his HUC scholarship by teaching Hebrew in the Sunday school at Bene Israel,[38] the synagogue where Dr David Philipson, part-time HUC faculty member, was the rabbi. Over the winter of 1905 IIM increased his income further by assisting in a second Hebrew class at the Sunday school and teaching English to 'foreigners' (the Eastern European Jews) at the Jewish Educational Institute run by Dr Bogen. This gave him little time for charitable visiting, which did not disappoint IIM since this was not his 'long suit' (his strength).[39]

After a few months at HUC, IIM felt that he was relating more easily to the faculty. He thought that this was because they had come to know him better and had overcome the puzzling prejudice against him evident when he first arrived. They were now inviting him to meals in their homes[40] and life was now was 'a fairly pleasant affair', apart from his lack of skill in what he called the 'art of fussing' prevalent amongst the HUC students, which he hoped to learn eventually. 'After all', he quipped to Archie, 'Plato learnt Greek at eighty'.[41]

However, within a few months, IIM's comfortable life was unsettled. Because of sickness in the family with whom he boarded, he was forced to move out of his lodgings in Avondale. He told Archie that he had heard the command 'To your tent, O Israel', and eventually found a new 'camping ground' sharing with two other young men (one of whom was Joseph Gorfinkle)[42] a two-room flat in an uptown apartment block (33 South Warwick building in Avondale). No board was provided and the three young men were forced to lead a 'bachelor lifestyle', making their own meals and doing their own housekeeping, which appears to have amused IIM, although it was not a situation he wanted to prolong.[43] 'Can you imagine us washing our own dishes and making our own beds? If not I will take a picture – of somebody else doing it for I do not intend to do it anymore – and send it to you. Try it for yourself; it's a great sport.'[44] Just how far IIM had now travelled socially is apparent in the derogatory remarks he makes about the 'servant girl' who the roommates employed to clean their apartment.[45]

In addition to his accommodation problems, things were not going well at HUC. In April 1906, IIM and three of his fellow students, Joseph Gorfinkle, George Fox and Samuel Thurman,[46] submitted a formal complaint to Kohler and the faculty.[47] As well as criticising the atmosphere in the college, the students expressed their disappointment at the poor relations between the professors and students and the apparent 'constant suspicion as to the good faith of the students'. They also complained about the 'general disregard for the interests of the students', and the 'injustice' of being forced to join classes for younger and less well-educated students. They protested that they were not being given the instruction to fit them for their practical work as rabbis or to prepare themselves 'to combat the evils, moral and social, which we may find among our peoples'.[48] Their 'most discouraging' experience was that they had met with 'utter lack of sympathy towards Reform Judaism and the rabbinate on the part of the professors'.[49]

Given IIM's Orthodox background and his amazement on witnessing a Reform service in Boston just a few years earlier, the latter aspect of the students' complaint is very interesting. IIM's transition to radical religious thinking was obviously now complete and he evidently saw himself as more enlightened than the faculty of a Progressive seminary.

The students requested a more intensive course of study to enable them to graduate in 1907 rather than in 1908, a request that was narrowly rejected by the HUC faculty. In IIM's case, the reason given for the refusal was that he would not by 1907 have been present at HUC for the three years required by the college.[50] Using his casting vote, Kohler forced the faculty to reach a decision that, although they might feel 'grossly insulted' by the views expressed by the students, the charges they (the students) had made should be overlooked. In a power play against Kohler, the three professors who dissented from this decision (Malter, Schloessinger and Margolis) forwarded the students' letter, over the president's head, to the HUC Board and asked for the matter to be investigated. By the following year, all three professors had left the college.[51]

In June 1906, the four students submitted a further request that they be allowed to choose their courses, as three of them had been able to do at Harvard. This request was again refused by the faculty on the grounds that 'ample provision is made for elective work' in the new curriculum.[52] While his complaints were being considered, IIM appears to have attempted to make the most of his time in Cincinnati. He became involved in communal organisations such as the Jewish Students' Literary Society, held at the Jewish Educational Institute, where he read papers on topics such as Bernard Shaw's *Man and Superman*,[53] and expounded on books and plays such as Ibsen's *An Enemy of the People* and Edward Bellamy's *Looking Backward*'.[54]

For many years, philanthropy was the hallmark of Jewish life in Cincinnati[55] and its many innovations in that sphere of 'scientific charity' became the exemplar for Jewish communities across America. IIM was drawn into a number of welfare activities: he acted as a 'Jewish Probation Officer' for two 'delinquent Jewish boys' who did not have a mother,[56] and started to work at the Jewish Settlement in Elm Street.[57] It is somewhat ironic that IIM was part of the German-Jewish effort to assimilate Eastern European Jews as quickly as possible at the same time as he himself was being socialised as the result of living in the German-Jewish milieu of Cincinnati.

IIM much preferred his 'practical work' to his studies on 'Jewish philosophy or similar things' at the college, about which he was 'not able to wax eloquent'. He felt it unlikely that his future congregations would be entertained by Hebrew quotations from Maimonides. He told Archie: 'I can see my listeners bow low in humble adoration of my great philosophical training and offer me – a leave of absence for an indefinite length of time.'[58]

Lincoln, Nebraska

By July 1906 IIM had reached the decision to leave HUC.[59] Over the summer months, he travelled around America having a 'delightful time'.[60] It later emerged that he had suffered some kind of breakdown on his departure from HUC,[61] and he had borrowed money from his friend, Archie, to tide him over while he sought employment.[62] He stayed for a while in Edgecombe, Maine where he met up with his HUC friend, Gorfinkle, which made livelier his otherwise 'quiet though not dull existence'.[63] He later moved on to Cleveland, Ohio where he applied for but failed to obtain a position there due to his lack of experience.[64] He met up with a friend from Harvard[65] who took him 'automobile driving' around the city and to a nearby amusement park,[66] both of which were totally new experiences for IIM. After spending time in Chicago, in September 1906 he accepted an appointment in Lincoln, Nebraska (he described Lincoln as 'the prettiest town you want to see')[67] to officiate over the High Holydays at the Reform synagogue, B'nai Jeshurun.

Known as the 'South Street Temple', B'nai Jeshurun had been founded in 1884. The first synagogue building was erected in 1893 when the community had just twenty-eight members. The congregation was principally made up of a number of inter-related German-Jewish families, who had settled in the city in the late 1860s. They were merchants who were mainly involved in the clothing industry and in various types of manufacturing. IIM pronounced that the members of the congregation, then numbering about fifty, were 'just right' and he obviously made a strong impression on them (he was probably the only Ivy League graduate in Lincoln at this time), because he was asked to stay on for a year as the full-time rabbi at a salary of $1,200, which he felt was 'not bad for a beginner'.[68] He wrote to Kohler at HUC confirming his decision to discontinue his studies 'for reasons well known to you'.[69]

IIM was a little in awe of the fact that he had been appointed to 'take charge of people's souls'.[70] He was also a little intimidated by the intellectual calibre of the congregation, which included many women who were ex-teachers and belonged to literary clubs:

> So you can imagine what I am up against. In one of my sermons I got Buddha's date wrong and one of the women afterwards asked me about it – and the men are not so backward either. I cannot impress them with long words – they use longer ones than even I dreamt of handling. They are a critical set but fine nevertheless.[71]

IIM quickly settled down to preaching and organising the Sunday school. Within a few months of his arrival he also set up a social club for single people, with the intention that the club would take an interest in Jewish affairs as well as providing social opportunities.[72] This was in line with emerging thinking within the Reform movement about the role of synagogues as places to meet as well as places to pray, and the increasing emphasis that was being placed on activities for young people.[73] By January 1907 it was reported in the *American Israelite* that, as a result of his work, the size of the Lincoln congregation had increased rapidly.[74] However, IIM confided to his friend Archie that, despite all this progress, he felt somewhat 'betwixt and between', and that he still planned to finish his studies at some future time but not, he stressed, at HUC.[75]

As well as his routine rabbinic activities and visiting congregants, IIM spent time reading and studying. He was lodging in the home of a synagogue member. The house, at 1436 'C' Street, was 'very fine' and well located for the synagogue. IIM had once more found himself congenial accommodation.

In December 1906, the HUC Board became aware of IIM's absence from the college[76] and instructed Isaac Bloom, the Secretary of HUC, to write to IIM advising him that he was contravening college rules by taking on himself the office of rabbi without having been ordained. The letter pointed out forcefully that one of HUC's main purposes was that of 'making it impossible in the United States the incumbency of pretenders in the rabbinical office [sic]'.[77]

IIM found Bloom's letter 'very uncomplimentary' and wrote back to say that, although he was carrying out the role of rabbi, he had not been using the title of rabbi and the community was well aware that he had not been ordained.[78] He outlined his reasons for leaving HUC, saying that the fault may have been partly his own 'in expecting too much because of my previous schooling experience', yet he couldn't help thinking that things were 'out of joint at the school'.[79] His main grievances were that the professors at HUC were haughty and 'un-American' in their outlook, that he disliked the 'petty jealousies' amongst faculty members, the 'ungentlemanly' aspersions cast by the professors on 'Reformed Judaism and the rabbis', and their opposition to Dr Kohler.[80] It was clear from this letter that IIM's argument was with the professors rather than with the president, and that he fully supported the changes that Kohler was seeking to introduce. He concluded rather loftily:

> Therefore, much as I desired the title of Rabbi, yet would I not sacrifice precious time for its immediate acquisition. I have stated my reasons rather harshly, but frankly with the hope that these, to my mind, existing evils will soon be eradicated from the school towards which the Progressive Jews of this country hopefully lift their eyes.[81]

The correspondence between HUC and IIM ceased for about twelve months, during which time IIM was overcome by a sense of 'irresoluteness' and was dwelling on what he perceived to be his shortcomings, which he tried hard to shake off.[82] He was feeling quite lonely, but found it helpful to read the works of Emerson.[83] His dark mood seems to have improved over the summer months of 1907, when he went home to Worcester for a visit and also spent some time at Lake Sebago in Maine.[84] He returned to Nebraska with more enthusiasm for his role, but remained nostalgic about his time at Harvard. He wrote to Archie Hillman, now studying at Harvard Law School saying, 'If you meet anybody who knows me or knew me just tell them that I am still on the earth but not kicking'.[85]

IIM used the opportunity of his re-election to the South Street Temple in November 1907 to set out some of his aspirations for the community. Although the congregation was considered to be 'in the front' and one of the 'most advanced' in the country, he hoped that this position would be maintained and improved upon by the adoption of more inclusive practices, such as the active participation of women and unmarried synagogue members, and by inviting into membership those who could not afford to pay the full synagogue subscription rate. He said that he wanted to prevent young men from withdrawing from synagogue life because of the many forces that were luring them away from Judaism.[86] He also pointed out that in Reform Judaism, women were regarded as men's equal, arguing that 'we need women's direct influence in all matters pertaining to religion and religious institutions'.[87] He chided the congregation on some of its 'exclusive' practices, such as their provisions on burial rights and attendance of services by visitors during the High Holydays, which he found 'completely at variance with the preachings and teachings of our religion'.[88] These were bold words indeed from a young man standing before an established and well-to-do congregation. IIM's suggested measures, which he insisted were based on religious rather than political beliefs, appear to have found favour with the congregation. At a meeting held shortly after his re-election, the synagogue board agreed to his recommendation that women be admitted as full synagogue members.[89]

IIM also tried experimenting with different types of sermon at the synagogue.[90] His sermons and addresses of this time are redolent with the themes that dominated the agenda of classical Reform Judaism – modernity, moral conduct and social justice. For example, he spoke on 'Modern Idols', 'The Meaning of Progress', 'Organised Charity and the Individual', and 'The Teachings About Justice and Love in Judaism and Christianity'[91] as well as topical issues of the day such as the education of women and children.[92]

Of particular interest is his address on the subject of immigration restriction,[93] in which he spoke poignantly about the circumstances that caused Eastern European Jews to emigrate to America and argued forcefully that they were a great benefit to the American economy. However, he had few solutions to suggest on overcoming the problems of squalor and overcrowding that faced the large Jewish communities in the big cities (especially in New York) other than their dispersal. He had clearly absorbed, apparently without question, the line being taken by the majority of German Jews towards their co-religionists. It is interesting to note that in his address he did not mention his first-hand knowledge of the problems facing immigrants.

It is possible that IIM's early sermons on social issues were influenced by Emil G. Hirsch, the rabbi at Sinai Temple in Chicago, one of the most prominent, radical and influential Reform congregations in America. Like Kohler, Hirsch was the son-in-law of David Einhorn and, alongside Kohler, was one of the two main architects of 'classical' Reform Judaism. It was as a result of Hirsch's urging that the Pittsburgh Platform included a commitment to addressing 'the evils of the present organisation of society'.[94]

At the time of Hirsch's death some years later, IIM referred to him as a 'towering figure in American Jewry'[95] and paid tribute to his commitment to social causes. It is probable that IIM heard Hirsch speaking during his 1906 visit to Chicago. However, it is also clear from IIM's later comments that, although he was a great admirer of Hirsch, he realised that the radical reforms he pursued – particularly in relation to Sunday services[96] and the removal of both the scroll and ark from his synagogue – placed him at the extreme edge of American Reform Judaism, and he considered that Hirsch did not give enough attention to outward symbols.[97] IIM may have aspired to Hirsch's oratorical standards and his success in gaining the attention of non-Jews, but in his religious belief he was closer to the Progressive outlook of Kohler than the unswerving radicalism of Hirsch.

Outside the Lincoln synagogue, IIM became a vice-president of the local Jewish lodge, the Independent Order of B'nai B'rith,[98] and worked successfully with the Lincoln School Board to set up a night school.[99] He was also involved in various charitable activities in the city and was invited to preach at the synagogue in Omaha, including at its dedication service in May 1908,[100] and at the Unitarian Church in Lincoln.[101] In January 1908, he addressed the Lawyers' Club of Lincoln. From these activities it is evident that IIM was fully accepted in both the well-to-do, highly assimilated, German-Jewish community, and also by the non-Jewish community of Lincoln.

While working at B'nai Jeshurun, IIM became acquainted with Simon Mayer, a former president of the synagogue, who was then its treasurer and a member of the synagogue's Board of Trustees. Mayer was of German descent but had been born in New York. For a number of years he and his brothers Charles and Henry had been involved in frontier trading in Plattsmouth, Nebraska,[102] before moving to Lincoln to set up a highly successful shoe shop which made them the leading tradespeople in the city.[103] It was Simon Mayer's daughter, Edna Minna Mayer, whom IIM was to marry.[104] Edna Mayer was born in Plattsmouth in 1888. She was Simon Mayer's daughter with his first wife, Rachel Hesse, whom he married in 1883. Edna had an older brother, Louis (born in 1884),[105] and also a younger brother, Alfred (born in 1891). After the death of Rachel Hesse, Simon Mayer married Sarah Kline in 1899; she died in childbirth a year later.[106] Simon Mayer was married for a third time in 1902 to Jeanette Kline (possibly Sarah Kline's sister), who died in 1904.

Edna moved with her family to Lincoln when she was a small child. The family lived in what was described as a 'mansion' in 'H' street in the city. Edna was well known in both Jewish and non-Jewish circles in the city because of her 'many accomplishments'.[107] Her activities, such as giving piano recitals at society events, were regularly reported in the local newspapers.[108] She initially attended the high school in Lincoln, but completed her education at a finishing school in New York.[109] She and IIM met as a result of Edna's involvement in the Sunday school held at B'nai Jeshurun.[110] Their engagement was announced on 1 April 1908 at a dinner party given by the Handy Club at the home of Edna Mayer's friends, the 'Misses Schlesinger'.[111]

It may have been IIM's engagement, or perhaps the influence of his future father-in-law, that prompted IIM to rethink his position regarding his rabbinic training. In March 1908 he wrote to Kohler indicating that he was considering returning to HUC, since his health had improved during his stay in Nebraska.[112] Now that he was engaged, IIM had an added incentive to shorten his time at HUC and to start earning a living, but Kohler was adamant that, in order to be ordained, he would need to be resident at HUC for a minimum of two further years. Kohler said that, if IIM were to agree to this, his scholarship would be reinstated, a privilege no longer granted to HUC students.[113] 'As a *friend* [Kohler's emphasis] warmly interested in your welfare and success', he advised IIM against going to study in Berlin, which it seems he was also considering as an alternative to returning to HUC.[114] Kohler was of the view that studying in Berlin would not assist IIM in obtaining an American pulpit. He concluded:

> Personally I felt very sorry that in leaving and taking the attitude that you did you thwarted your prospects and the great hopes that I built on you. But it is not too late to resume the course which promises a bright future for you. Therefore I say take courage חֲזַק וֶאֱמָץ and success will crown you with God's aid.[115]

This response seems somewhat disingenuous, bearing in mind the prominence of some Reform rabbis, such as Stephen Wise,[116] who were not ordained by HUC. It obviously did not satisfy IIM, who objected to spending two years of residence at the college. Kohler indicated that this was non-negotiable.[117] Nevertheless, IIM carried on negotiating. He suggested that, if he were to remain with the college for two years, he might be awarded a Doctor of Divinity degree (DD) in addition to being ordained. On being told this was not a possibility since doctoral degrees were only awarded to those who had graduated from HUC,[118] IIM proposed that he apply for admission to the senior class for a year, during which time the college could judge whether his progress was such that it might consider deviating from the three-year rule.[119] If the rule could not be changed despite his progress, IIM's suggestion was that he might spend a further year carrying out 'graduate work' at the end of which he could be ordained.

This latter suggestion appears to have found favour with the HUC Board; IIM would be granted 'special privileges' to spend his third year preaching in neighbouring towns and pursuing other postgraduate activities.[120] An agreed course of study for the senior year was drawn up by Kohler, which it was arranged that IIM would commence after the High Holydays that year. Despite the way in which he had departed from the college and his bold negotiations over the terms of his return, Kohler assured IIM that he retained the 'good will of the faculty in looking after your interests'.[121]

IIM took leave from B'nai Jeshurun synagogue over the summer of 1908, during which time he preached at Temple Israel in Far Rockaway, New York.[122] He returned to Lincoln for a short while, but made his final departure from the South Street Synagogue on 1 September 1908.[123] He was complimented by the board for his 'accomplishments during his tenure with the congregation' and was elected as an honorary member of the synagogue.[124] Before re-embarking on his studies, IIM gained further pulpit experience at Temple Adath Israel, in Owensboro, Kentucky, where he was engaged to officiate over the High Holydays.[125]

Beneh Abraham

IIM seems to have resumed his studies at HUC with the best of intentions. However, his return proved to be only a stepping stone to ever-improving employment opportunities. After two years of leading a growing congregation in Nebraska, and having experienced a taste of leadership, returning to being a student was probably untenable for IIM.

Back in Cincinnati, he took lodgings at 555 Hale Avenue in Avondale, Cincinnati,[126] became involved in the communal life of the college and worked in the local community. He also taught at the religion school at the Plum Street Temple[127] where Dr Grossmann, a part-time professor at HUC, was the rabbi, and lectured at the Bene Israel Temple.[128] In November 1908 he was elected as President of the HUC Isaac Wise Literary Society, a forum for 'discussing such problems as are of interest to rabbinical students'.[129] However, shortly after his return, IIM accepted a full-time appointment at Beneh Abraham, a Reform synagogue in Portsmouth, Ohio, 100 miles to the east of Cincinnati. From 1 December 1908 he held this pulpit at a salary of $1,000 per annum[130] while continuing to study at HUC.[131]

The Beneh Abraham community, originally known as Kal a Kodesh Beneh Abraham, was established in 1858 to cater to the Jewish families who were moving to the area as a result of the industrialisation that radiated out from Cincinnati along the banks of the Ohio River.[132] Beneh Abraham never became a large community, and experienced difficulty in retaining a professional rabbi. The synagogue remained loyal to UAHC when it had shed its moderating influences in 1885, and in 1895 voted unanimously to adopt the widely publicised *Union Prayer Book*.[133]

IIM's experience of working in this Reform community appears to have had a significant impact on his developing views on the organisation of synagogue life. Many facets of the way in which Beneh Abraham operated

– such as the prominence of women in synagogue life, the emphasis placed on 'decorum' in services,[134] the way in which the congregation consciously positioned itself in the mainstream of the local community, the opening of the synagogue doors to non-Jewish people and the facilitation of the conversion process to bring new people into the congregation[135] – were all replicated by IIM when, a few years later, he became the rabbi of the Liberal Jewish Synagogue in London.

Although he had agreed to serve the community for a year, in May 1909 IIM terminated the agreement after just six months,[136] perhaps finding the travel to and from Cincinnati and working full-time while continuing to study too onerous. Correspondence between IIM and the college shows that he was failing to deliver work to an acceptable standard. Kohler was particularly critical of the thesis on which IIM was working, which he said was 'rather superficial' and 'not worthy of you'. Kohler urged him to 'present a paper for which you can get a high credit.'[137]

By early 1909 IIM had decided to disregard his agreement with HUC about his final year and started to seek permanent rabbinic positions. In May 1909 he put himself forward for the vacancy that had arisen at Temple Israel in Far Rockaway, where he had preached the previous summer. In Kohler's absence, Professor Grossmann advised IIM to check that he was in a position to make this application because of his agreement with HUC about residency.[138] IIM ignored this advice and attended the interview, which included preaching at the synagogue.[139] He accepted 'the call' and took up the post at Temple Israel in September 1909.

The Pulpit in Far Rockaway

Far Rockaway is a beach community in the Borough of Queens, New York, which borders on Nassau County. Temple Israel (known as the 'White Schul') was a large synagogue with a colonial design, which had just been opened at the corner of Roanoke and State Streets. Until then the congregation, which had been founded in 1908, had met in rented rooms. The synagogue served a growing, mainly Reform, community. By 1910, some 200 Jewish families lived all year round in Far Rockaway, with an additional 2,000 Jewish households spending their summer holiday in the area. Later there was to be a steady influx of Orthodox Jews, which ultimately transformed Far Rockaway into a 'Torah Suburb by the Sea.'[140]

In addition to it being a permanent and well-paid appointment, the pulpit in Far Rockaway was advantageous to IIM for several reasons. As a developing community, it offered him scope for putting his own stamp on communal life and for implementing the ideas he had been developing in Lincoln and Portsmouth. More importantly from IIM's point of view, the location of the synagogue in New York brought him into contact with a new tranche of influential people to assist him in his career, as well as placing him within reach of several well-known congregations, including Temple Emanu-El, involvement with which IIM had plainly set his sights. In New York, IIM came of age and his future success was virtually assured.

IIM took lodgings in Shinden Boulevard in Far Rockaway and, according to one of his congregants, within a few months of his arrival had established himself both as a popular rabbi with the embryonic congregation, and also as someone held in high esteem by the wider community.[141] While working in Far Rockaway, IIM was ordained and married Edna Mayer.

Ordination

Kohler was very displeased when he learned of IIM's appointment. On Kohler's recommendation, the HUC faculty had agreed to reduce further the requirement for IIM to attend the college full-time from one year to six weeks but then, without consultation, IIM had accepted the post at Temple Israel.[142] The board instructed Kohler to write to IIM to tell him that he must resign from his position and return to Cincinnati and remain there until his graduation. Kohler pointed out to IIM that the difficulties would not have arisen had he remained in Portsmouth, from where it had been possible for him to continue to attend HUC. He urged IIM to return to Portsmouth where the position was still open. He warned IIM that his future was at stake and that he had the 'knowledge and capacity to attain a higher standing than Gorfinkle and Thurman' (two of the fellow-students, with whom he had made a complaint to the HUC Board in 1906).[143]

In his reply IIM satisfied Kohler that there were mitigating factors and Kohler suggested that IIM write at once to the HUC Board saying that, having been granted 'special privileges', he (IIM) was under the impression that he had been acting loyally and in good faith.[144] Kohler assured IIM that he would support his position. The HUC Board meeting of 21 December was a stormy one, but Kohler succeeded in convincing the board to reverse its ultimatum that IIM must return or forfeit his ordination. The agreement was that IIM should ask his congregation for leave of absence to attend the college from January to May (*Pesach* excluded) and graduate in June. Kohler realised that this would be disagreeable to IIM and indeed it was because, in response, IIM continued to negotiate to spend less time in Cincinnati. Kohler felt that this showed ingratitude for his efforts and insisted he return to Cincinnati immediately.[145]

At this point IIM called on the services of the president of Temple Israel, Joseph Fried, who wrote to the board saying that IIM could not be spared for the length of time that he was being asked to reside at the college. Joseph Fried must have been a very influential man, because the board not only agreed to hold a special meeting to consider IIM's case but, when it met, its decision was to reduce the prescribed term of residence of September to June to two months and 'to accommodate you even in that to the period agreeable to yourself',[146] a remarkable concession. In addition, it appears that IIM was not required to complete his thesis, 'An Account of the Jewish Eschatology in the Sibylline Oracles', about which Dr Kohler had previously been so critical[147] and, by the time of IIM's graduation, was still 'hardly up to the standard'.[148] Nor was IIM asked to take the final examination, although the HUC faculty did decide that no grade should be recorded on his diploma of ordination.[149]

IIM eventually returned to Cincinnati for just a few weeks before his ordination.[150] The commencement service took place at the Plum Street Temple on the morning of 16 April 1910. It opened with a brief, but 'very much to the point', salutatory by Edward Heinsheimer, the new president of the Board of Governors of the college. Rabbi Julian Morgenstern followed with an invocation and Rabbi Louis Grossmann preached the Baccalaureate sermon on the subject of 'The Work and Duty of the Rabbi'. Kohler conferred the degree of rabbi on IIM, concluding by bestowing on him the priestly blessing. IIM then delivered the valedictory on 'The Sanctification of the Ideal', which was described in the local press as 'far above the average, both in substance and in manner of delivery'. The service closed with a benediction by Professor G. Deutsch.[151]

Reflection on IIM's Time at HUC

The foregoing account of IIM's time at HUC reveals interesting facets of his character, his commitment to Reform Judaism and the high regard in which he was held from an early age. Throughout his time at HUC, those corresponding with IIM (perhaps with the exception of Professor Grossmann), did so in the most amicable of tones and remained in admiration of him despite his headstrong and independent behaviour, the protracted negotiations regarding his residency and his scant regard for the agreements he reached with the college. It appears that IIM viewed himself as being in a special category of student, perhaps as the result of a sense of superiority instilled in him during his time at Harvard.

After he was ordained, IIM's teachers, including Rabbi David Philipson, praised his intelligence and capabilities.[152] A contemporary who later emigrated to England to work in Liverpool, and who presided at a lecture given by IIM, recalled: 'Several years ago, in a cafeteria in Cincinnati, Ohio, my companion nudged me and said, indicating a serious-looking young Jew [IIM], 'There's a kid you will hear about some day'.[153] In contrast, IIM was not complimentary about either his fellow students (he appears to have associated mainly with those who had a similar educational background) or about the HUC professors, who clearly did not meet his expectations. The one person IIM seems to have respected as someone worthy of dealing with was Kohler. IIM apparently knew how to win Kohler over to his way of thinking and, since he was president of HUC, that was important.

It is clear that Kohler heavily influenced IIM. On Kohler's death in 1926, IIM described him as a 'giant' and 'the chief intellectual force in the formulation of the principles of Reform Judaism in America'. He regarded Kohler as 'a teacher and a friend who, in diverse ways, influenced my life; and his memory is bound up with feelings of reverence and affection'.[154]

IIM's high estimation of Kohler appears to have been mutual. During his early days in Far Rockaway, IIM completed his first piece of significant research on 'The Levirate Marriage in Jewish Law'. The research, which he had been invited to undertake by HUC, was published in a collection of studies compiled in honour of Kohler at the time of his 70th birthday.[155] In his essay, IIM argued that the principle underpinning the concept of the Levirate marriage was 'out of consonance' with modern thought and therefore should no longer be applied. Kohler wrote to IIM congratulating him on the article, which he said showed 'a fine scholarly spirit and a penetrating mind'.[156] However, a review in the *Jewish Exponent* suggested that IIM's arguments lacked logic.[157]

Although we know quite a lot about IIM's time (or rather the lack of it) at HUC, we are nevertheless left with some unanswered questions, such as why exactly the college capitulated on the issue of his residency and why he was not required to complete his thesis. Kohler and his colleagues may have wished to avoid too many examples of Reform rabbis who succeeded in spite of not having been ordained at HUC. However, this is not a very adequate explanation of the board's almost complete reversal of its stance. IIM's letters setting out the reasons for his actions and arguments for exceptions being made to HUC policies are interesting but not outstandingly persuasive. A more plausible explanation is that HUC recognised the extent of IIM's potential and wanted to be able to claim him as one of their protégés. This theory is supported by some of the statements that were made retrospectively about his time at HUC, such as that of David Philipson ('He left an excellent record at the college'),[158] which is patently a gloss on events.

Another lingering question is, what may IIM have missed out on as a result of not completing his rabbinic studies? In terms of Judaic learning, the answer is probably not a great deal, given his Orthodox upbringing and the tuition provided by his learned father. However, he might have benefitted from being subjected to challenge from his peers and the faculty. At certain points in his future career, he was to be unduly weighed down by criticism of his views and by adverse reactions to his candidness.

All in all, IIM seems to have gained little from his time at HUC, apart from his friendship with Kaufmann Kohler and David Philipson, his experience of working in the local community and some social skills, which facilitated his entry into the upper echelons of American Jewish society. To IIM, HUC was more of a finishing school than a seminary. His time at Harvard appears to have been much more influential in terms of developing his religious outlook, and the time he spent away from HUC working in Reform pulpits more significant in developing his rabbinic skills.

Marriage

After he left Nebraska in 1908 to resume his rabbinic studies at HUC, IIM made several trips back to Lincoln to see his fiancée, sometimes preaching at the synagogue, such as during his stay in February 1909.[159] After a prolonged engagement, the couple were married there on 3 November 1910 in Lincoln, when Mattuck was 27 and had begun to establish himself professionally. They had what was described by the local press as an 'impressive society wedding', which was celebrated at noon in the home of Edna's uncle, Charles Mayer, 'a wealthy local resident'.[160] The wedding service, which included a 'double ring ceremony', was led by Gustave Lowenstein, a rabbinic student from HUC, who was now leading the congregation in Lincoln, and the witnesses included Henry Schlesinger, the synagogue president.[161]

For their honeymoon, the couple visited 'places of interest' on the east coast of America. The Mayer family, who were described as 'occupying a high position in Jewish circles',[162] supported IIM as he established his career.[163] The circumstances of his marriage were therefore not dissimilar from those of his parents, albeit in an American setting. Around the time of the wedding, IIM was offered the post of the permanent rabbi at the synagogue in Lincoln for an annual salary of $1,800, but this he refused, perhaps seeing greater prospects in New York.[164] IIM and Edna set up their home in Crescent Street, Far Rockaway, close to Temple Israel.[165] Their son, Robert, was born there on 4 September 1911. At the end of 1911, IIM was living in a substantial house in Far Rockaway, with a wealthy wife, and a nanny to help look after his son – a world apart from the *shtetl* in Lithuania, where he was born, and the semi-ghetto of Worcester, where he grew up.

While some contemporary Reform rabbis with Eastern European backgrounds had misgivings about marrying into the German-Jewish community for fear they might be looked down upon and the marriage might not therefore be successful,[166] IIM appears to have harboured no such fears. He was determined to marry well.

Moving on

During the latter part of 1910, IIM seems to have reached a decision to increase his professional profile. He began to preach in other synagogues in New York, including at the prestigious Temple Emanu-el in Manhattan,[167] and to write articles on religious topics for Jewish newspapers and periodicals, such as the article on 'A Liberal Attitude to Tradition', which was published in the California-based Progressive Jewish journal, *Emanu-El* in 1910.[168] In this article, he argued that 'Progress makes inadequate traditional ideas'. However, he criticised both those who 'stuck to the old' as being 'dreaming romanticists', and those who rejected tradition altogether, whose attitude he saw as an 'absurd iconoclasm'. He advocated a liberal outlook that involved examining 'reverentially all tradition has brought', discarding what was useless and retaining traditions still relevant.[169] In maintaining that 'liberalism makes possible progress', IIM was truly a man of his age.

Despite his popularity and his progress in developing the congregation of Temple Israel,[170] IIM was obviously set on achieving higher things. Early in 1911, he was considered for the position of Assistant Rabbi to Rabbi Joseph Silverman at Temple Emanu-el, where he had previously preached. Temple Emanu-el was described as being 'the foremost Reform synagog [sic] in New York' and 'one of the wealthiest in the United States', with a congregation that included many 'Hebrew millionaires'.[171] IIM failed to impress the congregation when invited to preach there in March 1911,[172] but shortly afterwards he received an invitation to visit England with a view to being considered for the vacancy of 'minister' (as rabbis in Britain were referred to at this time) at the newly established Liberal Jewish Synagogue in London. This invitation was to seal his career.

NOTES

1. Stories abound on whether or not Wise was an ordained rabbi. See Hasia Diner, *A New Promised Land: A History of Jews in America* (New York: Oxford University Press, 2003).
2. A prototype of the new college, Zion College, had opened and closed in Cincinnati in 1855 due to lack of support and funding.
3. Alan Silverstein, *Alternatives to Assimilation, The Response of Reform Judaism to American Culture,* 1840–1930 (Boston, MA: Brandeis University Press, 1994), p.62.

4. Kaufmann Kohler was born in Fürth, Bavaria, in 1843. He was a descendant of a family of rabbis. His PhD thesis of 1868, 'Der Segen Jacob's', was one of the earliest Jewish essays in the field of the higher Biblical criticism, and its radical character had the effect of closing to him Jewish pulpits in Germany.
5. Michael A. Meyer, *Hebrew Union College-Jewish Institute of Religion: A Centennial History 1875–1975* (Cincinnati, OH: HUC, 1992), p.255.
6. Ibid., p.279. According to Meyer, Einhorn's prayer book was more in keeping with the mood and theology of Reform Judaism in its 'classical' phase.
7. Gerald Sorin, *A Time for Building: The Third Migration, 1880–1920 (Vol. 3 The Jewish People in America)* (Baltimore, MD and London: Johns Hopkins University Press, New Edition, 1995), p.172.
8. Jason Lustig, 'Resigning to Change: The Foundation and Transformation of The American Council for Judaism' (unpublished MA thesis, Brandeis University, 2009), p.17.
9. The term 'classical' Reform became used to distinguish this phase from the Neo-Reform phase that arose in reaction to it.
10. Michael A. Meyer, *Response to Modernity – A History of the Reform Movement in Judaism* (New York: Oxford University Press, 1988), p.262.
11. See Silverstein, *Alternatives to Assimilation*, p.67.
12. See Meyer, *Response to Modernity*, p.265.
13. 'The Beginnings of Liberal Judaism in America', sermon given by IIM at the LJS, 5 April 1919, Montagu Centre Collection (MCC).
14. See Meyer, *Hebrew Union College*, p.47.
15. By 1903 there were only thirty-six students in the college, less than half as many as there were just five years earlier. Ibid., p.52.
16. Ibid., p.57.
17. Joan S. Friedman, 'The Making of a Reform Rabbi: Solomon B. Freehof from Childhood to HUC', *American Jewish Archives Journal*, 58, no.1–2 (2006), p.17.
18. Yaakov Ariel, 'Kaufmann Kohler and His Attitude Towards Zionism: A Re-examination', *American Jewish Archives Journal*, 43, no.2 (1991), p.216.
19. In Britain it would be referred to as a 'prospectus', but this is what HUC called it.
20. Quoted in Meyer, *Hebrew Union College*, p.59.
21. Quoted in ibid., p.60.
22. Described as 'the greatest social agency find that had ever been made in America', Bogen was responsible for the professionalisation of social work, not only in Cincinnati, but throughout America, establishing the Jewish Social Service Bureau, the School of Jewish Social Service and the National Conference of Jewish Charities. Nancy Klein, 'Cincinnati Jewish History': www.jewishcincinnati.org. It is interesting to note that Bogan was an Eastern European employed by German Jews.
23. After graduating from Harvard in 1903, Gorfinkle went into business for a year, but gave that up to study for the rabbinate. Thurman graduated from Harvard the same year as Gorfinkle. He then studied for two years at Harvard Law School, but abandoned his studies because of a lack of finance and interest. He was initially offered a post as a lecturer at HUC, but when he arrived he decided to become a student instead. Information from Harvard College yearbooks for the 'Class of 1903', *U.S. School Yearbooks* [database on-line]. Provo, UT, USA: Ancestry.com Operations, Inc., 2010.
24. See Silverstein, *Alternatives to Assimilation*, p.149.
25. Ibid., p.117. This might have been out of necessity rather than a belief in these Eastern European students, since at this time very few students from German Jewish origin were attracted to the rabbinate.
26. See Friedman, 'The Making of a Reform Rabbi', p.12.
27. Letter from IIM to Archie Hillman, 27 October 1905, American Jewish Archives (AJA), SC-13649.
28. The historian Henry Howe quoted in Jonathan Sarna, 'A Sort of Paradise for Hebrews: The Lofty Vision of Cincinnati Jews', in Henry D. Shapiro and Jonathan Sarna (eds), *Ethnic Diversity and Civic Identity: Patterns of Conflict and Cohesion in Cincinnati Since 1820* (Chicago, IL: University of Illinois Press, 1992), p.131.
29. He lived at 3550 Rosedale Place, just a mile or so away from HUC. Avondale was then in the process of becoming the largest Jewish neighbourhood in Cincinnati. Students either took the trolleybus to the college or walked if they did not have the money to pay fares. See Meyer, *Hebrew Union College*, p.102. He lived with Helen Lowenstein and her family.

She was the widow of Henry Lowenstein, a former wealthy manufacturer in the city. See City Directory for Cincinnati for 1906.

30. Ibid., p.59.
31. See letter from IIM to Archie Hillman, 27 October 1905, AJA, SC-13649.
32. The faculty at this time saw it as part of their role to educate students socially and invited them into their homes to help develop their table manners. Conversation with Michael Meyer, 3 May 2012.
33. See Friedman, 'The Making of a Reform Rabbi', p.16.
34. See Sarna, 'A Sort of Paradise for Hebrews', p.144.
35. Shortly before IIM arrived in Cincinnati, HUC had started to build a new college in Clifton, a more salubrious part of the city, but it was not opened until 1912.
36. See Meyer, *Hebrew Union College*, p.59.
37. See Friedman, 'The Making of a Reform Rabbi', p.14.
38. Bene Israel was at that time the largest Reform synagogue in America.
39. Letter from IIM to Archie Hillman, 4 December 1905, AJA, SC-13649.
40. Letter from IIM to Archie Hillman, 17 January 1906, in ibid. These invitations obviously flattered IIM, but they may have been motivated by a desire to acculturate rather than by a desire for his company.
41. Letter from IIM to Archie Hillman, 4 December 1905, in ibid.
42. Letter from IIM to Archie Hillman, 1 October 1906, in ibid.
43. Letter from IIM to Archie Hillman, 16 April 1906, in ibid.
44. Ibid.
45. Ibid.
46. Joseph Gorfinkle went on to gain a PhD from Columbia University in 1909. In an obituary it is stated that he graduated from HUC, but this is not so. George Fox stayed at HUC and graduated in 1908 and Samuel Thurman went on to be a rabbi in Michigan, but he did not graduate from HUC. IIM appears to have maintained contact with Gorfinkle for at least a few years after he left HUC. In 1911, Gorfinkle was the witness for IIM's American Citizenship. National Archives and Records Administration, Washington DC; Petitions for Naturalization of the U.S. District Court for the Eastern District of New York, 1865–1937; Series: M1879; Reference: (Roll 141), vol. 27, p.14 – vol. 28, p.182.
47. In the Mattuck Family Archive kept by Jill Mattuck Tarule (MFAa) there is a draft of the letter dated February 1906, but the letter was not formally submitted until 12 April 1906. The actual letter is in AJA, Manuscript Collection 5, D-2, Folder 16.
48. Ibid.
49. Ibid.
50. Regular Meeting of the Faculty of HUC, 28 April 1906, AJA, HUC Records, MS-5, Box B-3.
51. See Meyer, *Hebrew Union College*, pp.101–3. While some historians have suggested that the three faculty members were dismissed because they were Zionists, faculty minutes show that it was more to do with Kohler dealing with challenges to his leadership of the college. Ideological differences may have caused tensions between Kohler and the other professors, but they were not the main reason for their departure. See minute books for regular meetings of the faculty, AJA, HUC Records, MS-5, Box B-3.
52. Regular Meeting of the Faculty of HUC, 18 June 1906, in ibid.
53. *American Israelite*, 23 November 1905, p.6.
54. *American Israelite*, 26 April 1905, p.6 and 14 December 1906, p.6.
55. Jonathan Sarna and Nancy H. Klein, *The Jews of Cincinnati* (Boston, MA: Center for the Study of the American Jewish Experience, 1989): www.cincinnati-cityofimmigrants.com/cci/pdf.
56. Letter from IIM to Archie Hillman, 16 April 1906, AJA, SC-13649.
57. Letter from IIM to Archie Hillman, 3 June 1906, in ibid.
58. Letter from IIM to Archie Hillman, 16 April 1906, in ibid.
59. In a letter that IIM wrote to Archie Hillman, it is clear that he had left Cincinnati by then. He talks about being visited by Joe Gorfinkle, one of his roommates from Cincinnati, but no address is given. Letter from IIM to Archie Hillman, 31 July 1906, in ibid.
60. Letter from IIM to Archie Hillman, 15 September 1906, in ibid.
61. The first mention of his breakdown is made in an undated letter from IIM to Kaufmann Kohler, MFAa.
62. See letter from IIM to Archie Hillman, 1 October 1906, AJA, SC-13649. He was able to repay the money once he obtained a rabbinic position.

63. Letter from IIM to Archie Hillman, 31 July 1906. There is no explanation on why he was in this place, which did not have a Jewish population.
64. Letter from IIM to Archie Hillman, 15 September 1906, AJA, SC-13649.
65. The friend was Harry Kangisser, who was to become a prominent lawyer in the city.
66. IIM visited Luna Park, an early American that operated from 1905–29.
67. Letter from IIM to Archie Hillman, 27 September 1906, AJA, SC-13649.
68. Minute book of Temple B'nai Jeshurun in the possession of Bob Nefsky, a current member of the synagogue.
69. Letter from IIM reproduced in the minutes of the meeting of the HUC Board, 23 December 1906, p.129, AJA, HUC Records, MS-5, Box D-22.
70. Letter from IIM to Archie Hillman, 27 September 1906, AJA, SC-13649.
71. Ibid.
72. Letter from IIM to Archie Hillman, 6 December 1906, in ibid.
73. See Silverstein, *Alternatives to Assimilation,* pp.84–5.
74. *American Israelite*, 3 January 1907, p.3.
75. Letter from IIM to Archie Hillman, 23 October 1906, AJA, SC-13649.
76. It is interesting that Kohler did not report this to the board at the time he received IIM's letter saying that he wasn't returning.
77. Letter from Isaac Bloom to IIM living at 1436 'C' Street, Lincoln Nebraska, 28 December 1906, MFAa.
78. Draft letter from IIM to Isaac Bloom, 7 January 1907, MFAa.
79. Letter from IIM reproduced in the minutes of the meeting of the Board of Governors of HUC, 26 February 1906, p.149, AJA, HUC Records, MS-5, Box D-22.
80. Ibid.
81. Ibid.
82. Letter from IIM to Archie Hillman, 8 April 1907, AJA, SC-13649.
83. Ibid
84. Letter from IIM to Archie Hillman, 1 August 1907, in ibid.
85. Letter from IIM to Archie Hillman, 31 December 1907, in ibid.
86. Copy of a letter from IIM to the congregation B'Nai Jeshurun, Lincoln, Nebraska, 6 October 1907. Mattuck Family Archive kept by Robert Edgar (MFAb). His proposals were discussed at a meeting of the congregation held on 3 November 1907.
87. Ibid.
88. Ibid.
89. See minute book of Temple B'nai Jeshurun.
90. Letter from IIM to Archie Hillman, 31 December 1907, AJA, SC-13649.
91. See sermons in MCC.
92. Ibid.
93. 'Immigration Restriction', an address given by IIM to the Lawyers' Club of Lincoln, Nebraska on 7 January 1908, MCC.
94. Quoted in Meyer, *Response to Modernity*, p.269.
95. Rabbi I.I. Mattuck, 'Emil Gustav Hirsch', *Jewish Guardian*, 2 February 1923, p.3.
96. The services at Temple Sinai were the main services at the synagogue. When IIM introduced Sunday services in England in the 1920s, he stressed that they were additional services. He never considered, as Hirsch did, abandoning the Jewish Sabbath.
97. See Mattuck, 'Emil Gustav Hirsch', p.3.
98. Jewish lodges aimed at enhancing Jewish identity. Simon Mayer, IIM's future father-in-law, was a prominent member of the lodge.
99. These classes may have been for the Eastern European immigrants settling in Lincoln.
100. At this service he gave a sermon on 'Constructive Judaism', MCC.
101. Letter from IIM to Archie Hillman, 31 December 1907, AJA, SC-13649. On 26 April 1908 he spoke on 'A Jewish View of Jesus', on 17 May 1908 on 'A Practical Religious View of Life', and on 14 June 1908 on 'Education and Life', MCC.
102. Manuscript by unnamed author, 'Lincoln, Early Settlers', AJA, SC-7262. Apparently the Mayer brothers maintained their business in Plattsmouth alongside the new venture until 1898.
103. His father was David Mayer, who originated from Staudernheim south-west of Frankfurt in Germany. Private family tree made available by Dr Michael Starrels. When the shop was sold in 1914 to Eli Shire it netted around £200,000, which was a considerable amount for that time. See 'Lincoln Early Settlers'.

104. It was not uncommon for young rabbis to marry the daughters of leading congregants. It was often a mutually acceptable arrangement. For many young men, like IIM, it helped their social advancement, but it also enhanced the standing of the lay leaders in their congregations. Information provided by Dr Amy Shevetz.
105. According to notes made by Robert Mattuck, Louis Mayer had psychological problems, MFAb.
106. Her baby also died. Information from family plot in Lincoln, Nebraska, www.findagrave.com.
107. Unidentified newspaper cutting, MFAb.
108. See for example *Nebraska State Journal*, 1 June 1901, p.8.
109. Naomi Capon (née Mattuck), *Snippets From the Past – a Childhood from the Twenties* (unpublished manuscript, undated, c.1975).
110. See minute books for the B'nai Jeshurun.
111. *American Israelite*, 9 April 1908, p.2. It is interesting to note that when the engagement was announced in the *American Israelite*, the announcement came from Mr and Mrs Simon Mayer, even though Mayer's third wife had died four years earlier.
112. Undated draft letter from IIM to Kaufmann Kohler, MFAa.
113. Letter from Kaufmann Kohler to IIM, 18 March 1908, in ibid.
114. Ibid.
115. Ibid.
116. See later discussion of Rabbi Stephen Wise.
117. Letter from Kaufmann Kohler to IIM, 19 March 1908, MFAa.
118. Letter from Kaufmann Kohler to IIM, 5 April 1908, in ibid.
119. Draft letter from IIM to Kaufmann Kohler, 13 April 1908, in ibid.
120. Letter from Kaufmann Kohler to IIM, 29 April 1908, in ibid.
121. Letter from Kaufmann Kohler to IIM, 15 May 1908, in ibid.
122. He gave a sermon on 'What is Reform Judaism' on 4 June 1908, MCC.
123. See minute book of Temple B'nai Jeshurun.
124. Ibid.
125. *American Israelite*, 24 September 1908, p.3.
126. This house seems to have consisted of a series of rooms that were let out to professional people rather than IIM lodging with a family as he did previously. See Cincinnati City Directory for 1909.
127. *American Israelite*, 10 June 1909, p.6.
128. *American Israelite*, 26 November 1908, p.6.
129. *American Israelite*, 12 November 1908, p.6.
130. Minute book of the congregation Beneh Abraham (later B'Nai Abraham), AJA, Congregation B'nai Abraham (Portsmouth, Ohio) Minutes, 1896–1957, X-62.
131. Note provided by IIM for *Harvard College, Secretary's Second Report, Class of 1905* (Cambridge, MA: Harvard University Press, 1911).
132. List of former rabbis contained in the programme for the dedication of the new temple, 25 April 1975, AJA, Congregation B'nai Abraham (Portsmouth, Ohio), Nearprint Geography.
133. Amy Hill Shevitz, *Jewish Communities on the Ohio River, A History* (Lexington, KY: , 2007), p.142.
134. Ibid., p.89.
135. Ibid., p.112.
136. See minute book of the congregation B'nai Abraham.
137. Letter from Kaufmann Kohler to IIM, 14 May 1909, MFAa.
138. Letter from Grossmann to IIM, 30 August 1909, in ibid.
139. His sermon, given on 21 May 1909, was on 'Universal Peace', MCC.
140. In 1930, Temple Israel moved to its new quarters on Central Avenue in Lawrence. The old synagogue building was sold to Congregation Knesseth Israel, an Orthodox congregation founded in Far Rockaway in 1922: leimanlibrary.com.
141. Letter from Charles A. Brodek, Counsellor at Law, to Dr Stephen Wise, 17 March 1911, LJS Archives, Box 1/2.
142. Letter from Kaufmann Kohler to IIM, 1 December 1909, MFAa.
143. Ibid.
144. Letter from Kaufmann Kohler to IIM, 12 November 1909, in ibid.
145. Letter from IIM to Kaufmann Kohler, 6 January 1910, in ibid.

146. Letter from B. Bettman on behalf of the HUC Board to IIM, 2 February 1910, in ibid.
147. Only two incomplete versions are in evidence, one in the library of HUC and the other in the LJS Archives, Box 1/2.
148. Regular Meeting of the Faculty of HUC, 28 March 1910, AJA, HUC Records, MS-5, Box B-3. The supervisor for IIM's thesis was Professor David Neumark and the co-supervisor was Kaufmann Kohler.
149. Ibid.
150. Undated newspaper cutting 'Eight Rabbis', MFAb.
151. 'Hebrew Union College Commencement', *American Israelite,* 21 April 1910, p.4.
152. Letter from Rabbi David Philipson to Dr Maurice Harris, 15 March 1911, LJS Archives Box 1/2. David Philipson (1862–1949) was an American Reform rabbi, orator, and author. The son of German-Jewish immigrants, he was a member of the first graduating class of HUC. He became a leader of American Reform Judaism.
153. 'Clericus', 'Clerical Cameo, Rabbi Israel Mattuck', *Liverpool Evening Echo*, 24 March 1928, p.6.
154. Rabbi I.I. Mattuck, 'Dr Kaufmann Kohler, American Liberal Leader, Memoir and Tribute', *Jewish Guardian*, 5 February 1927, p.7.
155. Rabbi I.I. Mattuck, 'The Levirate Marriage in Jewish Law', in Julian Morgenstern, David Neumark, David Philipson (eds), *Studies in Jewish Literature*: *Issued in Honor of Professor Kaufmann Kohler, Ph.D, on the Occasion of his Seventieth Birthday, May the Tenth, Nineteen Hundred and Thirteen* (Berlin: Georg Reimar, 1913).
156. Letter from Kaufmann Kohler to IIM, 15 June 1913, LJS Archives, Box 1/2.
157. Joshua Bloch, 'Studies in Jewish Literature', *Jewish Exponent*, 31 July 1914, p.9.
158. Letter from Rabbi David Philipson to Dr Maurice Harris, 15 March 1911, LJS Archives, Box 1/2.
159. *American Israelite*, 25 February 1909, p.6.
160. Simon Mayer's third wife had died five years earlier, which is probably why his brother and sister-in-law hosted the wedding.
161. Schlesinger was a founding member of the Anti-Defamation League set up in 1913 to combat anti-Jewish rhetoric and behaviour.
162. Unidentified newspaper cuttings, MFAb.
163. Information provided by Arthur Mattuck, and May (Monie) Salkin, daughter of Rose Mattuck.
164. See minute books of Temple B'nai Jeshurun.
165. This was the address given in his naturalisation papers of that year. National Archives and Records Administration (NARA), Washington DC; Petitions for Naturalization of the US District Court for the Eastern District of New York, 1865–1937; NARA Series: M1879; Reference: (Roll 141), vol. 27, p.148 – vol. 28, p.182.
166. See Friedman, 'The Making of a Reform Rabbi', p.29.
167. He preached there on 30 September 1910 on 'A Liberal Attitude to Religion', MCC.
168. *Emanu-El*, 30 September 1910, New York Edition. It was based on the sermon he gave at Temple Emanu-El, and at Far Rockaway on 9 September 1910, MCC, both in ibid.
169. Ibid.
170. 'Rabbi Mattuck, Rabbi of Temple Israel Far Rockaway', undated newspaper cutting, MFAb.
171. 'May Go to New York. Rev Dr Israel I. Mattuck Preaches. Temple Emanu–El wants assistant. Worcester young man has a chance', undated newspaper cutting, in ibid.
172. The letter that Kaufmann Kohler wrote to IIM, 29 May 1911, suggested that the sermon he had given at Temple Emanu-El had lacked enthusiasm, LJS Archives, Box 1/2. IIM preached on 'Some Evidences of Divinity' on Saturday morning 18 March and on 'The Worth of the Individual' on Sunday morning 19 March 1911. See *American Hebrew and Jewish Messenger*, 17 March 1911, p.583.

CHAPTER SEVEN

The 'Call' to England

Because it was such a watershed in his career, it is worth examining how IIM came to be appointed to the important post of rabbi at the Liberal Jewish Synagogue in London and to lead elite Liberal Judaism for the first half of the twentieth century.

The Setting up of the Jewish Religious Union and the Liberal Jewish Synagogue

While Reform Judaism had spread quickly, if unevenly, across Germany from the turn of the nineteenth century, in Britain the 'modernisation' of Judaism had been slower to develop. Repeated attempts to introduce changes were bitterly opposed and it was not until 1840, when a resolution was passed by a group of wealthy Jews to set up what became known as West London Synagogue of British Jews (consecrated in 1842), that the first step was taken towards Progressive Judaism.[1]

The setting up of the new synagogue did not result from the teachings of the Jewish enlightenment (*Haskalah*), or the emancipation of Jews, as was the case for Reform synagogues in Central Europe, but was the outcome of the upward mobility and acculturation of some English Jews. As they had become more integrated into English Society, the elite of London's Jewry had moved from the overcrowded Jewish enclaves of the east and the City to the more salubrious areas of the West End of the capital. Walking to the synagogues – all still situated in the East End – became an inconvenience. At the same time, the acculturated Jews began to desire modifications in synagogue services to make them more akin to those of their gentile neighbours. Their concern was less for changes in theology than for changes in standards of behaviour during services to give them more decorum.

The changes introduced at the West London Synagogue (an abbreviated Sabbath morning service, the abolition of the Second Day of the major festivals, sermons in English, discontinuation of the practice of being called up and the formation of a choir) were relatively minor, but they were the cause of great acrimony in the Anglo-Jewish community and were referred to as 'the Great Schism'. When the synagogue's first minister, David Woolf Marks, questioned the value of the Oral Law, the criticism became a furore and a *cherem* (excommunication) was demanded. Since the reformers were part of an influential and close-knit social circle, the majority of whom remained attached to Orthodox synagogues, this was impractical. A religious 'caution' was issued instead, which was lifted in 1849.

Although the membership of the synagogue grew rapidly, it followed a highly exclusive and a very conservative new path and attendance of services was very poor. In the latter half of the nineteenth century, two Reform synagogues were established in Bradford and in Manchester, but no further Reform congregations emerged in London. At the turn of the twentieth century, the writer Israel Zangwill saw the West London Synagogue as 'a body that has stood still for fifty years admiring its past self'.[2] The reality was that those who had established the synagogue would have preferred not to have seceded from orthodoxy and would have liked changes to have been made within the established communal organisation.

More progressive thinking began to emerge during the final decade of the nineteenth century, mainly as a result of the dissatisfaction with resistance to change in both the Orthodox and Reform camps. The first indication of the new thinking was the series of Sunday afternoon services held in West Hampstead Town Hall in 1890. However, the main catalyst for change was an article, 'Spiritual Possibilities of Judaism To-day', written by 25-year-old Lily Montagu, daughter of a rigidly Orthodox Jew, Samuel Montagu (later Baron Swaythling).[3] The article, which appeared in the *Jewish Quarterly Review*[4] in January 1899, articulated the problem that was concerning certain quarters of Anglo-Jewry at the time – the apathy and lack of spiritual awareness amongst Jewish people resulting from Jewish emancipation, Anglicisation and secular education, referred to by Lily Montagu as Anglo-Jewry's 'spiritual degeneration'.[5] She argued that changes should be made to Jewish worship to 'lift Judaism from its desolate position'.

Lily Montagu's article aroused an enthusiastic response and led to the establishment of an organisation named the Jewish Religious Union (JRU). The members of the JRU did not at that time see themselves as a breakaway movement; rather, they hoped to liberalise existing synagogues by changing them from within. They wanted more English to be used in services, men and women to sit together, organ music to be used to accompany a mixed choir, and greater congregational participation in worship. These ideas were, at the time, both radical and contentious.

The first leadership committee of the JRU included Lily Montagu, who became Vice-President, Dr Claude Montefiore, an eminent scholar, who had been a significant influence of Lily Montagu's, and who became President only after much persuasion by her, a number of Orthodox ministers and others who were both well-informed and influential in Jewish affairs. The first Sabbath service organised by the JRU was held at the Great Central Hotel, Marylebone Road on 18 October 1902. It was attended by over 300 people and was conducted by the Orthodox minister, the Reverend Simeon Singer.[6] After the service, the JRU approached the then Chief Rabbi, Herman Adler, to discuss holding future services in an Orthodox synagogue. This overture was rejected and the JRU denounced.

Prayer books were written, publications were issued, lectures were organised and children's religion classes were established in Hampstead. Contact was made with other Liberal and Progressive congregations in Europe and America. Services continued to be held at the Great Central Hotel, in various halls in the West End, and also in the East End of London. The JRU found itself faced with fierce opposition, including from Lily Montagu's father, who described the JRU as 'a menace to Judaism'.[7] It was widely seen as being schismatic in intent and encountered a highly critical press. Pressure was placed on those JRU members who were Orthodox ministers, forcing them to resign.

By 1907, the impetus behind the JRU was waning and divisions within the leadership were becoming apparent. Initially the movement had concentrated its attention on forms of service rather than articulating the principles that underpinned the changes being introduced. This avoided potentially divisive differences of opinion being aired but, as time progressed, it was no longer possible to ignore a discussion of beliefs. At a conference held in November 1908, it was acknowledged openly for the first time that the beliefs of the JRU differed from those of both Orthodox and Reform synagogues, and that the only means for ensuring the survival of a modern view of Judaism was to establish a separate 'Liberal Jewish' movement.

In January 1909 the JRU decided that the time had come to set up a Liberal synagogue in Britain. This proved to be a step too far for those holding more traditional beliefs, who as a result left the JRU. Members who remained committed to the JRU were forced to relinquish their positions elsewhere. Despite these setbacks, the JRU pressed ahead with plans to establish a new congregation, to be called the Liberal Jewish Synagogue (LJS). The JRU published a 'manifesto', written by Claude Montefiore, together with a pamphlet, *The Jewish Religious Union – Its Principles and Its Future*. These publications created a great deal of interest and, by the autumn of 1909, applications for membership of the proposed synagogue, together with the annual subscriptions promised, were sufficient for a viable congregation to be formed.[8] In March 1910 premises for a synagogue were acquired in Hill Street, Marylebone in a building that had previously been a Mount Zion Baptist Chapel. It had seating for 232 on the ground floor and a further 192 in the gallery. The first service was held there on 4 February 1911.

The Search for a 'Minister'

One of the first tasks facing the leaders of the LJS was to find a religious leader. This proved to be far from straightforward. In 1910 an advertisement was placed in the *Jewish Chronicle* for a 'minister'. When no suitable candidates presented themselves,[9] a decision was taken to look further afield. Claude Montefiore, together with Charles Singer, a prominent JRU member and son of the Reverend Simeon Singer, embarked on a month-long trip to America to identify potential rabbis. They visited New York, Chicago, Pittsburgh, Philadelphia and Cincinnati and spent several days at the annual meeting of the Central Conference of American Rabbis (CCAR).[10] After considering many possibilities, including Charles Fleischer from Boston,[11] whom IIM had encountered during his time at Harvard, offers were made to Rabbi Hyman Enelow (a prominent New York rabbi) and to Rabbi Gerson Levi in Chicago. Both declined to be considered, a source of embarrassment to the LJS leaders.[12]

At this point, Montefiore and Singer enlisted the help of three prominent American rabbis (dubbed by Claude Montefiore as the 'Committee of Three'), Dr Stephen Wise, rabbi of the Free Synagogue of New York,[13] Dr Kaufmann Kohler, from HUC and Dr Maurice Harris, a prominent spokesman on Progressive Judaism and rabbi of Temple Israel, Harlem, New York.[14] They regarded their task as a 'very high responsibility'.[15] Wise, the leader of the triumvirate, had recently addressed ten crowded JRU meetings in London and therefore had some understanding of the LJS community. He urged Montefiore not to advertise the vacancy publicly as he felt that this would 'cheapen' the role. He argued that candidates should be identified as the result of personal recommendations.[16] He also suggested that, given the nature of its congregation, the LJS should be looking for someone more 'conservative'.[17]

The committee first turned its attention to Dr Joseph Stolz, an early graduate of HUC and, by then, the long-standing rabbi of Isaiah Temple in Chicago. It also approached Rabbi Louis Mendoza of Norfolk, Virginia.[18] However, both refused to consider the position because they were reluctant to leave America, where they had strong roots and family ties. The committee therefore decided to seek out potential candidates who were less well established, and possibly more likely to consider a move to England. One of the first young men their attention alighted upon was one who had recently taken up a pulpit close to New York – IIM. He had been recommended by Rabbi Louis Bernstein (a contemporary of IIM's at HUC) of Temple Adath Joseph in Kansas City, Missouri, who had written to Stephen Wise suggesting that there was a man 'at your very door' who was 'admirably fitted in all ways'. He described IIM as:

> mentally a man of very superior qualities. Excellent training both from a Jewish and secular standpoint. An earnest speaker and a polished writer. Reared in an Orthodox atmosphere but thoroughly of the Progressive school by inclination and choice.[19]

IIM's candidature was endorsed by Kaufmann Kohler, who wrote to IIM to explain that he had done so since he felt that he (IIM) possessed 'many of the qualities that fit you better than others for the position as leader of the Reform Union in London'. In particular he mentioned IIM's 'natural oratory', 'resourcefulness' and his 'positive views concerning Reform Judaism'.[20] Given the troubles surrounding IIM's time at HUC, these comments were very generous. Further support for IIM came from Professor Toy of Harvard University, who wrote: 'Of his scholarship I have only praise. As a student with me he showed qualities of a high order – accuracy, breadth, freshness and power of formulating and stating his views clearly and strongly.'[21]

IIM was invited by Dr Harris to meet with him and to 'occupy his pulpit' at Temple Israel in March 1911. After IIM had preached, Dr Harris commented: 'I was very favourably impressed. He had a quiet manner, expresses himself well and shows scholarship behind him.'[22] IIM also met with Stephen Wise, who found him to be 'earnest, thoughtful and well-poised'.[23] The 'Committee of Three' therefore suggested to Claude Montefiore that IIM should be invited to London to give the LJS congregation the opportunity to become acquainted with him. When this suggestion was put to IIM, not only was he comfortable with the proposal, but felt that no other plan would be 'fitting and equitable'.[24] However, shortly after his meeting with IIM, Dr Harris received a letter from Rabbi Louis Grossmann[25] at HUC, in which Grossmann was less than complimentary about the young rabbi:

> I cannot say that he is a man of scholarship or that even the natural and elementary 'gift' of public address is strikingly strong. He is a young man of average calibre. As to spirituality (and I know that, whatever that may be, that is the quality which is looked for in the candidate for the London Position) I can say that I have never regarded Mr Mattuck as possessing it in any degree.[26]

Grossmann also made some more personal remarks about IIM: 'As to 'social' fitness, I mean as to tact and courteous manner, Mr Mattuck has much to learn.'[27] Despite his poor opinion of IIM, Grossmann claimed that he had secured for him the post in Far Rockaway. As we have seen, Rabbi Grossmann had actually written to IIM discouraging him from applying for the vacancy,[28] and it subsequently emerged in a letter from Stephen Wise to Montefiore that one of Grossmann's reasons for making derogatory comments about IIM may have been that he had hoped to be considered himself for the role at the LJS. Grossmann did not have a good relationship with Kohler and others at HUC and was looking for alternative employment.[29] To ensure his views were heard, Grossmann also wrote to Stephen Wise saying that IIM:

> is not a man of refinement, nor of tact and Mr Montefiore looks to that very much, and justly. The man in that place [the LJS] ought to be the most courteous and courtly gentleman possible. … Mr Mattuck is simply a fairly good common-place young man.[30]

There is a suggestion of social condescension in this statement, but a more personal dispute may have been the cause of his comments. Because of Grossmann's comments, further references were sought from Kohler, in which Kohler did not abate one iota from his high opinion of IIM.[31] Soundings were also taken from other sources. Charles Brodek, a prominent New York lawyer and a friend of both IIM and Stephen Wise, spoke of him in glowing terms:

> His personality is attractive and he is blessed with a fine sense of humour. He is modest with a slight tendency towards shyness; slow and deliberate in his habits of thought including his estimate of persons … He is earnest and sincere. In fact, the thing that impresses me most forcibly about him is his honesty of thought, I have never observed the slightest tendency on his part to veer or shift. I do not mean obstinacy but merely a habit of honest thought.[32]

IIM's Visit to London

Montefiore appears to have been reassured by these additional references. On 29 March he wrote a long letter to IIM setting out in detail what would be required of him during his visit to England, stating that it should not be seen as any form of commitment on either side, and making it clear that the LJS was still considering other candidates.[33] He explained that the congregation was looking for 'a Leader and not an Echo' and that the person appointed would find 'a free pulpit'.[34] IIM does not seem to have been at all daunted by Montefiore's candid letter, and accepted the invitation with enthusiasm, saying he was strongly attracted by the opportunity to 'work in the cause of Liberal Judaism that serving your community would offer'.[35] Despite the caveats Montefiore had placed on IIM's visit to England, he was optimistic about IIM's candidature. He sang IIM's praises to the lay leaders of the congregation, but warned them not to become too excited, in case IIM decided not to accept the post.[36]

In readiness for his visit, IIM completed the process of becoming a naturalised American Citizen, which he had started while still living in Cincinnati, in order to obtain a passport.[37] Because of the difficulty of arranging for his pulpit to be covered during his absence, IIM was unable to make the May dates suggested by Montefiore, but agreed to a visit in June. While preparations were being made for his arrival, the 'Committee of Three' continued to put forward names of possible candidates, and further correspondence between Stephen Wise and Claude Montefiore suggests that IIM did not, at least initially, have Wise's full support.[38]

Perhaps in an attempt to raise his standing and display his credentials in advance of his interview in London, in May 1911 IIM penned a lengthy article on Liberal Judaism, published in the *American Israelite*.[39] Shortly before his departure, he received a letter from Kohler wishing him a memorable and pleasant trip and encouraging him to endeavour to inspire his audience.[40] IIM left America for England on 6 June, arriving in Plymouth six days later. The journey and the prospects ahead must have been very different from his long sea journey from Lithuania to America two decades earlier. However, his later recollection of his arrival in England reveals that he still had misgivings:

> I well remember the scene which greeted me in June 1911, when coming to you [the LJS] on a visit, I first saw the shore of England. A haze hung over as the boat stopped outside Plymouth. All was grey except where the red cliffs of Cornwall stood out, but all was suffused with the golden light of the early morning sun, piercing its way into the haze, soon to dispel it; and I saw in that vision a symbol – a symbol of the hope, of light dispelling doubts, dispelling obscurantism.[41]

Although the LJS had encountered difficulties in making some of the arrangements because IIM's visit coincided with the Coronation of King George V as a result of which London was unusually full of visitors, IIM's schedule for the next two weeks was a busy one. It included addresses at the Saturday afternoon services held at the LJS on both 17 and 24 June, attending a children's service on the morning of 17 June, conducting the children's service on 24 June, and meeting with members of the congregation at the Great Central Hotel on 18 June when he was to give an address. He was also invited to several 'At Homes' and evening meals with leading synagogue members. Charles Singer arranged for him to be seen by a physician in Harley Street for a health check. (The doctor found IIM to be in good health but 'poor in physique' and 'highly strung'.[42]) The visit was to conclude with a formal committee meeting on 26 June, at which a decision would be taken on whether to offer the position to IIM.[43]

IIM seems to have heeded Kohler's advice. From the outset he made a favourable impression, including on Lily Montagu:

> [He] spoke to us on 'Faith'. I well remember that first sermon and the serious, ardent face of the young man who delivered it. He told us that faith in God and faith in man were the basis of his work; that through faith in God, man was exalted, and the possibilities of his work were infinite.[44]

Lily Montagu wrote to IIM the following day saying that she had prayed for a long time that God would send the JRU '*the* right man [her emphasis]' and believed that he now had.[45] She later recalled the feeling of intense anxiety that preceded the meeting on 18 June and the extreme thankfulness that followed it.[46] By the end of the fortnight, the decision of the appointment committee was unanimous: IIM was to be 'called' to London. As gratified as he might have been by this outcome, IIM did not give an immediate response to the committee. Shortly after his return to America he wrote to Montefiore thanking him for his kindness and the hospitality he had experienced during his time in London, but asking for time to make up his mind.[47] The *American Hebrew* interviewed IIM on his reactions to his time in England. He said that the Jewish population of London was much smaller than he was used to in American cities and 'decidedly more Orthodox in theory, but becoming liberalised by contact with more liberal brethren'.[48]

IIM Accepts the 'Call'

Having not received a response from IIM, on 19 July the LJS sent a telegram asking for an urgent decision as a committee meeting was due to take place the following day. It appears IIM's delay in making up his mind may have been partly due to some initial doubts on the part of Edna Mattuck. She became reconciled to the move,[49] but IIM apparently continued to have misgivings of his own as recorded by Rabbi David Philipson:

> It was during my stay at Far Rockaway, Long Island that Rabbi Mattuck consulted me on the matter of his going to England. Naturally he hesitated. The prospect was very alluring but there were difficulties to be considered. I urged him very strongly to accept. I felt that a young man of fine abilities would have a superb opportunity for service in the cause of Liberal Judaism in England, notably that he would have as co-workers such capable and devoted spirits as Claude G. Montefiore, Lily Montagu and Israel Abrahams. 'However', said I to him, 'there is one most important factor to be considered; is your wife willing to make the venture?' 'Yes she is altogether willing to go'. 'Then', said I, 'go. I am sure that you will make good.'[50]

IIM may have been finding it difficult to make the choice between being one of many bright stars in the constellation of the American Reform movement and becoming a 'big fish in the small pond' of Anglo-Jewry. However, he heeded Philipson's advice and by the time that the telegram arrived from the LJS he had made up his mind. He telegraphed his acceptance within hours.

It is interesting to reflect on why IIM was attracted to a position so far away from his home and family and to lead a congregation the future of which was far from certain. In an interview published in the *Jewish Chronicle* two months after his arrival in England, he explained that he had accepted the role because he saw the potential for what he referred to as 'missionary work' in England.[51] Later in life, looking back over his career, he shed further light on the decision, saying that he had regarded the role as an 'adventure' and had been excited about the fact that the job was to be more than leading a congregation – 'being at the centre and fountain head of the Liberal Jewish Movement in this country'.[52] Knowing what we do about the extent of his ambition and his desire to be amongst the intellectual elite, the opportunity for working with the renowned scholars Claude Montefiore and Israel Abrahams was probably also an important factor in his decision.

Several decades after his appointment IIM was described as 'a young rabbi with a pioneer spirit'[53] and, looking back over his career, Lily Montagu recognised what a momentous decision IIM and his wife had taken:

> Since my visit to the USA I realise a little better something of what the decision must have cost our friends. Big synagogues, great

> congregations, with all their vitalising influence; a multitude of friends; recognised leadership; a youthful and enthusiastic country; and we asked them to leave all this.[54]

However, family members have wondered if the move was partly about push as well as pull; a continuing rebellion against his Orthodox background and his desire to distance himself from his family.[55]

Complications

There were to be two further developments before IIM took up his post at the LJS. The first was the matter of his contract with the synagogue. On 16 October A. Lindo Henry, Honorary Secretary to the LJS, wrote to IIM saying that a draft agreement had been prepared covering the main terms of his appointment, which was enclosed for his perusal.[56] IIM appears to have been taken aback by this; he wrote back saying that such agreements did not exist in America and raising issues about some of the points detailed in the draft contract. However, his main objection was that the contract might fetter the freedom of his pulpit:

> Furthermore, the Council should hardly expect me to bind myself to whatever regulations it may exact in the future. I doubt that the Council would exact any that would be distasteful – but possibilities can be conceived. ... You must appreciate my reluctance to forgo any part of my freedom to which I am accustomed.[57]

IIM's spirited response was considered by the LJS Council on 29 November. The decision was that, although it was still inclined to have some sort of contract, it was willing to let the matter rest temporarily until IIM arrived in England, when they would be able to talk the matter over with him face-to-face.[58] It is interesting to note that a formal contract does not appear ever to have been issued. In March 1912 IIM was sent a letter that confirmed 'the terms of a verbal agreement' on the date of the commencement of his employment and a salary of £800 per annum.[59] Subsequently the lay leadership of the LJS may have realised that this episode was an early indication of IIM's strength of character.

Although his congregation was reluctant to see him depart, it was agreed that IIM's last day of work at Far Rockaway would be 1 January 1912, or earlier if a new rabbi could be identified before that date. By the beginning of December 1911 Temple Israel had recruited a successor,[60] and on 15 December a farewell reception was held to thank IIM for his services to the synagogue. He was presented with a bound volume that recorded the gratitude of his 'loving congregation' for his 'splendid labors'.[61] The reception included a musical service in his honour given by the choir. On behalf of the mothers of the congregation, Mrs Rosenbaum thanked him in 'heartfelt words' for his services to the Sunday school and with young people.[62]

After spending a few days with his parents in New York,[63] IIM set sail for England on 6 January with his wife and baby son on the SS *Amerika*, bound for Plymouth. If the Mattucks had any anxieties about leaving America, these must have intensified as they crossed the Atlantic and Robert was taken seriously ill. By the time that the boat docked in Plymouth, he had developed bronchial pneumonia.[64] The couple booked into a hotel while their baby was treated and until his health improved sufficiently to allow the family to continue their journey to London to fulfil a number of engagements. The LJS was very supportive of the Mattucks – it paid for the hotel accommodation and made relevant onward travel arrangements – but after a few days, IIM was pressed on his likely arrival date.[65] He had been expected to arrive on 14 January, but he finally reached London only just in time for his inaugural service on 20 January.

NOTES

1. Much of the account which follows is based on Anne J. Kershen, '1848–1990: One Hundred and Fifty Years of Progressive Judaism', in Anne J. Kershen (ed.) *150 Years of Progressive Judaism in Britain* (London: the London Museum of Jewish Life, 1990).
2. Quoted in ibid.
3. The following account is based on information contained in Pam Fox, *A Place to Call My Jewish Home, Memories of the Liberal Jewish Synagogue 1911–2011* (London: Liberal Jewish Synagogue, 2011).
4. This periodical was jointly edited by Claude Montefiore and Israel Abrahams, the best-known Jewish scholar in England. It was devoted both to scholarship and to the liberalisation of Judaism.
5. The Hon. Lily H. Montagu, 'Spiritual Possibilities of Judaism Today', *Jewish Quarterly Review*, 11 January 1899.
6. Simeon Singer was the rabbi at the synagogue where Lily Montagu was brought up and also editor of the famous 'Singer Prayer Book.'
7. Cited in Edward Kessler (ed.), *A Reader of Liberal Judaism: The Writings of Israel Abrahams, Claude Montefiore, Israel Mattuck and Lily Montagu* (London: Vallentine Mitchell, 2004), p.7.
8. The minutes of the JRU for 1909 note that 110 applications for membership of the new synagogue had been made, LJS Archives.
9. Lily Montagu was later to disclose that the JRU had been placed under some pressure (she did not say from where) to accept a candidate who would have been unsuitable. See Lily H. Montagu, *The Jewish Religious Union and Its Beginnings* (Papers for Jewish People, No. XXVII) (London: JRU, 1927), p.24.
10. Lucy Cohen, *Some Recollections of Claude Goldsmid Montefiore, 1858–1938* (London: Faber and Faber, 1940), p.62.
11. Daniel R. Langton, *Claude Montefiore: His Life and Thought* (London: Vallentine Mitchell, 2002), p.98. Rabbi Fleischer was recommended by Israel Zangwill.
12. See letter from Dr Stephen Wise to Claude Montefiore, 20 March 1911, in which he refers to the need to avoid 'a repetition of the Enelow-Levi refusals', LJS Archives, Box 1/2.
13. Dr Wise launched his career in 1900 as the rabbi of Portland, Oregon. Typical of the activists of the era, he attacked many of the social and political ills of contemporary

America. In 1893 he was appointed assistant to Rabbi Henry S. Jacobs of the Congregation B'nai Jeshurun, New York, and later in the same year, minister to the same congregation. In 1906 Wise made a major break with the established Reform movement following a disagreement about freedom of the pulpit. In 1907 he established his and the Free Synagogue movement. Wise was an early supporter of Zionism, and founded the Jewish Institute of Religion in New York City in 1922 to train rabbis in Reform Judaism. It was merged with HUC after his death in 1949.

14. Dr Harris was appointed in 1882 as the congregation's first permanent rabbi and, over a forty-eight-year period of service, transformed Temple Israel of Harlem into a major cultural institution and became one of the most prominent spokesmen of Progressive Judaism. During his ministry Temple Israel became Temple Israel of the City of New York, which was first located in a former church at 125th Street and Fifth Avenue, then in a grand limestone building which still stands at 120th Street and Lenox Avenue.
15. Letter from Dr Stephen Wise to Dr K. Kohler at HUC, 24 January 1911, LJS Archives, Box 1/2.
16. Letter from Dr Wise to Claude Montefiore, 2 January 1911, in ibid. He went on to say: 'In our country, a man worth while would not respond to such an advertisement'.
17. Ibid. Since both Dr Wise and Dr Harris visited England and preached at JRU services (Dr Harris in 1908 and Dr Wise in 1910), they were acquainted with the nature of the movement. See Montagu, *The Jewish Religious Union*, pp.18, 23.
18. Letter from Dr Stephen Wise to Dr Kohler, 24 January 1911, LJS Archives, Box 1/2.
19. Letter from Rabbi Louis Bernstein to Dr Stephen Wise, 8 February 1911, in ibid.
20. Letter from Kaufmann Kohler to IIM, 5 March 1911, in ibid.
21. Letter from Professor Crawford Toy, 18 February 1911, in ibid.
22. Letter from Dr Maurice Harris to Claude Montefiore, 6 March 1911, in ibid.
23. Ibid.
24. Letter from Dr Stephen Wise to Claude Montefiore, 16 February 1911, LJS Archives, Box 1/2.
25. Letter from Rabbi Louis Grossmann to Dr Harris, 16 March 1911, in ibid.
26. Ibid.
27. Ibid.
28. Letter from Rabbi Grossmann to IIM, 30 August 1909, Mattuck Family Archive kept by Jill Mattuck Tarule (MFAa).
29. Letter from Dr Stephen Wise to Claude Montefiore, 17 March 1911, LJS Archives, Box 1/2.
30. Letter from Rabbi Grossmann to Dr Stephen Wise, undated, in ibid. Rabbi Grossmann later wrote directly to Claude Montefiore recommending another candidate who he did consider to have a 'refined manner' (Rabbi Abraham Cronbach). See letter, 20 April 1911, in ibid.
31. Letter from Dr Maurice Harris to Claude Montefiore, 21 March 1911, LJS Archives, Box 1/2.
32. Letter from Charles A. Brodek, Counsellor at Law, to Dr Wise, 17 March 1911, in ibid. Dr Wise considered Brodek to be 'a man of good mind and astute judgement', see letter from Dr Stephen Wise to Claude Montefiore, 17 March 1911, in ibid.
33. Letter from Claude Montefiore to IIM, 29 March 1911, in ibid.
34. Ibid.
35. Letter from IIM to Claude Montefiore, 11 April 1911, LJS Archives, Box 1/2.
36. 'Memento of a Great Occasion', *LJM*, XX, no.6 (March 1949), p.29.
37. See National Archives and Records Administration (NARA), Washington DC; Petitions for Naturalization of the U.S. District Court for the Eastern District of New York, 1865-1937; NARA Series: M1879; Reference: (Roll 141), vol. 27, p.148 – vol. 28, p.182. Given his strong allegiance to America, it is interesting that IIM did not complete the naturalisation process until this time. Later he was to explain that he had understood that when his father was naturalised in 1905, this covered his offspring. He only discovered subsequently that as he was by then over 21, he had to make an application to be naturalised in his own right.
38. Letter from Dr Stephen Wise to Claude Montefiore, 22 December 1911, LJS Archives, Box 1/2.
39. Israel I. Mattuck, 'The Emancipation of Israel', *American Israelite,* 11 May 1911, p.1.
40. Letter from Kaufmann Kohler to IIM, 29 May 1911, LJS Archives, Box 1/2.

41. 'Five Years of the Liberal Jewish Synagogue', sermon given by IIM at the LJS, 20 January 1917, Montagu Centre Collection (MCC).
42. Letter from Dr Rankin of 9 Harley Street to Charles Singer, 19 June 1911, LJS Archives, Box 1/2.
43. Letter from A. Lindo Henry, Honorary Secretary, to IIM, 23 May 1911, in ibid.
44. The Hon. Lily H. Montagu, 'Rabbi Dr Israel I. Mattuck, Memorial Tribute', *LJM, In Memoriam of Israel I. Mattuck, 1883–1954* (June 1954), p.1.
45. Letter from Lily Montagu to IIM, 19 June 1911, London Metropolitan Archives, ACC/3529/002/018.
46. Quoted in 'Israel I. Mattuck – His Life and Work', *LJM, In Memoriam of Israel I. Mattuck, 1883–1954* (June 1954), p.9.
47. Letter from IIM to Claude Montefiore, 3 July 1911, LJS Archives, Box 1/2. It later emerged that this was partly because of the need for him to give his attention to the dedication of the new synagogue and also because of the need to consult the lay leaders of the congregation. See letter from IIM to Claude Montefiore, 1 August 1911, LJS Archives, Box 1/2.
48. *JC*, 14 July 1911, p.16.
49. A letter from Stephen Wise to IIM, 1 August 1912, has a handwritten note on the typed letter saying that the content showed that, by then, Edna Mattuck had agreed to move to England ('EMM changed her mind on this one'), LJS Archives, Box 1/2.
50. David Philipson, *My Life As An American Jew – An Autobiography* (Cincinnati, OH: John Kidd and Son, 1941), pp.225–6.
51. *JC*, 8 March 1912, p.13.
52. Letter from IIM to Miss Marjorie Moos, 30 January 1948, LJS Archives, Box 1/2.
53. Article in celebration of Rabbi Mattuck's Seventieth Birthday, *LJM*, XXV, no.2 (February 1954), p.25.
54. Lily Montagu, 'Dr Montefiore's Discovery', quoted in *LJM*, XX, no. 6 (March 1949), p.29.
55. Conversation with Jill Mattuck Tarule, 13 November 2011.
56. Letter from A. Lindo Henry to IIM, 16 October 1911, LJS Archives, Box 1/2.
57. Letter from IIM to A. Lindo Henry, 30 October 1911, in ibid.
58. Letter from A. Lindo Henry to IIM, 1 December 1911, in ibid.
59. Draft letter from A. Lindo Henry to IIM, undated but attached to a letter dated 24 February 1912, saying that the draft will be considered at the next meeting of the LJS Council, in ibid.
60. His successor was Rabbi Ephraim Frisch, a graduate of HUC. See *New York Times*, 16 June 1912.
61. Date unknown. Volume in MFAa.
62. 'Farewell to Rabbi Mattuck', *American Hebrew and Jewish Messenger*, 22 December 1911, p.255.
63. *Jewish Advocate*, 22 December 1911, p.7.
64. See letters from IIM to A. Lindo Henry, LJS Archives, Box 1/2.
65. Letter from A. Lindo Henry to IIM, 15 January 1912, in ibid.

CHAPTER EIGHT

Early Years at the LJS

Induction Service

Despite the stresses surrounding his arrival in England, IIM's inaugural service was a triumph. The LJS was crowded on that Saturday afternoon: in addition to the JRU leaders, the Reverend A.A. Green from Hampstead (Orthodox) Synagogue attended the service and Mr H.G. Lousada represented West London Synagogue.[1] Claude Montefiore read the service and also a special 'induction prayer', which was largely a statement of the advantages that he saw as accruing from IIM's appointment.[2]

IIM then read a short passage from the Sefer Torah before he gave a sermon on 'What is Liberal Judaism', commencing with a tribute to Montefiore and other JRU leaders.[3] In the course of the sermon he made a statement that he was to use again and again and which was to epitomise his forty-year career at the LJS: 'To sacrifice principle to conformity would jeopardise our cause. Falsehood is ever an evil.'[4] Implicit in IIM's sermon was his belief that the form of Judaism to which he was committed represented the most enlightened expression of the Jewish religion to date. It is interesting to note that, despite his allegiance to the American Reform movement, IIM readily adopted the English term 'Liberal Judaism'. A year or so later he was to explain that he preferred 'Liberal' to 'Reform' because it cast 'no aspersion on that which preceded it.'[5]

IIM's induction service was widely reported in the Jewish press, including by the *Jewish Chronicle*, which conveyed a vivid picture of the young rabbi:

> Mr Mattuck is certainly a striking figure in the pulpit. He has a young ascetic-looking face, with piercing eyes, and makes frequent use of very affective gestures. His speech is deliberate, except when he is carried away by the flow of his ideas when he bursts out into an exceedingly rapid stream of language.[6]

Although the reporter was uncomfortable with some of IIM's pronouncements on Orthodox Judaism (IIM said that it was 'incased [sic] in the wrappings of a mummy'), he clearly found IIM very impressive and said there was no denying the impact that he had made.[7] IIM had spoken for forty-five minutes without consulting a note and the congregation appeared 'gratified with the minister who had been selected for them'. Other commentators attending the service observed that IIM was obviously going to add 'an ardent spiritual force to the communal life of Anglo-Jewry'[8] and, even if one did not agree with what he had to say, it had to be acknowledged that he was 'a forceful personality'.[9]

The Anglo-Jewish Community

Before embarking on an exploration of the development of IIM's career in Britain, it is worth considering the setting in which he was to work and how it compared to the Jewry he had come to know in America. When he visited England in 1911, what had struck IIM most was the difference in the scale of Anglo-Jewry both in overall terms and in the size of its component congregations. He was later to remark that while it was common for synagogues in major American cities to have an attendance of 400 or 500 congregants, this would be unthinkable in Britain.[10]

However, on his arrival in 1912, he quickly became aware of a range of other significant differences between the British and American Jewish communities. As in America, the profile of Anglo-Jewry was changing because of the rapid influx of Jews from Eastern Europe, but whereas the dominant community in America until the early part of the twentieth century was mainly Germanic in origin, in Britain the Jewish establishment included a significant number of Sephardic families, some of whom were represented in the lay leadership of the LJS. Until he came to Britain, IIM would probably have met very few Sephardic Jews.[11] The make-up of the Anglo-Jewish community led to customs and practices that were new to IIM, but it was also reinforced by the English class system, with which IIM was to struggle in trying to bring coherence to the LJS congregation.

While many acculturated American Jews were keen to demonstrate that they were good American citizens, in a land largely made up of immigrants, the pressures to leave Judaism, and what IIM referred to as the 'temptations of the Jew of intermarriage',[12] were not as acute in America as they were in Britain. Whereas in America, 'perhaps by mutual agreement', Jews and Christians kept themselves apart socially,[13] in England there was no 'clear line of demarcation between Jew and non-Jew'.[14] Unlike in other parts of Europe, English Jews were accepted socially in aristocratic circles even before they gained full political emancipation,[15] adopting the manners and lifestyle of those with whom they associated. IIM remarked that the Anglo-Jewish community was strong in charitable institutions and community dinners and there was a great deal of interest in individuals and the Jewish press, but disinterest in 'Judaism itself.'[16] On the whole, IIM appears to have preferred the American situation, fearing that the social closeness of Jews and Christians in Britain risked reducing Jewish identity.[17]

According to IIM, the reason for the social closeness of Jews and non-Jews in Britain was the low level of anti-Semitism.[18] He referred to anti-Semitism in Britain as 'practically unknown' and 'limited to a small coterie of people'.[19] He perceived that anti-Semitism was 'repellent to the Englishman, he loves fair play', and saw this aspect of English culture as acting as a counterbalance to the other factors leading to the drift away from Judaism.[20] However, his perception of British anti-Semitism was something of a rosy one. He appears to have overlooked the strength of the anti-alien agitation that had led to the 1905 Act of Parliament curtailing the flow of immigration of Jews from Russia, the anti-Semitism associated with Hilaire Belloc and G.K. Chesterton and the so called 'pogrom of the valleys' that erupted in Wales in 1911 just prior to his arrival.

IIM came of age in a country that prided itself on its intellectual liberalism, individualism, rationalism, spirit of democracy and a willingness to break sharply from the past. In America there was no government control over religion and a multitude of denominations competed for adherents in a free market of religions; religious belief was a matter of voluntary choice. As a result, Progressive Judaism thrived in a way it had been unable to in Europe, from where it had originated. IIM commented:

> One of the causes that made for the tremendous development of Liberal Judaism in America, is that there was something in the American atmosphere, perhaps because the country was new, perhaps because [in] the Puritan tradition there was a strong impulsion to religious thought and a deep love for religious freedom, that made him [the Jew] eager for religious freedom, that made him eager for a Judaism that was living and was ready to accept it when it was offered to him.[21]

The continuing arrival in America of large numbers of Jews from Eastern Europe meant that Reform Judaism was soon to lose its hegemony,[22] but at the time IIM left, American Reform Judaism was still the main form of organised Jewish religious life. According to IIM, Orthodox Judaism appealed only to 'immigrant Jews', not to Jews who were 'assimilated' American citizens.[23] By contrast, as previously mentioned, in the second decade of the twentieth century, Progressive Judaism had barely gained a toehold in Britain; opposition to it was virulent and, as IIM later remarked with feeling, 'used all kinds of methods'.[24] Trained in an environment where Reform rabbis believed that they were the rightful leaders of the Jewish community, this must have been a real culture shock.

IIM attributed the opposition to reform to the deeply conservative nature of Anglo-Jewry. This was a reflection of the nature of British society in general but, more particularly, a result of the influence of the Church of England – its traditionalism served to encourage a similarly conventional Jewish religious establishment. IIM was discomfited by the strong desire to retain 'old paraphernalia and forms',[25] which he saw as pervading even progressive-thinking circles in Anglo-Jewry: 'In England that which is old is justified by its very antiquity, that which is new still requires justification. In America that which is new is justified by its novelty, that which is old requires defence.'[26]

Although the Orthodox community in England lacked the learning and the Talmudic fervour to which IIM would have been accustomed in his formative years, it was firmly anchored to synagogue ritual. IIM noted that, even when it did not observe old forms, the community satisfied itself by upholding them in theory. As he saw it, many Jews nominally belonged to an Orthodox synagogue 'to have the mark of respectability given by a religious label'.[27] To illustrate what he regarded as a tendency towards hypocrisy in Anglo-Jewry, he later recounted:

> I had a humorous example of this attitude early on in my ministry. A group of university students invited me to speak to them on Liberal Judaism. It was a Friday evening in December, and several of those who criticised Liberal Judaism for ignoring some traditions were smoking![28]

This conservatism of Anglo-Jewry was further reinforced by the way in which synagogue life was organised in Britain. While in America synagogues were highly autonomous, the extremely centralised United Synagogue and its leader, the Chief Rabbi, demanded subordination and religious conformity. Disputes were reprimanded on the basis that they split the community and the somewhat sentimental belief in a united Anglo-Jewry was often more paramount than theological differences. IIM had some difficulty coming to terms with the concept of a chief rabbi given the pluralistic nature of American Jewry and its resistance to adopting the hierarchical structure of Europe.[29]

IIM was disappointed not only by the comparative under-development of Progressive Judaism in Britain, but also by its lack of influence in public life, especially in respect of social and philanthropic work and on the thinking of non-Jews.[30] He found it difficult to understand why the Anglo-Jewish community maintained a low profile and tended to opt out of debates on which Jewish thought and experience could make a valuable contribution. On a number of occasions, he commented on the lack of dialogue and friendly relations between Jewish and non-Jewish religious bodies. In America, non-Jews often preached in synagogues, rabbis were frequently invited to preach to a congregation of non-Jews and very different religious congregations united on Thanksgiving Day to pray together. By comparison, IIM said, when Jews in Britain heard about non-Jews preaching in synagogues they were horrified.[31]

IIM's Reception

Although the challenges facing him were enormous, IIM threw himself into the task of providing spiritual leadership to the LJS with single-minded devotion, energy and zeal. He was later to admit that he had underestimated the amount of opposition he would face in Britain, and it took him a while to realise that the forces against him would test his mettle for many years to come.[32] Looking back ten years after his arrival, he admitted both to his 'folly in walking where better men may have feared to tread' and the 'temerity' of his decision to make the move from America.[33] Coming from a country where pioneers and rebels were revered, he had clearly had some uncomfortable lessons to learn about his new environment.

As the first Liberal minister, he experienced considerable difficulty in establishing his credibility in the Anglo-Jewish community. On 3 March 1912, the Reverend I. Raffalovich of Liverpool devoted his sermon to belittling IIM's early addresses and to a personal attack on the young rabbi:

> The unconcern displayed by the community at the process of dejudaising Judaism betokens not broadmindedness but sheer apathy and indifference. We protest against missionary efforts and yet actually connive at a worse heresy preached by Jews to Jews. ... The American interpretation of Judaism, which is only a repetition of the old Pauline doctrine, is a menace to English Judaism ... a great menace to the Judaism of the young ... that they may discard all bonds of the Jewish religion and yet be Jews – 'Liberal' Jews.[34]

IIM was surprised by the level of antipathy directed against him personally. He commented that he had not encountered such opposition in America, where he had been able to preach in Orthodox synagogues 'without in any way disturbing anyone's religious sensibilities'.[35] However, some of IIM's early statements did not help the situation. When he had been at the LJS for less than a year, he said that traditional Judaism 'concealed its beauty under heavy trappings',[36] and a few months later he castigated the dishonesty and hypocrisy, particularly intellectual dishonesty that destroyed spiritual life.[37] His reference to *kashrut* (Jewish dietary law) as 'an ancient Jewish prejudice' proved to be particularly inflammatory.[38] His words echoed Emil Hirsch's contemptuous reference to 'kitchen Judaism', but the sentiment was even less well received in England than it had been in America.[39] IIM referred often to the 'missionary work' he had come to carry out, which became the source of satire in the Jewish press:

> Rabbi Mattuck, the latest subject of the *Jewish Chronicle* interview, believes that England offers much scope for his missionary work. He thinks there are many Jews in London and the Provinces who are attached by the slenderest ties to their faith, to whom the old order of religious things does not appeal. Rabbi Mattuck's acquaintance with Anglo-Jewish conditions is of the slenderest, and we think that we are well within the mark of truth when we say that the Liberal Jewish order of religious things does not appeal to by far the vast majority of English Jews and Jewesses. Rabbi Mattuck, however, is a true alumnus of the Cincinnati Rabbinical College in his *serious* [journalist's emphasis] contemplation of his own work in London as in the nature of a 'mission'. The Hebrew Union College has in the course of the past thirty years, graduated more 'prophets' and 'missionaries' than are included in the canon of the Old Testament. Rabbi Mattuck, formerly of Lincoln, latterly of Far Rockaway, and now of London, is the latest candidate for the mantle of Amos.[40]

The early hostility towards IIM was partly a reaction to his outspokenness and the insensitivity of some of his remarks, but also due to the fact that he was a fully trained rabbi. At that time Jews' College, which trained Orthodox ministers, gave them the title of 'reverend'. Under the chief rabbinate of Herman Adler only a small number of Jewish ministers received *s'michah* and were entitled to call themselves 'rabbi'.[41] It was naturally difficult for older, better-established and well-respected ministers to refer to a young man from America as 'rabbi' when they themselves were called 'reverend'.

In his early days in England, IIM was rarely addressed as Rabbi Mattuck in the Jewish press and if the title of rabbi was used, it was given in inverted commas. Over the first ten years of his ministry, IIM's right to take the title of rabbi was repeatedly questioned in the pages of the *Jewish Chronicle*, despite the spirited support of Claude Montefiore,[42] and the more grudging comments of the editor of the newspaper, who opined that IIM had more right to the title than some 'obscure rabbi in Eastern Europe'.[43] Anglo-Jewry remained unconvinced and, as IIM pointed out on one occasion, his contribution was more warmly welcomed by some non-Jewish clerics such as the Bishop of London, who remarked that Liberal Judaism made it more difficult to convert Jews to Christianity because Liberal Judaism strengthened the loyalty of the Jewish people to their faith.[44]

Notwithstanding communal hostility, IIM was invited to attend the inaugural service for the new Chief Rabbi, Joseph Hertz, which took place at the Great Synagogue in April 1913.[45] Hertz was to become a harsh critic of Liberal Judaism and IIM may have later regretted the cordial welcome he gave to his appointment. He wished Hertz:

> every success in his new sphere. I heartily welcome any new force, personality or institution which has close at heart the interests of Jews and Judaism, and I trust that Dr Hertz – in the task he has set himself of enthusing new life and hope, and of strengthening the old love for the ancient faith that has been handed down to us – will meet all the success he deserves.[46]

In his dealings with the new Chief Rabbi, IIM's mentor, Kaufmann Kohler, urged him to draw on his bank of Jewish learning and to 'ignore the hollow protestations of the Chief Rabbi, the little man in the high chair'.[47]

Within the LJS, IIM also faced difficulties in dealing with the powerful lay leaders who had become accustomed to making all the decisions relating to the movement. Prior to IIM's appointment they had employed someone whom they referred to as the 'curate' (Mr M. Epstein, later Dr Epstein), whose role was confined to preaching at services. On a number of occasions, IIM found it necessary to exert his rabbinic authority. For example, in 1913, he pointed out firmly that decisions relating to conversion to Judaism should be made by him as the rabbi rather than by a committee of lay people as had been the case until that time.[48] Before IIM's arrival the JRU had taken a firm stand against mixed marriages, although the policy was to admit into Judaism those who accepted sincerely Jewish teachings. However, the rules drawn up by the JRU for conversion were quite stringent. IIM saw the requirements as counterproductive to the cause of Liberal Judaism, because they encouraged people to 'marry out' of the faith and to drift away from Judaism. He argued for a more welcoming approach and established a Rites and Practices Committee under his chairmanship to deal with conversions.[49]

Building Synagogue Life

As well as demonstrating the force of his personality and his self-assurance, IIM soon proved to be a good organiser. In the twelve months following his appointment he arranged for marriages to take place in the synagogue by applying to the Superintendent Registrar to have the Hill Street building registered as a place of worship for the conduct of weddings. He also addressed the issue of burials. After a long search for a suitable site, in 1913 a cemetery was established in Pound Lane, Willesden. In addition to a prayer hall, the cemetery had a columbarium[50] where ashes could be placed and there was the facility for ashes to be buried under a rose bush, both of which represented a major break with Jewish tradition.

When inviting IIM for an exploratory visit to England, Montefiore had stressed that the congregation was keen to retain the style of services established by the JRU. He told IIM that he was particularly keen to avoid the introduction of Sunday services, which had been adopted in the more radical American synagogues.[51] However, soon after his arrival, IIM began to experiment with both the structure and timing of services. The general format of preaching at the LJS (and in most other British synagogues) prior to his arrival had been for the minister to read a biblical text, to give an explanation of it and to conclude by drawing a moral lesson from the reading. IIM varied the style of his sermons from one week to the next seeking to maintain congregational interest and to engage those whom others had been unable to reach.[52]

IIM set to work on producing a new prayer book since those previously used by the JRU for Saturday afternoon and children's services were not appropriate for a synagogue with an Ark. A liturgy subcommittee had started to update the JRU prayer book in 1910, but had delayed completing the task until the appointment of a rabbi to allow him to add his views. IIM's new prayer book, *Sabbath Afternoon Services*, appeared towards the end of 1912. It contained a cycle of six Saturday afternoon services rather than, as previously, just an anthology of prayers. The inclusion of six services meant that no service was used more than once in a calendar month. After the services there were a number of 'Prayers for Silent Devotion'.

IIM's prayer book introduced more Hebrew, included the *Shema*, which had until then only been read at morning and evening services and, for the first time, services were planned to include readings from the scroll and the Prophets. However, the prayer book made no attempt to replicate the traditional sequence of prayers and bore very little resemblance to worship in any other part of Europe other than in Berlin's long-established *Reformgemeinde* and a small congregation in France, the Union Libérale Israelite led by Rabbi Louis-Germain Levy.[53] Thus just as rabbinical calls were beginning to be heard in America for the recovery of tradition, IIM was setting the LJS on a very radical course from a liturgical point of view. The prayer book was widely welcomed by the LJS congregation.[54]

IIM's second prayer book, *Sabbath Morning Services*, did not appear until 1916, demonstrating the priority the congregation still attached to

Saturday afternoon services compared to Saturday morning services. This second prayer book contained just four services, which again bore little resemblance to traditional liturgy.

Before IIM was appointed there had been no set ways for celebrating festival and High Holydays at the LJS. Arrangements remained largely experimental for his first year at the synagogue, but within two years of his appointment he had established a pattern for High Holyday services based on the model of Reform synagogues in America, which endured for many years. He was later to record that he retained a fondness for the traditional form of High Holyday services but recognised that 'unless much changed it cannot suit'.[55] During 1912, IIM produced three slim prayer books to be used at major festivals – one for Pentecost (*Shavuot*), one for Tabernacles (*Sukkot*), and one for Passover (*Pesach*).

Like his Reform counterparts in America, IIM placed the utmost importance on 'decorum' in services. His daughter, Dorothy, recalled, 'my father telling the women of the congregation what he thought of them for wearing furs and jewellery to a service. It took many years to expunge some of the less desirable Orthodox behaviour.'[56] IIM was also opposed to 'dressy' wedding parties and one of his objections to *B'nei Mitzvah* was the ostentatious celebrations associated with them.

In America, IIM had not been accustomed to covering his head in services and some of his sermons reflect his disinclination to do so.[57] In one he argued that it did not feel 'natural' for men to wear 'skull caps' and that worship should 'introduce forms consistent with the manners and circumstances of our daily life'.[58] However, he bowed to the pressure of the more conservative LJS congregation and to appeals from Montefiore. He compromised by encouraging men to wear hats on the *bimah* and introduced birettas for rabbis and laypeople leading services.[59] On one occasion early on in his tenure, he failed to ensure that confirmation students (see below) wore head coverings on the *bimah* and he felt the need to write to Montefiore to apologise for this.[60]

As well as general synagogue matters, IIM concerned himself with the needs and interests of individual congregants. He was available for consultation every Thursday afternoon from 3–5 p.m. or from 3.30–6 p.m., and also sometimes on a Sunday morning and other times by appointment. However, one-to-one meetings were usually discontinued over the summer months.

The Religion School

One of IIM's highest priorities was the development of the LJS's embryonic Religion School (or the 'Sunday School' as it was then known).

At the time of his arrival, nine children were enrolled in the school. Within two months he had drawn up detailed plans for religious education, which were launched at a packed meeting held at the Great Central Hotel in March 1912. IIM spoke for an hour (again without the aid of notes) setting out his vision for the school, stressing the importance of religious education for young people and the need to develop a 'faith-creating capacity' in children.[61] He explained that the emphasis in the school would be on providing information on 'the wonderful pronouncements of the Prophets' rather than on dogma, rites and rituals, and on ideals and hopes rather than acquiring facts.[62]

By the end of 1913 the Religion School had expanded to thirty-six pupils.[63] IIM organised it into grades, mirroring the American public school system. To begin with the children were taught by IIM himself, and he sent weekly letters on progress to parents. However, he gradually gathered around him a team of voluntary teachers who 'gladly gave' their Sunday mornings to teaching as well as time during the week to be trained by him and to prepare lessons.[64] Recognising that the task of educating young people in Judaism was more challenging in Britain than in America because of the tradition of sending children to boarding schools at the age of 9 or 10 that existed among upper- and upper-middle-class families (of which there was a disproportionate number in the membership of the LJS), IIM also established a 'correspondence course' for those unable to attend the Religion School. Although he gave time to designing and developing the correspondence course, IIM saw 'a lesson a week [as] a poor substitute for the permanent home and religion school influence'.[65]

In America, the Reform movement had established the Hebrew Sabbath School Union as a means for coordinating and raising standards in supplementary schools run in synagogues, to emulate the success of Protestant churches both in attracting students and retaining them as members of their congregations.[66] With this in mind and his own experience of working in and developing Sabbath Schools in Cincinnati and elsewhere, IIM had very high expectations of the teachers. One early teacher recollected:

> I know I found it difficult to attain the standard that Dr Mattuck rightly expected. None of us had ever taught before in a Religion School. I was a teacher by profession and I had studied the Bible and Hebrew, and I was a member of the synagogue. This gave me help, but how hard I had to read![67]

Even when he had the help of well-trained teachers, many of whom had passed through the LJS Religion School, IIM remained very involved in directing the school and organising its curriculum, discussions of which were judged by those participating to have been an 'unforgettable experience'.[68] He later divulged that he had tried delegating development of the curriculum to the teachers, but that the experiment had proved unsuccessful so he had retained a firm hand on it for some time.[69] He instituted 'School Assemblies' as an integral part of the Religion School, which enabled young people to pray under his leadership. IIM apparently knew every child by name and was considered by the pupils to be 'quite wonderful'.[70]

Religion School students (both boys and girls) graduated at the age of 16 with a confirmation ceremony. Although Confirmation services had been held in some British synagogues since the nineteenth century, those introduced by IIM were for children who were older than had been the norm. This idea was probably based on the advice of one of his mentors, David Philipson, who had promoted the idea that Confirmation, which had generally been substituted for Bar Mitzvah at the age of 13, should be delayed until students were old enough to understand their religion sufficiently to carry it into future generations.[71]

The first LJS Confirmation service was held in 1912 and, from the outset, IIM expected of Confirmation students a high understanding of Judaism and discussion of its significance. Over the next few years he experimented with the format and timing of Confirmation ceremonies, but he always conducted the ceremonies personally until his partial retirement after the Second World War. His early 'Confirmees' (as they were referred to) remembered his 'deeply spiritual teaching'.[72]

Social Responsibility

We have seen that since his days as a rabbinic student, IIM had been involved in philanthropic and charitable activities. Soon after his arrival in England he began to stress to the LJS congregation the importance of their involvement in social work. Just a few days after his inauguration he preached:

> The Synagogue ... should play no small part in the attempt to improve social conditions – You may do that as individuals in a measure, but you can do it infinitely better as a fellowship. I do sincerely hope that when this congregation shall attain a sufficient degree of strength, it will undertake as a unit, something in this direction.[73]

A few months later he declared himself in favour of the then fashionable scientific approach to charity with which he had become acquainted during his time in Cincinnati. As he described it, this involved teaching the poor to 'free themselves from the causes of their low estate'.[74] Later in the year he oversaw the establishment of a Guild of Social Service to work with disadvantaged children and fundraise for both Jewish and non-Jewish charities. At his first Rosh Hashana service with his new congregation, IIM chastised Jews who did not contribute to 'the progress of the human race',[75] and at the first Annual General Meeting of the LJS in November 1912, he argued forcefully that the role of the synagogue in serving the wider community was as important as its role in serving the spiritual needs of its members.[76] Soon afterwards he preached:

> Judaism was ever a social religion. It recognised the individual, recognised his worth, recognised his importance and it demanded of him that he utilise what powers he possesses for the welfare of humankind, that his salvation depends on the salvation of society, and if there is one note more insistent than another in the hopes expressed by the Jewish prophets it is that human society will be saved ultimately from all that is ugly and miserable in it, that the crooked places will be made straight, and that the tortuous paths will be made even, that men, yes even the beasts, will live together in peace, secure in the law that which God does send to his children.[77]

In 1913 IIM invited Basil Henriques, a prominent LJS member, to talk about his work in the East End of London and urged synagogue members to fundraise for and help in the running of a Jewish Boys' Club in St George's-in-the East, which Henriques was setting up. In his introduction to Henriques' address, IIM was enthusiastic in his support for the venture.[78]

However, IIM did not confine himself to encouraging ameliorative social welfare activities. Shortly after he took up his position at the LJS, the congregation noticed that social issues were discussed more frequently than they had been formerly.[79] Within a year, IIM had also shown his support for 'the working man'. He told the congregation:

> Justice as applied to social or industrial conditions means the recognition of the rights of every individual. It means fair treatment for all alike; it means that the fruits of labour must go to the labourer; it means that he who gives his life and his energy in some service, however humble to society, has a right to a living wage, for himself and for those who depend upon him … [80]

During the industrial unrest of 1913 IIM commented on the disputes, which he insisted were not motivated simply by the greed of the workers.[81] He noted with satisfaction the 'intellectual evolution of the labouring class into a consciousness of its own social value', and the growing self-respect and independence of working people:

> The realisation that has dawned on the working man has changed him from a yoked ox into a serving man. He is no longer the machine without a soul that responds to the push of the lever or the turn of the wheel, but a child of God, aspiring, hoping, thinking and trusting.[82]

IIM said that the phrase 'the dignity of labour' had evolved from being 'a cant phrase' to becoming 'a living truth and inspiring reality'. He counselled the congregation to 'recognise the blessing of God in whatever raises the estate and condition of men'.[83] In a lecture he gave at a meeting of the Jewish Working Men's Club at Lily Montagu's West Central Club later in the year, IIM said:

> The association of labour with the ideal means that in the humblest piece of work a great purpose may express itself and it may conduce to the achievement of some great goal. You may have heard the story of the young housemaid who was asked by a good parson what she was doing for God and she answered 'I sweep the corners clean.' There is a great truth revealed in this humble answer. The lowliest act, when done with the intent of serving a great cause becomes a great act. The cobbler who pegs at his shoes or the tailor who works with his needle, feeling that they are doing a service to society in helping to clothe human beings; the mechanic who forges a plough and the farmer who drives it into the soil with a consciousness that they are helping to supply an answer to human wants are transfiguring their work and ennobling it by their consciousness of the social services they are doing.[84]

Had any of the many businessmen represented in the LJS community been present at the address, they would probably been discomfited by IIM's support for organised labour:

> The binding together of the men engaged in the several industries to protect, as far as possible, the rights of each individual, has finally resulted in giving to labour in general a strength in the control of industry and in the development of society.[85]

IIM went on to urge working people to use their increased power not only to improve their personal lot or that of their class alone, but to think about how they could contribute to social improvement generally. He admitted to being puzzled about why working men were involved so little in organised religion, saying that the synagogue had as much to give the working man as to any other member of society.[86]

The Impact of IIM's Leadership

IIM's early progress attracted many new members to the synagogue. In 1912 there were just over 100 members, but within two years membership had more than doubled. Some people joined the synagogue because of the well-organised and increasingly effective Religion School or because of the strong emphasis that IIM placed on ethical behaviour. However, many were attracted by the sheer power of his oratory, which appealed to both young and old. One young congregant was enthused by his dramatic sermons, saying 'no one would move. He was more like an actor really; everyone was mesmerised'.[87] In their congregations, 'classical' Reform rabbis in America were first and foremost preachers. Ability in the pulpit was invariably the criterion of success or failure. The most eminent combined great oratory with a broad knowledge of contemporary intellectual issues. IIM was therefore clearly a product of the environment in which he trained.

With the growth of its membership, the LJS found it necessary to appoint paid staff. The first appointment was Isaac Michael ('Jack') Duparc as Synagogue Secretary. He replaced A. Lindo Henry, who had until then been carrying out the role on a voluntary basis. A former reporter with the *Jewish Chronicle*, Mr Duparc remained employed by the synagogue for over sixty years. He had a particularly close relationship with IIM, with whom he worked for thirty-five years. Mr Duparc's initial duties included delivering the sermon at the Saturday afternoon service when IIM was unavailable. In his later years, Mr Duparc recollected that sometimes when he and IIM were discussing synagogue problems involving human frailty and fallibility, IIM would say to him: 'You and I are men of the world'.[88] However, IIM evidently was not always the easiest person to work with: 'Mattuck and I never had a quarrel, though often I would say a thing was white and he would argue that it was black, but, in the end, we always compromised and made it grey.'[89]

IIM was fair in his dealings with LJS staff and had a flair for making the best use of those who worked with him.[90] However, he was also quite demanding. Being capable himself of working long hours under pressure and with 'unremitting dedication',[91] he expected the same of others. Ivor Warren, the LJS choirmaster during IIM's early years at the LJS and himself the son of a famous cantor, looked on IIM with admiration and affection and described him as 'unforgettable',[92] but also commented that he 'expects grand opera on tuppence halfpenny'.[93]

Spreading Liberal Judaism

Before taking up his post, IIM indicated that he relished the prospect of spreading a 'liberal understanding of Judaism' and, from the outset, he devoted a great deal of effort and enthusiasm to doing so and to fostering new communities in London and elsewhere. Lily Montagu commented that he: 'felt the urgency of every call that came to us', and was determined that 'no group should starve because of the delay in satisfying their spiritual hunger'.[94] He addressed JRU conferences, at which he was often heckled. Harry Lewis, an early supporter of the JRU, resigned from his position as the radical minister of Manchester Reform Synagogue after the synagogue's lay leadership refused to sanction an invitation for IIM and Montefiore to give a sermon at the synagogue.[95] IIM was not deterred and adopted a policy of not replying to 'the catalogue of sins, from apostasy to atheism', which appeared to him to be 'driven by malice'.[96] Through the power of reasoned argument, he soon proved to be a 'winner of disciples'.[97] With his guidance and support, by 1914 embryonic Liberal communities had been established at Lily Montagu's West Central Girls' Club located near Soho and in Golders Green.

Because of his oratory, IIM began to be in demand as a preacher, speaker and lecturer at many different types of events. For example, in May 1912 he gave well-attended lectures at the LJS on 'The Message of Liberal Judaism to the Individual' and on 'The Social Teaching of Liberal Judaism'[98] In November 1912 he travelled to Glasgow[99] to give a talk to the Jewish Literary and Social Society on 'Judaism Tomorrow',[100] and in January 1913 he addressed the Adler Society at Oxford University on 'The Need for a Liberal Interpretation of Judaism.'[101]

IIM's addresses were soon being mentioned in the Jewish press. 'ML' writing in the *Jewish Chronicle* in May 1912 commented that he had 'an actor's voice' with a 'suggestive tremor' and that his 'monotone delivery' was relieved by 'beautiful elocution and perfect clarity'.[102] The same commentator described his addresses as 'apt' and 'not flowery'. The editor of the *Jewish Chronicle,* Leopold Greenberg, writing under the pen name of 'Mentor'[103] also said that 'Mr Mattuck, preaching orthodoxy, could fill any Orthodox Synagogue in London'.[104]

Within eighteen months of IIM taking up his post, his addresses started to be reproduced in full in the pages of the *Jewish Chronicle* and other Jewish newspapers. His first sermon to be printed in full was on 'The Ideal of Universal Religion in Liberal Judaism'. It was delivered at the first of a series of 'propaganda meetings' held at West Hampstead Town Hall in May 1913, which was attended by 600 people.[105] Later in the year, Leopold Greenberg wrote to him as a 'recognised religious leader in Anglo-Jewry' asking him to submit an article on the form of Judaism followed by the LJS, to be printed alongside articles from other religious leaders including the Chief Rabbi and Morris Joseph, rabbi of West London Synagogue.[106] For reasons that are unknown, the piece he submitted on 'Judaism and the Synagogue' was not published.[107]

To help raise the profile of Liberal Judaism, IIM joined a variety of Jewish and non-Jewish organisations including the Committee for the Home for Aged Jews, the Birmingham Jewish Young Men's Association (of which he was President in 1913 prior to the appointment of the Chief Rabbi), the Jewish Maternity Society and the Jewish Peace Society. At the inaugural meeting of this latter body, held in June 1914, which was presided over by Chief Rabbi Hertz, IIM supported a motion proposing a celebration of 100 years of peace between Britain and America, which he said had profound significance for Jewish people because the two great nations were 'imbued with the spirit of the ancient Prophets'.[108]

The 'Three Ms'

In consolidating the LJS congregation, IIM worked very closely with Lily Montagu and Claude Montefiore, for both of whom he developed a deep respect and with whom he had what he described as a 'firm and significant bond'.[109] He later acknowledged their guidance, influence and untiring zeal.[110] Retrospectively IIM, Lily Montagu and Montefiore became known as the 'Three Ms'. Described as the 'forceful and ideological progenitors of Liberal Judaism in England',[111] they shared an abiding commitment to Liberal Judaism, but they were very different from each other. Lily Montagu took an interest in cricket, tennis and films and had contact with people from all walks of life at her West Central Girls' Club and as a Juvenile Court magistrate. However, she remained 'awe inspiring in her piety and morality'[112] and retained her Victorian ways throughout her lifetime. While IIM was scholarly, Lily Montagu spoke and wrote as a preacher, almost always choosing the first person plural in her addresses. Theory was less her concern than practical commitment and action.[113] She deferred to IIM 'almost completely',[114] referring to him constantly as 'our leader'.[115] She regularly discussed her problems with him, which he 'straightened out by his clear intellect and practical sympathy'.[116] At the reception held at the LJS on 9 December 1922 to mark the twentieth anniversary of the founding of the JRU she said:

> I did tend to prophesy once; it was at a drawing room meeting held at my sister's house. I ventured to hope then that one day we should have a minister of high intellectual power and humanity, one possessed of sympathy and indomitable courage and with a magnetic personality. Well, today, we have such a one in Rabbi Mattuck.[117]

Correspondence between IIM and Lily Montagu was formal and businesslike. It was only towards the end of IIM's life that Lily Montagu consented to address him as 'Dear Friend' rather than as 'Dr Mattuck'.[118]

IIM's relationship with Montefiore was less straightforward. Montefiore had a well-developed sense of humour and was known to sprawl on the floor to play with children. However, he lived in the rarefied and remote world of the Anglo-Jewish aristocracy and Oxford academia. His background and outlook could not have been more different from IIM's. With his American upbringing, IIM continued to struggle with the English class system while Montefiore, despite his religious liberalism and tolerance, was imbued with it. Montefiore once wrote to IIM: 'My world – the world of Emancipation and Mr Marks and Sir Francis Goldsmid and Lord Palmerston – was a good world – and a far better world than some of you think – but it is so different from this world in which we live.'[119]

Given their divergent origins, inevitably there were some tensions between IIM and Montefiore. As president of the synagogue, Montefiore expressed his views 'quite forcefully, and with his own authority'.[120] On day-to-day matters, the disagreements between Montefiore and IIM were relatively minor, such as on the covering of heads in the synagogue, which was a matter of ongoing debate for a number of years.[121] However, IIM and Montefiore disagreed more significantly on spiritual matters, especially on the way in which they viewed Christianity. Despite his regard and affection for IIM,[122] Montefiore complained 'often and at considerable length' about what he saw as IIM's 'unwarranted hostility towards Christianity'.[123] For example, Montefiore once wrote to IIM:

> The something else which I object to, and consider fallacious, in your sermons is common to you and heaps of other Jews. It is common to most American Rabbis, so far as I know, common to their Teachers, common to the Teachers of their teachers ... It is a constant side reference to, and depreciation of, Christianity. It is a constant attempt to make up differences between Judaism and Christianity, to the great advantage of Judaism ... I wish, when you revise your sermon, you could blot out from your mind the very existence of Christianity! I wish you could imagine yourself in a purely Buddhist or Confucian majority, or that you could forget all other persons but Jews![124]

On his part, IIM was never fully reconciled to or in agreement with Montefiore's sympathetic fascination for Christianity,[125] nor comfortable with the Bible commentators to whom Montefiore introduced him, who he said 'still have to learn that what some of the ancient rabbis taught, that the language of the Bible, is the language of man'.[126]

As we will learn later, on several occasions the two men clashed on the content of IIM's sermons, which Montefiore appears to have scrutinised in detail. Montefiore was seemingly troubled by what he saw as IIM's dogmatism and his desire to make religious pronouncements on socio-political issues. Montefiore once wrote: 'I am inclined to think that you do hanker after a collective, definite Jewish attitude – a categorical pronouncement – towards social, political and international questions.'[127] He regularly wrote to IIM seeking clarification and commenting on IIM's sermons. In one instance he ended a five-page critique by asking, 'Do you like getting these long letters? If not, beware of sermons which provoke them! Or pray for a deaf day for me when I happen to be present.'[128]

One theme in IIM's career was his concern for the fate of Russian Jews, which is unsurprising given his background. Montefiore, on the other hand, took a reticent approach to the sufferings of Russian Jews. The solution to the 'Russian problem' he felt could only be found in Russia and he saw little benefit in organising protests in Britain. As president of the Anglo-Jewish Association, he was reluctant to do anything to protect Jewish interests abroad.[129] This must have been a disappointment to IIM.

Notwithstanding these differences, the two men generally got on well and respected each other's perspectives.[130] The two shared a sense of humour and their correspondence contains a great deal of wit and banter. IIM revered Montefiore's ecumenical work,[131] and after his death, missed him sorely; he said that he was 'one of the greatest Jews of our time, and of all time'.[132]

Montefiore was quite aware of his own limitations in drawing a crowd and holding its attention.[133] He admitted publicly that IIM's sermons were much preferred to his own,[134] and repeatedly wrote to IIM to commend him on his lucidity.[135] On one occasion, Montefiore told IIM how he worried for weeks beforehand about synchronising the timing of his sermon with the one given by IIM, when on the High Holydays they were preaching simultaneously at the LJS. IIM blithely replied that Montefiore should not worry since he, IIM, was quite able to go on speaking for five minutes longer or to cut his sermon if necessary. Leonard Montefiore later disclosed that his father regarded this as 'a kind of modern miracle'.[136] In a letter to IIM, Montefiore summarised his views of his colleague thus: 'You are a wily, excellent, naughty, persuasive, juggling, beguiling, wicked, virtuous, alluring, troublesome and charming man.'[137] When Montefiore published his book, *The Old Testament and After* in 1923, he dedicated it to IIM 'in gratitude and affection'. Given Montefiore's standing, this was seen by David Philipson as a great honour.[138] IIM not only had an enduring relationship with Montefiore, but also appears to have been close to his second wife, Florence, who wrote to him praising him on his work.[139] In later chapters we will see how IIM fared without the support and guidance of Montefiore.

NOTES

1. 'Liberal Jewish Synagogue, the New Minister, Induction of Revd Israel I. Mattuck', *JC*, January 26 1912, p.28.
2. Ibid.
3. 'What is Liberal Judaism?', sermon given by IIM at the LJS, 20 January 1912, Montagu Centre Collection (MCC).
4. Ibid.
5. 'The basis for a Liberal Interpretation of Judaism', sermon given by IIM in Birmingham, 9 November 1913 (unfinished draft), MCC.
6. See 'Liberal Jewish Synagogue, the New Minister'.
7. Ibid.
8. *JC*, 26 January 2012, p.7.
9. *JC*, 29 March 2012, p.17.
10. 'Liberal Judaism in the United States', sermon given by IIM at the LJS, 27 January 1923, MCC.
11. A Sephardi Jew is a Jew descended from, or who follows the customs and traditions followed by, Jews who lived in the Iberian Peninsula (Portugal and modern Spain), before their expulsion in the late fifteenth century.
12. 'A Century of Modern Judaism in America. What has it achieved?', sermon given by IIM at the LJS, 22 November 1924, MCC.
13. 'Some Aspects of American Life', sermon given by IIM at the LJS on 16 October 1927, in ibid.
14. See 'A Century of Modern Judaism in America'.
15. Stephen Sharot, 'Reform and Liberal Judaism in London: 1840–1940', *Jewish Social Studies*, 41, 3/4 (Summer–Autumn, 1979), p.214.
16. 'Liberal Judaism and the Community', address given by IIM at a JRU conference, 25 October 1914, MCC.
17. See 'Some Aspects of American Life'.
18. Based on his travels in America, IIM had found anti-Semitism to be particularly evident in New York and other eastern cities, and to be more evident in social rather than economic spheres of life, which IIM dismissed as 'insignificant'. See his comments in his article on 'The American Jew and His Neighbor', undated (c.1913), draft article written for the magazine of the Birmingham Jewish Young Men's Association, MCC.
19. 'The Jews in Great Britain', draft article written by IIM to be published in American newspapers, 20 February 1925, MCC.
20. For example, see 'Liberal Judaism in Britain', sermon given by IIM at the LJS, 19 August 1928, in ibid.
21. See 'Liberal Judaism in the United States'.
22. Michael A. Meyer, *Response to Modernity – A History of the Reform Movement in Judaism* (New York: Oxford University Press, 1988), p.292.
23. See 'Liberal Judaism in the United States'. According to IIM, more than three-quarters of those Jews born in America belonged to Reform communities.
24. 'Rabbi Dr Mattuck's Fortieth Anniversary Address', in *LJM*, XXIII, no.2 (February 1952), p.17.
25. See 'Liberal Judaism in the United States'.
26. See 'Some Aspects of American Life'.
27. 'Ten Years in the LJS Ministry', sermon given by IIM at the LJS, 21 January 1922, MCC.

28. See 'Rabbi Dr Mattuck's Fortieth Anniversary Address'.
29. Jonathan D. Sarna and Jonathan Golden, 'The American Jewish Experience through the Nineteenth Century: Immigration and Acculturation', Brandeis University, National Humanities Centre: nationalhumanitiescenter.org/tserve/nineteen/nkeyinfo/judaism.htm
30. See 'Liberal Judaism in the United States'.
31. See 'The American Jew and His Neighbor'.
32. See 'Ten Years in the LJS Ministry'.
33. Ibid.
34. 'Liberal Judaism in England', *American Israelite*, 14 March 1912, p.7.
35. Ibid., pp.8–9.
36. 'Return O Israel to Your God', sermon given by IIM at the Rosh Hashana service at the LJS, 13 September 1912, MCC.
37. 'The Need for a Liberal Interpretation of Judaism', sermon given by IIM at the LJS, 31 January 1913, in ibid.
38. *JC*, 29 March 1912, p.17.
39. Hirsch declared: 'The Dietary laws are a survival of a species of totemism' and 'The Abrahamitic rite, the dietary and levitical laws, sacrificial ritualism, the festal cycle and the like are not indigenous to the Jewish soil'. See Meyer, *Response to Modernity*, p.273.
40. Unnamed and undated news cutting (likely to be 1912 as it refers to an interview that appeared in the *JC* shortly after IIM's arrival), LJS Archives, Box 1/2.
41. The lack of Orthodox rabbis at the time of IIM's arrival is explained in a letter IIM later wrote to an American colleague. Letter from IIM to Rabbi Sidney Unger, January 1951 London Metropolitan Archives, ACC/3529/002/011. The number of rabbis ordained gradually increased under subsequent Chief Rabbis.
42. *JC*, 9 January 1914, p.1.
43. *JC*, 16 January 1914, p.9.
44. 'Liberal Judaism and the Community', sermon given by IIM at the LJS, 25 October 1914, MCC.
45. *JC*, 18 April 1913, p.26.
46. *JC*, 21 February 1913, p.34.
47. Letter from Kaufmann Kohler to IIM, 15 June 1913, LJS Archives, Box 1/2.
48. Lawrence Rigal and Rosita Rosenberg, *Liberal Judaism*: *The First Hundred Years* (London: Liberal Judaism, 2002), p.49.
49. Ibid., p.49.
50. A columbarium is a wall with niches into which ashes can be placed. The niches are covered with plaques with inscriptions.
51. Daniel R. Langton, *Claude Montefiore*: *His Life and Thought* (London and Portland, OR: Vallentine Mitchell, 2002), p.89.
52. See Rigal and Rosenberg, *Liberal Judaism,* p.45.
53. See Meyer, *Response to Modernity*, p.221.
54. First Annual Report of the Liberal Jewish Synagogue, 1913, LJS Archives.
55. Tape recording of the diary kept by IIM between January and April 1918, read by IIM's daughter, Dorothy Edgar, née Mattuck, Mattuck Family Archive kept by Robert Edgar (MFAb).
56. ULPS Oral History Project 1994–5, interview with Dorothy Edgar, LJS Archives, Box 139a.
57. See 'Our Attitude to Ceremonies', sermon given by IIM at the LJS, 11 April 1913, MCC.
58. 'The Place of Tradition in Liberal Judaism', sermon given by IIM at the LJS, 14 February 1920, in ibid.
59. See ULPS Oral History Project 1994–5, interview with Dorothy Edgar.
60. *LJS newsletter*, 14 April 1916.
61. *JC*, 15 March 1912, p.26.
62. Ibid.
63. These numbers included the children of both members and non-members of the LJS.
64. Marjorie H. Moos, 'His Greatness As a Teacher', in *LJM, In Memoriam of Israel Mattuck 1883–1954* (June 1954), p.15.
65. 'Liberal Judaism in Britain', sermon given by IIM at the LJS, 19 August 1928, MCC.
66. Alan Silverstein, *Alternatives to Assimilation, The Response of Reform Judaism to American Culture, 1840–1930* (Boston, MA: Brandeis University Press, 1994), p.55.
67. Rose Solomon, 'The Religion School in Hill Street', in *The First Fifty Years – A Record of Liberal Judaism In England, 1900–1950* (London: Liberal Jewish Synagogue, 1950), p.8.

68. Ibid., p.15.
69. See tape recording of the diary kept by IIM.
70. Transcript of interview with Denise Franklin, LJS Archives, Box 139a.
71. Michael C. Hilton, *Bar Mitzvah: A History* (Lincoln, NE: Jewish Publication Society, University of Nebraska Press, forthcoming).
72. 'Rabbi Dr I. I. Mattuck', *JC*, 1 January 1954, p.13.
73. 'The Place of the Synagogue in Modern Life', sermon given by IIM at the LJS, 26 January 1912, MCC.
74. 'The Pursuit of Righteousness', sermon given by IIM at the LJS, 26 April 1912, in ibid.
75. See 'Return O Israel to Your God'.
76. *JC*, 20 November 1912, p.24.
77. 'Judaism and Social Problems', sermon given by IIM at the LJS, 15 December 1912, MCC.
78. Taken from the diary of Sir Basil Henriques, quoted in an introduction to Henriques Music Archive produced by Sally Civval, 2011.
79. Lucy Cohen, *Some Recollections of Claude Goldsmid Montefiore 1858–1938* (London: Faber and Faber, 1940), p.63.
80. See 'Judaism and Social Problems'.
81. 'The Challenge to Our Religious Institutions of the Industrial Unrest', sermon given by IIM at the LJS, 8 March 1913, MCC.
82. Ibid.
83. Ibid.
84. 'The Ideals of Labour', address given at meeting of the Jewish Working Men's Club, 3 November 1913, in ibid.
85. Ibid.
86. Ibid.
87. Transcript of interview with Aileen Davis, LJS Archives, Box 139a.
88. Letter from Rabbi John Rayner to Dr Ellen Umansky, Emory University, 9 December 1982, LJS Archives, Box 1/2.
89. Pamela Fletcher Jones, 'Mr Duparc remembers', special edition of *ULPS Focus* to celebrate the first seventy-five years of Liberal Judaism, Autumn 1977.
90. 'Leader of Liberal Judaism in England', *The Times,* 5 April 1954.
91. 'The Spirit of Israel Mattuck', sermon given by Rabbi John Rayner at the LJS, 25 January 1992, LJS Archives, Box 135c.
92. Ibid.
93. Quoted in ibid.
94. The Hon. Lily H. Montagu, 'Address given at the Memorial Service on Tuesday April 8th 1954', in *LJM, In Memoriam of Israel Mattuck, 1883–1954* (June 1954), p.2.
95. D. Langton 'A Question of Backbone: Contrasting Christian Influences Upon the Origins of Reform and Liberal Judaism in England', *Melilah; Manchester Journal for Jewish Studies*, Vol. 3 (2004), p.36.
96. 'Review of the Year', sermon given by IIM at the LJS, 20 January 1914, MCC.
97. 'Worcester Man Who Became One of the World's Great Rabbis', undated news cutting kept by the American Antiquarian Society, Worcester, MA: www.americanantiquarian.org
98. *JC*, 17 July 1912, p.8.
99. This journey may have been quite an emotional one since he changed ships at Glasgow on his way from Lithuania to America as a 7-year-old child.
100. *JC*, 29 November 1912, p.30.
101. 'List of Reviews, Lectures, etc. (other than sermons), 1913–1932', MS, MCC.
102. *JC*, 12 July 1912, p.20.
103. See further discussion of IIM's relationship with Leopold Greenberg later in text.
104. *JC*, 4 October 1912, p.8.
105. *JC*, 23 May 1913, p.18.
106. Letter from the editor of the *JC*, Leopold Greenberg, to IIM, 4 December 1913, London Metropolitan Archives, ACC/3529/002/018.
107. Copy of unpublished article, May 1914, MCC.
108. *JC*, 12 June 1914, p.16.
109. Letter from IIM to Marjorie Moos, 30 January 1948, LJS Archives, Box 1/2.
110. See Rabbi Dr I. Mattuck, 'Liberal Judaism in Great Britain', in *The First Fifty Years – A Record of Liberal Judaism in England, 1900–1950* (London: Liberal Jewish Synagogue, 1950), p.9.

111. Anne J. Kershen and Jonathan A. Romain, *Tradition and Change: a History of Reform Judaism in Britain, 1840–1995,* p.103 (London and Portland, OR: Vallentine Mitchell, 1995).
112. See letter from Rabbi John Rayner to Dr Ellen Umansky.
113. See Meyer, *Response to Modernity*, p.218.
114. See letter from Rabbi John Rayner to Dr Ellen Umansky.
115. Email from Ellen Umansky to author, 2 September 2013.
116. See Montagu, 'Address given at the Memorial Service', p.2.
117. *JRU Bulletin*, January 1923, X, 8, p.9.
118. See correspondence in the London Metropolitan Archives, ACC/3529/002/009.
119. See Langton, *Claude Montefiore*, p.90.
120. See letter from Rabbi John Rayner to Dr Ellen Umansky.
121. See correspondence at the London Metropolitan Archives, ACC/3529/004/002.
122. See Cohen, *Some Recollections of Claude Goldsmid Montefiore*, p.63.
123. See Langton, 'A Question of Backbone', p.45.
124. Letter from C.G. Montefiore to IIM, undated. American Jewish Archives (AJA), Sheldon and Amy Blank Papers, MS 165/1/12.
125. See Langton, *Claude Montefiore*, p.91.
126. See tape recording of diary kept by IIM.
127. Letter from Claude Montefiore to IIM, 5 January 1935, London Metropolitan Archives, ACC/3529/004/02.
128. See Langton, *Claude Montefiore*, p.90.
129. Ibid., p.17.
130. See letter from Rabbi John Rayner to Dr Ellen Umansky.
131. See 'The Jews in Great Britain'.
132. 'Claude Montefiore and Liberal Judaism', sermon given by IIM at the LJS, 18 June 1944, MCC.
133. See Langton, 'A Question of Backbone', p.31.
134. See Cohen, *Some Recollections of Claude Goldsmid Montefiore,* p.63.
135. See letter from Claude Montefiore to IIM, 12 October, year unknown, in which he wrote 'I wish all you said could have been taken down stereographically; it was so wonderfully lucid', London Metropolitan Archives, ACC/3529/004/002.
136. *Synagogue Review* (West London Synagogue), XXVIII, 9, p.20.
137. Letter from Claude Montefiore to IIM, 15 February, year unknown, London Metropolitan Archives, ACC/3529/004/002.
138. Letter from David Philipson to IIM, 17 October 1923, London Metropolitan Archives, ACC/3529/002/18.
139. See letter from Florence Montefiore to IIM, May 1922, London Metropolitan Archives, ACC/3529/002/010.

CHAPTER NINE

The First World War

Reactions to the War

In the years that followed the Mattuck family's emigration, America had a growing economic role on the world scene. The Spanish-American War helped to establish the country as a formidable force in world events and boosted American nationalism. Having weathered successive cycles of depression during the latter part of the nineteenth century, the American economy emerged with fresh confidence epitomised by the quest for new markets abroad. Whereas in the past ideas and goods had flowed from Europe to America, foreign trade agreements now reversed the flow. At the time that IIM left, the country was on the crest of a wave of optimism. IIM was therefore badly shocked when Britain was plunged into a world war just two years after his arrival. The First World War brought to an abrupt close an era of uninterrupted progress and security. Much that had been thought immutable was thrown into the melting pot, and although strenuous efforts were made to restore the status quo after 1918, the past proved irrecoverable.

For a time, the war threatened to undermine IIM's core religious beliefs. As a liberal minister he had confidence in the capacity of human beings to improve their society through the determined pursuit of progressive ideas. Within weeks of arriving at the LJS he had reminded the congregation that the belief that 'this is a good world'[1] was a basic Jewish belief. He averred:

> Yes, there is misery in the world; all too much misery but there is much more good than there is evil. When there are hundreds of cures for almost every ill, when there are uncounted balms for every sore, when there is a powerful social conscience contending against social wrong, when there is a mighty force of righteousness struggling against all injustice, surely this is none but a good world.[2]

By contrast, IIM's initial wartime writings and addresses resound with disillusionment.[3] He first preached on the subject of the war on Rosh

Hashana 1914, having been out of London at the start of the war. In his sermon he referred to the disastrous toll on human life, 'the hearts and homes crushed and shattered by its titanic blows'.[4] He condemned the war as a 'great evil' and drew attention to what he saw as its deeper significance, that 'centuries of human effort in civilisation are threatened with complete destruction'.[5] He appears to have felt that any belief in the inevitability of progress, which was paramount in his pre-war sermons, was naively misguided. He valiantly searched for a rationale for the war beyond narrow national interests, but it was not until a year later that he was able to see beyond the rampant confusion surrounding the onset of war and identify what he viewed as the true issues and ideals behind it. Looking back he explained:

> During the first year of the war, when the issues were not clear to me, and I suspected the aims of both sides, I refrained from any actions that indicated or implied the moral of one side, and the condemnation of the other, For the attitude I eventually adopted – whether it was right or wrong – I can claim that it was the result of a serious effort to make a fair judgement on the issues, not a mere acquiescence in popular clamour.[6]

As the result of his deliberation, IIM identified causes for the war 'reaching back into history and rising out of the spiritual faults in human character' (he does not expand on this statement).[7] He was clearly relieved to have found this explanation, because the consequences of accepting that the war was based on mere national interests would have been for him too difficult to bear.[8]

IIM did not shirk from speaking about the theological crisis presented by the war. The agonising challenge is articulated most poignantly in one sentence in his Yom Kippur morning service in 1915: 'Why has God permitted so great an evil to come into the world?'[9] He responded to the question by shifting responsibility away from God and onto human beings, who are bestowed with the freedom of choice and control over historical events.[10] Nevertheless, in his sermon following the Armistice on 16 November 1918, IIM does invoke some of the more traditional rhetoric of divine providence:

> With gratitude we greet the coming of victory and peace, gratitude to God Whose guiding hand lies on the events in human history, from Whom alone comes the strength men use. Even as we prayed to Him and stayed our hearts on Him when things seemed to go ill for this country and those associated with it, and the deep darkness of anxiety

> brooded over our spirits, so now that light has shined forth let us see in it the flashings of God's arm and in all humility praise and thank Him.[11]

In several of his wartime sermons, IIM emphasised the positive by-products of the devastation that served to counterbalance the negatives, though still acknowledging the evils of the war. The benefits of the war he cited included an enhanced sense of national social unity and interdependence that transcended the self-interest of special social units,[12] the 'heroism and self-sacrifice of the men in the fighting line, the fortitude, and humble resignation of those who at home bear their part of the burden',[13] and the challenge and opportunity of sharing in the creation of a new world that would follow the termination of the bloodshed.[14]

Some of what IIM referred to as his 'congenital optimism'[15] had obviously reasserted itself, but he was not sanguine about the prospects for national self-determination or of justice and peace being achieved once war ended. In a sermon, 'The War and Character', delivered at the LJS in December 1916, he warned that historical precedents were not encouraging about the capacity of war to transform society for the good. Speaking from his knowledge of American history he said:

> The greatest war in the last century, and one which has been referred to again and again in connection with the present war as a sort of parallel, the American Civil War, holds out both a promise and a warning. While it produced the actual aims for which it was fought in spite of the great odds against which Lincoln and his associates had to contend and the early discouraging defeats, it was, however, followed by a period of great confusion and what was worse, the play of some of the worst passions. It has taken America many decades to overcome the evil of the period of reconstruction which followed the civil war, and perhaps that evil is not yet altogether overcome.[16]

However, he was firmly convinced that it would be universal religious values that would heal the damage caused by the war. He declared that 'whilst no universal religion now exists', all faiths were moving towards:

> ... the religion which all peoples will, in the end, come to recognise ... I cannot mean that the time will come when the Judaism which we know now will be the religion of the whole world. But what I mean is that the spiritual facts upon which Judaism insists ... will ultimately receive universal acceptance.[17]

With characteristic meticulousness and even-handedness, in 1916 IIM turned his attention to the highly contentious issue of conscientious objection to participating in war. While the issue was being debated in the political arena, IIM had felt it was inappropriate for him to comment, but once it was decided to introduce a special form of national service for conscientious objectors, he had no compunction in doing so. He could find nothing in traditional Jewish teachings to support not participating in war, only prescriptions on the way war should be conducted. He concluded that even the Prophets were somewhat ambivalent on the subject. While he recognised that some conscientious objectors based their objections on their religious belief, he felt that 'even this right, great and precious that it is, cannot be granted without limitation'. Individual beliefs sometimes had to take second place to 'the salvation of the state'.[18] He admitted that the issues involved in conscientious objection were confused and confusing to him, but nevertheless pronounced:

> With all due deference to the many honest people who believe that the salvation of humanity lies in non-resistance, it must still be said that now in the midst of war the salvation of the nation and of humanity cannot be produced by the laying down of arms by that nation or nations who believe that they are contending with what is right.[19]

IIM felt that the state would have been justified in insisting that citizens should comply with the laws about national service, whatever their views, and in imposing penalties on those who refused to do so. He deemed it fortuitous that the government had 'allowed those men who had conscientious scruples about sharing in the war to take on a form of national service which did not violate those scruples'.[20] The grandees of the LJS were probably relieved by IIM's pronouncements on conscientious objection (which mirrored those being made by American Reform rabbis), at a time when it was important for Jews to be seen to be as patriotic as anyone else.

Evident in IIM's early wartime sermons is the ambivalence he felt about Britain's alliance with Tsarist Russia against Germany and Austria. As the war progressed, IIM drew attention to reports of the wave of patriotism that was sweeping over Russian Jewry. He noted that notwithstanding the horrors of persecution they had suffered under successive Tsars, the Russian Jews were 'prepared to forget them and to sacrifice all for their country which, in spite of its past treatment, they still love'.[21] His hope was that this noble sacrifice would lead to an improvement in conditions for the Jews of Tsarist Russia.

However, by 1917 it was apparent that IIM's hopes were not going to be realised. The exposure of the autocratic Russian Empire to the liberalising influences of France and Britain was to have no impact on the lot of Russian Jews. For a short while IIM anticipated instead that the longed for transformation might be achieved by revolution. Preaching in March 1917, he greeted the abdication of the Tsar and the formation of the Provisional Government with enthusiasm, seeing exciting new hopes for the seven million Jews living in the Russian Empire.[22] His hopes were again to be crushed. By the beginning of 1918 he was wishing fervently that the Russian people would 'overthrow their duplicitous leaders'.[23] He criticised *The Times* for failing to comment on the negotiations at Brest-Litovsk and for not supporting the show of democracy in Russia.[24] Probably as a result of his own early life, IIM felt acutely the hardships suffered by Jewish communities in Russia, which bore the brunt of the fighting in the territories that were fiercely contested throughout the war. He made a plea for Jews living in more secure circumstances to cultivate a sense of unity with their co-religionists living so precariously in Eastern Europe.[25]

IIM's attitude towards Germany and its allies is interesting. He insisted on the humanity of the enemy and criticised those who were exulting in a military victory while ignoring the costs for those who had been defeated.[26] His refusal to demonise the enemy, which was consistent throughout the war, would not have pleased everybody in the LJS congregation, especially those who considered themselves to be loyal British citizens. This included Montefiore, who wrote in a letter to IIM, possibly in response to IIM's sermon saying: 'Again, for instance, there is a rumour tonight that a German battleship has been sunk. I rejoice ... Even if all have gone down, I rejoice that there is one German battleship less.'[27]

IIM may have felt somewhat compromised because he had married into a German family, but he also felt that he viewed the war differently because he was American:

> When war broke out in 1914 I refused to believe that all wrong was on one side and all right on the other. My English friends did not like my attitude. Because I was not English my judgement lacked a quality they wanted: but, as I sometimes reminded them, because I was not English my judgement possessed a quality theirs lacked – the quality of fairness.[28]

He also perceived that hostility towards him as an American citizen intensified before America entered the war:

> Somehow I have a feeling that the listeners are subconsciously thinking 'he is not an Englishman' … I thought that I felt actual antipathy in the atmosphere whenever I spoke of the war or any subject connected with it. Perhaps they are right. What business do I, an American, have to criticise or discuss national matters? But if they want me to pray with them for the nation, they must have the sermons too.[29]

IIM continued to make powerful statements on the subject of war, but appeared somewhat relieved when America joined force with the allies against Germany.[30] He ensured that the LJS congregation understood the significance of America's entry to the war:

> I don't know whether many outside of America realise the vastness for America of this step. It is a complete reversal of fundamental policy rigidly, almost jealously, maintained since its national beginnings, the policy of aloofness in international affairs outside the American continent. The United States had no desire to take part in world politics but rather felt that participation in them would jeopardise the principles for which it stood. It is, however, a new world into which it now enters, a world fighting for some of those very principles. The reversal of the policy of unconcern means that there is a new spirit in the world.[31]

IIM's war sermons significantly increased his public profile. His sermon on 'War and Reality' given at a JRU conference was praised by the *Jewish Chronicle*[32] and published subsequently as a pamphlet. Claude Montefiore, who had presided at the JRU conference, commented that he had not heard or read a finer treatment of the subject.[33] IIM's public profile was also raised by the two addresses he gave at the Steinway Hall in London as part of a series of lectures on 'Judaism and the War' in February and March 1917.[34] Both were published in a booklet and again reproduced in full in the *Jewish Chronicle*.[35]

However, IIM's addresses on war issues were not unfettered or their messages universally welcomed by the LJS congregation. On one occasion, Montefiore warned IIM against being overly polemical in his public statements, advising him: 'Our time will come'.[36] Montefiore particularly counselled IIM against expressing his views on the issue of 'Universal Military Service'.[37] IIM himself stated that he would have preferred to remain silent on some issues, but felt impelled to speak out on those issues that were 'out of accord with the teachings of our religion'. He recognised that some congregants found some of his statements uncomfortable but argued: 'Whether my opinions are worth heeding or not, you have put me here to express them; though you asked me to come at a time of peace it were [would be] wrong to be silent in a time of war.[38]

Maintaining Synagogue Life

The growth of the LJS under IIM's leadership abated after the outbreak of the First World War. The LJS had a high proportion of young members, many of whom served in the Armed Forces, including Mr Duparc, the choirmaster, the sexton and several council members. IIM had anticipated the loss of synagogue members to the Armed Forces, but he was surprised that the war had deflected the interest and enthusiasm of the remaining congregation away from religion.[39] The hostilities also delayed the synagogue's move to larger and more conducive premises that had been agreed just a few days before war was declared.[40]

However, IIM continued to shape the LJS community. With its other activities temporarily suspended, IIM encouraged the Guild of Social Service to support a home for Jewish refugees from Belgium. At his behest, members of the guild also found longer-term accommodation for the refugees, visited them in their new homes and helped them to become self-supporting. IIM continued to give his attention to increasing the profile of the LJS and Liberal Judaism in general. In January 1916 he started to invite distinguished speakers to give lectures at the synagogue on Sunday afternoons. These events commanded large audiences and were widely reported in the Jewish press. He also wrote a number of pamphlets that were published as part of the collection of the JRU's *Papers for Jewish People*. Several of his wartime sermons delivered on High Holydays and at festival services were published and widely circulated, such as his sermons on 'Religion and the Children', and on 'Religion and Society'.

IIM was not always satisfied with the spiritual progress of the congregation during the war years. He was saddened by the social distinctions that militated against the spiritual unity of the congregation,[41] and disliked what he described as the 'self-satisfaction' of some in the LJS community, who hated 'to be disturbed by sermons and want only their intellects tickled or impressed'.[42] He recorded in his diary 'I preach and preach and still there are few results'. He sometimes feared himself 'unequal to the task both in ability and attitude'.[43] It appears that he may have overestimated the motivation of those who joined the LJS, supposing that they were like him thirsting for an intellectual form of Judaism and waiting eagerly for someone to provide it. Later on he confided that during these years he had struggled to impart to the congregation that Liberal Judaism was a legitimate form of Judaism in its own right rather than 'just Orthodox

Judaism diluted'.[44] He battled against making 'sacrifices of principle' even though this occasionally brought him into conflict with some members of the LJS.[45]

Towards the end of the war, IIM set up a youth group 'with an integral place in the life of the congregation'.[46] The Alumni Society, as it became known, was the first of its kind in an English synagogue but mirrored developments in America. Since the late 1880s, Reform synagogues there had been organising activities intended to hold the generation of young people born in the country who were becoming increasingly disaffiliated. A number extended their buildings to provide space for young people to congregate.[47]

The first meeting of the Alumni Society was held on 13 January 1918, when twenty-six young people discussed 'The Conscription of Women'. Shortly afterwards the society began to publish its own magazine, the *Alumni Gazette* (subsequently the *Alumni Digest*).[48] IIM encouraged Alumni members to become involved in welfare activities in the local community, to give them a sense of social responsibility.[49] The development of the Alumni Society was at first 'beset with difficulties', including, according to IIM, the class differences between the young people participating in its activities.[50] At times it appeared to IIM that the society might not succeed and would have to be replaced by a 'study circle'.[51] However, with IIM's determined support, it moved forward, albeit hesitantly at first,[52] to become one of the main pillars of synagogue life for almost fifty years.

Shortly before the end of the war, the LJS established a Social Services Committee under the chairmanship of council member Lionel Jacobs, to provide a focus for the synagogue's external social welfare work. The setting up of the Social Services Committee followed a long debate by the LJS on the role of the synagogue as a focus for social action, a function that was strongly advocated by IIM. Claude Montefiore was not initially convinced by what he referred to as 'Mr Mattuck's Scheme',[53] but he eventually agreed it should go ahead. IIM was singularly unimpressed when some lay leaders suggested that his name should not appear as a committee member since this might prejudice its standing in the wider Anglo-Jewish community.[54]

With the setting up of the Social Services Committee, the Guild of Social Service concentrated its attention on the training of voluntary social workers. Speaking at the launch of a series of lectures on social work devised by the guild, IIM reminded those present that social work was not just about helping the poor of the East End, but should be regarded as a two-way process to 'instil the West End with a larger social outlook and imparting them sympathy'.[55] The war had sharpened some of the differences between the native and immigrant sections of the Jewish community and IIM urged the would-be social workers to recall that 'all Jews similarly emerged from the furnace of suffering', that 'all Jews are one' and the 'Jewish poor are our poor, and we are the first to be called to help them'.[56] Speaking as one who had 'devoted his life to the problem of Jewish social service', IIM argued that the poverty of the Jewish immigrant was unique – it was usually only temporary 'and with effort and help he can throw it off'.[57] He also made the case for dedicated Jewish social workers, who would understand the specific circumstances of those Jews in need of welfare:

> The Jew who has come from Russia has an outlook upon things that Englishmen cannot understand because they cannot appreciate the conditions under which they live and which produce certain moral and mental links ... That psychology can be best understood, because it is different, by Jews.[58]

IIM is almost certainly talking from personal experience on this subject.

Egalitarianism

Shortly after his arrival in England, IIM became Vice-President of the Jewish League for Women's Suffrage,[59] an organisation demanding parliamentary suffrage for women on the same basis as men, as well as supporting their equal involvement in religious life. In taking on the role, he stressed that the league was a Jewish body, not just a branch of the National Women's Suffrage Movement; it had been established because Jews believed that their religion taught them ideals on which the suffrage movement was based and that 'Judaism impelled them to support universal suffrage'.[60] He preached on women's suffrage at the LJS:

> ... the women's movement has a spiritual or religious basis. Controversy has raised [sic] so furiously and become so keen, and sent up such a cloud of dust as to obscure that which is fundamental and which is most essential for the comprehension of this movement. The vote is a very good and a very desirable object, and I hope that the time will speedily come, when it will be granted to those who ought to have it regardless of difference in sex.[61]

Although IIM cited religious reasons for his belief in women's equality, his background also probably shaped his views. As we have seen, in the

Eastern European community in which IIM grew up, it was not unusual for women to play the role of breadwinner. During the First World War, the strength of IIM's views on the religious equality of men and women became fully apparent. In the latter part of 1915 the Board of Deputies of British Jews approached Claude Montefiore proposing that the LJS should be represented on the board. Although this was a positive sign of the synagogue's recognition by Anglo-Jewry, after discussion, the LJS decided not to accept the invitation due to the fact that, at that time, only the male seat holders in a synagogue elected representatives to the board. A report of the Rites and Practices Committee, which was drafted and signed by IIM, stated that the board's voting practice was 'at variance with the attitude adopted by our synagogue, in whose privileges and duties men and women share alike'.[62] It was only when the board changed its constitution to allow women to vote that the LJS joined in 1922.

Following a debate at an LJS Council meeting, in 1918 IIM wrote to synagogue members seeking their views on his recommendation that women be allowed to preach in the synagogue. His suggestion was almost unanimously supported and Lily Montagu became the first woman to speak from the pulpit at the LJS. She had previously preached at the children's services held on a Saturday morning, but on 15 January 1918 she gave her first sermon to an adult congregation at the main service on a Saturday afternoon.[63] On IIM's recommendation, two years later women started to read on the *bimah*, and at its AGM in March 1920 the synagogue agreed unanimously the principle of admitting women to the ministry. IIM subsequently elaborated on this decision in the *JRU Bulletin*:

> If, indeed, a suitable woman should present herself for the ministry of the LJS, she would not be in the least handicapped by her sex. For it is evident that a ministry composed of men and women would be one of increased usefulness to the congregation.[64]

IIM was not to see his expectation come to fruition in his lifetime. In his approach to women's equality IIM was a few years in advance of his rabbinic colleagues in America. CCAR twice turned down resolutions in support of women's suffrage and it was not until 1917, only three years before the adoption of a US constitutional amendment allowing women to vote, that CCAR passed such a resolution. According to the historian Michael A. Meyer, even then many Reform rabbis remained ambivalent about the issue of women's equality, denying that men and women were equal in their natural competencies. As a result, women's rise to positions of leadership in the Reform movement was very slow, while in England a number of women were represented on both the LJS Council and the JRU executive committee.[65]

Although IIM may have been ahead of his American Reform colleagues, his views on equality were a logical consequence of his liberalism rather than being a central cause. His writings on the subject of religious equality give the impression that he was more concerned with purging Judaism of its 'Oriental' origins than with gender equality per se. In addition, while IIM spoke often about the religious and legal status of women, he had little to say about the advancement of their social status.[66] In fact his views on the role of women were quite traditional; he criticised women who pursued careers outside the home at the expense of the welfare of their children and expressed his dislike of feminism:

> Equality of the sexes is to my mind a cardinal principle of religious thought and religious life. I am afraid, however, that there has been a tendency to make equality mean similarity. We can be equal and yet be different. A woman need not be like a man in order to maintain a position in every way equal to his. I am afraid that the movement that went under the name of feminism has gone either too far or is altogether wrong in confusing likeness with equality. The home has to suffer for this.[67]

IIM saw feminism and the attitudes of what he referred to as 'the new woman' as undermining marriage.[68]

As early as 1913, he criticised the arrangement in the LJS of charging for named seats, which was favoured by the prosperous businessmen who constituted a large proportion of the congregation. He pronounced this policy as 'good business' but 'very bad religion'.[69] In the latter part of 1915 he argued forcefully against those members who criticised the LJS's policy of congregants making voluntary contributions dependent on their means, and who were proposing that the synagogue move towards the more standard practice of a fixed membership fee:

> We do not grieve over the fact that there are many people who cannot afford to buy diamonds, and we do not open special institutions to make it easier for them to acquire these delectable objects. But we should be less than short-sighted if we were content with affairs, which would keep any number of people from worship simply because they could not afford to pay a specified sum for a seat in a place of worship, which means for the right to worship.[70]

His arguments were heeded and, on IIM's recommendation, the LJS Council agreed to retain the system of voluntary contributions. This move reflected the pattern of democratisation developing across the Reform Movement in America, following the example set by Stephen Wise in his Free Synagogue in New York. Speaking about the organisation of the synagogue in 1915, IIM stated that he found it impossible to conceive of any form of liberalism that was not democratic.[71] IIM continued to argue against the designation of seats that would often remain vacant, but it was not until several years after the First World War that the LJS Council eventually agreed to unassigned seating.[72]

JRU Bulletin

During the war, IIM continued to chair JRU meetings held at the LJS, but there were few practical developments in the movement. He regretted the fact that 'there is no money to do anything and therefore very little interest in it [the JRU]'.[73] To help maintain the profile of Liberal Judaism, in 1914 IIM founded the *Jewish Religious Union Bulletin* (*JRU Bulletin*), which after seventeen years became the *Liberal Jewish Monthly (LJM)*. The content of the *JRU Bulletin* was largely written by IIM. In every issue there was a lengthy article on a faith issue and several pages of commentary on topical events both in Britain and abroad. It documented in detail developments in Anglo-Jewry and Jewish life in America, Russia, Poland and Germany and commented on non-Jewish affairs. IIM also often wrote and spoke about current social conditions, never hesitating to challenge traditional views from a prophetic perspective.

Although the editor of the newspaper was later to regret its existence,[74] the *Jewish Chronicle* greeted the appearance of the *JRU Bulletin* warmly: 'Rabbi Mattuck, the editor [of the *JRU Bulletin*] deserves congratulations, for the *Bulletin* is a useful record of activities and an able statement of views. Such a periodical might become a useful congregational bond.'[75]

Jewish Identity and the Balfour Declaration

We have seen that from an early age IIM was opposed to Zionism,[76] and soon after his arrival at the LJS he made his views known to the congregation when he preached on 'The Modern Nationalist Tendency in Judaism'.[77] During the war years IIM continued to contend the 'classical' Reform position that Jews were not a nation as the Zionists claimed, rather that the 'presence of Jews in the various countries is not an accident, but in accord with Israel's destiny'.[78] At this time he was also adamant that it was impossible for Liberal Jews to support Zionism completely:

> There are, it is true, some who are both Liberal Jews and Zionists, but a reconciliation of two contradictory ideas must involve some sacrifice or weakening on the part of both ideas. The universal hopes of Liberal Judaism and the national hopes of Zionism are opposed to one another.[79]

However, IIM did not dismiss all aspects of the Zionist cause. He was willing to consider one expression of the Zionist ideal as an appropriate solution to the problems faced by Jews during the war: the notion of Palestine as a place of refuge.[80] For this reason IIM was, at this stage, prepared to work alongside Zionists.

Prior to the war, the World Zionist Organisation (WZO) battled in the wilderness following the death of Theodor Herzl, and on the eve of outbreak of war it was in a state of disintegration. However, as the war progressed the Zionist cause gained momentum. This was partly as a result of the rise of anti-Semitism, but the growth of Zionism was even more apparent after the British occupation of Palestine in 1917, which made the Zionists more hopeful of achieving their goal. The British Government believed that significant propaganda value could be gained both against Germany and in America if it were to indicate its support for a Jewish national entity after the ending of the war. After considerable debate, what became known as the 'Balfour Declaration' was signed in November 1917 despite the protests of the influential Cabinet member, Edwin Montagu (brother of Lily Montagu), who was then Secretary of State for India in Lloyd George's First World War Cabinet.[81]

Although the official stance of the JRU towards Zionism was neutral, many of its leaders were opposed to the founding of an independent Jewish state. Along with both Lily Montagu and Claude Montefiore, IIM wrote to the Government voicing his opposition to the Balfour Declaration. Notwithstanding his opposition to the nationalist aspect of the Balfour Declaration, IIM was subsequently to reject vehemently any claims that it was the result of a bargain with Jews, regarding it as a deep insult to their integrity.[82]

IIM noted with growing concern that the war had 'turned many Jews into nationalists,[83] and in his Yom Kippur sermon in 1918, he returned to challenging Zionism forcefully rather than seeking to work with it. He now contended that the most insidious danger facing the Jewish people was Zionistic interpretation of Judaism in non-religious terms.[84]

The Ending of the War

By the beginning of 1918 IIM was feeling very jaded by the war, especially by the closing down of institutions he held dear, such as the British

Museum – 'the greatest museum in the world'.[85] He was distressed that air raids had driven children out of London and away from the Religion School, and by the 'barking of guns' close to the synagogue.[86] It seemed to him for a while that Britain was losing the war:

> The Germans are steadily approaching the Channel ports. Why can't they be stopped? Sometimes I wonder whether the leaders of the Allied armies have some strategic trick up their sleeves, but the thought cannot stay long. The present advances of the German army are too serious. What an agonising anxiety. Every gain of the enemy cannot but mean the promulgation of war.[87]

He visited the treatment centres set up for those wounded in the bombing of London to offer comfort and support. However, he sometimes found himself turned away because he was not recognised as a minister since he did not wear a dog collar.[88] On occasion, his visits led to discomfiting experiences, such as encountering prostitution:

> What struck me most was that the 'patient', the young girl seemed to have no self-respect. She seemed eager to speak of her past and only with now and then a faint trace of shame. Must learn if possible to understand the psychology of such people.[89]

Within a month or so, however, IIM was beginning to 'feel the breath of the Angel of Peace' and appears to have been gratified to receive an invitation to the House of Commons to speak with 'Mr L' and 'Mr B' about the peace process.[90] He began to preach at the LJS on ideas for reconstruction following the end of the war. Although he perceived that the war had 'destroyed the normal sequence of our life' and 'disarranged our ideas about nearly all important things', he felt that some good might yet come from this because it would 'restore the intellectual and even spiritual freedom which old habits and prejudices have encrusted'.[91] In particular, he hoped that the radical disturbance of the war would lead to new ideas for dealing with social problems, especially those arising from the way in which industry was organised.[92]

In his sermons IIM warned against the sentiment of conceptualising reconstruction as an attempt 'to produce in the nation a great military efficiency for the next time its military prowess might be challenged'.[93] Writing in his diary, IIM confided his fear that his anti-militaristic stance might lead some to conclude that he was a socialist,[94] and that he had been advised by Montefiore to avoid becoming associated with any proposed social reforms that might prove to be controversial.[95] Nevertheless, IIM returned to the topic of post-war reconstruction in a sermon he gave at the Wigmore Hall on Rosh Hashana in September 1918. This sermon contained a warning, which in retrospect, seems frighteningly prophetic: 'An unscrupulous or deluded demagogue with plausible tongue and violent sincerity, seeming or real, could make out of the present susceptibility to new ideas and change a spirit of evil.'[96] It is unclear whether IIM was thinking of Germany or England, but it was certainly a nightmare that two decades later he must have been devastated to see become a reality.

NOTES

1. His indirect quote is taken from the Book of Genesis, 1:31.
2. 'This is a Good World', sermon given by IIM at the LJS, 8 February 1912, Montagu Centre Collection (MCC).
3. Much of the following analysis is based on a reading of IIM's war sermons together with a helpful paper written by Professor Marc Saperstein, 'Normative Judaism' in 'the Crisis of the War: Sermons by Abraham Cohen and Israel Mattuck', in *Melilah*, Manchester Journal of Jewish Studies, Normative Judaism, Jews, Judaism, and Jewish Identity, Proceedings of the British Association for Jewish Studies (BAJS) conference 208, Supplementary Volume No. 1 (2012), eds Daniel R. Langton and Philip S Alexander, pp.52–65.
4. 'The Comprehension of the Reality in Life', Rosh Hashana sermon given by IIM at the LJS, 21 September 1914, MCC. The 'ruin of town and sacred houses' probably alludes to the devastation of Louvain at the end of August, and the German bombardment of the Rheims Cathedral just two days before the sermon was delivered.
5. Ibid.
6. 'The Part That Religion Took in the War: How Shall We Judge it?', sermon given by IIM at the LJS, 12 November 1933, MCC.
7. 'The War and Spiritual Progress', sermon given by IIM at the LJS, Rosh Hashana, 9 September 1915, in ibid.
8. Ibid.
9. 'God's Healing', sermon given by IIM at the LJS, 18 September 1915, MCC.
10. 'What Can Religion Do?', sermon given by IIM at the LJS, 28 November 1914, in Ibid.
11. 'Victory and Peace', sermon given by IIM at the LJS, Thanksgiving Service, 16 November 1918, in ibid.
12. 'The War and Social Conscience', sermon given by IIM at the LJS, 24 October 1914, in ibid.
13. See 'What Can Religion Do?'.
14. 'Faith and the National Crisis', sermon given by IIM at the LJS, 2 January 1915, MCC.
15. See 'Anti-Semitism, Some Causes and Remedy', sermon given by IIM at the LJS, 21 May 1921, in ibid.
16. 'The War and Character', sermon given by IIM at the LJS, 9 December 1916, in ibid.
17. 'Judaism as a Universal Religion', address given by IIM at the Glasgow Literary Society, 12 December 1915, in ibid.
18. 'Conscientious Objection', sermon given by IIM at the LJS, 16 September 1916, in ibid.
19. Ibid.
20. Ibid.
21. 'The War and the Jews', sermon given by IIM at the LJS, 23 January 1915, MCC.
22. 'The Larger Conception of Jewish Duty', sermon given by IIM at the LJS, 17 March 1917, in ibid.
23. Tape recording of the diary kept by IIM between January and April 1918, read by IIM's daughter, Dorothy Edgar, née Mattuck, Mattuck Family Archive kept by Robert Edgar (MFAb).
24. Ibid.
25. See 'The War and the Jews'.
26. See 'What Can Religion Do?'.

27. The undated letter is quoted in Daniel R. Langton, *Claude Montefiore: His Life and Thought* (London and Portland, OR: Vallentine Mitchell, 2002), p.9. A pamphlet that Montefiore wrote in 1918 with Basil Henriques, 'The English Jew and his Religion', has a xenophobic feel to it.
28. 'Post War America', address written by IIM, purpose unknown, day not specified July 1927, MCC. It is possible that he gave this address after his trip to America in that year.
29. See tape recording of the diary kept by IIM.
30. 'A Free Israel', sermon given by IIM at the Wigmore Hall at the Morning Service of the First Day of Passover, 7 April 1917, MCC.
31. 'After Four Years', sermon given by IIM at a special service at the LJS, 3 August 1918, in ibid.
32. *JC*, 30 October 1914, p.15.
33. Ibid.
34. The two addresses he gave were on 'Providence and Human Life', 18 February 1917, and on 'Prayer', 4 March 1917, MCC. The two sermons were reproduced in *Judaism and the War*, published by the JRU in 1917.
35. *JC*, 4 March 1917, p.14.
36. Letters from Claude Montefiore to IIM dated 21 and 28 October, year unknown, London Metropolitan Archives, ACC/3529/004/002.
37. Letter from Claude Montefiore to IIM, dated 28 October, year unknown, in ibid. It is not clear here whether Montefiore was referring the general male conscription or the legislation of 1917 to conscript naturalised Russian nationals in the British Army, which was a highly contentious issue, but it was probably the latter.
38. 'Five Years of the Liberal Jewish Synagogue', sermon given by IIM at the LJS, 20 January 1917, MCC.
39. Ibid.
40. Ibid.
41. 'Ten Years in the LJS Ministry', sermon given by IIM at the LJS, 21 January 1922, MCC.
42. See tape recording of the diary kept by IIM.
43. Ibid.
44. 'Rabbi Dr Mattuck's Fortieth Anniversary Address', in *LJM*, XXIII, no.2 (February 1952), p.16.
45. See tape recording of the diary kept by IIM.
46. Rabbi Dr I. Mattuck, 'Liberal Judaism in Great Britain', in *The First Fifty Years – A Record of Liberal Judaism In England, 1900–1950* (London: Liberal Jewish Synagogue, 1950), p.10.
47. Alan Silverstein, *Alternatives to Assimilation, The Response of Reform Judaism to American Culture, 1840–1930* (Boston, MA: Brandeis University Press, 1994), p.84.
48. Lawrence Rigal and Rosita Rosenberg, *Liberal Judaism, The First Hundred Years* (London: Liberal Judaism, 2002), p.64.
49. Article in celebration of Rabbi Mattuck's Seventieth Birthday, in *LJM,* XXV, no.2 (February 1954), p.26.
50. See tape recording of the diary kept by IIM.
51. Minute book of the LJS Organising Committee, meeting held on 7 January 1919, LJS Archives, Box 1/2.
52. See Mattuck, 'Liberal Judaism in Great Britain', p.10.
53. Paper written by Claude Montefiore, 'Mr Mattuck's Scheme', 9 May 1917, LJS Archives, Box 1/2.
54. See tape recording of the diary kept by IIM.
55. 'Social Service Training Class, Lecture 1', undated (c.1919), given by IIM at the LJS, MCC.
56. Ibid.
57. Ibid.
58. Ibid.
59. *JC,* 15 November 1912, p.18.
60. *JC,* 14 March 1913, p.34.
61. 'The Spiritual Meaning of the Women's Movement', sermon given by IIM, undated (c.1913), MCC.
62. See Rigal and Rosenberg, *Liberal Judaism,* p.59.

63. Lily H. Montagu, *The Jewish Religious Union and Its Beginnings* (Papers for Jewish People, No. XXVII) (London: JRU, 1927), p.27. The subject of her sermon was 'Kinship with God'.
64. Leader, *JRU Bulletin*, X, No. 8, April 1920, p.9.
65. Michael A. Meyer, *Response to Modernity – A History of the Reform Movement in Judaism* (New York: Oxford University Press, 1988), p.285.
66. See *Jewish Ethics*, published towards the end of IIM's life in 1953, when he was still largely concerned with the religious position of women and their role in the home.
67. 'The Problem of the Divorce Laws', sermon given by IIM at the LJS, 25 November 1922, MCC.
68. Ibid.
69. *JC*, 21 February 1913, p.20.
70. 'The Ideals of Our Synagogue', sermon given by IIM at the LJS, 18 December 1915, MCC.
71. Ibid.
72. See 'Liberal Judaism and the Future ii – Our Congregation', sermon given by IIM at the LJS, 12 January 1919, MCC. In this sermon IIM is still expressing his unhappiness with the allocated seating policy in operation in the synagogue.
73. See tape recording of the diary kept by IIM.
74. See later discussion of the relationship between IIM and the *JC*.
75. *JC*, 'Books Supplement', 1 May 1914, p.11.
76. See Chapter Five on IIM's time at Harvard, which describes his reaction to Zionist meetings in Boston.
77. 'The Modern Nationalist Tendency in Judaism', sermon given by IIM at the LJS, 9 May 1913, MCC.
78. 'Liberal Judaism and the Future of the Jews', sermon given by IIM at the LJS, 28 October 1916, in ibid.
79. Ibid.
80. See 'The War and the Jews'.
81. Edwin Montagu said that he had striven all of his life to escape the ghetto to which he now faced possible relegation as a result of the proposed declaration. Peter Egill Brownfeld, 'The League of British Jews: Challenging Nationalism in Behalf of Jewish Universalism', *Journal of the American Council for Judaism,* Fall 2001: www.acjna.org
82. 'The New British Policy', draft article by IIM submitted to *John Bull*, 5 November 1930, MCC.
83. See tape recording of the diary kept by IIM.
84. 'The Problem of Judaism', sermon given by IIM at the LJS, 16 September 1918, MCC.
85. See tape recording of the diary kept by IIM.
86. Ibid.
87. Ibid.
88. Ibid.
89. Ibid.
90. Ibid. Correspondence between IIM and Montefiore at this time suggests that he was referring to the war Cabinet Conservative politicians Lansdowne and Baldwin. See correspondence in the London Metropolitan Archives, ACC/3529/004/002.
91. 'The War and Social Service', sermon given at the LJS, 4 March 1916, MCC.
92. Ibid.
93. 'Ideals in Reconstruction', sermon given by IIM at the LJS, 19 January 1918, in ibid.
94. See tape recording of the diary kept by IIM.
95. Ibid.
96. 'New Life', sermon given by IIM at the Wigmore Hall, Rosh Hashana, day of Memorial, 7 September 1918, MCC.

CHAPTER TEN

After the First World War

Victory and Peace

IIM's relief on the ending of the war was profound. When he spoke at the Thanksgiving Service held at the LJS in November 1918, his joy was palpable:

> After more than four years of a war unequalled in the sacrifices it demanded, in the desolations it wrought, in the sufferings and sorrows it inflicted, we have come unto peace with the victory we yearned and prayed for. There were times during these years when hope drooped, and darkness threatened the soul. Hope has now reached its realization, there is light. We strive hard to grasp the full meaning of the event, to measure its grandeur. We open ourselves out to feel it, to feel all of it, as when a body is brought near to a source of warmth ... We watched thrones totter and fall, empires crumble, haughty powers laid low. The climax of them all came last Monday morning with the glad tidings: Victory and Peace. The heart could only swell with all its fervour into one prayer: Thank God![1]

However, IIM was at pains to point out that victory was not just about winning, or about one power showing itself to be superior to another; it was about a triumph for righteousness and the vindication of justice. He celebrated the achievements of the British allies, but also highlighted the capitulation of Germany despite the fact that it retained its military might, which showed that the German people recognised the wrongness of their country's cause. IIM hoped fervently for peace based on justice, humanity and the rights of nations. The world had experienced a 'gigantic war'. Now what was needed was a 'gigantic peace'.[2]

IIM was acutely aware that the Jewish people had a particular interest in the peace negotiations. He noted that a large proportion of world Jewry lived in the countries whose future would be under discussion – especially those that were once part of the Russian Empire – and that the subject of Jewish immigration was likely to arise. Also, because the Peace Conference was charged with establishing justice, there was now an opportunity to address the rights of those Jews who had long endured suffering and deprivation. He considered the implications for Jews of the Peace Conference in three sermons that he gave at the LJS during January and February of 1919. In these sermons he argued that the way to improve the condition of the Jews in Eastern Europe was not by the establishment of a Jewish state, but to raise their status in the lands where they lived. They should be emancipated in the same way as the Jews of the Western world.[3]

However, he accepted that this measure alone would not solve the problems of Eastern European Jews; unless the Peace Conference imposed on the new Eastern European states the condition that they allow entry to Jews from elsewhere in the former Russian Empire, many Jews would continue to live a ghetto-like existence. He recognised that the dispersal of the Jews from the former Pale of Settlement would cause initial upheaval and called for economic support to help them settle in their new lands.[4] IIM's hopes of the Peace Conference ran high:

> We do not expect the Peace Conference to inaugurate the final millennium, but we do look to it to bring out of this chaos a world order better than the one that has crumbled, better because it is more just. I believe that hope will not be disappointed. A spirit of idealism is dominating the Council in Paris that augurs its fulfilment. For the Jews the Day of Justice will become the day of a new deliverance. And with the fortune of the Jews is intertwined that of their religion. When all Jews shall be freed, a new era will begin for the faith by which the Jew lives and for which he will live.[5]

Rebuilding the Congregation

With the war over, IIM began to rebuild synagogue life. An Organising Committee was set up under his chairmanship, charged with identifying ways of encouraging synagogue attendance and engaging the congregation. The measures he and his colleagues devised included holding local meetings with members, advertising the subjects of sermons in advance of services and involving the congregation in synagogue decision making.[6] As a result of these measures and IIM's determined leadership, membership of the synagogue rose rapidly, and by 1919 the LJS had one of the largest congregations in England.

However, IIM was not satisfied with the mere numerical growth of the congregation. He regarded the congregation as 'a man-sized baby', perceived that it was 'encumbered with much dead wood' and expressed his disappointment in the lack of communal consciousness amongst LJS members.[7] He recognised that attendance at services was better than for most other synagogues in the country, but that this was, however, 'far from satisfactory'; he expected 'something much better'. IIM perceived that, to many of his congregants, religion was no more than an ornament of respectability. In his usual forthright manner he said:

> For why did those whom we see rarely, if ever, at our services, join us? If it was to stay away from our services, they could just as well have done it in their old congregations. If it was to be buried, the older synagogues would have done that for them with no less chance for salvation of their souls, and it may be added with no greater expense to their purse.[8]

He answered his own question by suggesting that some people behaved in this way because, in Orthodox Judaism, they had been 'trained' to stay away from services and that it was hard for Liberal Judaism to break this habit. He also blamed low attendance on the example set by the Anglican Church – it had given people permission to 'play fast and loose with religious matters and institutions', and 'practically made it permissible to belong to a Church without believing in the cause for which the Church stands'.[9] He was later to record his view that one of the big differences between American and English Jews was in the balance between personal religion and communal consciousness: while English people saw religion as something they did in private, for Americans it was 'something that you did with your society'.[10]

Seeing it as a role model for future Liberal synagogues, IIM refused to allow the LJS to become an institution that demanded little of its affiliates and renewed his efforts to encourage the congregation to become involved in social action. As a result, LJS members, working in cooperation with the West London Synagogue, provided financial and other forms of assistance for the first Jewish settlement established in the East End by Basil Henriques on his return from active service. The St George's Jewish Settlement was modelled on the Christian settlements Henriques had seen operating in the East End prior to the war. When Clement Atlee, then the Mayor of Stepney, officially opened the new settlement on 18 January 1920, IIM led the service along with Montefiore.

Having made progress on the involvement of young people in the synagogue with the establishment of the Alumni Society, IIM turned his attention to the participation of women. Since the LJS's establishment, a Needlework Guild had taken care of the synagogue linens and had made clothes for children's charities. IIM now encouraged women to assume more prominent and more varied roles, taking as his model the Temple Sisterhoods that had been set up in Reform synagogues from the 1890s.

In 1923 The Women's Society was established under the chairmanship of Lady Sassoon. It had two main purposes: 'to deepen the corporate life of the community by promoting a spirit of fellowship amongst its members' and 'to undertake such tasks in connection with the synagogue itself, or in connection with any social work that might be promoted, as fell naturally within the scope of women's activities'.[11] Edna Mattuck was one of the founding committee members. She became very active in the affairs of the Women's Society, especially its work in catering for major LJS functions and in the preparation of the synagogue for festivals and High Holydays. Her skills, patience and tact as a hostess were quickly recognised.[12]

In 1916 IIM had started adapting the Saturday morning children's services for adult audiences and by the early 1920s a full Sabbath Service was held at the LJS on Saturday. Saturday afternoon services continued for people who worked on Saturday mornings. Although IIM was prepared to make changes to Saturday services, Sabbath eve services were not introduced until much later (1945) since he firmly believed, as had his mentor Kohler,[13] that good Jews should spend Friday nights at home with their family. Friday evening services he said had a tendency to destroy the Friday evening home atmosphere.[14]

Eastern European Immigrants

We have seen that while studying at Harvard, IIM appeared to take no interest in the influx of vast numbers of Eastern European Jews to Boston. However, by the time that he reached Britain he clearly saw it as one of his roles to reach out to the large numbers of Eastern European immigrants living in London's East End. His early speaking engagements included addressing meetings in this part of London, where he found a community very similar to the one he had left behind in Worcester. His audiences were largely made up of Jews from Russia and other parts of Eastern Europe, with whom IIM was able to converse in Yiddish.[15] In the years following the First World War, IIM took an even keener interest in the circumstances of Eastern European Jews. On occasion, he visited the Jews' Temporary Shelter,[16] and was saddened by what he saw:

> About two years ago [1921] I had some business that took me to the Jewish shelter. There I saw a number of men and women and children sitting about with the promiscuous empty look which showed complete ignorance of plan. When I asked what they were waiting for and where they were going, the answer was that they did not know, but that they would go to any country where the ship companies would take them with a chance of them being admitted.[17]

IIM may have reflected on the fact that just thirty years earlier the Mattuck family had not experienced such limited opportunities.

On 1 April 1922 a conference on 'The Immigrant Parent and His English Child' was held at the LJS chaired by IIM, and in January of the following year he chaired a second conference on the 'The Alien Jew and His Child'. While the first conference appears to have been unreported, the second event proved to be highly controversial. After heated discussions, the conference was adjourned and its proceedings attracted criticism in the Jewish press. The Reverend A.A. Green of Hampstead Synagogue, who was normally supportive of the LJS, expressed disappointment at what he heard of the disparaging attitude of those who had spoken at the conference towards immigrant Jews, which he feared would provide fodder for anti-Semites.[18]

When the conference was reconvened, IIM voiced his concern about the way in which the proceedings of the previous meeting had been misreported and misconstrued. He also contested suggestions appearing in some Jewish newspapers that his attitude to 'alien Jews' savoured of snobbery. He pointed out that this was unlikely since he was an 'alien Jew' himself. While some of those who were present at the conference did exhibit condescending attitudes towards the Eastern European Jews, IIM's remarks displayed a much greater empathy with their hardships.[19] He opined, with a degree of bitterness, that any initiative pursued by the LJS was viewed in a negative light by certain sections of the Anglo-Jewish community regardless of its merits.[20]

Although the situation was beginning to change, the Jewish communal organisations that led, financed and ran the social welfare activities in the East End were dominated by the well-to-do families who had lived in England for many generations. Alongside their concern for the welfare of their co-religionists, less altruistically, they were keen to see them become respectable, middle-class English citizens to ensure that they did not detract from the status and comfort that the Anglo-Jewish establishment had achieved. It has already been mentioned that the families that made up the Anglo-Jewish establishment were well represented in the congregation of the LJS, and it may have been as a counter to their cultural arrogance and social condescension that in his many of his sermons on the subject of charity and philanthropy, IIM stressed the religious basis of social welfare activities and challenged common misconceptions of Eastern European Jews.

In a notable sermon delivered at the LJS in December 1924, IIM criticised *The Times* for viewing Jewish immigrants as a problem and for ignoring their tragedy. While expressing his disagreement with the Zionist tendency amongst new arrivals, IIM sought to explode the myth that all

Russian Jews were Bolsheviks and drew attention to the general 'sobriety, thrift and industriousness' of the immigrants as well as their intelligence and ambition, all of which pointed to a strong likelihood of their eventual assimilation. With more than a hint of reference to his own background, he alluded to the conflict that often arose between immigrants and their offspring.[21]

Despite his empathy with and understanding of Eastern European Jews, he had little patience with the Yiddish-speaking subculture they brought with them to England. He said:

> But there are some habits and manners that characterise some Jews which are objectionable. They do not make their morals – they just affect their acceptability as associates – I almost say their aesthetic quality. Ornateness in dress and loudness in speech can serve as illustrations. Neither of these are Jewish faults; they are faults which some Jews have brought with them from their countries of origin and which material success in other lands brings to the surface.[22]

IIM's pronouncements on Eastern European Jews are redolent of those made by his mentors, Kaufmann Kohler and David Philipson,[23] who probably helped to shape IIM's views when he was in Cincinnati. IIM was particularly critical of those Eastern European Jews who refused to abandon what he referred to as their 'Ghetto mentality', which was epitomised as a 'tendency to see great value in little things and little value in great things, the neglect of new truths, and a general separation from the current of civilisation that in ways produced anachronisms and worse things'.[24] IIM's comments are somewhat anomalous, uttered as they were by someone coming from the same background as the immigrants about whom he was speaking, and who was ostensibly overlooking the fact that he had left the semi-ghetto ambience of Water Street in Worcester less than a generation earlier. However, to IIM, the 'Oriental trappings' of his co-religionists detracted from his deeply held belief that Jews were different from other citizens only in their religion; he felt that they obscured the essence and beauties of Judaism to Jews and non-Jews alike (see further discussion in Chapter Seventeen).[25]

IIM's Prayer Books

After his initial work on the LJS prayer books, it was several years before IIM carried out any major work on developing the liturgy of the Liberal movement. His prayer books of 1912 and 1916 had been followed in 1918 by *Services and Prayers for Jewish Homes*, which included daily, Sabbath and festival prayers and services, as well as life cycle rituals such as the marriage service. Noteworthy features of this prayer book included a slightly abridged Sabbath Eve *kiddush* in Hebrew and in English, a considerably shortened 'Grace After Meals' and the Liberal Jewish movement's first Passover Haggadah covering just twenty pages.

It was in the early 1920s that IIM set about preparing the significantly different liturgies that became known as the *Liberal Jewish Prayer Books for Sabbaths, High Holydays and Festivals* (or more informally, 'Mattuck's prayer books'). Volume II for the High Holydays appeared first in 1923 alongside a pamphlet containing sixty-five hymns in English. Volume I, 'Services for Weekdays, Sabbaths, etc.' and Volume III, 'Services for Passover, Pentecost and Tabernacles' were both published in 1926. Volumes I and II were both revised by IIM in 1937, when the number of Sabbath services was increased from fifteen to twenty-six and the services were reworded, recast, and enriched by newly composed prayers. IIM also added readings and meditations, which aimed at preparation for services by contemplation, a custom from older prayer books that IIM chose to readopt. Volume III was never revised.

As he began the task of producing the new generation of prayer books, IIM engaged with the congregation on the role of liturgy. He saw the aim of the prayer book as being to 'express the faith of those who use it for worship' and 'to bring more fully the influences of religion to bear upon life'.[26] The intention was not to express a creed or dogma, but rather to express the common beliefs of the congregation.[27]

In producing the new prayer books, IIM did not start from scratch, but built on David Einhorn's *Olat Tamid* and the UAHC *Union Prayer Book* mentioned in Chapter Six. By the time that IIM produced the new prayer books, the LJS was well established and IIM obviously felt able to be more radical in his liturgy. He removed traditional concepts including the return to Zion as a religious hope, the coming of a personal messiah, sacrifices and the desirability of their restoration and the idea that the world was created in six days. He articulated the concept of progressive revelation that might not be limited only to the Jewish people.

Volume I of IIM's prayer books is unique amongst Progressive Jewish prayer books because of the number of different services it contains. Some of the services were designed for use either on a weekday or a Sabbath; IIM probably had in mind their use for the Sunday services he introduced in 1920 (see below). It is also of interest that some of the services focus on particular themes. For instance, in Service 8 there is an emphasis on nature and in Service 9 there is an emphasis on justice. This feature of IIM's prayer books was to be developed more systematically by Rabbis John Rayner and Chaim Stern in the 1960s.[28] The services at the beginning of

Volume 1 are more traditional than those towards the end, where drastically abbreviated material from the Bible, the Apocrypha and later Jewish literature appears alongside the writings of Plato, Shelley, Browning and many of IIM's own compositions. These demonstrate his deep piety, as illustrated in the following extract:

> O thou Infinite Spirit of the Universe, whom men serve in diverse ways, and whom men acknowledge in diverse faiths, do thou come unto us impelling us to seek for truth, to strive for righteousness, to show love unto all men, and to rejoice in the beauty of the world.
>
> Though we must be far from the realisation of perfect truth, yet may the love of truth be the guide of our thoughts, and the desire of truth be the impulse in our striving. Though we cannot attain to complete righteousness, yet may the desire for righteousness be the force controlling and directing our actions. Though the realisation of perfect love is too hard for us, yet may love be the guiding light in our hearts.
>
> Though the full joy of beauty is beyond us, yet let us learn to appreciate more and more the beautiful in the universe and in the works of men. O give us the help of thy spirit wherein is the knowledge which is above all human knowledge, the wisdom which is greater and deeper than all human wisdom, so that by thy guidance we may come to see the way to the highest life, and seeing, walk therein. By goodness, truth, love and beauty teach us to live, and through them lead us to knowledge of thee.[29]

In his introduction to Volume I, IIM explained that his purpose in including a variety of prayers and readings was not only to demonstrate the ideas of Liberal Judaism but also to produce a unity, which would 'satisfy the historic feeling and the religious thought of the modern Jewish consciousness'.[30]

As with his earlier prayer books, IIM changed the traditional order of the prayers that were retained. None of the services contains the entire 'Seven Benedictions'. Volumes II and III of IIM's prayer books are more traditional than Volume I. Since they covered occasions that occurred only once a year, IIM's urge to provide variety and variation may have been less strong.[31]

In a sermon given in 1926 just after Volume II appeared, IIM defended the radical nature of his prayer books by saying that the purpose of a prayer book was 'not to maintain tradition but to maintain life'.[32] He also explained the inclusion of writings by non-Jews, which he saw as a demonstration of the universalism of Liberal Judaism, and of the poems he said: 'Religion is poetry. Religion is a poetical understanding of the universe'. Of the other writings he had included he said: 'If Plato and Shakespeare can help Jews to God, they have a place in Jewish Worship'.[33]

IIM's prayer books were hailed with great approval by the leading American rabbi and well-known historian of the Reform Movement, David Philipson, as being 'fully expressive of the modern religious spirit' and as meeting 'the needs of the modern worshipper much more adequately than does the traditional prayer book.'[34] However, despite the time he spent in producing the new prayer books, IIM was not totally satisfied with the product of his labours. When conveying his gratitude for the permission he had been granted to use prayers from the UAHC prayer book, IIM confided to his American colleagues that although he was pleased the movement now had its own prayer books, he would have preferred to use the American Reform prayer book.[35]

IIM's prayer books were to be used throughout the Liberal movement for more than forty years but, to begin with, some of the developing Liberal congregations such as the St George's Settlement in the East End and the North London Liberal Synagogue found Mattuck's liturgy too modern, and produced their own versions.[36] Although ideologically the prayer books belong to the left of the Progressive Jewish spectrum, they did contain some more traditional elements when judged by American Reform standards. In 1927 Rabbi Feldman from Connecticut, who was himself a neo-reformist, wrote to IIM to challenge him on his liturgy that accompanied the new festival celebrations, which IIM had established at the LJS in 1926.[37] Rabbi Feldman questioned IIM's reintroduction of processions of children as well as the procession of the scrolls on the last day of *Sukkot* and was worried that IIM's reintroduction of *Hakafot* might be regarded just as a 'means for saving the day'.[38]

IIM was very gratified when his new prayer book of 1937 was reviewed favourably by Professor Ismar Elbogen, 'a foremost authority on Jewish Liturgy'.[39] Elbogen praised the variation that IIM introduced to the new edition, which he said demonstrated IIM's 'possession of very great religious wealth and of intensive religious labour'.[40] However, Elbogen did question whether the prayer book placed too much emphasis on the primacy of the individual, and whether the value of the community had been underrated. He also challenged the prominence that IIM had given to doctrine, and suggested that since IIM was known for not reasoning dogmatically and for his readiness to modify his work, he would in time alter his liturgy.[41] Elbogen also commented that the variation in services that IIM had introduced was testament to the strength of the congregation he had moulded, it being simpler to use a more traditional prayer book where the content is repeated continually.[42]

IIM Becomes a National Figure

The public profile IIM had begun to establish during the war years further heightened in the immediate post-war period. The Sunday services he introduced in 1920 were to be pivotal in making him a national figure.[43] Concerned that an increasing number of congregants were, for financial reasons, finding it necessary to work the whole of Saturday rather than just Saturday morning, in January 1919 IIM mooted the possibility of holding 'Supplementary Sunday Services'. After lengthy consideration, the LJS Organising Committee decided to endorse his suggestion despite fears that the LJS might be laying itself open to 'misunderstanding and unjust criticism' from Anglo-Jewry.[44]

The LJS Council ratified the proposal, and early in 1920 Sunday services commenced in the Mortimer Hall near Regent Street. They were later transferred to the synagogue when the new building opened in St John's Wood Road in 1925 (see below).[45] The Sunday services included very little liturgy and consisted mainly of biblical readings chosen to complement a speech or discussion given after the service. There was neither music, nor a choir, and the ark was not opened. The ambience was more homiletic and academic than celebratory. After the service IIM talked on contemporary issues or invited prominent public figures, some of whom were not Jewish, to give addresses. Advance notice of the topics to be covered at the Sunday services was posted in the *New Statesman*. This may partly have been the result of IIM's desire to attract non-Jews, but it was also through necessity, for in the early years of their existence, some Jewish publications refused to publish details of the services because of opposition to them.

IIM's talks were often followed by question-and-answer sessions, with the younger members of the synagogue acting as 'runners' to bring written questions for IIM to answer from the *bimah*.[46] The post-service sessions were very informal with IIM taking off his gown and biretta before answering questions.[47] These were sometimes so numerous that IIM was only able to deal with a fraction of them.[48] The subjects IIM covered at the Sunday services were often quite controversial and drew large audiences of over 1,000 people, including a large proportion of non-Jews, which led to them becoming an arena for interfaith dialogue. There were no events quite like them in either the Jewish or non-Jewish religious communities. The Sunday services were also attended by large numbers of Orthodox Jews who reportedly were 'proud to have heard Mattuck speak'.[49] IIM went to great lengths to stress that the Sunday services were additional to Sabbath services and should be regarded as weekday services.

Once they were firmly established, IIM's addresses were widely reported in both the Jewish and non-Jewish press.[50] A frequent topic was contemporary literature and plays dealing with political and philosophical issues, which he discussed from a Liberal Jewish point of view. In general he found the writings and addresses of the period unduly miserable:

> It is well-nigh impossible to take up any recently published book without finding in it some forebodings on the future of civilisation or a reference to such forebodings in somebody else. The panaceas are many – from anti-waste clamourings to the preaching of new psychologies and new religions. The condition cannot better be described than in the old simile, 'like a sheep without a shepherd' or in the description applied by a prophet to a smaller world: 'Ephraim is like a silly dove'.[51]

IIM cited the works of authors throughout the world, but he commented most frequently on the writings of H.G. Wells and George Bernard Shaw, because they were having a significant impact on public attitudes. He took issue with Shaw's rejection of political democracy, for example. Commenting on *The Apple Cart* and *Back to Methuselah*, IIM said scathingly, 'Unless I am greatly mistaken, Mr Shaw never did believe in Political democracy but in government by an oligarchy composed of experts ... he would give the role to sanitary engineers'.[52] IIM was not blind to the shortcomings and failings of democracy, but he continued to believe that the world was a better place because of the existence of democracy and to defend it against the alternatives advocated by H.G. Wells:

> Mr Wells in 'William Clissold' and other books wants the management of the whole world entrusted to a group of men like the late Lord Melchett ... science and business to constitute a combination for regulating the lives of nations; and by science he means the technical sciences only, and by business he means factories and shops. Now, if life meant only manufacture and consumption, that method might be a good one, if we had some infallible mark that would reveal with perfect precision who the scientific business man or commercial scientist were who would be best for the job. But since there is no such mark, I suppose we should have to ask the people about it or parliament, or something like that which would be contaminated by the original sin of democracy.[53]

The Sunday services displayed the extent of IIM's scholarship and just how widely read he was. He was increasingly recognised as a man of great intellect, reflected in his increasing involvement in English universities, especially Oxford[54] and Cambridge Universities, the University of London and Manchester University,[55] in all of which there was by now a significant Jewish undergraduate presence. In November 1920 IIM was invited to give a paper to the Schechter Society in Cambridge on 'Judaism and the Future',[56] and in February 1921 he lectured at the London University Students' Union on Liberal Judaism and the Future'.[57] The event was presided over by Maurice Perlzweig, who was soon to become well known to IIM.

IIM's growing prominence as a religious leader and an intellectual force led to many invitations to speak at events organised by both Jewish and non-Jewish organisations such as the City Temple Literary Society, where in December 1920 he made a 'lasting impression' with his talk on 'Religion and Democracy',[58] and where his talk in February 1922 on 'The World's Work and the Individual' resulted in 'a chorus of approval'.[59] Three years later he was invited back to the Literary Society to give an address on 'An Old Solution for some Modern Problems'.[60]

As well as speaking on theological issues, IIM was in demand as a speaker on wider Jewish themes. In June 1920 he addressed the Jewish Historical Society at Toynbee Hall on 'The Settlement of the Jews in America'.[61] This lecture was very long and meticulously researched.[62] IIM also spoke at meetings of bodies as disparate as the Hampstead Jewish Literary and Philharmonic Society,[63] the Adler Society at Oxford,[64] the Wesleyan College in Richmond,[65] the Indian Students' Union,[66] and Mr Rocke's Working Men's Club.[67]

IIM was now writing more frequently in the Jewish press, both in England and in America. A number of his articles and letters were published in the *Jewish Guardian,* which was the official proponent of Progressive Judaism in England.[68] His articles published in America included, 'Judaism and the Belief in Progress' (*Menorah Journal*, February 1922), 'Judaism in England' (*American Hebrew*, October 1929) and 'America Revisited' (*American Israelite*, October 1929).[69]

With increasing frequency, IIM wrote in the non-Jewish press on both Jewish and more general issues, such as his 1927 article in the *Westminster Gazette* on 'A Philosophy for Worry', in which he advocated religious belief as a means for facing worries calmly and courageously,[70] his article on 'Marriage and Divorce', which appeared in the *Daily Express* in September 1929, and his article on 'Moneylending and Moneylenders', published in *John Bull* on 7 July 1925.[71] He became a frequent contributor to *The Spectator* (his article on 'Back to Moses or Have We Outlived the Laws of Moses' was published in May 1926, and 'Liberal Judaism and the Modern State' was published in May 1926, for example)[72] as well as to publications with a more limited circulation, such as *The Outline*, which published his article on 'What Jews Believe' in February 1928.[73]

New Congregations

IIM continued to devote significant time to advancing Liberal Judaism and founding new Liberal communities. During the 1920s, he supported the embryonic community in Finsbury and Highbury – which later became the North London Liberal Synagogue based in Belfast Road in Stamford Hill – and the developing West End Central section of the JRU. The North London Liberal Synagogue was consecrated by IIM in April 1927 with much ceremony, it being only the second Liberal synagogue in Britain. In 1928 the West End section of the JRU, which had been holding meetings and services for many years, became a full congregation – the West Central Liberal Synagogue. IIM was also very prominent in establishing the Liberal communities in Liverpool (formally constituted in 1928), and the South London Liberal Jewish Synagogue, which held its first service in Streatham in 1929. During 1929 IIM sought the help of his brothers George and Bernard in identifying a suitable minister for the new Liverpool congregation. The man eventually appointed was Rabbi Morris Goldstein, whom George had been to see preaching in his pulpit in Niagara Falls.[74]

Renewed Criticism

The period following the First World War was a time of great anxiety for the Anglo-Jewish community because of the outbreak of a wave of anti-Semitism. Jewish status suffered during the war, partly as a result of the controversy over the conscription of Jews who were not naturalised,[75] but even more damaging were events in Eastern Europe. The involvement of Jews, albeit Jews who had left Judaism, in the leadership of the Bolshevik Party and their association with the brutal assassination of the Russian imperial family led to a widely held belief in the existence of a Jewish conspiracy to destabilise the Western world. Attacks against Jews regularly appeared in leading newspapers such as *The Times* and even the most assimilated Jews came under suspicion. Instead of uniting the Anglo-Jewish community, there was great dissension on the correct response and under the pressure of hostility the communal solidarity that had existed during the war soon waned. In the post-war years IIM was faced with again having to defend himself, the LJS and the Liberal Jewish movement against a fresh onslaught of criticism. In March 1919 the *Jewish Chronicle* published a lengthy article penned by IIM, 'Liberal Judaism and its Critics', in which he explained the philosophical basis of Liberal Judaism.[76] The article provoked many months of largely disparaging correspondence to the newspaper.

IIM was outspoken on proposals for a Jewish war memorial scheme to mark the end of hostilities. The scheme involved moving Jews' College to either Oxford or Cambridge University, fostering religious education and improving the status of Jewish ministers. IIM's criticism was that the proposals excluded the Liberal Jewish wing of Anglo-Jewry. His views were articulated in a sermon given at the LJS in December 1919 and subsequently reproduced in the *Jewish Chronicle* in juxtaposition to the more positive attitude of the West London Synagogue to the communal scheme.[77] IIM asserted that 'mere honesty' prevented the participation of Liberal Judaism in the scheme. His opinions again led to a great deal of correspondence and heated controversy. Deadlock was reached on the form that the war memorial should take and, in the event, the scheme failed to materialise.[78]

As members of the LJS Organising Committee had predicted, IIM was lambasted by some of his critics for intending to shift Sabbath to a Sunday when he established his Sunday services, and despite his ever-increasing prominence, he was not universally welcomed as a speaker. His talk on 'Citizenship and Religion', scheduled to take place in Leeds Town Hall on February 1924 was cancelled due to the objections of Orthodox congregations in the city (described as a *force majeure*), who had taken the advice of the Chief Rabbi.[79] However, IIM was made more welcome in nearby Bradford; on the afternoon of 11 May 1924 he spoke at the Reform congregation on 'Judaism and the Future' and in the evening he gave an address on 'The Jew as a Citizen' at a public meeting held at the Masonic Hall.[80]

While IIM was largely able to deal with the barrage of criticism against him, it did sometimes lead him to doubt himself, and sapped his energy. Montefiore frequently tried to offer his reassurance. On one occasion he wrote to IIM saying, 'Jones may criticise this small thing, Smith that, Robinson the other, but Smith, Jones, Robinson and CGM and all love you and honour you very much. Do not be over sensitive. Few ministers are more respected and loved than you.'[81] IIM's efforts were also bolstered by praise from Israel Abrahams:

> I wish so much to express our indebtedness to you, to your talents, your addresses, your sincerity and your whole personality. It was a fortunate hour for us when you sacrificed a brilliant career in America to take on the leadership of a small and doubtful experiment. You

> have turned it into a big and assured accomplishment. Judaism in England owes more to you than any of us can repay.[82]

Noting IIM's flagging spirit, during 1924 a 'well-meaning' member of the LJS sent him a cheque as a contribution towards a holiday, which IIM gracefully refused.[83]

Notwithstanding the attacks on him, or perhaps because of them, in December 1926, IIM preached a long sermon on 'Jewish Differences and Jewish Unity',[84] in which he declared 'Diversity is the heritage of our tribe'. To IIM the differences between Jews – Orthodox or Progressive, Zionists or non-Zionists – were real and important. He challenged those who tried to hide Jewish differences of opinion, whom he suspected were ashamed of their part in them.[85] However, he maintained that differing views did not destroy the 'unity of Israel', and rejected Jewish unity based on a 'sloppy sentimentality, which can melt all sorts of contradictions and opposites'.[86] Nevertheless, he admitted he did not always find Jewish unity easy:

> I do not like all Jews; and I am not going to pretend that I do. I do not like all non-Jews, but those I do not like have no interest for me. But in the case of the Jews, even though I do not like them, they have an interest for me. They make me uncomfortable and even ashamed. But in spite of all that, they are my fellow-Jews; because the unity of Israel is a dynamic fact. It is something that exists; and upon it depends the power of Israel. The Jew feels his relation to other Jews, that feeling is part of his Jewishness. From its presence in individual Jews, the House of Israel draws its strength.[87]

The Move to St John's Wood

By the early 1920s membership of the LJS was more than double the number of seats available in the synagogue[88] and visitors from all over the world regularly attended its services. On one Saturday morning in 1920 for example, the congregation included people from America, Canada, New Zealand and Russia.[89] As early as 1916, IIM had identified the need for a 'second minister' at the LJS. He sought the assistance of HUC, Stephen Wise and Leo Wise, publisher of the *American Israelite*,[90] in identifying possible candidates, but none of those he approached proved willing to cross the Atlantic,[91] and it was to be several years before IIM was able to obtain the support he needed to lead the growing congregation. The Reverend Maurice Perlzweig, whose career at the LJS will be explored further below, was appointed in 1921 and the American rabbi, Solomon Starrels, was appointed in 1928.[92] Starrels trained at HUC and, like IIM before him, became the rabbi at the South Street Synagogue in Lincoln, Nebraska. He came to London for the inaugural conference of the World Union for Progressive Judaism in 1926 (see below) where he met IIM, which influenced his decision to move to London.

With a move to larger premises now a priority, a Building Committee was set up to conduct the search. Attempts to find a building that could be converted into a synagogue were fruitless and the LJS Council therefore decided to construct purpose-built premises. A suitable site was eventually identified in St John's Wood Road opposite the Grace Gates of Lord's Cricket Ground.[93] Although he was diffident about fundraising, IIM spearheaded a building appeal amongst the synagogue's membership that raised enough money (£40,000) within a year to finance most of the new building. According to his daughter, Dorothy, IIM 'almost worked himself to death over collecting the money for it'.[94] The fundraising activities included a dinner held at the Savoy in April 1923 at which IIM presided, causing much merriment by opening his after-dinner speech with an anecdote about being rebuked by Claude Montefiore (himself a 'calligraphic sinner') for his poor handwriting. According to IIM, Montefiore had sent him a letter addressed to the Reverend B. Kettle saying 'If one Mattuck lives near you, will you please tell him he writes a wretched handwriting'. The letter was signed 'B. Pot'.[95]

IIM was fully involved in the design and layout of the new building. He saw it as an opportunity to realise his ambitions for the development of synagogue life until then circumscribed by the inadequate premises at Hill Street, which IIM described as 'stifling' and 'depressing'.[96] He decided that there should be space for 'every possible congregational activity' and gathered around him men and women who could help him achieve his 'great scheme'.[97] The new synagogue, then by far the largest in London, was 'quite a novelty' and created a sensation in the Anglo-Jewish community.[98] It had seating for nearly 1,500, a hall for congregational activities (named the Montefiore Hall), offices and dedicated classroom accommodation. It was equipped with a state-of-the-art organ. Montefiore laid the foundation stone in January 1925. The sermon that IIM preached at the consecration service on 13 September 1925 sought to strike a balance between thankfulness and hope, but also challenged the congregation to further endeavour. IIM was clearly moved by the occasion:

> In the simple, the almost austere beauty of this Synagogue, I feel a token of our faith. It has for us the beauty of simplicity, and it is austere in the demands that it makes. All religion when, true to

> itself, calls for the best that men can give, shows itself austere. The beauty, which is simple to austerity, like the beauty of a sunlit mountain, that is the beauty of our religion; and I feel its presence here.[99]

IIM received many letters of congratulation from various colleagues and friends and from many organisations in Britain and elsewhere, especially America, including from a large number of Reform rabbis.[100] Interestingly, before the new synagogue was opened, IIM wrote to Kaufmann Kohler, now Honorary President of CCAR, encouraging him to write formally to congratulate him at the time of the dedication service.[101] It is not clear why he should feel the need to do this; perhaps he was seeking to emphasise his continuing links with the Reform Movement in America.

Following the move to St John's Wood, discussion groups, a drama society and educational activities were all established, as well as study groups led by IIM.[102] In promoting the role of the synagogue as a centre for community life, IIM was breaking new ground in Britain, but was following developments taking place in Reform synagogues in America. When visiting there in 1927 (see later mention), IIM wrote an article for the *American Hebrew*, in which he praised with enthusiasm those synagogues that were encompassing 'all forms of social activity', describing these 'Synagogue-Centres' as 'the central institution of American Jewish life'.[103]

Social Issues

We have seen that IIM declared his support for the working man soon after his arrival at the LJS. During the war he gave a number of sermons that demonstrated his support for the various social reforms then being considered, such as the introduction of a minimum wage, the establishment of industrial pensions and the maintenance of widows and their children by the state, all of which he saw as consonant with Jewish teachings.[104] Particularly potent were his calls for state action to be taken to address the high infant mortality rates that existed in certain areas. In June 1917 he opened a sermon dedicated to this topic with a reference to the prophet Elijah asking of the Shunammite woman (II Kings 4:26) 'Is it well with the child?'.[105] He then noted that over 28 per cent of under-fives had died between 1911 and 1914, a death rate that was higher than that of British soldiers in France. He deplored the fact that many infant deaths occurred as the result of avoidable infections due to overcrowded and unsanitary housing. He denounced greedy landlords who continued to let 'hovels' that had been condemned by the London County Council.

He was ashamed that some of these landlords were Jewish, commenting scathingly that they had no right to call themselves good Jews.[106]

During the 1920s when the dislocation caused by the war led to a prolonged economic depression, IIM applied prophetic ethics more directly and radically to social issues such as housing, education, industrial unrest and unemployment. By this time CCAR had adopted a 'declaration of principles', and had set up a Commission on Social Justice. IIM's pronouncements were very much in line with the CCAR platform. He felt that the time for 'leisurely' discussion of social reorganisation had now passed; the war and its consequences had made social reform 'acutely necessary'.[107] While he was not totally convinced by calls for increased wages for working people, he was emphatic in his support for changes that would restore dignity to the lives of the 'industrial classes'. With passion he preached:

> The labourer has become in very many cases but an adjunct of the machine. Individuality is destroyed. One man may work more quickly than another, or take care of more machines, but one man's production will be as like another's as two machines are alike. Modern industrial methods have crushed personality and individuality out of work. Society may be the gainer through increased production and greater efficiency; but the working man has lost what is most valuable to any human being, the sense of doing something that is distinctly his own.[108]

IIM was determined to confront the LJS congregation with the harsh realities of life and seemingly ignored the desires of those whom he perceived 'come to public worship with a desire for removal from the affairs of the world to the point of forgetfulness'.[109] In October 1920 IIM reminded his listeners that the ten shillings a week being demanded by coal miners was more than simply a wage; it represented food, clothing, education and enjoyment. As a direct challenge to the class-conscious members of the LJS he preached:

> And some who did not know before have learned since the war when they found themselves more and more working in social and governmental affairs side by side with just ordinary working men. … I cannot help feeling that many of us – perhaps without really knowing it – form our judgment with a feeling that the working man is an inferior being – less reasonable, and perhaps even less civilised than ourselves! Fairness requires that we see them for what they are – human beings quite like ourselves! That may be good, bad, or

> indifferent – but the same natures, desires, reasons work in all of us and we all respond to the same ideals.[110]

IIM felt most strongly that people had the right to work and he had an almost idealised view of labour and the working man as shown by an anecdote contained in one of his sermons:

> Some time ago I was on a railway carriage, when I noticed one of my neighbours, a man, who by his appearances belonged to what you call the working classes, nimbly working at something he had in his hand. My curiosity was aroused. I had seen people reading newspapers in railway carriages, I had seen and even heard some talking, and at times sleeping, but I don't think I had ever seen anybody doing real work in a railway carriage. This man was evidently doing so, and on a Sunday afternoon, too. Well curiosity is aroused to be satisfied, so first I looked and then asked. He had brought with him in his pocket, evidently he carried about with him, all the time, bits of leather torn, and a kind of awl or needle, and he was making little leather purses. 'Do you make your living by this sort of work' I impertinently asked. 'Oh no', said he, 'I am a carpenter, but I do this in my odd moments for the fun of it. I give these purses, sometimes I make bags, to a friend, or a charity bazaar or things of that sort'. Suppose the author of Ecclesiastes had asked that man what profit he had in his labour, he would have smiled into the questioner's glum face and with a good-natured laugh have answered, 'for the fun of it'.[111]

Contemplating the high unemployment of the early 1920s and the failure of various governmental measures to abate it, he said 'the problem is grave, grave to the point of being terrible'.[112] In a sermon delivered later in the year, he described with great pathos his feelings on coming into contact with unemployed people:

> One of the most touching things that I have seen in recent years was the march of the unemployed along Oxford Street. Here, surrounded by all the signs of a pleasurable activity, of an eager and happy pursuit of things needed for living, the small group of men walked on in sombre, almost stern silence. No roll of drums or sound of trumpet to announce their coming, but only the monotonous tramp, tramp of their feet, which only heightened the serious effect. One inscription stood out prominently, and that was an improvised one which bore the words, 'we demand the right to work'.[113]

He felt particularly strongly about unemployment because many of those without work were men who had recently served their country during the war.[114] IIM cared not just about the impact of unemployment on individuals and their families, but also its effect on social wellbeing – the fracturing of relationships between employers and employees, between those employed and those not employed. To IIM the labour disputes of the early 1920s suggested that both workers and owners were often selfish advocates of their own particular collective interest and were not influenced by the religious principle of the common good and the advancement of society. He perceived the time was ripe for state intervention.[115]

IIM returned to this subject a year later during an engineering dispute, suggesting a new way of understanding industry other than the existing dichotomy between the creation of profit and wealth (capitalism) or earning wages (socialism). He called for a religious understanding of the joint venture between owners and workers for the common good and commended a religious or social conception of industry as a joint undertaking with joint responsibility and sharing of power that would satisfy 'natural longing for freedom'.[116] In his sermons and addresses IIM did not explicitly favour socialism or directly attack the capitalist system. However, as early as 1914 he had declared: 'It is undoubtedly true that men of property and wealth owe more to society than those of their fellows who are less well off in the matter of material possessions', and that taxation is not 'taking from one class to give to another, but is taking from those who are deriving most benefits from society ... not a tax but an investment.'[117]

During the 1920s IIM's political perspectives discernibly moved left and he became one of the most left-leaning religious leaders in the country. This was illustrated not only by his views on unemployment, but also by the views that he expressed when housing became a prominent electoral issue at the end of 1922 and as the Housing Bill went through Parliament in 1923. He told the LJS congregation that, due to a major shortage of housing, people were living crowded into one or two rooms 'very much as pigs [are] huddled in the sty or sheep herded in the fold'.[118] The problem was not limited to the lack of housing, but also 'the character' of the housing available. Many houses were, he said, 'unfit for human habitation'. He was concerned not just with the health implications of dilapidated housing but also its possible impact on morality. He asked the congregation to:

> Imagine the case of a young woman living under these conditions. She has to work all day. When she returns in the evening there is no place where she can sit down to rest quietly; there is no place where she can have a friend with her all to herself. Can she be blamed if she

> prefers the glamour of the street life and the freedom of the pavements to such a home? Can we blame her if she dares to face its dangers and the temptation of the streets in order that she might escape from the stuffy, disturbing, cheerless, turbid atmosphere of such a home? And if you prove too weak in the face of these temptations, can she be altogether blamed?[119]

He argued forcefully for state intervention to 'remedy the evil' of the housing problem,[120] and challenged those who suggested that people who could not afford to provide their own home should take what they were given, arguing that the working man not only had a right to a home but to a decent home so that he might take a pride in it and gain self-respect.[121]

IIM was greatly relieved when the Government decided to reject the proposals put forward by the Geddes Committee on how savings might be made in expenditure on education. He had objected particularly to the committee's suggestions that teacher salaries should be reduced and that education should be curtailed for children of infant school age. He argued that teachers were already underpaid and their worth inestimable:

> For who can measure the worth of influences which pass from the teacher to children? How much do we owe to the men or women, who mixed with the influences in our homes, revealed to our sleeping eyes the greatness and wonders of the world, or to our wondering minds the places and in literature and history where they might find the best proof, or to our almost unconscious hearts bring forces, which stimulate them to noble hope and varying endeavour.[122]

IIM felt that it was 'almost ludicrous' that the 'committee of businessmen' (the Geddes Committee) had argued that, since children who had attended an infant school seemed to be no further intellectually developed than those who had not, infant school education should be discontinued. He contended that the purpose of education was not only to develop children intellectually, but also to shape their moral outlook and imagination and that this latter task was a vital ingredient of early years education. If the committee had measured the moral and physical good resulting from infant education they would have come to a very different conclusion.[123] While IIM admitted that expenditure on higher education was harder to defend to the taxpayer, he argued that free higher education should nonetheless be made available for the general good of society and particularly to ensure that children from the poorest families could have the opportunity to be educated: 'There are few things in the world more pitiable, I think, than a young man or woman desiring education and unable to get it. Next to being hungry and without food, this is perhaps the saddest sight.'[124] IIM probably realised that his arguments were likely to be understood by his Jewish audience, but they were all the more forceful because they contained strong hints of his own experience – the jeopardy in which his own higher education had on occasion been placed due to a lack of income (see Chapter Five).

Montefiore did not always share IIM's views on social issues but, in his open-minded way, was usually willing for both sides of any question to be put before the LJS congregation.[125] IIM's comments on the miners' strike in 1920[126] appear to have been received without demur, but the sermon that he gave on the General Strike of May 1926, in which he described the miners' strike as a 'lock out',[127] was too contentious even for Montefiore. Although IIM had stated in his sermon that he was disturbed by the power of organised labour demonstrated by the General Strike and had prayed for national unity,[128] Montefiore, via Mr Duparc, suggested that IIM should temper the political content of his sermons. IIM is reported as having been disturbed by Montefiore's comments.[129] However, he remained resolute[130] and went on to preach twice in the same year on the issues involved in the 'Mines Dispute'. He was perhaps thinking of his own position when he staunchly defended the Christian bishops who had been criticised for commenting on the dispute.[131]

IIM regretted that the miners had rejected the report of the Coal Commission because they (the coal miners) had not been given any guarantee that mine owners would implement the Commission's conclusions regarding the reorganisation of the industry, and was saddened by the mutual hostility between the two sides involved in the dispute. Nevertheless, his sympathies were clearly with the miners:

> It is an economic fight, but the economic position of one side is immeasurably stronger than the economic position of the other side. While the pits lie idle, the coal owners are losing profits, they are also in danger of losing the capital which the pit represents, but they are not in danger of losing their daily bread; whereas the miner is not only losing his present wages – the loss of these wages may mean to him partial or complete starvation. It is, therefore, strife between unevenly matched sides and religion must answer whether this is not the time for the utmost exercise of its function to support the weak.[132]

IIM condemned those who, through 'the blindness due to class prejudice',[133] failed to recognise the weak bargaining position of the miners. He was acutely aware of the impact that the dispute was having on wider society and called for the setting up of a body that could arbitrate in future industrial disputes to overcome the disbenefits for the community that resulted from the adversarial nature of collective bargaining.[134]

Montefiore's latitude reached its limits five years later, when IIM preached on the subject of communism,[135] which Montefiore considered a wholly unsuitable topic for a synagogue sermon. On this occasion Montefiore spoke with IIM directly about the matter in strong terms. IIM's response was to dictate his letter of resignation.[136] After a long discussion, the letter was withdrawn. IIM had made his point about the principle of rabbinic freedom to which he was so much committed but, as we shall see, the matter had not yet been laid to rest.

In 1929 IIM instigated and personally oversaw the collection of money and clothes for the coal miners,[137] and in the four months leading up to the General Election of that year, IIM again defended his right to speak out on issues of the day following a leading article in *The Times*, in which it was suggested that ministers should confine themselves to stirring feelings of piety and goodwill and not involve themselves in economic and political matters. While recognising the necessity of avoiding party prejudice, he argued:

> In the election we are facing there are several issues, which reveal how great the duty lies on religion and its spokesmen to consider political questions. There is, first and foremost, the problem of unemployment, an economic problem it would seem, but only on paper. No one faced to their face [sic] with the unemployed themselves would think it an economic problem. If we could see the unemployed miner with his family living in a poverty whose gloom is unrelieved by hope, unless we are ourselves much less than human we should not think of him and his family as an economic problem but as a human problem. And let us remember that unemployment does more than deprive men, women and children of their means of living, it deprives them of their life, their moral stamina, their spiritual self-respect, their dignity. To the materialist these things may mean nothing, to religion they mean everything, and therefore religion is prepared to say: I allow the value of economics in dealing with unemployment but I cannot leave to economics the last word.[138]

He saw unemployment as the pivotal electoral issue and advised the congregation to vote for the candidate they could most trust to help the unemployed.[139]

IIM and Maurice Perlzweig

In 1921 Maurice Perlzweig became the 'second minister' at the LJS. The son of the eminent Ukrainian cantor, Asher Perlzweig, he graduated from London University in 1921 and embarked on postgraduate historical research at University College at the same time as being employed to carry out bibliographical work for an American university.[140] He came to Montefiore's attention as the result of his involvement in various Anglo-Jewish organisations. Perlzweig was to become the first Liberal rabbi to be trained in England. Since there was no seminary for training Progressive rabbis, an ad hoc arrangement was established whereby Perlzweig was employed by the LJS, which paid for his tuition at Christ College, Cambridge, where he studied what was then termed 'Oriental languages'. He also received regular tuition from Israel Abrahams, Reader in Rabbinic Studies at Christ College.[141] In return for his tuition fees and a small stipend, Perlzweig preached on Saturday mornings at the LJS. He also preached on Saturday afternoons for the embryonic North London Liberal congregation and taught at the LJS Religion School on a Sunday morning. On his graduation from Cambridge in 1924 he was ordained as Associate Minister at the LJS and took the title of 'Reverend'.[142]

Since Perlzweig was one of the leaders of the Zionist movement in England and IIM was profoundly non-Zionist, it is often assumed that tensions between the two men arose from their opposing views. However, it appears that their differing opinions were not the only cause of dissension between them. While acknowledging that IIM had stated publicly that Perlzweig was to be given freedom of the pulpit as far as his views were concerned,[143] Perlzweig later questioned the veracity of IIM's pledge, saying that 'whenever a chink appeared which enabled Mattuck to weaken my position in a bad light, he would do so'.[144] Perlzweig also claimed that IIM had tried to prevent the publication of a pamphlet that he (Perlzweig) and Claude Montefiore had penned to show how Zionism and anti-Zionism could coexist under the umbrella of Liberal Judaism,[145] *Why the Jewish Religious Union Can Be, and Justifiably is 'Neutral' on Zionism.*[146] Perlzweig attributed the acrimony between himself and IIM to the fact that IIM had imported from America 'some of the bitterness of the struggle ... between Zionists and anti-Zionists'.[147]

However, many years later, when IIM was approached by the Chief Rabbi, Dr Hertz, to give his views on Perlzweig (who had applied for the position of rabbi of the congregation in Far Rockaway, where IIM had started his career),[148] IIM disclosed to Hertz that his real concerns related to Perlzweig's 'tendency to neglect his congregational duties' and his 'lack of an appropriate sense of responsibility', for which he had rebuked him on several occasions.[149] He mentioned some of Perlzweig's virtues but concluded his assessment by saying that Perlzweig was 'able, likeable, plausible and unreliable', and also 'a careerist, without any profound regard for principles'.[150]

Anti-Zionism

A petition by the English Zionist Federation (EZF) to the Peace Conference in 1919, asking for the implementation of the Balfour Declaration 'to reconstitute Palestine as [the Jews'] national home' was signed by 77,000 Jews in the United Kingdom out of a total Jewish population of around 300,000.[151] The Zionist movement grew significantly after the announcement of the British Mandate for Palestine in 1920 and the appointment of Herbert Samuel as the High Commissioner, which had captured the imagination of a large number of British Jews. Membership of the EZF rose from 4,000 in 1917 to over 30,000 in 1921. Even the traditional Jewish communal organisations were not immune to this sea change. From 17 June 1917 Zionists started to percolate the Board of Deputies and began to condemn the anti-Zionism of the old ruling elite.[152]

Faced with this rising tide of Zionism, IIM voiced his misgivings about Jewish nationalism more forcefully and more regularly. He was relieved at the end of the war when, as he saw it, the Balfour Declaration was 'reduced so that national homeland came to mean only an economic agency whose sole function to its brethren was to help in the economic restoration of the country'.[153] In May 1919 he invited Mr Michael Green to the LJS to give a lecture on 'The Claims of the League of British Jews', at the end of which IIM said that he had some sympathy for the 'non-Zionist' perspective of the league, which had been set up in 1917 by Claude Montefiore and others to counter the Zionist claim that 'the Jew is an alien in the land of his birth'.[154]

IIM's supportive comments attracted negative reports in the Jewish press.[155] However, it is interesting to note that IIM does not appear to have become closely associated with the league and in one editorial of the *JRU Bulletin* he openly questioned its stance in denying the solidarity of the Jewish people.[156] Unlike Montefiore and his colleagues who emphasised their British citizenship, thereby setting themselves apart from the immigrants from Eastern Europe, IIM's objection to Zionism was that it threatened the religious content of Jewish life and interfered with the universal message of the Jews. IIM was also uncomfortable with the fact that Eastern European Jews were excluded from the League.[157] His unease sprang from the fear that, if the new generation of Eastern European Jews were not engaged with others, they would increasingly be drawn into sectarian rather than observation-based movements.

IIM objected strongly to an article that appeared in *The Times* in May 1920 in which it was stated by the newspaper's Washington correspondent that 90 per cent of Jewish people in America were Zionists. IIM's letter to the editor correcting this assertion concluded by saying that, as a result of a recent visit to America, he was convinced that the main body of American Jewry was 'out of sympathy' with Zionism.[158] Later that year a lengthy article by IIM on 'Palestine and Judaism' was published in the American publication *Emanu-El*. In this article he 'confessed' that he could see value in a Jewish state if it were to be run according to the social ideals of Judaism. However, he could not perceive that this was a possibility, since no Jewish state was yet being mooted and Palestine's limited capacity for receiving immigrants meant that Jews would always be in a minority; more was to be gained for Judaism by Jews living throughout the world.[159]

During the 1920s, British policy in relation to Palestine was relatively uncontroversial, and responses to it were mainly confined to the WZO now based in London. The Board of Deputies at this time was still officially non-Zionist; it gave its general support to the Mandate, but was not deeply involved in furthering the advance of the Jewish national home. When the Churchill White Paper of 1922 rejected the idea of imposing a Jewish state on the inhabitants of Palestine, anti-Zionists felt able to cooperate with Zionists in the development of Palestine. The Jewish Agency was established for the purpose of advising and cooperating with the Administration of Palestine on which both Zionists and non-Zionists sat. IIM now predicted (wrongly):

> The Jews have not got Palestine as their homeland and it is as unlikely as ever that they will ever have it. The Jewish nation has not been re-established in the land which was once their home, and it is not likely that it will ever be established.[160]

Although he hoped fervently that political Zionism was now dead,[161] he kept himself well informed about happenings regarding Palestine and Zionist organisations and for several years his 'Commentaries' in the *JRU Bulletin* (then the *Liberal Jewish Monthly*) were preoccupied with such matters. Every Zionist conference received full comment, with IIM going into great detail on the internal politics of the Zionist movement. From time to time, IIM preached on Zionism and commented on developments in both the Jewish and non-Jewish press. For example, during 1926 he voiced his opinions on the 'Crimea Project', which involved the settlement of Russian Jews as farmers on a large tract of land in the Crimea. IIM condemned the lukewarm welcome given to the project by Zionists in general, and by Stephen Wise in particular, whom he felt were placing their 'nationalist ambitions' before the needs of impoverished Russian Jews.[162]

However, overall his sermons displayed a balanced assessment of the interests of the Jews, the Arabs and the British authorities. It was to be almost another five years before there were to be major developments on which he felt impelled to comment with vigour and at length.

IIM and the Chief Rabbi

In 1925 Chief Rabbi Hertz shunned IIM by not inviting him to attend a conference of Anglo-Jewish preachers that he had convened, despite the fact that IIM was a member of the Preachers' Union. The majority of the union's members felt that the Chief Rabbi was acting ultra vires in not extending an invitation to IIM, but Hertz was apparently resolute in his decision to exclude him. Muted criticism of the Chief Rabbi's action appeared in the *Jewish Chronicle*.[163] However, the *Jewish Guardian* was more damning of Hertz and published a large number of letters of protest at the speech that he gave at the beginning of the conference, in which he accused the leaders of Liberal Judaism, including IIM, of 'joining hands with the maligners of the Jewish People in the campaign of anti-Semitism against the Jewish method of slaughter.'[164] IIM shrugged off his exclusion from the Preachers' Conference[165] as a 'matter on which I feel no personal concern', commenting pithily that it would have been enough if Hertz had simply said 'I do not like Liberal Jews!'[166]

Following the Preachers' Conference, the Chief Rabbi went on to deliver even harsher criticisms in a series of three sermons he preached in December 1925 and January 1926. He attacked Liberal Judaism as 'a rebellion against the Jewish faith'.[167] According to IIM, the sermons 'combined fair criticisms with appeals to prejudice',[168] and gave an impression of Liberal Judaism designed to deter people from joining the movement. In Hertz's opinion, Liberal Judaism would lead to Christianity and he used his often-quoted description of Liberal Judaism as 'a moving staircase carrying those, who have taken their stand on it, out of Judaism'.[169] On behalf of the JRU, IIM responded to the attacks by submitting to the Jewish press a sharp but effective reply. Although his response largely consisted of a statement of facts about Liberal Judaism, and he made no attempt to argue with the Chief Rabbi's opinions, he did raise some trenchant questions about Dr Hertz's motivations:

> What did Dr Hertz mean to achieve by his rather violent attack on Liberal Judaism? Did he mean merely to do some damage to the Liberal Jewish movement or to the Liberal Jewish Synagogue? That would have been un-Jewish. Did he mean to strengthen the cause of Orthodox Judaism? It seems most inadequate to do so by denouncing Liberal Judaism. Or did he mean to give a warning against the

dangers of joining a Liberal Jewish congregation. What then is a Jew to do who does not believe in some of the teachings of Orthodox Judaism? ... The weakness of the attack on Liberal Judaism shows the strength of Liberal Judaism.[170]

The Spectator Controversy

When the *Jewish Chronicle* leader writer praised the Chief Rabbi's attacks, there were no letters in defence of Liberal Judaism; IIM was obviously seeking to avoid an undignified quarrel with Hertz. However, the following year IIM became embroiled in another bitter and damaging disagreement within Anglo-Jewry – what has been referred to as the '*Spectator* controversy'.[171]

By the mid-1920s, IIM was writing regularly in the national press. Many of his articles and letters increased support for the LJS and for the Liberal Jewish movement, but also gave rise to howls of protest from the more Orthodox sections of the Jewish community. IIM's article, 'Liberal Judaism in the Modern State', which appeared in *The Spectator* in October 1926 and in which he maintained that being a Jew was a matter of religion, not of race or nationalism, proved to be particularly controversial. The article was misinterpreted by a number of readers, including by Maurice Perlzweig at the LJS,[172] who thought that IIM was saying that an Orthodox Jew must either be inconsistent in religion or disloyal to his country. The Chief Rabbi wrote a letter of complaint to *The Spectator* the following week, and IIM subsequently replied that not only had he not made such a statement, but quoted a passage from his article to show that he had said the exact opposite.

The Press Committee of the Board of Deputies did not wait until IIM's rebuttal was published before writing to him rebuking him for his article, saying that it could be made use of as a weapon in the hands of anti-Semites by throwing doubt on the loyalty of the great number of Jews in England. IIM sent the Press Committee a curt reply in which he said that the Committee's censure did not in any way alter his views.[173] The Press Committee referred the matter to a full meeting of the Board of Deputies, where there was 'a heated discussion'[174] during which IIM was condemned even though most delegates had not read either the original article or IIM's letter of reply to the Chief Rabbi.[175] The Council of the LJS issued a statement expressing its undiminished confidence in IIM.[176]

IIM was apparently undaunted by these differences of opinion with the Chief Rabbi and the Board of Deputies. The following year he announced that he was willing to remarry Jewish women who had not obtained a *Get* (divorce document). This provoked a further barrage of

1. Ship's manifest showing Mattuck family (mother and five children), bottom left. Note adjacent to names saying that father is a tailor in Boston. National Archives and Records Administration (NARA); Washington, DC, Crew Lists of vessels Arriving at Boston, Massachusetts, 1820–1943.

. Studio portrait in celebration of Israel Aattuck's Bar Mitzvah, 1896. Mattuck family rchives.

. Israel Mattuck leading the confirmation class at the congregation Sons of Israel nd David, Providence, Rhode Island where he was a temporary rabbi in 1905. Rhode Island Jewish History Association: http://www.rijha.org/wp-content/uploads/ 013/01/2-1-June-56-87-96.pdf.

4. Benjamin and Ida Mattuck outside their Argyle Road home, Brooklyn, New York, possibly on the occasion of Anna Mattuck's wedding in 1924. Mattuck family archives.

5. Formal portrait of Israel Mattuck taken at the time of his being awarded an honorary doctorate (Doctor of Hebrew Letters, DDL) by Hebrew Union College, Cincinnati, Ohio, 1925. Mattuck family archives.

6. Wedding photo, 3 November 1910. Mattuck family archives.

Hebrew Union College
Union of American Hebrew Congregations
Cincinnati, Ohio, U.S.A.

By authority of
The Union of
American Hebrew Congregations
We
The Faculty and Board of Governors
of the
Hebrew Union College
hereby certify that whereas
Israel Isidor Mattuck
has completed with all requirements for Graduation we have conferred upon him the degree of
Rabbi
and hereby authorize and license him to perform all Rabbinical functions in the name of God and Israel
Cincinnati, Ohio, United States of America
this Sixteenth day of April, 5670, A.M. (1910.)

ראש בית המדרש לרבנים
ישראל יצחק בן צבי בן ציון

The Faculty of the Hebrew Union College

7. Israel Mattuck's ordination certificate, awarded by Hebrew Union College (HUC), Cincinnati, Ohio, 1910. It is signed by Kaufmann Kohler (the president), Louis Grossman (HUC faculty member), David Neumark (HUC faculty member and Israel Mattuck's rabbinic thesis supervisor), Julian Morgenstern (future HUC president), E. Feldman (faculty member), Gotthard Deutsch (faculty member), Moses Buttenwieser (faculty member) and Edward Heischeimer (president of the HUC Board), Israel Bloom (secretary of the HUC Board). Mattuck family archives.

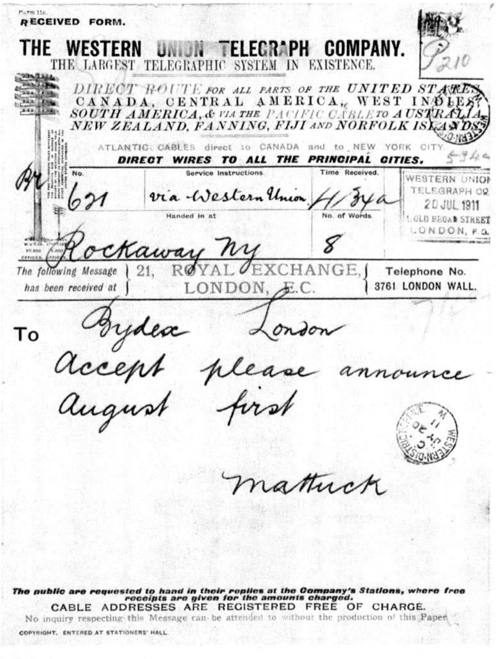
RECEIVED FORM.
THE WESTERN UNION TELEGRAPH COMPANY.
THE LARGEST TELEGRAPHIC SYSTEM IN EXISTENCE.
DIRECT ROUTE FOR ALL PARTS OF THE UNITED STATES, CANADA, CENTRAL AMERICA, WEST INDIES, SOUTH AMERICA, & VIA THE PACIFIC CABLE TO AUSTRALIA, NEW ZEALAND, FANNING, FIJI AND NORFOLK ISLANDS.
ATLANTIC CABLES direct to CANADA and to NEW YORK CITY.
DIRECT WIRES TO ALL THE PRINCIPAL CITIES.

No.	Service Instructions.	Time Received.
621	via Western Union	11/34a

Handed in at	No. of Words.
Rockaway NY	8

WESTERN UNION TELEGRAPH CO. 20 JUL 1911 OLD BROAD STREET LONDON, E.C.

The following Message has been received at 21, ROYAL EXCHANGE, LONDON, E.C. Telephone No. 3761 LONDON WALL.

To Brydex London
Accept please announce
August first
Mattuck

The public are requested to hand in their replies at the Company's Stations, where free receipts are given for the amounts charged.
CABLE ADDRESSES ARE REGISTERED FREE OF CHARGE.
No inquiry respecting this Message can be attended to without the production of this Paper.
COPYRIGHT. ENTERED AT STATIONERS' HALL.

8. Telegram dated 20 July 1911. Israel Mattuck's acceptance of the 'call' to England. LJS archives, St John's Wood London.

9. Mattuck family picnic. Left to right sitting: Robert Mattuck, Dorothy Mattuck (behind), Israel Mattuck, Naomi Mattuck, Edna Mattuck, Amy Kirschberger (later Amy Blank); standing: Simon Mayer, Israel Mattuck's father-in-law, c. 1927. Mattuck family archives.

10. Mattuck family home in Burke's Road, Beaconsfield c. 1916. Mattuck family archives.

11. Israel Mattuck working in his study at the family home, 'Wildwood', in North End, Hampstead, c. 1925. Mattuck family archives.

12. Mattuck family home, 'Wildwood', North End, Hampstead, c. 1935. Mattuck family archives.

13. Robert Mattuck, Israel Mattuck's son, c. 1935. Mattuck family archives.

14. Dorothy Edgar (née Mattuck), Israel Mattuck's older daughter, c. 1940. Mattuck family archives.

15. Naomi Mattuck (later Capon), Israel Mattuck's younger daughter, c. 1935. Mattuck family archives.

16. Cartoon of Israel Mattuck by 'Salon' (the well-known cartoonist, Ralph David Salon) that appeared in the Jewish Chronicle, c. 1950. Mattuck family archives.

17. The Mattuck country home, Bradden's Yard, Long Crendon, near Aylesbury, Buckinghamshire, 1950. Mattuck family archives.

18. Israel Mattuck relaxing in his Long Crendon garden, c. 1940. Mattuck family archives.

19. 'The Doll's House', Israel Mattuck's study in the garden of the family home, Bradden's Yard, Long Crendon, near Aylesbury, Buckinghamshire. Mattuck family archives.

20. Israel Mattuck preaching at the Liberal Jewish Synagogue. On the *bimah* from left to right: Rabbi Leslie Edgar (Senior Minister at the synagogue), Reverend Philip Cohen (Associate Minister at the synagogue), Israel Mattuck, and Lily Montagu (synagogue Council member and President of the Union of Liberal and Progressive Synagogue), c. 1945. Mattuck family archives.

1. Service of re-consecration after ıe repair of the Liberal Jewish ynagogue, 23 September 1951.)n the *bimah* from left to right: ɪrael Mattuck, two unknown eople, Sir Louis Gluckstein (LJS resident), Rabbi Leslie Edgar, Basil Ienriques, Reverend Philip Cohen, ily Montagu. LJS archives, St ɔhn's Wood, London.

22. Meeting of Jewish delegates at International conference of Jews and Christians held at Lady Margaret Hall College, Oxford 1946 of which Israel Mattuck was one of the leaders. Those identifiable include Israel Mattuck (seated centre), Leslie Edgar (behind him seated below portrait), Rabbi Alexander Altman, USA? (seated to IIM's right), Rabbi Moses Cyrus Weiler, South Africa (seated far right next to his wife), Rabbi David Wice, USA (standing immediately behind IIM), Rabbi Ephraim Frisch (seated next to Leslie Edgar). Mattuck family archives.

23. Israel Mattuck chairing the Executive Committee of the World Union for Progressive Judaism (WUPJ) c. 1950 in the Council Room at the Liberal Jewish Synagogue. To his left is Lily Montagu, Deputy President of WUPJ and to her left is Jessie Levy, Lily Montagu's long-standing secretary. Others unknown. Mattuck family archives.

24. Presentation of portrait painted by Sir Arthur Pan, January 1948. On the *bimah* at the Liberal Jewish Synagogue from left to right: Sir Arthur Pan, Reverend Philip Cohen, Sir Louis Gluckstein (president of the Liberal Jewish Synagogue), Edna Mattuck, Israel Mattuck, Leslie Edgar, Lily Montagu. Mattuck family archives.

25. Presentation of anthology of writings on the occasion of Leo Baeck's eightieth birthday, the compilation of which Israel Mattuck had overseen and to which he contributed, 1953. Left to right: Israel Mattuck, Edna Mattuck, Leslie Edgar, Dorothy Edgar (née Mattuck) Dr Charles Lewsen (LJS Council member) and Leo Baeck. Mattuck family archives.

protest, including this time from Dr Asher, Dayan of the Beth Din.[177] IIM's main reaction to the criticism and hostility of the Chief Rabbi and other community leaders was disappointment at their apparent lack of religious tolerance. In a sermon given by Hertz on the suppression of religion in Russia, he pointed to what he saw as the double standards of the Chief Rabbi in condemning religious intolerance in Russia while seeking to halt the spread of Liberal Judaism in England.[178]

Despite these public disagreements, it was later acknowledged that privately Dr Hertz was more cordial in his relations with the leaders of Liberal Judaism, including IIM, whose advice and views he occasionally sought.[179]

IIM and the *Jewish Chronicle*

As we have seen, from the time of his arrival in Britain, IIM featured regularly in the pages of the *Jewish Chronicle*. His sermons and lectures were often quoted at length or reproduced in full. He wrote letters to the newspaper on issues about which he felt particularly strongly or in response to criticisms that had been made of him in the *Jewish Chronicle*. IIM also had frequent exchanges of views with Leopold Greenberg,[180] editor of the *Jewish Chronicle* between 1907 and 1931. Greenberg was a committed Zionist and he and IIM often clashed on the topic of an independent Jewish state. Writing under the pen name of 'Mentor', and in his weekly column 'From the Armchair', Greenberg repeatedly challenged IIM's stance on issues.[181] For example, he was scathing about IIM's dialogue with other religious groups (see below),[182] and the principled position IIM took on moneylenders in 1925.[183] He claimed that although IIM had stated that he had debarred moneylenders from membership of the LJS, he (IIM) had sought funding for the new synagogue in St John's Wood Road from a well-known moneylender.[184]

IIM sometimes replied to Greenberg's criticisms through the pages of the *JRU Bulletin*; Greenberg scathingly referred to this publication as IIM's 'parish newsletter' and accused IIM of 'pea shooting' at him from 'behind the puny cover of the dwarf hedge' of the *JRU Bulletin*.[185] However, despite their differences of opinion, Greenberg respected IIM as a congregational leader and praised his work in building the LJS community. He was keen for the LJS and the West London Synagogue congregations to be united under IIM's leadership. Greenberg saw IIM as a 'born leader of men', a 'fine preacher', and 'a man of great personal merit'.[186] Even when he disagreed with IIM's views, Greenberg was prepared to find space in the *Jewish Chronicle* to allow IIM to express his opinions. In 1921 he wrote to IIM:

> Have I ever refused any communication of yours, or any article submitted to us of your particular creed … I know quite well that you would never submit to us anything unfitted to be inserted in the 'Jewish Chronicle' however much I may disagree with the views that you express.[187]

Greenberg was moved to defend IIM when he thought that IIM had been misinterpreted. In May 1932 he disputed 'Watchman's distorted report'[188] of IIM's 'eloquent discourse' on Jesus Christ of Nazareth, which had appeared in a previous issue of the *Jewish Chronicle*.[189]

Ecumenical Activities

One of IIM's main ventures in the post-war years was to establish a dialogue with Christian leaders to promote understanding between Jews and Christians. Just after the First World War, IIM joined the organising committee of the short-lived League of Religions for World Peace, which was set up in Oxford in November 1919[190] to 'hold out a hand of fellowship' to 'Christians, Mohammedens [sic], Buddhists and others',[191] and to work for world peace. Emanating from the Jewish Peace Society, IIM saw the league as a religious counterpart, 'the propelling power', to the League of Nations. He was hopeful that it might succeed in raising spiritual values above all others as the guide to human life.[192]

IIM gave lectures at the league's meetings held at the Friends Meeting Place in Euston Road.[193] Based on his experience in America where he had witnessed different religious groups worshiping together, 'all saying the same prayers, all singing the same hymns, listening to the same sermon',[194] IIM was optimistic that the different groups involved with the league might gain from their association with other religions. However, he was emphatic that the aim of the league was 'not to eradicate religious differences or to establish a universal religion'. Nor was it a 'vague conglomerate of religious teachings.'[195] Its constitution stipulated that it should not interfere with the religious tenets of any of its constituent bodies.

The League of Religions was chaired by Dr Maud, the Bishop of Kensington, and its membership included a number of prominent Oxford professors and religious leaders, such as the Bishop of Oxford and the Chief Rabbi. However, as IIM subsequently recorded, the Archbishop of Canterbury, Dr Davidson, refused to give the league his blessing and 'it quickly came to a peaceful end'.[196]

Building on his leading role in the League of Religions, in 1924 IIM encouraged a number of leading members of the LJS Social Service Committee to make contact with other religious bodies. They set up an organising committee to convene an interfaith conference, the aim of which was to provide 'an opportunity for Jews and Christians to confer together on the basis of their common ideals and with mutual respect for differences in belief'. The theme of the conference was 'Religion as an Educational Force'.[197] IIM was gratified that the conference, which he chaired, was supported by the Bishops of London, Liverpool and Kensington, as well as by the leaders of Christian churches 'of all shades'.[198] All sections of the Jewish community were present even though they were not 'officially connected' to the embryonic organisation that had organised the conference.[199] IIM was struck by the uniqueness of the event and commented that during the nineteen centuries of their coexistence, this was the first time that representatives from all forms of Judaism and Christianity had come together to exchange views on religious matters.[200]

Some Orthodox leaders, who regarded the initiative as a step on the road to converting Jews to Christianity, were highly critical of IIM. He replied to this criticism in a sermon given at the LJS in which he objected to the 'contemptible suggestions about the character of the conference', which he said had been based on 'half truth'. This, to IIM's mind, was 'worse than a lie'.[201] He deplored the fact that critics of the conference had focused on the first part of its aims ('to confer together on the basis of their common ideals'), while neglecting to mention the second part ('with mutual respect for differences in belief'). He also railed against his main detractor, the editor of the *Jewish Chronicle*, Greenberg, who had been critical of Jews and Christians organising a conference together when he himself had relatively recently complained that Jews had not been invited to attend gatherings of Christian clergy examining topical issues.[202]

IIM was not deflected by criticism of the interfaith conference and went on to chair a second conference the following year on the topic of 'Religion and the Race Problem'. The conference, which was held in the Hinde Street Wesleyan Church in Manchester Square, was attended by nearly 400 delegates. IIM gave the opening address, in which he acknowledged the differences that existed between the various denominations represented at the conference, but drew attention to their common faith in God.[203] When he continued to be criticised for his interfaith initiatives, IIM averred:

> I believe in the value of religious differences. The light shining through many-colours is not poorer but richer than the light shining through one colour. And the light of truth as it reveals humanity must be coloured, in its purity man cannot live, else he be God. I believe in religious differences but with equal conviction I believe in religious unity.[204]

The two interfaith conferences led in 1927 to the founding of the London Society of Jews and Christians, which became a platform on which leading Jewish and Christian theologians expounded to one another their respective faiths. For over twenty years it was co-chaired by IIM and either the Dean of Westminster Abbey or the Dean of St Paul's Cathedral. IIM delivered several addresses on Judaism and on theological language at its meetings,[205] some of which were later published in a book, *In Spirit and in Truth, aspects of Judaism and Christianity*,[206] including his address on 'The Jewish Approach to God'.

IIM was frequently invited to address other religious groups, such as the Hampstead Churchman's Union (on 'Co-operation between Jews and Christians' in 1929), Reverend Ackroyd's Men's Group (on 'Liberal Judaism' in 1927), a group of Wesleyan Ministers (on 'The Jewish Attitude to Jesus' in 1926), the Presbyterian Theological Club (on 'Traditions and Progress in Judaism' in 1928) and the Society for the Study of Religions (on 'The Conception of Man, or Human Personality, in Judaism' in 1921).[207] He was the first rabbi in the country to participate in a church service[208] (at St Bartholomew's the Great in the City of London in May 1930, when he spoke on 'Jew and Christian').[209] He subsequently preached at various churches throughout England and was also invited to speak at churches in Scotland and Wales.[210] In his addresses he was candid about his objections to some aspects of Christianity, especially the Christian dogma on making Christians of Jews:

> Judaism had originally a missionary motive, it claimed to be and expected to be recognised as the universal religion. But it never adopted missionary methods. It certainly never sent missions to Christians. Perhaps we should do so to show Christians how Jews feel about Christian missions to the Jews. The Jews object to missions because they do not show respect for, let alone appreciation of, this religion. The missionary practically says two things to the Jews – you individually would be better if you were Christians, and the world would be better without your religion.[211]

IIM believed that this dogma militated against cooperation between Christians and Jews, and he was therefore mainly drawn to dialogue with liberal Christians who were prepared to reject the claim to finality or absolute truth and who recognised that other religions had 'something of spiritual value to give to the world'.[212]

As a result of his interfaith involvements, IIM became 'one of the leaders of religious thought in our generation'[213] and 'an incomparable interpreter of Judaism to Christians'.[214] The Very Reverend W.R.

Matthews, Dean of St Paul's, with whom IIM worked closely for many years commented:

> Mattuck was very well equipped to further the cause of understanding [between Christians and Jews] for he was a first-rate Hebrew scholar and versed in Rabbinical writings, while at the same time he was well read in history and philosophy and the literature of Christianity. I often admired his manner and spirit in discussion.[215]

However, not all of IIM's interfaith endeavours were successful. In October 1928 IIM was invited by the Reverend Dr J. Abelson, the minister at Belgrave Street Synagogue (the Old Hebrew Congregation) in Leeds to speak at an interfaith event being organised in the city.[216] The event was vetoed by the Chief Rabbi and, despite the intervention of the Mayor of Leeds, had to be cancelled. IIM was embarrassed by the 'annoyance and worry' Dr Abelson had experienced in organising the visit and unimpressed by the Chief Rabbi's behaviour, which he felt was intent on causing rifts in the Anglo-Jewish community and lowered its standing with non-Jews. He observed that while *Chillul Ha Shem* (desecration of the name of God) was a strong expression, the Chief Rabbi's actions almost deserved it.[217]

Although IIM formed close links with and was admired by many churchmen, he did not always agree with their outlook. IIM frequently questioned the opinions of the then Dean of St Paul's Cathedral, William Inge. He was highly critical of Dr Inge's *Romanes Lectures* of 1920, 'The Idea of Progress', because the lectures emphatically denied the possibility of progress.[218] IIM found such pessimism 'un-Jewish' and drew attention to how Jews had maintained an unquenchable idealism notwithstanding their sufferings.[219] He challenged Dr Inge's misconceptions of Judaism, such as in 1929 when he said:

> The Dean of St Paul's recently informed the world that his notebook contains this note: Christianity looks at life (or the future) with faith and resignation; Judaism with hope and fear. That view is based, I fear, on both theological and congenital dispositions of the Dean. Theological – because Christianity is the religion of faith, Judaism the religion through the Law. Congenital – because the Dean approves of the resignation he gives to his religion; he thinks hope folly, so he associates it with fear. If the Dean had, however, consulted history, I fear that he would have found much fear among Christians and not so much among Jews. The fear of hell did for a time dominate Christian theology.[220]

An 'International JRU'

IIM's other major endeavour in the post-war years was in helping to establish the 'International JRU'. As early as 1914, the leaders of the German Liberal Association approached IIM to suggest the formation of an international body that would include Liberal Jews from Germany, England, America and France.[221] However, due to the First World War and the tensions it created, this initiative was held in abeyance until 1925. Building on her success in establishing a Liberal community in Bombay and with IIM's backing, Lily Montagu submitted to the JRU Council a proposal for setting up a worldwide organisation of Progressive Jewish communities. Consultation with colleagues in America, Paris and Berlin was encouraging, and in July 1926 a conference was held at the LJS at which the World Union for Progressive Judaism (WUPJ) was launched. Its purpose was to 'affirm the universal character of Progressive Judaism and to encourage cooperation between Progressive communities in different countries to further Progressive Judaism, both in thought and in practice'.[222]

More than 100 delegates attended the inaugural conference, representing Progressive communities in France, Germany, Great Britain, India, Czechoslovakia, Romania, Sweden and America. Claude Montefiore was nominated as President of WUPJ, Lily Montagu became its Honorary Secretary and IIM was elected as Chairman of the Executive Committee as well as one of its Vice-Presidents. This meant that within fifteen years of his arrival in England, IIM was now the guiding spirit of three major religious organisations: the JRU, the London Society of Jews and Christians and the WUPJ.

The task that IIM took on in chairing the WUPJ Executive Committee was not an easy one, because the organisation was made up of communities of many shades of opinion and religious belief. However, he was not daunted by these differences. Speaking at the inaugural conference service he said:

> There are many differences among us, and none would wish for their complete removal. For differences issue from freedom, and freedom is as the life of the human spirit ... The way of God cannot be walked in chains ... I perceived the richness of our Judaism as the differences among us, as its power in the unity that comprehends [sic] us.[223]

IIM was repeatedly re-elected to the position of Chairman until his death, having proved himself to be highly effective. According to one contemporary commentator: 'a man and a place had happily found each other'.[224] Another said:

> There [at meetings of the WUPJ] he was at his best, among the widely differing viewpoints of delegates from many different lands. He always grasped quickly the trend of a debate and his lucid mind penetrated unerringly to the heart of the matter. He was patient, tactful, constructive, with a talent for analysis and synthesis. After a record output of words had descended on delegates at a Conference, Dr Mattuck's clear and immensely capable summary of a debate was always the highlight of the day.[225]

IIM's confidence in dealing with varying and conflicting views was demonstrated at the inaugural conference in 1926. Maurice Perlzweig raised the issue of Zionism, saying that Liberal Judaism and Zionism were not in opposition and claiming that an anti-Zionist movement could never hope to have influence in Eastern Europe.[226] Stephen Wise then pleaded passionately for the conference to show to the world, and particularly the younger generation of Jews, that its participants were not anti-Zionist. In the chair, IIM replied with the ruling that the conference would steer entirely clear of a potential minefield by taking no official stance on Zionism. He begged Zionists and non-Zionists alike 'not to wreck this first International Conference by beginning to discuss these issues'.[227] With this ruling, Zionism remained a bracketed question and was not debated by WUPJ for many years.

As well as chairing the private sessions of the inaugural conference, IIM gave an address on 'Bible Worship in Education'. American delegates attending the conference returned to America 'full of enthusiasm' and spoke 'in very high terms' of IIM's sermon and his conduct of the WUPJ meetings.[228]

The first official conference of the WUPJ was held in Berlin two years later. Its theme was 'The Message of Liberal Judaism and How to Give it'. The conference marked a high point in the early history of the WUPJ. Attired in formal dress, IIM and his fellow delegates gathered in the ornate chamber of the one-time Prussian Herrenhaus (House of Lords) and worshipped in the grand Neue Synagogue. During the conference, IIM reported on Liberal Judaism in England, which he said was radical when compared to Progressive Judaism in Germany, but conservative by American standards, especially in its ceremonies and outward trappings, which had been retained out of sentiment. He gave as an example the fact that Liberal Jewish ministers in Britain wore caps, gowns and *tallitot*. However, he argued that English Liberal Judaism was more radical in its thought. The subtext here may have been that while IIM had been willing to compromise on things that did not matter to him, he had remained resolute on matters of 'modern thought'.[229] Later in the conference IIM spoke on the 'Problem of Intermarriage' and also chaired the WUPJ business sessions.[230]

During his tenure as WUPJ Chairman, IIM was to give a number of further conference addresses: 'The Conception of Personal Piety' in 1930; 'Religion in Crisis' in 1946; and 'The Religious Approach to World Problems: The Need for a Spiritual Renaissance', in 1953. In WUPJ's early years IIM also arranged for rabbis to be appointed to develop Progressive communities. For example, in 1929 he travelled to Berlin to interview the young rabbi, Dr Koretz, with a view to his taking up work in Poland.[231]

IIM and America

Now he was firmly established as a leading religious figure in Britain, IIM was asked to participate in many committees and conferences organised by the American Reform movement, particularly those organised by CCAR, to which IIM was elected in 1915. In 1916 he was invited to join the CCAR Special Commission on Jews of Other Lands; a year later he joined the CCAR standing committees on Contemporaneous History and on Synagogue Music;[232] and in 1925 he became a member of a Special Committee on a Source Book of Reform Judaism. His activities in England were regularly reported in the American Jewish press and articles he had penned were often reproduced in various newspapers and periodicals in America. In 1922 he wrote an article on 'Judaism and Progress' for the *Menorah Journal*[233] edited by Henry Hurwitz,[234] and in April 1927 IIM was asked to write a tract for UAHC and CCAR on 'Immortality'.[235]

IIM was now regarded as one of the most prominent HUC alumni. In 1925 he joined the Executive Board of the HUC Alumni Association,[236] and in the same year HUC conferred upon him the honorary degree of Doctor of Hebrew Law – described as being 'richly deserved'[237] – in recognition of services rendered on behalf of Reform Judaism. The degree ceremony was held in the College chapel in Cincinnati on Saturday 24 October 1925, which was the second day of the Golden Jubilee celebrations of HUC. IIM received his degree from the president, Julian Morgenstern, alongside a number of other prominent Reform rabbis that included David Philipson and Hyman Enelow. In awarding the degree Dr Morgenstern said:

> Faithful minister of the Liberal Jewish Synagogue of London, who by wise, courageous and consecrated leadership has set Liberal Judaism in England on a firm foundation and thereby won for his Alma Mata honor and influence abroad.[238]

IIM and Edna Mattuck received an ovation from their 'numerous Cincinnati friends and admirers present in the chapel'[239] and IIM was sent many letters of congratulations, including one from a friend who pointed out that the degree would place him on a more equal footing in his disputes with the Chief Rabbi, Dr Hertz.[240]

IIM's time in America amongst his Reform colleagues seems to have wetted his appetite for spending more time there, and during 1926 he was in correspondence with Julian Morgenstern at HUC about the possibility of arranging an exchange of pulpits to allow him to stay in America for an extended period. Those considered for a possible exchange were rabbis Solomon Freehof and Felix Levy.[241] The proposal obviously proved unworkable, but the fact that it was being considered suggests that, with his doctorate under his belt and the building of a new synagogue to his credit, IIM may have had his sights set on a prestigious appointment in America.

When he went to America in 1925, IIM did not visit his family in New York, but in April 1927 he left Liverpool for a three-month trip, one purpose of which was to allow the Mattuck family to visit the friends and relations they had not now seen for eight years.[242] However, the journey had been occasioned by the invitations IIM had received from HUC and CCAR. On 28 May he delivered the Baccalaureate Address for that year's HUC graduates. In this address, 'The Ideal of Jewish Personality', he acknowledged the major institution the College had become and paid tribute to Kaufmann Kohler. He said he regarded Kohler with 'reverence and personal affection' and owed much to him for 'his instruction and inspiration'.[243] In his address he set out the three ideals that made Jews Jewish:

> … the appreciation of holiness, which is central to Jewish teaching, the love of learning which has been characteristic of the best of Jews of all ages, the practice of charity which has been a large part of Jewish life at its best.[244]

IIM saw it as the role of the Jewish minister to inculcate these ideals amongst Jews, to ensure that Jews lived up to them in their everyday lives and held them up as a model of humanity for the wider world.[245] His address was described by Julian Morgenstern as 'very forceful', and Morgenstern also praised IIM for the 'character and content' of its message.[246] IIM was the guest of honour at a dinner that followed the graduation service.

While in America, IIM also gave a 'sermon lecture' on 'The Jewish Concept of God in Relation to Some Aspects of Modern Thought and

Life'[247] to a CCAR meeting held at Cape May, New Jersey. At this conference IIM was invited to join a committee chaired by Rabbi David Philipson to plan the celebration of the 200th anniversary of the birth of Moses Mendelssohn.[248] IIM subsequently attended a number of other Jewish and non-Jewish gatherings,[249] which were organised by the James Pond Lecture Bureau of New York. His commitments included a dinner arranged by the New York chapter of the Independent Order of B'nai B'rith. His after dinner speech was acclaimed for its 'spontaneity' and 'vigor' and those present deemed him to be 'a brilliant, thoughtful and inspiring speaker'.[250]

During his twelve-week stay in America, IIM travelled 16,000 miles and visited 'a goodly number of cities' across the country, noting the perverse impact of the prohibition laws on American life (see Chapter Fourteen for more information).[251] Reflecting on his visit, IIM's overall conclusion about America in 1927 was that 'there have been many changes in American life but not much change'.[252] However, he perceived that there had been more significant developments in American Jewry. He noted that while he was growing up in America, Russian-Jewish immigrants held no positions of leadership in communal life, but that there were now many prominent and powerful Eastern European Jews.[253] He appears to have been pleased to see immigrants with the same background as himself becoming Americanised; he was less sanguine about the fact that their greater influence on communal life was leading to the growth of Zionism. IIM found it ironic that although they had experienced sufficient freedom to rise to prominence in America, the Russian Jews still burned with a desire to return to Zion.[254] He spoke of the growing Zionist Organisation, the American Jewish Congress, in the same disparaging way as he had described the Zionist Groups he encountered in Boston twenty-five years earlier:

> Though the Zionists in America are very loud, they seem to have an excellent publicity department, and politically very active, they are not as important, even in America, as they think themselves.[255]

He commented with apparent satisfaction that the Zionist organisations were failing to attract young people who (like himself) had received an American education and that large numbers of such young people were now joining Reform synagogues.[256] IIM was particularly impressed by the strong Jewish consciousness evident in America and the obvious attachment of American Jews to their synagogues. He was scathing of those Jews who retained their foreign qualities, especially 'the persistence of Yiddish in some sections of the large American cities'.[257]

During this visit to America, IIM was interviewed by the press. He spoke about the barriers he had encountered in developing Liberal Judaism in Britain: religious indifference, the antagonism of some Orthodox Jews, and the opposition of some Zionists, who thought that they saw in the Liberal Jewish movement 'an obstacle in the way of Zionist propaganda'.[258] However, he proudly pointed out that the LJS now had one of the largest congregations in the country and that this was not the result of the movement opposing any other form of Judaism or expression of Jewish life, but 'by its own strength'. He was gratified that people were joining from all walks of life.[259] He was full of enthusiasm for the developments he saw in the American Reform movement and its 'untraditionalism', which he contrasted to 'the conventions of the Jews in England'. The Reform movement remained his model. It was filled with 'the spirit of adventure in the new things it dares and does'. To him the American Jew was 'the latest development in Jewish life'.[260] As we shall see, he failed to identify some emerging currents.

NOTES

1. 'Victory and Peace', sermon given by IIM at the Thanksgiving Service at the LJS on 18 October 1918, Montagu Centre Collection (MCC).
2. Ibid.
3. 'The Jews and the Peace Conference, 3', sermon given by IIM at the LJS, 8 February 1919, MCC.
4. Ibid.
5. 'The Jews and the Peace Conference, 1', sermon given by IIM at the LJS, 25 January 1919, MCC.
6. See minute book of the LJS Organising Committee, LJS Archives, Box 1/2.
7. 'Liberal Judaism and the Future 11 – Our Congregation', sermon given by IIM at the LJS, 12 January 1919, MCC.
8. Ibid.
9. Ibid.
10. 'The Jew in America', second part of an address given by IIM to the North London Liberal Congregation Literary Society (day not specified) July 1927, MCC.
11. The Younger Members' Organisation of the Liberal Jewish Synagogue, *The Years Between 1911–1951, LJS exhibition catalogue* (London: ULPS, 1951), p.14.
12. Letter from Lily Montagu to Edna Mattuck, 18 July 1926 following the holding of the first conference of the World Union for Progressive Judaism, London Metropolitan Archives, ACC/3529/002/018.
13. Michael A. Meyer, *Response to Modernity – A History of the Reform Movement in Judaism* (New York: Oxford University Press, 1988), p.274.
14. 'The Beginnings of Liberal Judaism in America', sermon given by IIM at the LJS, 5 April 1919, MCC. See also letter from IIM to Marjorie Moos, dated 6 November 1945, in which IIM said 'Families with young children shouldn't attend them [Friday evening synagogue services], they should spend the whole Friday evening at home', LJS Archives, Box 1/2.
15. Isaac Landman, 'Dr Israel Mattuck Revisits America', *New York Times*, 27 May 1927, p.127. In this article IIM recalls his conversations in Yiddish with those who found it difficult to express themselves in English.
16. The Jews' Temporary Shelter was established in 1885 in the East End of London. It provided temporary accommodation, meals and assistance to poor Jewish immigrants and transmigrants arriving in London by ship from Eastern Europe.
17. 'Is Zionism Dead?', sermon given by IIM at the LJS, 20 October 1923, MCC.
18. A.A. Green, Letter to the editor, *Jewish Guardian*, 2 February 1924, p.4.
19. 'Immigrant Problems. Discussion at Adjourned Conference. Owners Defend Their Views', *Jewish Guardian*, 2 February 1924, p.3.
20. Ibid.
21. 'The Immigrant Jew, His Difficulties and His Possibilities', sermon given by IIM at the LJS, 13 December 1924, MCC.

22. 'The Jew and His Neighbour – A Problem of Social Relations', sermon given by IIM at the LJS, 19 May 1928, in ibid.
23. David Philipson is reputed to have said 'Oh the shame of it in this age of bath-rooms public and private!' when the growing Orthodox community settling in Cincinnati solicited funds for a ritual bath. Quoted in Meyer, *Response to Modernity*, p.292.
24. 'A Free Israel', sermon given by IIM at the Wigmore Hall, at the Morning Service of the First Day of Passover, 7 April 1917, MCC.
25. 'Assimilation and Intermarriage', sermon given by IIM at the LJS, 14 May 1921, in ibid.
26. 'Our Prayer Book', sermon given by IIM at the LJS, 24 January 1920, in ibid.
27. Ibid.
28. See Rabbi John D. Rayner and Rabbi Chaim Stern (eds) *Service of the Heart* (London: ULPS, 1967). It replaced IIM's prayer books in 1967.
29. *Liberal Jewish Prayer Book, Volume 1* (London: JRU, 1926), pp.94–5.
30. Israel I. Mattuck (ed.), *Liberal Jewish Prayer Book Vol. I (Weekdays and Sabbaths)* (London: Liberal Jewish Synagogue, 1936).
31. Jakob Pethuchowowski, *Prayerbook Reform in Europe: The Liturgy of European and Liberal Reform Judaism* (New York: World Union for Progressive Judaism, 1968), p.74.
32. See 'Our Prayer Book'.
33. Ibid.
34. Quoted in 'Israel I. Mattuck – His Life and Work', unattributed article in *LJM, In Memoriam of Israel Mattuck, 1883–1954* (June 1954), p.10.
35. CCAR yearbook, Vol. XXXII, Cape May, NJ, 1922, p.20.
36. According to Maurice Perlzweig, the Second Minister at the LJS, who was influential in the production of the *North London Prayer Book*, Israel Mattuck was not happy with this version because it included pro-Zionist material. *The Reminiscences of Dr Maurice L Perlzweig* (Oral History Research Office, Columbia University, 1993), p.262.
37. *LJM*, XI, no.45 (October 1926), p.45.
38. Letter from Abraham Feldman to IIM, 6 December 1927, American Jewish Archives (AJA), Abraham Feldman Papers, Box 24, Folder 4, MS-38.
39. Professor Isman Elbogen, 'The New Liberal Jewish Prayer Book', *LJM*, VIII, no.10 (March 1938), p.93. Elbogen was professor of history and Bible exegesis at the Höchschule für die Wissenschaft des Judentums.
40. Ibid., p.93.
41. Ibid., p.94.
42. Ibid., p.94.
43. Rabbi Dr Leslie I. Edgar, *Some Memories of My Ministry* (London: Liberal Jewish Synagogue, 1985), p.11.
44. Minute book of the LJS Organising Committee, meeting held on 7 January 1919, LJS Archives, Box 1/2.
45. Initially the Sunday services were held only in the winter months and collections were made after the services to help meet their cost, but they were mostly financed by a donation by the philanthropist and LJS member Bernhard Baron. They continued, albeit on an increasingly intermittent basis, into the 1940s.
46. ULPS Oral History Project 1994–5, interview with Ruth Ive, LJS Archives, Box 139a.
47. Ibid., interview with Maxwell Stern.
48. *LJM*, I, no.5 (October 1929), p.22.
49. Interview with Herbert Richer conducted by Rosita Rosenberg, 14/15 May 2012.
50. Rabbi Leslie Edgar, 'The Early Days and the Formation of the LJS', in Diamond Jubilee Celebration concert programme, 19 November 1972, LJS Archives.
51. 'The World's Work and the Individual', address given by IIM at the City Temple Literary Society, 16 February 1922, MCC.
52. 'Is the World Growing Better?', sermon given by IIM at the LJS, 16 February 1930, in ibid.
53. 'What Mr Bernard Shaw Thinks of Democracy (with reference to The Apple Cart)', sermon given by IIM at the LJS, 4 January 1931, in ibid.
54. For example, on 20 November 1926 he spoke on 'Personality and Religion'. See 'Reviews, Lectures, etc. (other than Sermons), 1913–1932', in ibid.
55. On 25 May 1924 he addressed the Manchester Jewish Students' Union on 'Liberal Judaism', in ibid.
56. *JC*, 29 November 1920, p.29.
57. *JC*, 4 March 1921, p.30.

58. See programme for the session of talks for the City and Temple Literary Society 1920–21, London Metropolitan Archives, ACC/3529/002/018.
59. Letter from the Hon. Secretary, Luke Cornforth to IIM, 20 February 1922, in ibid. He was subsequently invited to become a member of the society.
60. 'An Old Solution for Some Modern Problems', address given by IIM at the City Temple Literary Society, 29 January 1925, MCC.
61. *JC*, 4 June 1920, p.15.
62. See the handwritten notes that are archived with a copy of this lecture, MCC.
63. For example, on 9 May 1920 he spoke on 'Judaism and Democracy'. See 'Reviews, Lectures, etc.'.
64. For example, on 31 January 1913 he spoke on 'The Need for a Liberal Interpretation of Judaism'. See 'Reviews, Lectures, etc.'. See also 'Judaism and the Idea of Progress', address given by IIM to the Adler Society, 4 February 1921, MCC.
66. On 24 November 1929 he spoke on 'A Survey of Judaism'. See 'Reviews, Lectures, etc.'.
67. On 18 March 1930 he spoke on 'Some Jewish Characters in Recent Fiction and Drama'. See 'Reviews, Lectures, etc.'.
68. *The Jewish Guardian* was edited by Laurie Magnus, son of Sir Philip Magnus. It was the newspaper of the League of British Jews, and appeared weekly from October 1919 to 1931. Initially it challenged the *JC* because of its ability to attract high quality advertising, but eventually it proved unable to compete as its readership never exceed more than 1,200, mainly well-to-do Jews. See David Cesarani, *The Jewish Chronicle and Anglo Jewry, 1841–1991* (Cambridge: Cambridge University Press, 1994), p.140.
69. See 'Reviews, Lectures, etc.'.
70. Rabbi Israel Mattuck, 'A Philosophy for Worry', *Westminster Gazette*, 12 January 1927.
71. See 'Reviews, Lectures, etc.'.
72. Ibid.
73. Ibid.
74. Correspondence between George Mattuck and IIM during July 1929, LJS Archives, Box 1/2. It is interesting to note that in a letter dated 14 February 1928, IIM states that he did not feel that he could ask either Jacob or 'Birk' for their help.
75. This issue is discussed in Geoffrey Alderman, *Modern British Jewry* (Oxford: Oxford University Press, 1992), pp.237–8.
76. *JC*, 14 March 1919, pp.12–13.
77. *JC*, 19 December 1919, p.30.
78. Meir Persoff, *Faith Against Reason – Religious Reform and the British Chief Rabbinate, 1840–1990* (London and Portland, OR: Vallentine Mitchell, 2008), p.210.
79. Letter from the Reverend Abelson to IIM, 11 January 1924, London Metropolitan Archives, ACC/3529/002/018.
80. *LJS Weekly Circular*, May 1924.
81. Letter from Claude Montefiore to IIM, '17' month and year unknown (c.1922), London Metropolitan Archives, ACC/3529/004/002.
82. Letter from Israel Abrahams to IIM, 9 March 1924, LJS Archives, Box 1/2.
83. See correspondence from Julian Simon to IIM, March 1924, London Metropolitan Archives, ACC/3529/002/018.
84. 'Jewish Differences and Jewish Unity', sermon given by IIM at the LJS, 19 December 1926, MCC.
85. Ibid.
86. Ibid.
87. Ibid.
88. See The Younger Members' Organisation of the Liberal Jewish Synagogue, *The Years Between 1911–1951*, p.8.
89. Liberal Jewish Synagogue Annual Report, 1920, LJS Archives.
90. Correspondence in Mattuck Family Archive kept by Jill Mattuck Tarule (MFAa).
91. Those considered included the HUC senior rabbinic student, Jacob Marcus, who went on to be a major rabbinic figure.
92. Rabbi Starrels left the LJS in 1933 to become the rabbi at Alyth Gardens Synagogue. Maurice Perlzweig also moved to Alyth Gardens Synagogue in 1938.
93. Once it was established in its new location, A.A. Green, Minister at Hampstead Synagogue quipped, 'The Liberal Synagogue is in St John's Wood Road, but not on the Lord's side'.
94. See ULPS Oral History Project, interview with Dorothy Edgar.
95. *JC*, 20 April 1923, p.93.

96. Tape recording of the diary kept by IIM between January and April 1918. The diary is read by his daughter, Dorothy Edgar, née Mattuck. Mattuck Family Archive kept by Robert Edgar (MFAb).
97. The Hon. Lily H. Montagu, 'Rabbi Dr Israel I. Mattuck, Memorial Tribute', *LJM, In Memoriam, Israel I. Mattuck, 1883–1954,* p.1.
98. Letter from IIM to Rabbi Morris Lazaron, 15 May 1923, AJA, Morris Lazaron Papers, Box 5, Folder 34, MS-71.
99. Ibid.
100. See correspondence in the LJS Archives, Box 1/2. One of the letters he received was from his cousin, Israel Sarasohn.
101. Letter from Kaufmann Kohler to IIM, 30 August 1925, LJS Archives, Box 1/2.
102. Liberal Jewish Synagogue Annual Report 1927, LJS Archives.
103. 'America Revisited: Leader of Progressive Judaism in England Discusses Developments in Liberal Movement in America and the Jew's Place in American Life', *American Hebrew*, 28 October 1927, pp.121–4.
104. 'Judaism and Social Conditions', lecture given by IIM at the West Central Section of the JRU, 17 December 1916, MCC.
105. 'The Saving of Infant Life', sermon given by IIM at the LJS, 30 June 1917, in ibid.
106. Ibid.
107. 'Social Reform', sermon given by IIM at the LJS, 22 February 1919, in ibid.
108. Ibid.
109. 'On the Strike', sermon given by IIM at the LJS, 23 October 1920, in ibid.
110. Ibid.
111. 'Work and Reward', sermon given by IIM at the LJS 25 November 1922, in ibid.
112. 'The Problem of the Unemployed', sermon given by IIM at the LJS, 2 December 1922, in ibid.
113. 'The Right to Work', sermon given by IIM at the LJS, 28 November 1920, in ibid.
114. Ibid.
115. See 'The Problem of the Unemployed'.
116. 'The Religious Aspect of the Engineering Dispute', sermon given by IIM at the LJS, 23 March 1922, MCC.
117. 'The State and Social Reform', sermon given by IIM at the LJS, 9 May 1914, in ibid.
118. 'The Housing Problem and Social Reform', sermon given by IIM at the LJS, 28 October 1922, in ibid.
119. Ibid.
120. Ibid.
121. 'Homes or Slums', sermon given by IIM at the LJS, 5 May 1923, in ibid.
122. 'Economy and Education', sermon given by IIM at the LJS, 4 March 1922, in ibid.
123. Ibid.
124. Ibid.
125. Lucy Cohen, *Some Recollections of Claude Goldsmid Montefiore 1858–1938* (London: Faber and Faber, 1940), p.63.
126. See 'On the Strike'.
127. 'The Crisis', sermon given by IIM at the LJS, 8 May 1926, MCC.
128. Ibid.
129. See letter from Claude Montefiore to unnamed recipient, 17 May 1926, quoted in Cohen, *Some Recollections of Claude Goldsmid Montefiore*, p.63.
130. Pamela Fletcher Jones, 'Mr Duparc remembers', special edition of *ULPS Focus* to celebrate the first 75 years of Liberal Judaism, Autumn 1977.
131. 'The Religious Aspect of the Mines Dispute', sermon given by IIM at the LJS, 11 September 1926, MCC.
132. Ibid.
133. Ibid.
134. 'What I have Learned from the Coal Dispute', sermon given by IIM at the LJS, 5 December 1926, in ibid.
135. 'The Social Challenge of Russian Communism', sermon given by IIM at the LJS, 29 March 1931, in ibid.
136. Rabbi J. Rayner, 'Mattuck – *The* Boss', *LJS News,* January 1992, p.5.
137. *LJS Weekly,* 3 January 1929, p.3.
138. 'Parsons and Politics', sermon by IIM given at the LJS, 5 May 1929, MCC.

139. 'The Way to Vote', sermon given by IIM at the LJS, 18 May 1929, in ibid.
140. M.L. Perlzweig, 'Some Recollections of the First Minister', in M. Miller (ed.), *The First Fifty Years of Progressive Judaism at North London Progressive Synagogue, 1921–1951* (London: North London Progressive Synagogue, 1971), p.1.
141. See *The Reminiscences of Dr Maurice L. Perlzweig*, p.134.
142. He was formally inducted at a service held in November 1924.
143. See *The Reminiscences of Dr Maurice L. Perlzweig,* p.153. Reputedly IIM had said: 'You will have freedom of the pulpit, because if you don't have, then I might not have it, and therefore I will be your strongest supporter in seeing that you are free in what you say'.
144. Ibid., p.223. Perlzweig also compared IIM's apparent intolerance to the openness of Claude Montefiore. However, later correspondence reveals that Claude Montefiore had on occasion rebuked Perlzweig for using his status at the LJS to promote his Zionism. See letter from Louis Gluckstein to IIM, 27 March 1950, LJS Archives, Box 1/2.
145. Ibid., p.225.
146. Published in 1935 by the JRU.
147. See *The Reminiscences of Dr Maurice L Perlzweig,* pp.150–4. Perlzweig attributed IIM's anti-Zionism less to the influence of the Reform Movement in America than to the deeply Orthodox nature of his family: 'He was very anti-Zionist, the offspring of a very Orthodox family from whom he took his anti-Zionism. In those days the very Orthodox almost certainly meant to be anti-Zionist because the Zionists were trying to anticipate the Messiah, which was regarded as wrong'.
148. This synagogue had by then become Orthodox.
149. Letter from IIM to Dr Hertz, 11 April 1944, LJS Archives, Box 1/2.
150. Ibid.
151. V.D. Lipman, *A History of the Jews in Britain Since 1858* (Leicester: Leicester University Press, 1990), p.134.
152. Todd M. Endelman, *The Jews of Britain, 1656 to 2000* (Berkeley, Los Angeles, CA and London: University of California Press, 2002), p.218.
153. See 'Is Zionism Dead?'
154. The League of British Jews existed between 1917 and 1931. It enjoyed the support of most of the leading families in the English Jewish community including the Montefiores, the Montagus, the Rothschilds, and the Cohens. See Peter Egill Brownfield 'The League of British Jews: Challenging Nationalism in Behalf of Jewish Universalism', *Journal of the American Council for Judaism* (Fall 2001): www.acjna.org.
155. *JC*, 16 May 1919, p.24.
156. *JRU Bulletin,* 4, 9 (February 1918), p.3.
157. Non-naturalised Jews were debarred from membership of the league and since most Eastern European Jews had not naturalised, it meant that they were effectively excluded.
158. 'American Jews and Zionism', *American Israelite,* 27 May 1920, p.1.
159. Israel I. Mattuck, 'Palestine and Judaism', *Emanu-El*, 10 September 1920, pp.32–4.
160. See 'Is Zionism dead?'
161. Ibid.
162. 'Palestine or Crimea', letter from IIM, *American Israelite,* 28 January 1926, p.1.
163. Editorial article, *American Israelite,* 15 October 1925, p.4.
164. Notes of the Week, 'Chief Rabbi and Liberals', *Jewish Guardian*, 2 October 1925 p.1.
165. Ibid.
166. Letter from IIM to the editor, *Jewish Guardian*, 2 October 1925, p.9.
167. David Philipson, 'The Continuing Revelation of God', *American Israelite,* 4 March 1926, p.4. The three sermons were published in a booklet, J.H. Hertz, *The New Paths, Whither Do They Lead* (London: Oxford University Press, Humphrey Milford, 1926).
168. Rabbi Dr I.I. Mattuck, 'Liberal Judaism in Great Britain', in *The First Fifty Years – A Record of Liberal Judaism In England, 1900–1950* (London: Liberal Jewish Synagogue, 1950), p.8.
169. See Hertz, *The New Paths*.
170. John D. Rayner, 'Israel I. Mattuck', a talk given at the South London Liberal Synagogue, 28 June 1957, LJS Archives, Box 135a.
171. Lawrence Rigal and Rosita Rosenberg, *Liberal Judaism: The First Hundred Years* (London: Liberal Judaism, 2002), p.67.
172. See *The Reminiscences of Dr Maurice L Perlzweig*. According to Perlzweig, a letter appeared in *The Times* saying: 'How can Rabbi Mattuck say so and so and so and so, when one of his own colleagues in his own pulpit says something different?'.

173. 'Rabbi Mattuck Stirs up London Orthodox Forces, Board of Jewish Deputies Censures But His Congregation Sustains Action', *American Israelite*, 13 January 1927, p.1.
174. Ibid.
175. See Rigal and Rosenberg, *Liberal Judaism,* p.68.
176. See 'Rabbi Mattuck Stirs up London Orthodox Forces.'
177. *JC*, 23 October 1928, p.16.
178. 'What is Happening to Religion in Russia?', sermon given by IIM at the LJS, 5 January 1930, MCC.
179. Editorial comment, in *LJM*, XVII, no.2 (February 1946), p.11. An example of this was when he sought IIM's views when Hertz had been asked for a reference for Maurice Perlzweig.
180. Born in Birmingham, Greenberg worked as a journalist on the *Liberal Daily News* and the *Pall Mall Gazette* before forming a company to purchase the *JC*. David Cesarani, 'The Importance of Being Editor: The *Jewish Chronicle* 1841–1991', *Jewish Historical Studies*, 32 (1990), p.266.
181. See for example Mentor's piece on 'Rational Orthodoxy', in which he responded vigorously to IIM's (perhaps somewhat mischievous) suggestion that Greenberg was an adherent of Liberal Judaism, *JC*, 19 September 1924, p.11.
182. *JC*, 5 December 1924, pp.18–19. 'Mentor' was particularly critical of IIM for inviting Father Day (an East End priest well known for attempting to convert Jews to Christianity) to the meetings. He claimed that Father Day had been present at a conference even though Mattuck claimed that Father Day had not had a formal invitation, which he (Mentor) regarded as being hypocritical.
183. *JC*, 2 October 1924, p.8.
184. IIM was obviously not deterred by the criticism. The following year he wrote a lengthy article for a periodical called *John Bull* detailing his views on moneylending and moneylenders. *John Bull*, 18 July 1925, p.25.
185. *JC*, 17 October 1924, p.9.
186. *JC*, 11 May 1923, p.9
187. Letter from Leopold Greenberg to IIM, 10 February 1921, London Metropolitan Archives, ACC/3529/002/018.
188. 'Watchman' was the pen name of the columnist Simon Gilbert.
189. 'Dr Mattuck's Rhapsody', *JC*, 13 May 1932, p.9.
190. The idea of setting up the league was actually conceived during the war, but took some years to come to fruition. See 'A League of Religions', draft article by IIM (partly published in the *Sunday Evening Telegraph,* 2 November 1919), MCC.
191. *JC*, 19 November 1919, p.13.
192. 'A League of Religions', sermon given by IIM at Oxford, 8 June 1920, MCC.
193. *JC*, 11 June 1920, p.15.
194. See sermon 'A League of Religions'.
195. Ibid.
196. Letter from IIM to Lily Montagu, 29 April 1947, AJA, WUPJ Records, MS-16, D25/9.
197. Liberal Jewish Synagogue Annual Report, 1924, LJS Archives.
198. 'The Jews in Great Britain', draft of article written by IIM for publication in American newspapers, 20 February 1925, MCC.
199. 'Address for Conference', 27 November 1924, in ibid.
200. Ibid.
201. Untitled and undated sermon dealing with the criticisms to the 1924 interfaith conference, in ibid.
202. Ibid. IIM referred in particular to Greenberg's complaint that Jews were not invited to the Lambeth Conference held in 1918 on the subject of organised support for the League of Nations. *JC*, 6 December 1918.
203. 'Jewish-Christian Conference in London', *American Israelite*, 1 January 1925, p.8.
204. 'The Conference of Jews and Christians – from the Jewish Point of View', sermon given by IIM at the LJS, 24 October 1926, MCC.
205. For example, 'Religious Value of Nationalism and War', delivered at Council of Christian and Jews Conference, Friends Meeting House, 29 November 1927, *JRU Bulletin*, V, no.57 (December 1927), pp.6–7.

206. Reverend George Alfred Yates (ed.), *In Spirit and in Truth, Aspects of Judaism and Christianity* (London: London Society of Jews and Christians, 1934). This was the first Jewish-Christian symposium ever published in England.
207. See 'Reviews, Lectures, etc.'.
208. Draft of article by Dorothy Edgar, 'Some Recollections of Rabbi Dr Israel I. Mattuck and Rabbi Doctor Leslie I. Edgar', MFAb.
209. See 'Reviews, Lectures, etc.'.
210. He appears to have preached on a number of occasions at a church in Barry, Wales.
211. 'Co-operation between Jews and Christians', sermon given by IIM at a meeting of the Hampstead Churchmen's Union, 28 May 1929, MCC.
212. Ibid.
213. Montagu, 'Rabbi Dr Israel I. Mattuck, Memorial Tribute', p.2.
214. See John D. Rayner 'The Legacy of Israel Mattuck', in *LJM, In Memoriam, of Israel Mattuck 1883–1954*, p.17.
215. The Very Reverend W.R. Matthews, Dean of St Paul's, 'His Services Beyond the Jewish Community – Promoting Understanding between Jews and Christians', in ibid, p13.
216. Letter from the Reverend Abelson to IIM, dated 11 January 1924, London Metropolitan Archives, ACC/3529/002/018.
217. Letter from IIM to Reverend Abelson, 15 January 1929, LJS Archives, Box 1/2.
218. See 'The World's Work and the Individual'.
219. Ibid.
220. 'When the Jew Looks into the Future', sermon given by IIM at the LJS, 5 January 1929, MCC. See also address on 'Judaism and the Idea of Progress', given by IIM at the Adler Society, Oxford, 4 June 1921, in which he criticised Dean Inge for denying the validity of hope in his lecture on 'Progress', given at the LJS, 4 February 1921, MCC.
221. Rabbi Joel D. Oseran, Associate Director – The World Union for Progressive Judaism, in *Reflections on the World Union for Progressive Judaism Marking the 75th Anniversary of the First World Union Conference, Berlin 1928*, p.27.
222. Rabbi Dr I.I. Mattuck, 'Introduction', *The World Union For Progressive Judaism, The First Twenty-Five Years, 1926–1951*, p.2.
223. Quoted in John D. Rayner, 'Israel I. Mattuck', a talk given at the South London Liberal Synagogue on 28 June 1957, LJS Archives, Box 135a.
224. Rabbi Dr Leo Baeck, 'His Chairmanship of the World Union', in *LJM, In Memoriam, of Israel Mattuck 1883–1954*, p.12.
225. H.M. Sanger 'A Tribute to Dr Mattuck', produced at the time of IIM's 70th birthday for the *Temple Time* of Temple Beth Israel, Melbourne, Australia, sent to the LJS at the time of IIM's death in 1954, MFAb.
226. See Meyer, *Response to Modernity*, p.336.
227. Ibid., p.336.
228. Letter from Rabbi David Philipson to IIM, 14 April 1927, LJS Archives, Box 1/2.
229. Complete statement of IIM's address at the WUPJ Conference in Berlin, March 1928, sent to the German Telegraphic Agency, MCC.
230. 'Liberal Judaism Marches On In All The Occidental Lands: Antenatal Conference World Union for Progressive Judaism Has Second Annual Session in Berlin', *American Israelite*, 24 August 1928, p.1.
231. Minutes of the meeting of the Executive Committee of the World Union for Progressive Judaism, May 1929, AJA, WUPJ Records, MS-16, A1/2.
232. CCAR Yearbook, Vol. XXVII, Buffalo, New York 1917.
233. Letter from IIM to Henry Hurwitz, 7 February 1922, AJA, Henry Hurwitz Papers, Box 34, MS-2.
234. Henry Hurwitz overlapped with IIM at Harvard during 1904–05.
235. Letter in LJS Archives, Box 1/2. It was published by the Cincinnati Tract Commission as part of a collection of tracts in 1935 under the heading of 'Immortality in Judaism' by Rabbi Israel Mattuck. He was paid a fee of $100 for this article.
236. *Directory of Jewish National Organisations 1925* (New York and Boston, MA: American Jewish Historical Society, 1926), p.289.
237. Letter from Julian Morgenstern to IIM, 13 November 1925, London Metropolitan Archives, ACC/3529/002/016.

238. 'Golden Jubilee Hebrew Union College Celebrated at Cincinnati With Imposing Ceremonies', *American Israelite*, 29 October 1925, p.1.
239. *American Israelite*, 2 June 1925, p.6.
240. Letter from Reuben Levy to IIM, 26 October 1925, LJS Archives, Box 1/2.
241. Letter from Julian Morgenstern to IIM, 14 October 1926, in ibid.
242. It appears from the statement made in the *LJS Weekly Bulletin*, April 21 1927, at the time of his departure in 1927, that when he visited America two years earlier to receive his doctorate from HUC, he did not visit his family.
243. 'The Ideal of the Jewish Personality: Baccalaureate Sermon delivered at Graduation Exercises at Hebrew Union College, May 28th', *American Israelite*, 9 June 1927, p.1.
244. 'The Ideal of the Jewish Personality', sermon given by IIM at HUC, 28 May 1927, MCC.
245. Ibid.
246. Letter from Julian Morgenstern to IIM dated 9 June 1927, London Metropolitan Archives, ACC/3529/002/018.
247. This speech was reproduced in full in the *American Israelite*, 7 July 1927, p.5
248. Letter from I.E. Marcuson, Secretary of CCAR to IIM, 5 December 1927, LJS Archives, Box 1/2.
249. *JC*, 22 April 1927, p.25.
250. Letter from Charles Hartman to James Pond, 11 May 1927, London Metropolitan Archives, ACC/3529/002/018.
251. 'Some Aspects of American Life', sermon given by IIM at the LJS on 16 October 1927, MCC. He claimed that throughout his journeys he saw only one 'drunkard'.
252. 'America Revisited' (day not specified) August 1927, draft of article produced by IIM for the *Jewish Guardian* on his return from America, in ibid.
253. Ibid.
254. Ibid.
255. Ibid.
256. Ibid.
257. 'The Jew in America, Part Two', address given by IIM to the North London Liberal Congregation Literary Society (day not specified), July 1927, in ibid.
258. Isaac Landman, 'Dr Israel Mattuck Revisits America', *New York Times*, 27 May 1927, p.127.
259. Ibid.
260. 'The Jew in America, Part One', address given by IIM to the North London Liberal Congregation Literary Society (day not specified), July 1927, MCC.

CHAPTER ELEVEN

Between the Wars

The Great Depression

The Great Depression that originated in America in late 1929 quickly spread across the world. In Britain, the impact of the depression was immediate and devastating. At the depth of the depression in the summer of 1932, registered unemployment stood at 3.5 million, and many more people had only part-time employment. In some towns and cities in the north-east, unemployment reached as high as 70 per cent. While IIM was becoming increasingly preoccupied with international developments and matters impacting on Jewish people, he was clearly deeply moved by the plight of the unemployed and preached often on the economic crisis. His sermons displayed a detailed and thoroughly researched understanding of the factors that had led to the depression. He argued forcefully against the reintroduction of the gold standard, seeing its maintenance as having been responsible for widespread unemployment and many of the economic ills of the world.[1]

While he was acutely aware of the shortcomings of the capitalist system, which meant that 'starvation stands next to plenty, but cannot reach it',[2] IIM was not convinced that the solutions that were being offered as alternatives, particularly communism, were acceptable propositions. He recognised that communism might improve the financial lot of working people, but it represented a 'religious calamity'. He pronounced 'More money in the person cannot make up for poverty in the soul'.[3] He also rejected communism's emphasis on class struggle. Elimination of poverty was far more important than social reorganisation.[4]

IIM believed firmly that society would be improved by a reconsideration of the place of finance in society rather than dispensing with capitalism per se.[5] He argued for 'a society organised with political freedom for individuals and economic control by government in the interests of society'.[6] Although he was gratified that 'the working classes have been roused to aspirations for a better life', IIM regretted that the depression appeared to be having a socially divisive impact,[7] and was alarmed by what he saw as an increasing tendency for political parties to be identified with social classes:

> The dominating political parties have increasingly been identified with the two nations of which Disraeli spoke. The growth of the Labour Party has indicated and stimulated a growing class-consciousness among manual workers and others near them in economic status. The practical end of the Liberal Party gives further evidence of the same tendency. It has been squeezed out by the pressure of the two classes on either side of it.[8]

How the economic crisis should be handled and how the social and economic life of the nation should be regulated once the crises were over was the focal point of the 1931 election.[9] IIM felt that the Conservative government was best suited to deal with the current crisis, principally because financiers from America and France would not trust a socialist government, although he deeply regretted that 'there should be this need for consideration of the views of other countries', especially those that had 'not shown any effective social idealism'.[10] He was less categorical on which party offered the best answer to longer-term change:

> The question, I realise, is always difficult to answer. This time it has been made especially difficult because, while one side has stated its policy, the other asks for a 'doctor's mandate'; while one asks for trust in the honesty and competence of its leaders, the other asks that and approval of the policies the leaders will be expected to carry out.[11]

However, he did indicate that the answer to the question of which party might offer the best solutions to the current emergency might not be the same as the answer to the question of which party might be depended on to work for gradual social improvement.[12] This again illustrates his socialist leanings if not his socialist allegiance. He was clearly appealing to the better instincts of the wealthy members of the LJS when he acknowledged that pursuing solutions to promote a better world might raise conflicts with their material interests.[13] IIM was probably relieved when the general election delivered a cross-party National Government.

Religion and Party Politics

IIM was unapologetic about discussing economic issues at the LJS having, as he said, established with the congregation an agreement that 'religion must consider all matters that have a spiritual, moral or social significance' and that 'It is impossible generally to separate economic questions from social thought.'[14] However, many of the themes of his sermons of the 1930s had a political dimension, and although he declared himself free from party political affiliations, he was aware that not all of his congregants would perceive him to be so. He opened a sermon on 'Politics and Principles' in 1931 by saying:

> I feel myself confronted this morning with one of the most difficult tasks that I have ever attempted. The difficulty lies partly in itself, partly, too, in the fact, which I cannot and would not ignore, that some people think emphatically that nothing connected with politics should be mentioned in a place of worship. Holding, however, a different view I feel it is my duty to discuss the political issues which should now agitate the minds of men and women. And I may not use my own inadequateness and circumstances as an excuse for avoiding the task ... In spite of them, the congregation has given me its confidence, and I owe it such help as I can give to clarify the issues of the election at a religious judgement. In this task, I have one advantage, it is complete freedom [from] party affiliations.[15]

This sermon became the subject of a long, but apparently good-natured debate between IIM and Claude Montefiore. The debate was felt to be sufficiently important for it to be reproduced in a pamphlet, *Religion and Politics*, published later that year by the JRU.[16] This pamphlet merits a brief examination because of the light that it sheds on the relationship between the 'Three Ms'.

In his essay, 'Dr Montefiore's views', which appeared first in the pamphlet, Montefiore set out five different reasons why he felt it difficult for politics to be discussed in a synagogue. In 'his own inimitable way',[17] Montefiore put forward not only his own arguments but also their counter perspectives. He admitted that some of his arguments were more compelling than others and none were conclusive. He was clearly discomforted by IIM's insistence on discussing political issues, but recognised that 'the great preachers and prophets of all ages have by no means confined themselves to saying things which were pleasant and soothing', and that 'we do not come to churches and synagogues to be soothed and quieted'.[18] He challenged his readers to consider all sides of the question before coming to a decision. His conclusion suggests that his main purpose was less to do with curbing IIM and more with silencing IIM's critics in the congregation: 'I see no way out except to leave it to the judgement of the minister, who must weigh the advantages against the disadvantages for the course which, in any particular instance, he may choose to take.'[19]

Commenting on Montefiore's paper, IIM did not take issue with Montefiore's arguments individually, but with the overall risk they posed in dividing religious communities:

> … for a synagogue or church of poor people preaching socialism would not add much to the influence of socialism, and a synagogue or church of rich people preaching the justification and moral excellence of the present capitalist system could hardly expect its teaching to be efficacious except with those who already believe it. I do not maintain that religious institutions do now get anywhere near the ideal of a fellowship of rich and poor; their shortcoming in this respect is especially noticeable in cities. But I am prepared to admit that anything which would tend to interfere with the realisation of that ideal is objectionable.[20]

IIM rejected the premise that, although they might agree on their religious beliefs, the rich man and the poor man would, because of the differences in their material circumstances, come to a different conclusion when applying their religious beliefs to social and moral issues, and he defended robustly the role of religion in influencing its adherents to supplant party allegiance and other considerations with religious motive:

> The whole problem comes down to whether religious people are willing to have the guidance of religion even when it hurts, and whether they trust their churches and synagogues to give them such guidance. If the minister cannot be trusted to judge a political issue with freedom from party prejudices, then he does not belong in the pulpit. And if congregants cannot listen to religious teaching when it goes counter to their views or interests then they do not belong in the pews.[21]

Interestingly, when the pamphlet was reviewed in the *Liberal Jewish Monthly*, Lily Montagu, who was usually unquestioning of IIM's instruction, was not totally convinced by his treatise: 'I felt, if I may say so, with the greatest respect, that his survey of the influence of religion, was not sufficiently inclusive, and I wonder if any of his readers felt the same slight mystification as myself.'[22] In her review Lily Montagu also indicated that she had, on occasion, disagreed radically with IIM's pronouncements: 'I remember what agony I, as a pacifist endured, when listening to sermons during the years of the war, even from those whom I revered most.'[23] Like Montefiore, Lily Montagu nevertheless upheld IIM's right 'to examine political issues from a religious standpoint', and suggested that a notice be placed over the door of the LJS saying 'All you who enter in – drop ideas based on self-interest and prejudice outside'.[24]

The Pollitt Incident

While IIM and Claude Montefiore were generally able to deal with their differences of outlook in an amicable way, and Montefiore usually supported IIM in his occasional altercations with the lay leadership of the LJS, the dispute that erupted in 1934 was to prove much more acrimonious and far more intractable.

With the encouragement of IIM, in 1922 a Men's Discussion Group was set up at the LJS. Akin to the Brotherhoods being established at this time in Reform synagogues in America as a means for dealing with waning spiritual commitment, the Discussion Group met on a regular basis to discuss topical issues. Interestingly, at IIM's insistence, no women were allowed to participate in its proceedings.[25] The Discussion Group decided to invite the prominent and controversial communist politician, Harry Pollitt,[26] to speak at its December 1934 meeting.

Three members of the LJS Council – Montefiore, Sir Philip Hartog and Horace Myer – took great exception to a communist speaking at the synagogue and insisted that the invitation be withdrawn. IIM was incensed by this suggestion, not only because he believed strongly in freedom of speech, but also because he was concerned about the message that this would send to the membership of the Discussion Group. He feared that it would discourage younger members from participating in synagogue life and thus threaten the future of the LJS.[27]

The debate became quite heated with both IIM and Claude Montefiore offering to resign. While he accepted that the council had the right to decide whether or not a society should exist, IIM felt that it should not pronounce on what society members could or could not discuss.[28] On the other hand, Montefiore believed that his position would be 'untenable' if Pollitt were to enter the LJS building.[29] IIM resolved the impasse by suggesting that the invitation to Pollitt should not be withdrawn but that the meeting at which he was to speak should be held outside the LJS.

Although the immediate issue had been addressed, Claude Montefiore insisted on changes being made to the LJS constitution to make it clear that the council had ultimate authority over what went on in the synagogue. He wanted to prevent the reoccurrence of what he referred to as the 'Pollitt Affair'.[30] A lengthy exchange of letters ensued. IIM was deeply unhappy about the proposed constitutional changes as he felt that they undermined his right as a spiritual leader to rule on matters of principle. He said that the council was rejecting the 'authority of the Priest' and substituting it with 'the authority of the Presbyter'.[31] Claude Montefiore stated that he was not willing to be a mere figurehead whose views were negligible. Neither IIM nor Montefiore were able to change the position of the other but IIM did eventually, with some demur, agree to the wording of a constitutional amendment.

Claude Montefiore obviously felt wounded by the dispute, pleading to IIM in one letter: 'Do say a kindly word to me',[32] and IIM continued to believe that Montefiore's intervention had been unjustified and uncalled for, and that he (IIM) had been forced to compromise his principles. He complained, 'I don't feel very kindly about having it – this matter – forced on me'.[33] Eventually however, IIM and Claude Montefiore were able to put the affair behind them, and by October 1935 Montefiore was writing to IIM suggesting that the dispute had actually drawn them closer together and aided their understanding of each other.[34]

The Pollitt incident is interesting because of the light it sheds on the political differences between the two men. We have already seen that Montefiore was reluctant for IIM to become associated with the Labour party and socialism, so he naturally had an even greater distaste for communism and organised labour. This abhorrence was common in the aristocratic Anglo-Jewry milieu from which Montefiore came.

Moral Issues

A different feature of IIM's sermons and addresses in the 1930s was the attention he gave to the moral issues being debated at the time. Like other adherents of traditional religions, IIM seems to have found this decade a difficult period, because as the Victorian social order collapsed it was replaced by a new mass culture of consumption and new ideas such as those of Freud spread widely. The progressive impulse that had dominated IIM's early years gave way to cynicism:

> There are many signs of the world's unhappiness, varying in their character all the way from a mad and incessant pursuit of amusement, or physical pleasures among young people to the dabbling by dear old ladies in superstitious occultism which satisfied from a hidden world their cravings for what they cannot have in this one. Though there is a large traffic in pleasure, there is no satisfaction. The amount of money spent on amusements is unbelievably large. The kind of amusements is almost unbelievably tawdry. My criticism is not of the amusements but of the mentality that is satisfied with them.[35]

IIM abhorred what he saw as an increasing 'tendency towards destructionism', and the mood of the age that was 'rebellious against accepted standards without definitely formulating its own'.[36] He was saddened by the pessimistic attitude and spiritual despair of the people of that time, although he saw it as an inevitable consequence of the economic depression, and more especially of the development of scientific thought: 'It is hard to think that human life in general, and still less that any particular life, is worth anything, when we are told that man is an accident on earth that is an accident in a universe which is inexplicable.'[37]

In the face of these changes, IIM declared that he felt it incumbent on him to speak out against the defiant mood of the age and contribute to defining a 'new morality' fitting for the industrial era, which would 'include and strengthen the best that was in the old morality and go beyond it in the understanding of duty and right'. His fervent hope was that 'the conditions of our time will not mark the beginning of the end of our civilisation, but the beginning of a better era of our civilisation'.[38]

IIM felt that the morals of the young generation of the day were no worse than those of preceding generations, but society's values had shifted.[39] He cited the example of divorce. Although there were now more divorces, this was not because marriage was less sacred, it was because divorce was less of social disgrace.[40] IIM spoke and wrote candidly about a number of controversial issues such as birth control, marital fidelity, sexual relations and eugenics, which attracted to his addresses many young people. His liberal outlook on these matters echoed the arguments then being put forward by Reform rabbis in America.[41]

In 1927 IIM had stated forcefully that 'A marriage which from choice avoids the creation of new life, is religiously wrong', and that 'those who by choice avoid the responsibility of children transgress a religious law'.[42] However, a few years later he clarified his views. He argued that 'Jewish tradition does not oppose the practice of Birth-Control by the use of contraceptive methods', drawing attention to an old law (unnamed), which 'even seemed to command the practice of contraception in certain cases where pregnancy might be a danger either to the mother or a child'.[43] However, he condemned the 'frivolous use' of contraceptives.[44] A year later, now even more confident in his views, he asserted that large families could create social problems as well as difficulties between husbands and wives.[45]

IIM believed that similar arguments applied to abortion, but that the 'facts must be even more urgent'. He was also able to countenance sterilisation of those 'indubitably unfit' to bear children.[46] However, he disagreed strongly with those who argued for limiting the size of families among what they referred to as the 'lower orders', in order to reduce the burden to society. He saw this argument as being 'vitiated by an unhealthy class consciousness'.[47] In holding this view he was at odds with his American Reform colleagues who had recently passed a resolution which stated that birth control was especially important for the 'lower classes' of society because 'there is a growing and justified widespread opinion that the citizenship material ought to be more carefully and eugenically selected'.[48]

Despite these progressive attitudes towards birth control, abortion and sterilisation, there were some more reactionary aspects to IIM's views. He continued to argue against the spread of information on these topics, which, as a man of religion, he felt encouraged 'cohabitation outside the marital relation'.[49] He condemned George Bernard Shaw for suggesting in his play *Man and Superman*, that reproduction was the chief aim of women's existence.[50] He found distasteful Bertrand Russell's insistence on 'complete freedom of relation between the sexes' and deplored Russell's 'denying also to marriage the right to restrict it'.[51] IIM particularly abhorred Russell's view expressed in his 1929 book, *Morals and Marriage,* that the sole purpose of marriage was to perpetuate the human race and had little to do with the 'personal feelings of husband and wife'.

IIM was clearly discomforted by changing views of marriage. He continued to hold that marriage was 'a special relationship rooted in love' and that it was guided by standards of conduct that enabled man to express the good within him and achieve the highest fulfilment of his humanity.[52] He dismissed the suggestion that previous experience of relationships helped to make successful marriages with the comment: 'Judging by the number of times some people have been divorced and remarried, one would have judged there was sufficient evidence of the danger in variety!'[53] He opined that, 'those who flit from mate to mate, like a butterfly in a garden, are more conspicuous for their emotional emptiness than their happiness ... The morality advocated by Mr Russell means not even happiness, but simply more licence.'[54] However, he was willing to admit that, where marriages had irrevocably broken down, 'maintenance of the legal and even physical relation may be a sin against the spirit of man. Frivolous divorce is an evil; but so too is loveless marriage.'[55]

IIM did not confine himself to commenting on moral issues in England. He also examined changing morality in other countries such as in Bolshevik Russia. He was highly critical of what he saw as the laxity of the arrangements for divorce established by the Bolsheviks:

> When a couple want to live together as husband and wife, they appear together before the appropriate official to have their marriage recorded. If either one later finds that he or she has had enough of this marriage, he or she appears before the appropriate official to have a divorce recorded. The only difference between marriage and divorce is that it takes two to make a marriage, but only one to make a divorce. This is realism in morals carried to the full limits of logic.[56]

He was even more critical of the fact that in Bolshevik Russia, marriage was not necessary to permit relations which 'in other codes is considered immoral outside marriage', and which allowed 'complete freedom between the sexes'.[57] While reluctant to write these arrangements off as 'licentious', IIM did express his distaste for what he described as 'the morality of atheism'.[58]

West London Synagogue and Rabbi Reinhart

During his first twenty years in England, IIM fostered good relations between the LJS and West London Synagogue in Marble Arch, the history of which has previously been mentioned. He was assisted by the geographical proximity of West London Synagogue to the LJS and the close family ties between the two congregations. IIM was on good terms with the rabbis of West London Synagogue and met with them regularly to discuss matters of mutual interest.

The senior ministers of the LJS and West London Synagogue also preached at each other's synagogue. In IIM's case, this was not always without controversy. Morris Joseph, the senior minister at West London Synagogue, staunchly defended IIM out of 'fraternal feeling towards the Liberal Jewish Synagogue and its minister', after a small number of his more conservative congregants objected to some of IIM's remarks when he preached at the synagogue in April 1917.[59] The topic of his sermon was 'The Ideal in Human Life', in which he had counselled against materialism. IIM's presence had drawn a large crowd because of his reputation as a great orator.[60] However, some synagogue members complained that they had not been consulted about the invitation.[61] One correspondent declared in a letter to the *Jewish Chronicle* that IIM's sermon was 'outside Judaism', while Lionel Lucas, who called himself 'the oldest living member of the synagogue', said that he would rather have seen the Archbishop of Canterbury in the pulpit than IIM.[62] The controversy rumbled on for many months and reopened a debate about IIM's right to be called 'rabbi'. HUC was greatly offended that IIM's ordination should be called into question.[63]

Two years later, IIM was invited back to preach at West London Synagogue. This time the invitation came from the lay leadership rather than from the minister,[64] but again it caused disquiet. Whereas on the previous occasion the *Jewish Chronicle* had supported IIM, the newspaper now felt that it was inappropriate for IIM to preach at West London Synagogue given that he had recently affirmed publicly the differences between Liberal Judaism and the rest of Anglo-Jewry.[65]

Despite these controversies, the two synagogues continued to cooperate in supporting the St George's Jewish Settlement in the East End.

Changes in forms of worship and ritual at West London Synagogue during the 1920s brought its services closer to those of the LJS. However, the goodwill between the LJS and West London Synagogue diminished during the 1930s after Harold Reinhart became Senior Rabbi there. Rabbi Reinhart and IIM overlapped at HUC, from which Reinhart graduated in 1915. The leadership of the LJS knew Reinhart prior to his appointment to West London Synagogue because he had been approached in 1921 when the LJS was looking for a second minister. Reinhart, then a rabbi in Baton Rouge, Louisiana, had declined to be considered. This was due to his reluctance at the time to be separated from his parents and the LJS's unwillingness to offer him financial assistance for visiting them, rather than for ideological reasons.[66]

Having heard that Reinhart, now a rabbi in Sacramento, was being considered for the West London Synagogue pulpit, in 1928 IIM wrote to a friend, Rabbi Newman, in San Francisco saying that he knew Reinhart when they were students together and found him to be 'a charming fellow'.[67] IIM was subsequently involved in Reinhart's appointment to West London Synagogue when he was asked by the lay leadership of the synagogue to seek references for Reinhart from American rabbis.[68] Reinhart was appointed and prior to his arrival he wrote to IIM saying that his presence was 'going to be a tremendous help and comfort'.[69] IIM was equally fulsome about Reinhart coming to England, which he said would help relations between the two synagogues.[70]

IIM wrote to Julian Morgenstern at HUC, saying that he was sure that Reinhart was 'especially fit' for what was a difficult position. He asked Morgenstern if he would be prepared to write a letter to the *Jewish Chronicle* in support of Reinhart, to counteract the deprecatory remarks about him that had appeared in the newspaper and to help Reinhart establish himself in England.[71] Soon after Reinhart's appointment, the two rabbis started to discuss proposals for setting up systematic arrangements for training Progressive rabbis.[72] To IIM's gratification, Reinhart persuaded the lay leadership of West London Synagogue to reverse its previous decision not to participate in the World Union for Progressive Judaism (WUPJ).[73]

However, for reasons that are not clear, within a few years the relationship between IIM and Reinhart had cooled. Although they were both disciples of Kaufmann Kohler, they came from very different social backgrounds and were very different in their demeanours. While IIM was a refugee and had a Talmudic background, Reinhart came from an assimilated family from America's West,[74] was 'a poetic soul'[75] and 'a man of aristocratic bearing and autocratic tendencies'.[76] Unlike IIM, Reinhart never felt the need to rebel against orthodoxy imposed upon him as a child.

It has been argued by one writer that these cultural differences accounted for the eventual frosty relations between IIM and Reinhart.[77]

Despite the animosity, Rabbi Reinhart continued to preach at the LJS,[78] and in 1936 IIM and Reinhart attempted to put aside their mutual antipathy and sought to bring about closer cooperation between Liberal and Reform synagogues. However, after a few meetings the attempt was abandoned on IIM's recommendation,[79] the failure of the discussions being, in part, attributed to the uneasy relationship between the two men.[80] Subsequently, Reinhart's rancour towards IIM became so strong that it developed into an antagonism towards the Liberal Judaism he represented and prompted him to formulate his slogan of 'Non-adjectival Judaism', suggesting that his own synagogue represented the 'Authentic Tradition'.[81]

Spreading Liberal Judaism

During the 1930s, IIM supported developing Liberal communities in Birmingham and in Brighton, both of which were formally constituted in 1935. His work in developing Liberal Judaism in these years received an eloquent tribute from Claude Montefiore:

> He has immensely increased the strength and vitality of the Liberal Jewish Movement in this country, and by so doing he has increased the vitality and strength of Judaism as a whole. It is good to think that there are many outside the pale of Judaism who have been helped by his words, and there are still more who, through him, have come to understands better what Judaism stands for, and what Liberal Judaism means.[82]

IIM was also prominent in supporting new and developing Progressive communities in other countries, especially the community in Haifa led by Dr Elk and the community in Melbourne founded after Mrs Ada Philips, its lay leader, had visited the LJS in 1928 and had been inspired by IIM.[83] In his role as chairman of WUPJ, IIM travelled to many European countries, but especially to Holland, where he supported the development of the Progressive community in The Hague, and to Germany to attend conferences and meetings. While visiting these countries, he sometimes also preached, such as in July 1931 when he gave a sermon at the Berlin Reform Temple.

IIM's activities did not always have the total support of his American Reform colleagues. In January 1931, he was strongly criticised by Rabbi Solomon Freehof, a prominent rabbi from Chicago and contributing editor of the *American Israelite*, for sending Progressive Jewish missionaries into Orthodox communities.[84] Freehof argued that Reform Jews, by missionary efforts, 'open themselves to the same criticism, which the Reform Jews themselves level against Christians who seek to convert Jews'.[85] IIM was incensed by Freehof's remarks and there followed a series of acrimonious letters between the two rabbis, which appeared in the pages of the *American Israelite* during the early months of 1931. IIM pointed out that his letter – the one that had appeared in the *American Israelite* in November 1930 and had given rise to Freehof's comments – had not discussed the sending of missionaries into Orthodox communities; it had reported on the appointment of a Reform rabbi, Rabbi Mark, to work with an existing Progressive community in Melbourne to help them establish a synagogue. IIM chastised Freehof for being 'more eager not to hurt the religious intolerance of some than to satisfy the religious needs of others.[86] He clearly saw Freehof's remarks as hypocritical:

> Some time ago I read that Rabbi Freehof's congregation conducted a campaign to increase its membership. Where were the new members sought? I must of course exclude the possibility that they were taken away from other Reform Synagogues. I must assume that they were people not attending other Synagogues, whom Rabbi Freehof wanted to win for religious attachment. It was a good piece of missionary work; and justified, though these new members had not been, to use Rabbi Freehof's words, 'unattached electrons floating about in an empty cosmos', but belonged to the Jewish community of Chicago. I suspect that the people joining Rabbi Mark's congregation in Melbourne are very much like those that Rabbi Freehof's campaign brought to this congregation.[87]

Julian Morgenstern at HUC was drawn into the dispute. He claimed to be 'distressed indeed by the attitude which Freehof has taken' and saw his comments as being 'not a little malicious'.[88] Morgenstern sent several long letters to Freehof encouraging him to take a more supportive attitude to the work of the WUPJ, but they had no effect. He urged IIM to 'let the matter rest' having made his forceful argument about Freehof's Chicago campaign.[89] IIM heeded Morgenstern's advice and did not respond to Freehof's third editorial attack. He was convinced that Freehof's criticisms were personally motivated.[90] This incident is perhaps an early indication of IIM's divergence from mainstream CCAR rabbis, which was to become more apparent during the 1930s, and his continuing commitment to HUC, which was to remain wedded to the main tenets of 'classical' Reform Judaism for longer than CCAR.

As we have seen, IIM welcomed the overall diversity of views that existed amongst the members of the WUPJ. However he was sometimes downhearted by the views expressed by individual sections. In the years leading up to the Second World War, he was shocked when at a WUPJ conference, some young people from Germany said that they wanted 'to be told what to do just as the Nazi youth were told'. He saw this as a 'negation of liberalism'.[91]

As the 1930s progressed, the nascent WUPJ found itself starved of funding, and without the full support of its besieged German constituent, its activities were scaled down and IIM's WUPJ involvements became less demanding.

Jewish Communal Politics

During the 1930s, the Anglo-Jewish community faced three main interrelated challenges, all arising from outside the community: escalating anti-Semitism at home and abroad, the fate of the European refugees from Nazism, and the question of a Jewish homeland. Different sections of the Anglo-Jewish community took different positions on each of these issues and relations between the different factions were tense and often fractious.

The widely varying views that were voiced reflected not only differences in religious and political thinking, but also the changes that were taking place in the nature of Anglo-Jewry. The acculturated and patrician Jewish families who dominated communal organisations and Jewish affairs were gradually being replaced by first and second generation Jews with an Eastern European background now moving up the social and economic ladder. With the exit of the 'Cousinhood' (the Anglo-Jewish gentry), the latitudinarian orthodoxy that had grown up in the Victorian era began to break down and to give way to a more strident and sectarian traditionalism. The cohesion that Anglo-Jewry had valued proved increasingly difficult to maintain under the weight of the challenges facing the community. The changes did not happen as quickly or as dramatically as in America, with its more dynamic economy, but by British standards, the change was fairly rapid.

IIM played a highly prominent role in the many debates that took place during the decade. However, the arguments that he put forward did not confine him to either the 'activist' or 'moderate' camp. For instance, his consciousness of the urgency of the problems created by the rise of Nazism in Germany did not necessarily lead him to argue vociferously for the establishment of a Jewish national home. His views, as we shall see, were more complex and not always in tune with those of the lay leadership of the synagogue.

Many of IIM's views were articulated at the Sunday morning services – which reached the zenith of their popularity and efficacy during the 1930s

– and in the powerful and polemic lecture-sermons he gave elsewhere in these years. In 1936, by which time there was much on which IIM felt he needed to comment, the Sunday services were supplemented by mid-week services aimed at both Jewish and non-Jewish audiences. Noted for his articulacy since his arrival in Britain, IIM now reached his heights as an orator and used his skill to the full to convey his messages. He was an outstanding figure in Anglo-Jewry.

Anti-Semitism

Once the Bolshevik scare and xenophobia of the immediate post-First World War period had receded, adverse views on Jews during the 1920s were generally neither brutish nor shrill.[92] IIM was therefore at times inclined to think that anti-Semitism was 'best left unnoticed by Jews'.[93] He even perceived some positive impacts of anti-Semitism:

> Anti-Semitism, in so far as it emphasises the religious distinctiveness of the Jew, has its values for the Jewish consciousness. It stimulates loyalty, it keeps ever mindful of its peculiar possession and treasure, it also enforces a sense of responsibility to the Jewish brotherhood.[94]

With the onset of the Great Depression and the rising tide of anti-Semitism that accompanied it, IIM's messages on anti-Semitism became more challenging. He recognised that although prejudice against the Jews had always existed and was a price for their distinctiveness, the anti-Semitism he was now witnessing was totally different in its character. Whereas it was formerly an expression chiefly of religious intolerance, 'the result of resentment or variation', the new anti-Semitism was 'racial, economic, nationalistic'. Worryingly, it was also being 'used by some who hope to find in it a way to power which they have been unable to reach in other ways'.[95]

As early as 1930, IIM preached at the LJS on 'The Jewish Position – A Reply to the Anti-Semite', and on 'The Causes of Anti-Semitism',[96] drawing attention to events in Germany where a political party (the National Socialists), was making anti-Semitism a central plank of its political platform and had become the second largest party in the Reichstag. He also highlighted anti-Semitic outbursts in various Eastern European countries including Rumania and Czechoslovakia. He pointed to the lack of rationality of anti-Semitic reasoning:

> In one breath they accuse the Jews of responsibility for the Young Reparations plan which they describe as a method of exploiting

> Germany for the benefit of financiers and capitalists; in the next breath they fulminate against the Jews for being Marxists and capitalists.[97]

IIM's purpose was not merely to silence the anti-Semites, but to disprove their claims against the Jews, making clear the roots of political anti-Semitism. He saw it as 'the offspring of that German nationalism that culminated in the war', and which was once again threatening world peace.[98] He became increasingly concerned not just about the impact of rising anti-Semitism on the future of Jews, but also on their spirit and their thought:

> It is always one of the dangers of anti-Semitism that it may make the Jew narrow. And I fear that I can see the signs of the reality of that danger in some of the consequences of Hitlerism on Jewish thought. Not only in the development in religious life and thought, but in the exaggerated Jewish self-consciousness which some Jews express in a boisterous and belligerent Jewish chauvinism. Hitler has turned some bad Jews into bellicose Jewish nationalists and it has increased bellicosity in others.[99]

Given the violent anti-Semitism of the Nazis, IIM was at a loss to comprehend the small number of German Jews who supported Hitler. He condemned them both for their lack of self-respect in being prepared to 'make league with those who deny them the status they feel belongs to them' and, even more so, for supporting 'an immoral nationalism that openly declares its readiness to go to war for the sake of its economic interests'. He said that to 'kill for money is no less criminal when done in the name of national selfishness than when it is done in the name of individual selfishness'.[100]

In 1930 IIM was still celebrating the lack of anti-Semitism in England, which he saw as being the result of the English tradition of liberalism and tolerance of differences.[101] However, within two years Oswald Moseley and his British Union of Fascists (BUF) – commonly known as the 'Blackshirts' – were engaged in virulent anti-Semitic propaganda and provoking physical attacks on Jews in the East End of London. They became a regular topic of discussion at LJS Sunday services. IIM condemned Moseley and his followers for their 'attack at [the] weakest points in [an] effort to produce a semblance of truth for their accusations'.[102]

The urgency of IIM's messages contrasted sharply to the initial hesitancy of other communal leaders in condemning growing anti-Semitism in the East End and elsewhere. There was a readiness amongst most Jewish communal organisations to accept that the BUF was not anti-Semitic in principle.[103] IIM disagreed with the Board of Deputies when they continued to believe that anti-Semitic activities were 'conducted by agents under direct instructions from abroad'.[104] Although he perceived that 'anti-Semites everywhere have come out into the open under the dark shadows flung by Hitlerism', he was in no doubt that the seeds of British anti-Semitism lay closer to home.[105] The characteristic response of the Jewish establishment to concerns about anti-Semitism was that Jewish people should always be on their best behaviour to avoid providing fodder for anti-Semites, but IIM felt that this dealt with the symptoms of anti-Semitism rather than its underlying causes, especially unemployment.[106]

IIM was angered by instances of discrimination against Jewish people, which were spreading across the country. In 1932 he wrote to the *Daily Express*, the newspaper that uncovered the issue, protesting against the fact that leading insurance companies were refusing insurance to Jewish people. He railed:

> It is characteristic of the mentally blind that they base large generalisations on very limited experience. That is what the insurance companies are doing to discriminate against Jews. It is so easy. And some minds prefer easy falsehoods to fair judgements.[107]

When the *Sunday Express* asked why Jewish people were 'so touchy' about being discriminated against in this way, IIM explained that a 'mostly healthy body becomes sensitive through many blows' and centuries of persecution had made Jews sensitive.[108]

However, IIM was much more concerned about events in Germany. In the pages of the *Liberal Jewish Monthly* he drew attention to the increasing electoral victories of what he called 'the Hitlerists'. In May 1932 when Hitler failed to gain the presidency but captured nearly 40 per cent of the votes, IIM wrote in an editorial:

> The Jews of Germany have escaped from a serious danger. The defeat of Hitler at the German presidential elections saved them from a great political calamity. Hitlerism preaches the expulsion from Germany of all East European Jews and the denial of political and civil rights to the German Jews. Such threats sound so barbaric that it is difficult to take them seriously, even when they come from such unbalanced nationalist fanatics as Hitler and his followers. It is fairly certain, however, that had Hitler come to power, he would have closed all public offices to Jews, and he would have done all that government could do to restrict the economic opportunities of Jews ... He could have harassed and persecuted Jews.[109]

When Hitler became chancellor, IIM's fears proved grounded. His warnings on the fate of Jews in Europe were now given with increasing frequency and urgency to both Jewish and non-Jewish audiences.[110] At a large gathering of the Cardiff Business Club in March 1933, IIM delivered an address on 'Jews and Christians'.[111] He called for religions to come together to speak out against what was happening in Germany, which was 'falling back to the depths of the Russia of Nicholas II', thereby contradicting the chairman of the event who in his opening speech had placed doubt on the veracity of the reports of persecution of Jews emanating from Germany.[112]

A year later, a Sunday service at which IIM preached on 'Fascism in Germany' was covered in great detail by a periodical called *Truth*. The reporter, 'Eutychus', praised IIM for his 'penetrating sincerity' and his humanity, and noted the passion with which he spoke.[113] In an address he gave before the Hull Literary Society in March 1937, IIM said with great feeling 'You know of the Jew's treatment in Germany, but the worst you know is still not the worst as it is'.[114]

IIM was gratified that the British press ranging from the left-wing *Daily Herald* to the right-wing *Morning Post*, became united in their protests against acts of violence perpetrated by the Nazis. However, he felt frustrated that Jews in other countries were powerless to do anything to help their fellow Jews in Germany.[115] The fear was that if Jews were to organise against Nazism, they would open themselves to the false charge of an international conspiracy similar to the accusations that were made after the end of the First World War.[116] Because of this fear, IIM spoke out against the convening of a Jewish World Conference as advocated by Stephen Wise[117] and propounded that 'Christians and Christianity have a special responsibility in this crisis in Germany's life'.[118] Given his fears about conspiracy theories, we might wonder how IIM rationalised his own international work with the WUPJ.

Speaking shortly after the passing of the Nuremberg Laws, IIM was again critical of Stephen Wise:

> At the recent Zionist Conference, Dr Stephen Wise of New York informed the Jews of Germany that they would have been better off if they had not insisted on being German of the Jewish faith. Therein he agrees with Dr Goebbels and the other Nazis who also objected to the Jews calling themselves Germans.[119]

Although the Anglo-Jewish community failed to rouse the British government to the dangers of 'Hitlerism', IIM's personal exertions to keep what was happening in Germany in the public eye were outstanding and self-sacrificing. He was afraid that because no new anti-Jewish legislation had been enacted after the Nuremburg Laws, people might conclude that persecution against the Jews in Germany had ceased when in fact they were 'the whipping-boy for every failure of the Nazi regime'. He warned that new laws were not necessary for purpose of persecution; it was being carried out by 'party measures, police action, and the like'.[120]

While there is no evidence to show that IIM supported the call for an official boycott of German goods, he did see the need for more concerted action than did the Board of Deputies and the Anglo-Jewish Association (AJA). Both bodies were still reluctant to embarrass the British Government, whose policy was to appease Germany, or to do anything which might suggest that the interests of British Jews were any different from other citizens. IIM warned against 'the general attractiveness of non-interference'. German anti-Semitism was so evil and such a threat to civilisation, it called for 'emphatic and constant denunciation'.[121]

We have seen that, as a younger man, IIM had been somewhat phlegmatic about anti-Semitism in America. However, by the 1930s he was less sanguine about Jewish-Christian relations there. He particularly objected to the growing discrimination against Jews in American universities and colleges and the imposition of quotas. He perceived that there had been a 'significant change' in non-Jewish public opinion about Jewish people since the time he was growing up in America. Whereas Jews once revelled in the rights they had as American citizens, now they were on the defensive, and had to be satisfied with press articles which, 'as a sign of friendship', minimised Jewish influence on the economy.[122]

However, IIM was optimistic that the work being carried out by the American National Conference of Jews and Christians (which he said that, unlike interfaith bodies in Britain, did not confine itself to discussing religious issues) would help to abate increasing anti-Semitism and improve relations between Jews and their neighbours.[123] He took great heart when President Roosevelt appealed for friendship and harmony between Jews and Christians in the address he gave at a 'Brotherhood Day' organised by the National Conference in 1936.[124]

Faced with the rising tide of anti-Semitism in Britain, Europe and elsewhere, IIM became involved with the World Congress of Faiths, set up in 1936 under the leadership of Sir Francis Younghusband to 'make a contribution to a new world order by inculcating a better spirit between man and man and nation and nation and to promote world fellowship through religion'.[125] In July 1936 the Congress held twenty sessions over a two-day period at University College, London, one of which was led by IIM.

Even though IIM had for several years been predicting great atrocities in Germany, by 1938 he was admitting that his worst imaginings had been exceeded. He no longer believed that the German Jews were merely being forced back into a ghetto; they had now been 'practically destroyed'. They had 'only two possibilities of escape: death or emigration'.[126] When he preached at the Intercession Service held at the LJS on 17 July 1938, he referred to the Evian Conference held earlier in the month at which thirty-two nations had resolved to help the persecuted Jews to escape. IIM praised the 'spirit of willingness' shown at the conference, but felt that it had not gone far enough; too many people were still arguing that it was wrong to intervene in the internal affairs of other countries.[127] He was scathing about one 'Christian clergyman' (unnamed) who had defended the imprisonment of German clergy speaking out against National Socialism on the basis that they should have confined themselves to preaching the gospel. It was obvious that IIM felt that time was running out for European Jews.

European Refugees

IIM's profound sympathy for human suffering was evident from his arrival at the LJS. His support for the Belgian refugees and his weekly collections for Jewish people suffering in Eastern Europe during the First World War are just two early examples of his concern. He was involved in the intra-communal Federation of Ukrainian Jews (the Chief Rabbi was its President), which provided aid to those who suffered as the result of pogroms and made representations to Parliament about their plight.

IIM was acquainted with Lucien Wolf who, during the latter part of the nineteenth century, had played a prominent role in attempting to alleviate the suffering of Russian Jews by negotiating with the Tsars. This would have had personal meaning for IIM, and may have been what prompted him to invite Wolf to speak at the LJS in 1917.[128] In turn, IIM was one of the prominent guests present at the celebration of Wolf's 70th birthday hosted by the Jewish Historical Society in February 1927.[129]

As Vice-President of the Joint British Committee for the Reconstruction of Eastern European Jewry, the 'Ort-Oze', IIM attended an international conference held in Berlin in August 1930[130] and an Appeal Dinner held at the Savoy Hotel in October 1930, the guest of honour at which was Professor Albert Einstein. IIM sat on the top table alongside Einstein, H.G. Wells, Viscount Herbert Samuel, the Chief Rabbi, Sir Philip Hartog and Lady Sassoon (both of the latter were LJS Council members).[131] The following year, IIM appealed eloquently for intra-communal support for 'the stricken Jewries of Russia, Poland and other Eastern European countries' at an 'At Home' hosted by Henrietta (Netta)

Franklin, a sister of Lily Montagu and council member of the LJS. At this dinner he said with great empathy that he was aware of the 'morass of despair' amongst Jews in Eastern Europe and of their 'slough of hopeless despondency'.[132] IIM was moved not only by the ongoing plight of Eastern European Jews, but also by one-off crises such as the flooding in Poland in 1935 when he joined the committee of the Federation of Polish Jews in Britain, which appealed for donations to alleviate the suffering of the large number of Jews affected by the flooding.[133]

However, IIM's desire to alleviate hardship and oppression experienced by Jews was never more evident than in the way that he worked tirelessly to support German Jewry in the years leading up to the Second World War. In April 1933 IIM made his first appeal at the LJS on behalf of German Jews.[134] In July that year he occupied a platform with the Chief Rabbi at a Jewish Service of Intercession in support of German Jews coming to Britain. The service, held at the Royal Albert Hall was attended by hundreds of people from all sections of Anglo-Jewry.[135] In the same year he joined the Appeal Council of the Central British Fund for German Jewry based at Woburn House, alongside communal leaders such as Lionel de Rothschild, Viscount Bearsted, Sir Herbert Samuel, and Neville Laski as well as the Chief Rabbi.[136] In the following year he was one of the prominent speakers who appealed for financial support for the fund.[137]

IIM's response to the increasing number of refugees leaving Germany after Hitler became chancellor in 1933 was again more proactive and concerted than that of the Anglo-Jewish establishment in general, which was deeply ambivalent about Britain becoming a sanctuary for German-Jewish refugees, fearing that an increase in the size of the Jewish community would increase anti-Semitism.[138] While they were certainly not indifferent to the sufferings of German Jews, the 'communal notables' were committed to acting in a way consistent with their notion of correct political behaviour. IIM devoted a great deal of effort to raising money for the emigration and welfare of refugees, especially children and young people from Germany and other countries affected by Nazism.

After Kristallnacht on 9 November 1938, the British government agreed to allow 10,000 unaccompanied Jewish children into Britain provided the Jewish community made itself responsible for their upkeep. This called for an intensification of the local efforts for the reception and relief of refugees and, under the strain, a note of acerbity appeared to be growing in the relations between the parties involved. IIM preached a sermon at the LJS in which he asked the congregation to think seriously about providing a home for a child from the Kindertransport.[139] He established a fund known as 'Dr Mattuck's Refugee Fund', which provided guarantees for German Jews to come to Britain while waiting to emigrate to other countries.[140] In the first instance this fund was used to help those in the greatest danger to leave Germany, including a number of Liberal rabbis who were in concentration camps, and also friends and relatives of members of the LJS congregation.

IIM provided a role model for his congregants to follow. He personally sponsored a number of children who came to the country on Kindertransport. One such refugee was Marianne Dreyfus, the granddaughter of the foremost German Liberal rabbi, Leo Baeck, who later recalled:

> I was one of the children who sailed on January 18, 1939 from Hamburg to Southampton on a Kindertransport fearful that I might never again see my family. Edna and Rabbi Israel Mattuck welcomed me into their home, together with other refugee children. A few days later, Mrs Mattuck took me shopping for school uniforms, and sent me off to St Margaret's School in Westgate, Kent ...[141]

IIM also helped to bring a number of prominent people to England, such as the well-known scientist Ernst Chain, who was later awarded a Nobel Prize.[142] He also took into his own home a young German man, Gerhard Stein, from Breslau, whom he helped to obtain a place at Cambridge.[143] As IIM's work became widely known, the LJS was inundated by appeals for help from many different quarters.[144] IIM appointed Leslie Edgar, now assistant minister at the LJS and IIM's son-in-law (see Chapter Fourteen), to take charge of the committee established to identify which Jews would be assisted to escape from Germany, decide how they would be supported after their arrival and to deal with the relevant paperwork.

IIM was in regular contact with German rabbis and academics. According to his private secretary, Joe Foreman, IIM engaged in voluminous correspondence with colleagues across Europe to facilitate the process of bringing refugees to England. The work was not without its risks as Leslie Edgar recalled:

> I was asked by Dr Mattuck to attend a meeting of a small number of people at his private home – 'Wildwood' in Hampstead – and it was impressed on me that not only was I not to refer in any way to the fact that this meeting was being held but I was also to treat everything that happened as absolutely secret. I cannot now remember who were the few people who sat with Dr Mattuck around his dining table ... but after we were assembled, Dr Mattuck, re-emphasising the need for absolute secrecy since the person whom he was going to bring in

> could be in veritable danger if it were known that he had come from Germany to consult with us, then went to his study door (which led out of the dining-room) and brought in Dr Leo Baeck.[145]

At this clandestine meeting, IIM is said to have encouraged Leo Baeck to pass on his leadership of German Jewry to a younger person so that he (Leo Baeck) could come to Britain to support and lead the refugee community. IIM had already made discreet enquires about how this could be brought about and had arranged for Leo Baeck to be offered a position at an English university. Although he was moved by IIM's efforts, Leo Baeck was determined to be the 'the last Jew out of Germany'.[146]

Under IIM's leadership all other activities at the LJS were 'subordinated to helping Jews caught in the increasing tragedy of Germany under the Nazis',[147] and as a result, he was successful in arranging for 156 refugees to be settled in the country before the Second World War broke out.[148]

After Kristallnacht there was a measure of unity in the Anglo-Jewish community on the issue of fund-raising and coordinating the activity of the proliferating refugee agencies. By then even the most die-hard 'assimilationists' were willing to admit that there was no future for Jews in Germany. However, there remained acute divisions on other policy issues relating to refugees, including how they should be dealt with on arrival in Britain. The Board of Deputies took a fairly laissez faire attitude to welcoming refugees, limiting itself to publishing a pamphlet defending and praising them[149] and a booklet urging refugees to be loyal to Britain, not to criticise British institutions and to refrain from being conspicuous in public.[150]

In contrast, IIM appealed publicly for the refugees to be received with friendship and hospitality. IIM refuted the commonplace notion that German Jews were arrogant and 'too assimilated' and therefore deserving of their fate for having shed their Jewishness. Instead he pointed out that German Jews had shown a great deal of spirit and that, as a result of their experiences, many had returned to Judaism. He called for tolerance towards them.[151] By 1938 IIM felt that immigration for German Jews to Britain had become an 'urgent task' to save their lives and called for a 'vast effort' by the government to help the situation as Jews and Jewish charities could no longer cope and Palestine could offer no adequate escape.[152] He implored:

> The victims of persecution cannot be allowed just to die slowly under the torture. Herr Hitler may use all his strident emphasis to tell the other nations of the world that what is happening in Germany is none of their business, but unless all religious or humanitarian feelings are suppressed or destroyed in them, they must feel it their business to

> help when human beings are being killed more slowly, but no less surely, and, therefore, ever more painfully than by murder. It is time for the spirit of humanity to assert itself, by supplying refuge for those driven from their homes by unendurable oppression.[153]

IIM worked to help refugees adjust to British life, to find employment and to ensure that their religious and other needs were met. In January 1939 he wrote to *The Times* to say that Liberal Jewish synagogues in London and elsewhere were willing to provide instruction for refugee children regardless of whether they lived near a synagogue or not.[154] The LJS hosted a club for German refugees, which organised dances attended by as many as 200 young people. A room was set aside in the synagogue to enable older German refugees to meet together and in which they held lectures and music recitals, ran language lessons and started to hold their own services, because they wanted forms of worship more traditional than those of the LJS.

Palestine

The cooperation between Zionists and non-Zionists that existed during much of the 1920s was tested by the outbreak of Arab violence in Palestine in 1929 and by the White Paper that followed it. When the LJS received a request for a donation to the Palestinian Emergency Fund in October 1929 to deal with the impact of the hostilities in Palestine, IIM wrote a carefully constructed message to the congregation saying that although the LJS was officially neutral towards the general work of developing Palestine he urged them to consider making donations for the specific purpose of emergency relief work.[155]

It would seem that although IIM was keen to dissociate himself with the development of Palestine as a Jewish state, he could not ignore the suffering there, which he saw as being the result of 'nationalism inflamed, and inflaming itself with religious fanaticism'.[156] As IIM saw it, there had always been a risk of violence in Palestine since the signing of the Balfour Declaration with its apparently contradictory aims of establishing a Jewish Homeland in Palestine and at the same time safeguarding the interests of its present inhabitants. He asked: 'How can you establish a national homeland in Palestine for Jews without interfering with the Arabs?'.[157] IIM could not condone Britain's withdrawal from its assumed position of Palestine's 'special guardian angel', now being called for in some quarters. He felt that this would give 'a blow to international good faith' at a highly critical time.[158]

IIM appeared to be somewhat relieved when the Passfield White Paper was published in October 1930 following Hope-Simpson Commission's investigation into the causes of the 1929 Palestine riots. The White Paper clarified British policy in relation to Palestine and limited official Jewish immigration to a much greater degree. IIM welcomed the definition of future British aims for the sake of peace in Palestine. However, he was concerned about its pro-Arab and anti-Zionist tone, which he felt would inevitably lead to conflict between the two sides. Palestinian policy he said must be based on the principle of justice for both Arabs and Jews.[159]

Zionist organisations worldwide mounted a vigorous campaign against the Passfield White Paper, which as a result was eventually revoked. However, as the decade progressed, the modus vivendi between Zionists and non-Zionist came under ever more strain. Zionist bodies increased in size and numbers and became more militant as young people with radical views joined them. Tensions between Zionists and non-Zionists were brought to a head in 1937 when the Peel Commission concluded that the Mandate of Palestine established in 1922 had proved unworkable and recommended the partition of Palestine. IIM had condemned the Arab strike of 1936 because of the loss of life that resulted from it, but had recognised that the Arabs felt that they had a genuine grievance. He had been apprehensive that the British government might be inclined to concede to the Arab violence, which he said would make it guilty of a 'moral wrong'.[160] The findings of the Peel Commission confirmed his fears.

In September 1937 IIM gave a well-argued address at the LJS on 'The Jews in Palestine', which was reported in *The Times*. He said that his main objections to the solution put forward by the Peel Commission was that if Palestine were to be partitioned, the 'little state for Jews could not even admit a further 500,000', and that 'there would be all the dangers of a Jewish nation with little or none of its advantages'.[161] Partition was anathema to IIM because it contradicted his belief that people of different religions could and should live harmoniously together in the same state. Although he recognised that his comments might evoke disagreement and cause resentment, he contended that Jewish nationalism should be sacrificed in order to end the strife in Palestine.[162]

While admitting that what was happening in Germany showed the value of Palestine as a place of refuge for Jews,[163] IIM rejected the Zionist view that the solution to the persecution and suffering of Jews in Germany lay in the development of the Jewish homeland where Jews would have self-determination. He said that the needs of those who required a new home should be kept separate from political ends[164] and that, rather than relying on increased immigration to Palestine, the emphasis should be placed on ensuring 'the decent treatment of Jews in other lands, in the recognition of their rights and their status as citizens in the countries which are, and for many centuries have been their homelands.'[165]

Given his views, IIM is likely to have been very disappointed when in 1937 what is known as the 'Columbus Platform' (officially the *Guiding Principles of Reform Judaism*) was narrowly adopted by CCAR, the body of which he was a member and which he was proud to represent in England. While the platform reaffirmed the Jewish mission and the American Reform movement's universalism, it also endorsed both political and cultural Zionism and affirmed the obligation of all Jewry to assist in developing Palestine as a Jewish homeland, a haven of refuge and a centre of Jewish culture and spiritual life.[166] This major shift in policy was partly the result of the personal influence of the foremost Zionist rabbis, Stephen Wise and Abba Hillel Silver. It was also the result of a growing recognition amongst the Reform rabbinate in general that Jewish emancipation had not brought about the hoped-for golden age; Jews were still disadvantaged and persecuted, especially in Eastern Europe. Although Western Jews might not need a homeland themselves, they owed it to their less fortunate co-religionists to support the project.[167]

The Macdonald White Paper of 1939 that followed the Peel Commission proposed the partition of Palestine in ten years' time but, in the meantime, recommended a drastic reduction in the number of Jews emigrating to Palestine in a bid to reduce the escalating violence there. Zionists vehemently opposed the White Paper since it changed the issue of Jewish emigration to Palestine from an economic to a political issue. The Arabs of Palestine were now given the final say on Jewish immigration levels into the country thus ruling out the possibility of a Jewish majority in Palestine. Officially anti-Zionists such as IIM did not have a position on the White Paper because they regarded it as a political document rather than dealing with religious matters.[168] However, IIM found it hard to condone the possibility of no emigration to Palestine and felt that the White Paper constituted anti-Jewish discrimination.[169]

What are the Jews?

Possibly motivated by the Columbus Platform, IIM wrote his first full-length book, *What Are the Jews?*, published in 1939.[170] He said that he had produced it against a backdrop in which the publicity being given to the nationalist view of Jewish life was creating a false impression among non-Jews about the extent of its acceptance among Jews.[171] The most political of his books, *What Are the Jews?* sets out unequivocally IIM's views on Jewish identity and on the universal religious purpose of Judaism. IIM examined in turn theories often advanced about the nature of Jewish people. He rejected the idea that there is any trace of racial unity among modern Jews, arguing that Jews are as mixed a people as any in Europe and, even allowing for intermarriage among themselves, their racial origins are highly diverse.[172]

In his opinion, Jewish nationalism was not an inner product of Jewish life, but partly the impact of European nationalism upon the religious life of Jews and partly the product of modern anti-Semitism. He contended that since Jews were neither a race nor a nation, they must be seen as 'a people of religion', and that their treatment including anti-Semitism arose from their religious rather than national or racial distinctiveness.[173]

The book (which is examined in greater detail in Chapter Seventeen) was welcomed by many, but it also attracted criticism such as in a review that appeared in the *Jewish Chronicle*.[174] The reviewer, Leon Simon (Hebraist and prolific author), described the book as being 'ably-written' but 'provocative' for exaggerating the Agudist[175] opposition to the Jewish Agency and overstating the Zionist case. Simon also objected to IIM's assertion that no religious development of value would come out of the Jewish resettlement of Palestine. The article concluded by criticising IIM for putting forward his case at a time of crisis in Jewish history.

Some of IIM's arguments were also challenged by Progressive Jews, including by Sir Philip Magnus, who, writing in the *Liberal Jewish Monthly,* questioned whether IIM was justified in asserting that simply by remaining a Jew, the Jew becomes a witness of religious values and that to remain a Jew, the Jew has to resist his environment. However, Magnus did laud IIM's spirited defence of the need to retain a religious outlook on life.[176] The Reverend James Parkes, a distinguished non-Jewish scholar, described the book as being 'ably presented, but not always convincing', and disagreed with IIM in his total rejection of Zionism.[177]

The Mission of Israel

In 1933 IIM and Claude Montefiore published a pamphlet, *Jewish Views on Jewish Missions*,[178] which was circulated widely and eventually made its way to America. The pamphlet contained a detailed discussion about what the Jewish mission meant historically and what it could mean in the future. IIM's paper drew a distinction between a collective Jewish mission to better humanity and the individual, soul-saving campaigns of Christian missionaries, which he argued could never be the goal of Judaism.

IIM's views on the 'Mission of Israel' are explored in greater detail in Chapter Seventeen, but it is worth noting here some interesting aspects of this pamphlet. First, it was launched at a time that American Reform rabbis, who had been discussing mission theology during most of the 1920s, had become silent on the subject. In 1928, missionary plans became muted as the sense of insecurity engendered by the start of the Great Depression spread from financial matters to broader philosophical concerns about being Jewish in America.

Also interesting is the wide divergence of opinion between IIM and Claude Montefiore on the Jewish mission and how that was presented. Although the two agreed broadly about the difference between Jewish and Christian missions, Montefiore believed that the Jewish mission could not exist apart from a mission to civilise 'heathens', while IIM's aspirations were centred on spreading understanding of Judaism in the Western world. The pamphlet opens with a lengthy criticism, 'Jewish Views on Jewish Missions', by Montefiore of IIM's paper, 'Why the Jews Have No Missionaries', which is reproduced later in the pamphlet. The interchange of views is concluded by a reply from IIM to Montefiore's criticisms. It is not clear why Montefiore's criticisms are printed before IIM's original contribution, more especially because the reader is requested to read IIM's paper first.

The pamphlet may have been produced as an antidote to rising anti-Semitism, offering as it did a rationale for the Jewish presence in Britain and why Jews deserved respect and admiration. However, it does not appear to have gained much attention.

Looming War

During the 1920s IIM monitored avidly developments in international relations and for many years remained optimistic that the various initiatives would secure permanent peace. He held out great hopes for the success of the League of Nations, especially after it was joined by Russia and Germany, when his 'hopes ran high'.[179] Eventually IIM came to realise that, despite its potential, the league's impact was only ever going to be limited because of its curtailed powers and because it had been conceived as the result of two contradictory influences: idealism and cynicism.[180] In 1925 he welcomed the Treaty of Locarno as 'a new start for Europe', and believed it would be more effective than the Treaty of Versailles since it was agreed in discussion between all nations and 'dictated by a spirit of Give and Take' rather than being imposed 'without any generosity on vanquished countries'.[181] He also hoped that the Kellogg-Briand Peace Pact of 1928[182] would prove a step forward in the process of 'establishing a beautiful world on lasting foundations'.[183]

As a member of the Jewish Peace Society, IIM worked alongside other Jewish communal leaders to help promote peace in Europe and he spoke often at its meetings.[184] IIM was one of the prominent Jewish leaders invited to speak at meetings of the National Peace Congress,[185] and at the 'New Thought Conference' held in 1925.[186] He also addressed local bodies on the issues of peace and disarmament, such as the Leyton and District Council for the Prevention of War,[187] and the North West League of

Nations Union.[188] He put forward his views on peace in both the Jewish and non-Jewish press. For example, an article written by IIM on 'Disarmament and Security' appeared in the *Daily Mail* in December 1927.[189]

As an American citizen living in England, IIM was particularly interested in relations between the two countries. He was bitterly disappointed when the 1927 Geneva Naval Conference broke down because representatives from England and America could not agree on how many cruisers with what kind of guns each of them might have. This led to a strain on relations which IIM felt acutely because he had been in America when the conference was threatened with breakdown and back in England when the breakdown occurred.[190] IIM sorely hoped the rift would be mended when President Hoover and Prime Minister Ramsay MacDonald met in 1929. He spoke with humour of their meeting:

> The two men present an interesting contrast – Mr Hoover, the conservative in politics and the conservator of the present social order, Mr MacDonald, the progressive in politics and, almost, if not quite, radical in the desire to change the social order. Mr Hoover, the man who has lived and worked in silence, Mr MacDonald a man to whom speech – written and spoken – is as the truth of his life. I can imagine Mr Hoover making many speeches as little as I can imagine Mr MacDonald maintaining a long silence. Mr Hoover, the engineer who works with machines, Mr MacDonald the leader of men. One with a cold exterior almost like that ascribed to the English, the other with the warmth of an enthusiastic Scot.[191]

In his sermons, IIM frequently addressed issues around war and peace. It was clear that he abhorred war and yearned for its abolition,[192] but he was not a pacifist. By the 1930s an increasing number of American Reform rabbis had become absolute pacifists. In 1931 CCAR stated that 'it is in accord with the highest interpretation of Judaism conscientiously to object to personal participation [in warfare]'.[193] IIM did not follow suit. Just as during the early stages of the First World War he had refused to yield to 'unreasoning war fury', IIM resisted the general trend, seeking to retain a similar independence of judgement and avoiding being rushed into what he called 'unthinking pacifism'.[194] He said he was not one of those who believed that war was always wrong, 'it always is an evil but a lesser evil to reduce a larger one partakes of the quality of righteousness'.[195] When war arose men were impelled to 'do their share in it' through feelings of love of country.[196]

He argued that the refusal to fight could not prevent war and that peace would only be assured when every country felt secure. This could only be achieved by the establishment of a supranational authority tasked with guaranteeing security to each nation. To IIM, the League of Nations was not such a supranational authority; it was only the beginnings of what was needed. Britain and America, 'the two greatest democracies of our modern world', had a pivotal part to play in bringing about 'true peace' and it was essential that they worked with one another to achieve it. [197]

IIM viewed the failure of the various peace initiatives of the 1920s as mere setbacks. However, by the early 1930s, he was beginning to recognise the portents of another world war and called for collective action via the League of Nations, 'the guardian of European civilisation',[198] to secure 'an international organisation for peace rather than rearmament.'[199] In January 1932 IIM led a special Disarmament Service at the LJS to mark the commencement of the disarmament conference in Geneva (the League Commission on Disarmament), which had been planned for five years and the importance of which he said was difficult to exaggerate.[200] He detected that there was by now 'almost a pathetic longing to minimise the future danger of war'.[201] He argued that disarmament would not only reduce the threat of war; it would free resources to invest in social problems. He could not 'bear to contemplate the possibility of its [the conference's] failure'.[202] As the conference deliberated, IIM preached with increasing trepidation about the lack of progress. He perceived that 'on the more concrete and immediate questions of disarmament, there has been nothing but disagreements and confusion'. In his analysis the problems lay partly in 'the general psychology of nations', and 'partly in the actual position between France and Germany'.[203] He was bitterly disappointed when the conference eventually broke down having failed to find a basis for the limitation of arms.

In his Sunday addresses at the LJS, IIM spoke repeatedly of the dangers of the rising tide of fascism and communism, both of which he deplored because of their hostility to political and religious freedom. Fascism was undeniably evil in seeking to suppress the spirit of men, but IIM also found communism 'inadequate, unattractive, and even coldly repulsive'.[204] He commented on the irony that whereas the Russian Jews were now facing no discrimination civically and socially, their religion was faced with 'destructive opposition'.[205] Unlike Judaism, the two totalitarian regimes failed to 'recognise a supreme worth in human personality'.[206] He contended that both fascism and communism had 'shown how necessary religion is to give meaning to the life of man, and to give guidance and power in the individual and society to advance to higher ends' and that 'when a religious view predominates, as in England, there is no fear'.[207]

While recognising their differences, IIM saw in all totalitarian regimes the seeds of war. Of the Nazi regime in Germany he said:

> Since the establishment of the present regime in Germany, Europe has turned from exploring avenues for the permanent establishment of peace to the creation of armaments in preparation for war. There can be no question of Germany's large, if not complete, responsibility for the change. The things its Nazi rulers said before they came to power became with their accession to power a threat to the other countries of Europe.[208]

Although it was clear that the fascist regimes in Germany and Italy exalted war and posed the more obvious threat to the future peace of Europe, IIM found communist claims to internationalism unsatisfactory:

> The Communists have given up, in theory at least, loyalty to a nation and have put in its place not loyalty to humanity, but to a class. The best chance for humanity is not for it to take the place of nationality but to be beyond and above nationalities, not disobeying them, but joining them all together in a league of freedom and amity.[209]

As well as IIM's criticisms of fascism and communism, a repeated theme in his sermons and addresses of the 1930s was the distinction he drew between patriotism (or 'moral nationalism'), and bad or 'immoral nationalism'. Patriotism was a force that 'sees in a nation's life a thing of supreme value, transcending the selfish interest of individuals, and exalted in the righteousness which unifies them'.[210] Bad nationalism was the nationalism of the jingo who wanted his nation to dominate the world. Whereas good nationalism sought to establish lasting peace through covenants and pacts, immoral nationalism had produced the world's wars.[211] The extreme forms of nationalism to which IIM objected were, in his view, intrinsically associated with anti-Semitism. To him this was clear even before the advent of Hitler, but Hitler had made the association emphatically obvious.[212] IIM's analysis of international developments and the terminology he used was eerily prescient:

> between the ambitions of some nations moved by false nationalism and the principles of humanity there is an inevitable conflict. That is the conflict that has thrown Europe into turmoil and threatens its future with a holocaust of life and achievement.[213]

Until 1936 IIM continued to express his belief that the rising tide of aggressive German nationalism had its roots in the way that peace was handled in the aftermath of the First World War. Despite his profound criticisms and misgivings about the Nazi regime, IIM argued that the treaty of Versailles had wronged Germany and that 'her just grievances should be recognised and righted'.[214] However, in the face of Germany's increasing 'outlawry' and 'violations of international law', IIM felt that her actions were no longer excusable. He became convinced of Germany's 'warlike intentions' and the threat that 'Hitlerism' posed to world peace. For several years Hitler had been able to obtain his ends without recourse to war, but IIM predicted that the time would come when he wanted something for which he would fight.[215] However, at this stage, IIM still appears to have believed that war was avoidable:

> There must be no war in Europe, and we must rid ourselves of war-mindedness. The position is serious, and even grave; but we shall only aggravate it by thinking that war is inevitable. It is not inevitable, and it will be avoided.[216]

He was soon to change his mind.

Despite his deep attachment to America, IIM was not uncritical of its actions or unquestioning of its policies. In 1926 he expressed his concern about America's refusal to join the League of Nations, commenting that American idealism has not always shown itself equal to the practical demands made on it.[217] He averred:

> Now I should rejoice to see my country in the League of Nations. I can see the difficulties; I can see from the American point of view the objections, and even the dangers; but I feel that the aim of the League, and its potentialities for peace make the wish worthwhile.[218]

IIM saw America's reluctance to cancel the debts resulting from the First World War as a barrier to internationalism and hence to world peace. He felt that it would be in America's interests, as well as those of other nations, for the war debts to be cancelled. He was aware that this would be a big sacrifice for America, but one that it should be prepared to make 'for the sake of the society of nations'.[219] To IIM it was a bitter irony that the First World War, which was supposedly fought to make the world safe for democracy, had apparently had the reverse effect. In the confusion that followed the war, democracy disappeared in several countries and was threatened in many more. He pointed not only to what was happening in

Germany, Italy and Russia, but even in America where 'the President is taking as much of dictatorial power as his popularity and influence will allow'.[220]

During 1937 IIM redoubled his efforts to disseminate warnings about the threat of war. He participated in the Peace Week held in Marylebone in June that year,[221] and he was one of the signatories to a 'Statement on Religion and Peace' issued by the New Commonwealth Society in July 1937.[222] Preaching at the LJS in October 1938, IIM spoke out against Germany's annexation of the Sudetenland. He was by now clearly finding it difficult to maintain his optimism in the face of international events and desperately seeking positive aspects of terrible happenings. He said that, depressing as the present international crisis was, he could still see some grounds for hope. The moral conscience of humanity had been deeply shocked and mobilised by 'international brigandage', which must 'ultimately strengthen the forces supporting righteousness'.[223]

In May 1939 IIM was amongst 'the most eminent thinkers in the world – writers, scientists and artists', who spent two weeks in conference 'preparing weapons for use against Fascism'. The conference worked on a study that would provide an 'authoritative reply to the pseudo-scientific doctrines and propaganda of Fascism' in preparation for an International Conference on the Problems of the Defence of Democracy, Peace and Humanity to be held in Paris later in the month.[224] IIM, with a number of others, made a powerful appeal in the non-Jewish Press for British support for the Paris conference.[225] IIM was also one of a group of prominent leaders from all branches of Anglo-Jewry who wrote to *The Times*, calling for 'collective security' to safeguard those nations remaining outside the realm of Nazi domination,[226] and he put his name to a statement agreed by leaders of many religious denominations, including the Archbishop of York, the Reverend Dr Scott Lidgett, which was published in a pamphlet, *Religion and the Organisation of Peace*, by the Peace Book Company.[227]

Other Events and Developments

Although the 1930s was a time of immense effort and hard work, IIM still found time to engage in social activities and celebrations. During the decade the LJS celebrated both the fifth and the tenth anniversary of the opening of the new LJS building in St John's Wood Road. At the tenth anniversary celebration, Neville Laski, President of the Board of Deputies, was present as was Rabbi Reinhart, despite his tense relationship with IIM.

In 1933 an 'important function' was held to celebrate IIM's twenty-first anniversary as Senior Rabbi of the LJS.[228] To thank him for his teaching and his spiritual leadership, it was decided to ask IIM to sit for a portrait, and the artist chosen was Mr J.H. Amshewitz RBA.[229] Two portraits were presented to IIM, one to be hung in the Council Room at the LJS and a replica to be hung in his home. One of the portraits was exhibited at the London Portrait Society Exhibition at the New Burlington Galleries between 27 February and 11 March 1933.

Four years later, on 6 February 1937, a Thanksgiving Service was held to celebrate the twenty-fifth anniversary of IIM's ministry at the LJS. All the congregations of the JRU participated in the service.[230] Following his address on 'Problems and Progress', IIM was presented with an album recording the milestones of his ministry and the many letters of congratulations he received including from Neville Laski, President of the Board of Deputies.[231] A private celebration had previously been held in the home of Henrietta ('Netta') Franklin, to which past and present members of the LJS Council, Religion School teachers and chairmen of the various LJS societies were invited.[232]

Throughout the 1930s the Anglo-Jewish religious establishment remained generally hostile to IIM and to the LJS. In February 1931 Julian Morgenstern wrote to IIM and asked that he and Rabbi Reinhart represent HUC at the seventy-fifth anniversary of the founding of Jews' College, to be held on 23 and 24 March. Although Morgenstern notified the conference organisers who the HUC delegates were to be, Jews' College – of which Chief Rabbi Hertz was the President – failed to extend a formal invitation to IIM and Reinhart. IIM was not surprised; he said he refused to be upset by the snub,[233] and continued to expose what he saw as inconsistencies in Hertz's outlook and pronouncements.

There were, however, some signs of rapprochement. Early in 1934 Dr Hertz approached IIM asking for his cooperation in the acquisition of the Codex Sinaiticus for the British Museum,[234] and a few months later IIM sat alongside him at the ceremony held at the West London Synagogue to mark the opening of a major extension, which the *Jewish Chronicle* heralded as 'the lion laying down with the lamb – or, at any rate, the Chief Rabbi forgathered with Dr Mattuck'.[235] In 1936 IIM and the Chief Rabbi both spoke at the Memorial Meeting held at the Kingsway Hall to commemorate the tenth *Yahrzeit* of Israel Zangwill,[236] and when the LJS applied to the Board of Deputies for certification as a congregation authorised to perform marriages under the Marriage Act of 1936, Hertz approved the application. The Chief Rabbi said that that although he strongly disapproved of the principles and practices of the LJS, he would not be justified in declaring that the members of the LJS had left the Jewish faith.[237]

In 1937 IIM and Claude Montefiore were invited to participate in a communal service held in the Great Synagogue to celebrate the coronation of King George VI.[238] This was the first time that representatives of the LJS had been asked officially to attend a service in an Orthodox synagogue. Chief Rabbi Hertz conducted the service alongside IIM, Vivian Simmons from West London Synagogue and the Reverend Mayerowitsch, Reader of the Great Synagogue. A special youth service took place later in the day conducted by Dr Hertz assisted by IIM and Rabbi Reinhart.[239] A year later IIM and Reinhart were scroll bearers with Dr Hertz and Dayan Gollop at the Thanksgiving Service held at the Bayswater Synagogue to celebrate its seventy-fifth year.[240]

IIM was increasingly asked to participate in Jewish charities and cultural organisations such as the Society for the Protection of Girls and Women and the Jewish Drama League, of which he became a vice-president. IIM was now renowned for his oratory, and he was one of those featured in a series of sketches of nationally known figures that appeared in the periodical *Truth* under the pseudonym of 'Eutychus' (Muriel Harris). The sketches were subsequently brought together in a publication entitled *Pulpits and Preachers*.[241]

> A man about fifty. Enormous depths in the eyes; upper part of the head so developed that the face looks haggard, almost suffering from centuries of pain. Mobility of features, sensibility, complete range of voice modulations ... An orator? Yes, if oratory means projecting oneself by means of words past oneself into the consciousness of the listener.[242]

While IIM welcomed the increasing contact with other sections of the Anglo-Jewish community, he was only prepared to cooperate in intra-communal initiatives when Liberal Judaism as a distinctive interpretation of Judaism received full recognition. He refused involvement in schemes and events 'when there has been an implied obscuration of our principles'.[243]

Despite his increasing commitments, IIM managed to find time to study. In November 1932 he gave a lengthy and learned address on Spinoza at the fourth Horace Seal Memorial Lecture held at the Conway Hall in Red Lion Square. The event was organised by the Ethical Union to mark Spinoza's tercentenary. The Ethical Union subsequently published IIM's address, 'Spinoza's significance for religion'. In his paper, IIM concluded that Spinoza was a mystic, but that his mysticism had an intellectual as well as an emotional quality. He found several elements of Judaism that could be traced to Spinoza. Nevertheless, IIM felt that his reasoning 'appears to possess too many inconsistencies to merit full credit for rationality'.[244]

IIM continued his interfaith activities, making a number of visits to Wales, including to Barry and to Cardiff, to give addresses on Liberal Judaism at the church of St-Francis-on-the-Hill,[245] and to address meetings of Welsh Presbyterian Ministers.[246]

In July 1938 Claude Montefiore died, having retired as President of the LJS just one month earlier. IIM gave the address, 'Our Debt to Claude Montefiore', at a special service held at the LJS on 16 July. This was subsequently published, and was full of respect for the man with whom IIM had worked closely for twenty-six years:

> because of the inspiration that we found in him, we feel especially burdened by his death with a feeling that 'lies too deep for tears', but also we must feel especially grateful for his life. We are all the richer for being so greatly in his debt. His influence has become part of our congregational life and of our individual lives. It is an influence that will continue to bring inspiration and, God grant, blessing.[247]

Despite their disagreements, Claude Montefiore's death was a devastating blow for IIM. Not only did he face a future without a close colleague, but also without his intellectual peer, sponsor and mentor. When Claude Montefiore died, IIM lost a vital alter ego.

America

In 1936 IIM made a trip to America. This was mainly a family trip (see Chapter Fourteen), but he did make two public appearances during this visit, one at a reception held for him at the Hotel Astor in New York by the Directors of the American Ort,[248] and the other when he preached at Rodeph Sholom Synagogue in the city. He had planned to make another trip in the summer of the following year, having been invited to give the annual series of lectures to the faculty and students recently established by HUC.[249] However, in the event he was prevented from doing because Edna became ill and had to undergo surgery.[250] But the Mattucks did go to America in May 1938, returning to England via Canada on 25 June. Between 13–18 June, IIM attended the CCAR annual meeting held in Washington, where he spoke on behalf of the WUPJ, seeking increased financial support for its activities. Although he had been invited by HUC to give the Alumni lectures that year, again he had not been able to make the dates stipulated by the College.[251]

IIM was invited to give the lectures at HUC in 1939, but his commitments meant that he was again unable to accept the invitation. He did, however, make a ten-week private trip to America in May 1939.[252] The outbreak of the Second World War meant that it was to be a number of years before IIM was able to return to America to deliver the HUC lectures.

NOTES

1. 'The Present Crisis and the Future World', sermon given by IIM at the LJS, 3 October 1931, Montagu Centre Collection (MCC).
2. Ibid.
3. 'Fascism, Communism, and an Alternative', sermon given by IIM at the LJS, 13 January 1935, in ibid.
4. 'Politics and Principles', sermon given by IIM at the LJS, 18 October 1931, in ibid.
5. See 'The Present Crisis and the Future World'.
6. See 'Fascism, Communism, and an Alternative'.
7. See 'The Present Crisis and the Future World'.
8. See 'Politics and Principles'.
9. Ibid.
10. Ibid.
11. Ibid.
12. Ibid.
13. Ibid.
14. See 'The Present Crisis and the Future World'.
15. See 'Politics and Principles'.
16. Dr C.G. Montefiore and Rabbi Dr I.I. Mattuck, *Religion and Politics* (Papers for Jewish People No. XXIX) (London: JRU, 1931).
17. Lily H. Montagu, 'Religion and Politics', *LJM*, III, no.10 (March 1932), p.88.
18. See Montefiore and Mattuck, *Religion and Politics*, p.10.
19. Ibid., p.11.
20. Ibid., p.12.
21. Ibid., p.13.
22. See Montagu, 'Religion and Politics', p.88.
23. Ibid., p.88.
24. Ibid., p.88.
25. Letter from Mr Duparc to Claude Montefiore, 14 January 1936, London Metropolitan Archives, ACC/3529/004/009A. Given IIM's commitment to promoting the involvement of women in the synagogue, this is rather strange. A possible explanation is that he may have been keen to replicate the atmosphere of debate and discussion he had experienced himself as a young man at Harvard.
26. For information on Harry Pollitt see www.spartacus.schoolnet.co.uk/TUpollitt.htm.
27. See correspondence in the London Metropolitan Archives, ACC/3529/004/009a.
28. Letter from IIM to Claude Montefiore, 23 January 1935, Mattuck Family Archive kept by Robert Edgar (MFAb).
29. Letter from Claude Montefiore to IIM, 1 February 1935, in ibid.
30. Letter from Claude Montefiore to IIM, 19 January 1935, in ibid.
31. Letter from IIM to Claude Montefiore, 23 January 1935, in ibid.
32. Letter from Claude Montefiore to IIM, 1 February 1935, in ibid.
33. Claude Montefiore repeated this back to IIM, in ibid.
34. Letter from Claude Montefiore to IIM, 25 October 1935, in ibid.
35. 'The Special Need for Religion Today', sermon given by IIM at the LJS, 17 May 1931, in ibid.
36. Ibid.
37. Ibid.
38. 'The Modern Synagogue', sermon given by IIM at the Consecration Service of the LJS, 13 September 1925, MCC.
39. 'Is the World Growing Better?', sermon given by IIM at the LJS, 16 February 1930, in ibid.
40. Ibid.
41. See discussion in Michael A. Meyer, *Response to Modernity – A History of the Reform Movement in Judaism* (Oxford: Oxford University Press, 1988), p.312.

42. 'The Ethics of Marriage', sermon given by IIM at the LJS, 13 February 1927, MCC.
43. 'Birth Control, Sterilisation and Abortion – A Jewish View', draft of an article by IIM for DR F.... (name illegible), February 1934, in ibid.
44. Ibid.
45. 'Marriage and Morals – The Jewish View', sermon given by IIM at the LJS, 24 February 35, MCC.
46. See 'Birth Control, Sterilisation and Abortion'.
47. 'Marriage and Children', sermon given by IIM at the LJS, 30 March 1930, MCC.
48. See Meyer, *Response to Modernity*, p.312.
49. See 'Birth Control, Sterilisation and Abortion'.
50. Ibid.
51. 'The Morals of Marriage', sermon given by IIM at the LJS, 2 March 1930, MCC.
52. Ibid.
53. Ibid.
54. Ibid.
55. See 'Marriage and Morals – The Jewish View'.
56. 'Morality in Bolshevik Russia', sermon given by IIM at the LJS, 1 February 1931, MCC.
57. Ibid.
58. Ibid.
59. *JC*, 11 May 1917, p.16.
60. This controversy was reported both in the British Jewish press and in America. See *Jewish Daily News*, 23 May 1917, p.8.
61. *JC*, 4 May 1917, p.9.
62. Gotthard Deutsch, 'Foreign Affairs, A Weekly Review of Jewish Affairs Abroad', *American Israelite*, 19 July 1917, p.5.
63. Ibid.
64. Correspondence shows that IIM was reluctant to return to West London Synagogue due to previous opposition to his preaching there. He did not wish to do so if the only reason for the invitation was influence exerted by Claude Montefiore. See correspondence between IIM and Claude Montefiore, London Metropolitan Archives, ACC/3529/002/010.
65. 'Are "Liberal" Jews Jews?' *JC*, 9 January 1920, pp.21–2.
66. Minutes of the LJS Council, 21 March 1921, 19 June 1921 and 26 September 1921, LJS Archives.
67. Letter from IIM to Rabbi Newman, January 1928, LJS Archives, Box 1/2.
68. Correspondence in ibid.
69. Letter from Harold Reinhart to IIM, November 1928, in ibid.
70. Letter from Israel Mattuck to P.S. Waley, 29 October 1928, in ibid.
71. Letter from IIM to Julian Morgenstern, 29 October 1928, American Jewish Archives (AJA), Hebrew Union College Records, MS-5, Box A-18, Folder 14.
72. Letter from Harold Reinhart to IIM, 15 July 1929, LJS Archives, Box 1/2.
73. Jonathan Romain (ed.), *Great Reform Lives, Rabbis who Dared to Differ* (London: The Movement for Reform Judaism, 2010), p.72.
74. He was brought up in Portland, Oregon and was well known to Stephen Wise because Wise had led the congregation in Portland before his move to New York.
75. Rabbi Petuchowski, 'Who will take over from Reform?', *JC*, 21 December 1984, p.16.
76. John D. Rayner, 'Nonconformism in Anglo-Jewry', *Jewish Quarterly* (Winter 1999/2000), p.55.
77. See Petuchowski, 'Who will take over from Reform?'.
78. For instance, Reinhart preached at the LJS in November 1934 and again in March 1935. See *LJM*, V, no.7 (November 1934), p.61; V, no.10 (March 1935), p.96.
79. Anne J. Kershen and Jonathan A. Romain, *Tradition and Change: A History of Reform Judaism in Britain, 1840–1995* (London and Portland, OR: Vallentine Mitchell, 1995), p.158.
80. Ibid.
81. See Rayner, 'Nonconformism in Anglo-Jewry', p.55. Although the two men may have differed professionally, information from a contemporary source suggests that they may have maintained a personal friendship. Herbert Richer, who trained as a rabbi during the 1940s, remembers being told that IIM and Reinhart played golf together in Rickmansworth in the years leading up to the Second World War. Telephone interview with Herbert Richer conducted by Rosita Rosenberg 14/15 May 2012.
82. 'Israel I. Mattuck – His life and Work', unattributed article in *LJM, In Memoriam of Israel Mattuck, 1883–1954* (June 1954), p.10.

83. See Meyer, *Response to Modernity*, p.342.
84. 'Reform Jews Should Not Seek to Convert Orthodox, Says Dr Solomon Freehof', reported by the Jewish Telegraphic Agency, 12 November 1930: www.jta.org/1930
85. Ibid.
86. 'Rabbi Mattuck Responds', *American Israelite*, 12 February 1931, p.4.
87. Ibid.
88. Letter from Julian Morgenstern to IIM, 12 February 1931, AJA, Hebrew Union College Records, MS-5, Box A-18, Folder 14.
89. Ibid.
90. Letter from IIM to Julian Morgenstern, 2 March 1931, AJA, Hebrew Union College Records, MS-5, Box A-18, Folder 14.
91. Rabbi Dr Mattuck's Fortieth Anniversary Address, 'The Spirit of Liberal Judaism', *LJM*, XXIII, no.2 (February 1952), p.17.
92. Todd M. Endelman, *The Jews of Britain 1656 to 2000* (Berkeley, Los Angeles, CA and London: University of California Press, 2002), p.201.
93. Rabbi Israel I. Mattuck, 'Anti-Semitism and the Jewish Consciousness', *Hebrew Standard*, 2 June 1922, p.13.
94. 'Anti-Semitism and the Jewish Consciousness', sermon given by IIM at the LJS, 26 March 1921, MCC.
95. 'The Jews' Position Today', sermon given by IIM at the LJS, 4 November 1936, in ibid.
96. 'The Jewish Position – A Reply to the Anti-Semite', sermon given by IIM at the LJS, 12 October 1930, and 'The Causes of Anti-Semitism', address given by IIM to the Reviewers' Discussion Group, 25 November 1930, in ibid.
97. See 'The Jewish Position – A Reply to the Anti-Semite'.
98. Ibid.
99. 'The Jews and the World: ii Anti-Semitism', sermon given by IIM at the LJS, 14 October 1934, in ibid.
100. 'The Jew and his Neighbour's Opinion', sermon given by IIM at the LJS, 31 January 1931, in ibid.
101. See 'The Jewish Position – A Reply to the Anti-Semite'.
102. See 'The Jews' Position Today'.
103. In its 1932 annual report, the Board of Deputies printed a reassurance from Moseley to Lord Melchett: 'It is quite in accord with my definition of the BUF's attitude on this question to say that anti-Semitism forms no part of the policy of this organisation, and that anti-Semitic propaganda is forbidden', see V.D. Lipman, *A History of the Jews in Britain Since 1858* (Leicester: Leicester University Press, 1990), p.186.
104. Ibid., p.187. It was not until 1936 after the so-called 'Battle of Cable Street' that the Board of Deputies organised defence activities led by Neville Laski, which were still conducted with the reticence characteristic of the traditional Anglo-Jewish leadership.
105. 'A Review of the Year', sermon given by IIM at the LJS, 8 September 1934, MCC.
106. 'Religion and "The Coming Revolution" ', sermon given by IIM at the LJS, 22 April 1934, in ibid.
107. *Daily Express,* 18 June 1932, p.11.
108. 'Why are Jews so touchy?', article setting out IIM's response, copy of cutting from the *Sunday Express*, undated, MCC.
109. *LJM*, IV, no.2 (May 1932), p.9.
110. See his sermons 'Hitler and the Jews', 12 February 1933, 'Combatting Anti-Semitism', 3 December 1933 and 'What a Year of Hitlerism Has Taught the Jews and the World', 8 April 1934, all given at the LJS, MCC.
111. 'Plea for Mutual Understanding – Dr Mattuck on Persecution in Germany', *Western Mail*, 31 March 1933, reporting on the meeting of the Cardiff Business Club the previous day. The meeting at the Business Club was so large that many had to be turned away. See *LJM*, IV, no.12 (May 1933), notice inside back cover.
112. Ibid.
113. 'Eutychus' (Muriel Harris), 'Pulpits and Preachers – IV', *Truth,* 7 March 1934, pp.367–8.
114. *Daily Mail*, 11 March 1937, p.10.
115. 'The Position of the Jews in Germany', sermon given by IIM at the LJS, 19 March 1933, MCC.

116. 'Should there be a Jewish World Congress?', sermon given by IIM at the LJS, 27 January 1935, in ibid.
117. Ibid.
118. See 'The Position of the Jews in Germany'.
119. 'Germany's Return to the Ghetto', sermon given by IIM at the LJS, 20 October 1935, MCC.
120. Report of sermon by IIM given at the LJS, *Manchester Guardian*, 18 July 1938, p.7.
121. See 'A Review of the Year'.
122. 'Jewish-Christian Relations in America', sermon given by IIM at the LJS, 8 March 1936, MCC.
123. Ibid.
124. Ibid.
125. 'World Fellowship of Faiths, Plans for London Congress', *The Times*, 12 March 1936, p.20.
126. 'The Jews' Present and Future – (i) In the World', sermon given by IIM at the LJS, 30 October 1938, MCC.
127. 'A Crisis in Civilisation', sermon given by IIM at the Service of Intercession held at the LJS, 17 July 1938, in ibid.
128. *JC*, 25 May 1917, p.5.
129. Wolf's speech, which was well publicised in the Jewish press, condemned Zionism in vitriolic terms. See *JC*, 25 February 1927, p.24.
130. *JC*, 18 July 1930, p.19.
131. www.movinghere.org.uk.
132. *JC*, 3 July 1931, p.10.
133. *JC*, 27 July 1934, pp.14–15.
134. 'Report of One Who Left Germany', sermon given by IIM at the LJS, 21st April 1933, MCC.
135. *JC*, 14 July 1933, p.24.
136. *JC*, 16 June 1933, p.16.
137. *JC*, 6 April 1934, p.13. He led an appeal meeting held at New Cross Synagogue as part of the 'Second Appeal for Funds'.
138. See Endelman, *The Jews of Britain 1656 to 2000*, p.213.
139. Pam Fox, *A Place to Call My Jewish Home, Memories of the Liberal Jewish Synagogue 1911–2011* (London: Liberal Jewish Synagogue, 2011), p.21.
140. Following the depression of the 1920s and the years of high unemployment it created, Britain passed laws to limit the entry of refugees. The Government insisted that refugees had a guarantee of £250, and later £500, so that they would not be a burden on the state.
141. Marianne C. Dreyfus, 'Greetings from the Granddaughter of Rabbi Leo Baeck', in *Reflections on the World Union for Progressive Judaism Marking the 75th Anniversary of the First World Union Conference, Berlin 1928*, p.27.
142. Sir Ernst Chain was brought over from Germany in 1933. He was a biochemist and later won the Nobel Prize with Fleming and Florey for the discovery of penicillin. Email from Robert Edgar, 13 August 2011.
143. Gerhard Stein, later Gerard Stein, became a long-standing member of the LJS and close family friend of the Mattucks. Conversation with Dr Stein's daughter, Margaret Levin, 22 June 2012.
144. Letter from Henrietta Franklin to the editor, *JC,* 31 March 1939, p.20.
145. Rabbi Dr Leslie I. Edgar, *Some Memories of My Ministry* (London: Liberal Jewish Synagogue, 1985), pp.18–19.
146. Ibid., p.20. Leo Baeck subsequently became the 'hero of Judaism' because of his marvellous bravery and high spiritual conduct in the concentration camp.
147. Ibid, p.16.
148. See Fox, *A Place to Call My Jewish Home,* p.136.
149. *The Refugees: The Plain Facts*, see Lipman, *A History of the Jews in Britain*, p.196.
150. Ibid.
151. 'The Spirit of the Jews in the Face of Anti-Semitism', sermon given by IIM at the LJS, 9 March 1935, MCC.
152. See 'The Jews' Present and Future – (i) In the World'.
153. Ibid.
154. IIM letter to *The Times*, 11 January 1939, p.6.

155. *LJM*, I, no.5 (October 1929).
156. 'Shall Great Britain Get Out of Palestine?', sermon given by IIM at the LJS, 20 October 1929, MCC.
157. 'The New British Policy', draft article by IIM submitted to *John Bull*, 5 November 1930, in ibid.
158. See 'Shall Great Britain get out of Palestine?'
159. See 'The New British Policy'.
160. 'The Problem in Palestine', sermon given by IIM at the LJS, 18 October 1936, MCC.
161. 'Jews and Sacrifice of Nationalism', *The Times*, 4 October 1937, p.16.
162. Ibid.
163. See 'What a Year of Hitlerism Has Taught the Jews and the World'.
164. 'The Jews in Palestine', sermon given by IIM at the LJS, 1 January 1938, MCC.
165. See 'The Problem in Palestine'.
166. See Meyer, *Response to Modernity*, p.320.
167. John Rayner, *Progressive Judaism, Zionism and the State of Israel* (London: Liberal Jewish Synagogue, 1983), p.7.
168. Julian Franklyn, the Secretary of the Jewish Fellowship quoted in Rory Miller, *Divided Against Zionism: Anti-Zionist Opposition in Britain to the Jewish State in Palestine 1945–1948* (London and Portland, OR: Frank Cass, 2001), p.218.
169. See 'The Jews in Palestine'.
170. Israel I. Mattuck, *What Are the Jews? Their Significance and Position in the Modern World* (London: Hodder and Stoughton, 1939). According to his granddaughter, Jill Mattuck Tarule, it was symptomatic of IIM's sense of humour that the front pages of the book were arranged so that the title *What are the Jews*? appeared on the left hand page opposite the dedication on the opposite page 'To my wife' so that it could be read as 'What are the Jews to my wife'.
171. Ibid., pp.vii-viii.
172. Ibid., p.34.
173. Ibid., p.92.
174. Leon Simon, 'A Rabbi's She'elah', *JC*, 23 June 1939, p.5.
175. Agudat Yisrael was founded in Kattowitz (then Germany, now Poland) in 1912, to provide an umbrella organisation for observant Jews who opposed the Zionist movement. Eventually, at the eve of the Israeli Declaration of Independence 1948, Agudat Yisrael yielded to pressure from the Zionist movement and has been a participant in most governments since that time.
176. Sir Philip Magnus writing in *LJM*, X, no.3 (June 1939), p.26.
177. Reverend James Parkes, in ibid., p.27.
178. Israel I. Mattuck and C.G. Montefiore, *Jewish Views on Jewish Missions* (London: Jewish Religious Union for the Advancement of Liberal Judaism, 1933).
179. 'The Problem of International Peace', sermon given by IIM at the LJS, 7 November 1937, MCC.
180. 'The Meaning of the Treaty of Locarno', sermon given by IIM at the LJS, Armistice Service, 6 December 1925, in ibid.
181. Ibid.
182. The Kellogg–Briand Pact (officially General Treaty for Renunciation of War as an Instrument of National Policy) was a 1928 international agreement in which signatory states promised not to use war to resolve 'disputes or conflicts of whatever nature or of whatever origin they may be, which may arise among them'. It was signed by Germany, France and America on 27 August 1928, and by most other nations soon after. It is named after its authors, US Secretary of State Frank B. Kellogg and French Foreign Minister Aristide Briand.
183. 'England and the USA – Allies for Peace', sermon given by IIM at the LJS, 27 October 1929, MCC.
184. For example, in 1935 IIM appeared alongside Professor Bentwich, Chair of International Relations at the Hebrew University of Jerusalem, at a conference at which he spoke on 'The Spiritual Basis of Peace', *JC*, 12 July 1935, p.15.
185. Ibid. The National Peace Congress was a multi-faith body which included the Chief Rabbi and Sir Herbert Samuel.
186. It is not known what this conference was, but IIM spoke on 'The Peace Ideal in Judaism'. See 'Reviews, Lectures, etc. (other than Sermons), 1913–1932', MCC.

187. On 8 May 1928 he addressed this body on 'The Way to End War', in ibid.
188. 'America and the League of Nations', address given by IIM at a meeting of the North West League of Nations, 17 January, year not specified (c.1926 as there is a reference to the six years existence of the League of Nations), MCC.
189. See 'Reviews, Lectures, etc.'.
190. See 'England and the USA – Allies for Peace'.
191. Ibid.
192. 'A World Without War – is it practicable?, sermon given by IIM at the LJS, 18 December 1927, MCC.
193. CCAR Yearbook 88, 1931, p.76.
194. 'The Part That Religion Took in the War. How Shall We Judge it?', sermon given by IIM at the LJS, 12 November 1933, MCC.
195. 'Post War America', address written by IIM, purpose unknown, July 1927, MCC. It is possible that this is an address he gave at the LJS, or elsewhere, after his trip to America in that year.
196. See 'A World Without War – is it practicable?'
197. Ibid.
198. 'Germany's Return to the Ghetto', sermon given by IIM at the LJS 20 October 1935, MCC.
199. 'Germany and the Nations', sermon given by IIM at the LJS, 31 March 1935, in ibid.
200. 'The Disarmament Conference', address given by IIM at the Special Disarmament Service held at the LJS on 31 January 1932, in ibid.
201. Ibid.
202. Ibid.
203. 'The Troubles of the Disarmament Conference', sermon give by IIM at the LJS, 20 November 1932, MCC.
204. 'Nationalism: Good and Bad', sermon given by IIM at the LJS, 28 October 1934, in ibid.
205. 'The Jews in Russia', sermon given by IIM at the LJS, 1930, undated, in ibid.
206. 'The Challenge in Fascism and Communism', sermon given by IIM at Rodeph Sholom Synagogue, New York, 16 February 1936, in ibid.
207. Ibid.
208. See 'Germany and the Nations'.
209. See 'Nationalism: Good and Bad'.
210. 'Memories of the War and Hopes of Peace', sermon given by IIM at the Armistice Commemoration Service held at the LJS, 11 November 1934, MCC.
211. See 'The Jewish Position – A Reply to the Anti-Semite'.
212. 'The Jews and the Future (1) Our Place Among the Nations', sermon given by IIM at the LJS, 17 March 1935, MCC.
213. See 'Nationalism: Good and Bad'.
214. See 'Germany and the Nations'.
215. 'Germany's Outlawry and its Effect on International Morality', sermon given by IIM at the LJS, 15 March 1936, MCC.
216. Ibid.
217. See 'America and the League of Nations'.
218. Ibid.
219. 'What the Nations Expect from Japan and America', sermon given by IIM at the LJS, 5 February 1933, MCC.
220. 'Democracy or Dictators', sermon given by IIM at the LJS, 26 March 1933, in ibid.
221. *LJM*, VIII, no.3 (June 1937), p.26.
222. *LJM*, VIII, no.4 (July 1937), pp.30–1.
223. Report of sermon given by IIM at the LJS, in *Manchester Guardian*, 17 October 1938, p.13.
224. *The Daily Worker*, 2 May 1939, p.4.
225. *Yorkshire Post,* 29 April 1939, p.8. Other prominent signatories to the appeal included J.B. Priestly and John Gielgud.
226. Letter to the editor, *The Times,* 1 April 1939, p.10. The list of signatories to the letter included Robert Whaley Cohen, President of the United Synagogue.
227. *JC,* 21 July 1939, pp.32–3.
228. Liberal Jewish Synagogue Annual Report, 1934, LJS Archives.
229. John Henry Amshewitz (1882–1942) was a British painter, etcher, and cartoonist. He was born in Ramsgate, the son of a scholarly rabbi. He studied at the Royal Academy, 1902–7,

and won a prize for mural decoration in 1905. Amshewitz's output included portraits, still-lifes, Jewish subjects, and scenes of the theatre as well as book illustrations and cartoons, but he is best known as a muralist.

230. Liberal Jewish Synagogue Annual Report, 1937, LJS Archives.
231. Album in Mattuck Family Archives kept by Jill Tarule Mattuck (MFAa).
232. *LJM*, VII, no.10 (March 1937), pp.85–7.
233. Letter from Julian Morgenstern to IIM, 20 April 1931 and letter from IIM to Julian Morgenstern, 30 March 1931, AJA, Hebrew Union College Records, MS-5, Box A-18, Folder 14.
234. *LJS Monthly,* February 1934.
235. 'Burying the Hatchet', *JC*, 1 June 1934, pp.7–8.
236. *JC*, 23 October 1936, p.16. It is interesting to note that although Zangwill was an ardent Zionist, IIM had a deep admiration for him.
237. *LJM*, XX, no.6 (June 1949), p.76.
238. IIM gave a special address at the LJS at the time of the coronation celebrations, which Lily Montagu sent to Queen Mary. Marlborough House replied saying his address had apparently made a 'profound impression upon the Queen', Mattuck Family archive kept by Robert Edgar (MFAb).
239. 'Great memories of a noble institution', *JC*, 12 April 1991, p.2.
240. *JC,* 12 February 1965, p.32.
241. Muriel Harris, *Pulpits and Preachers* (London: Methuen and Co Ltd, 1935).
242. *JC*, 27 September 1935, pp.28–9.
243. 'Liberal Judaism in England', address given by IIM at the WUPJ conference in Berlin, 19 August 1928, MCC.
244. 'Spinoza's Significance in Religion', address given by IIM as part of the Horace Seal Memorial Lectures (London: Ethical Union, 1932).
245. For example, on 22 June 1930, IIM presided at the evening service at the church. The following day he addressed a meeting of ministers on the aims of the London Society of Jews and Christians and in the evening gave an address before a meeting of Copek on 'The Position of the Jew in the Modern World', see *LJM*, II, no.4 (July 1930), p.48.
246. See *LJM*, IV, no.1 (April 1932), notice inside back cover.
247. Rabbi Dr I.I. Mattuck, 'Our Debt to Claude Goldsmid Montefiore', special edition of *LJM* (September 1938), pp.4–5.
248. 'Dr Mattuck Endorses Ort Campaign', *Jewish Exponent*, 28 February 1936, p.6. Ort was an organisation set up in America in 1922 to provide training and education for Jews throughout the world. It was part of the World Ort organisation founded in the 1880s in Russia to provide vocational training for Russian Jews.
249. Letter from Julian Morgenstern to IIM, 28 March 1937, AJA, Hebrew Union College Records, MS-5, Box A-18, Folder 14.
250. Letter from Corinne Mattuck to her family, 20 October 1937, MFAa.
251. Letter from Julian Morgenstern to IIM, 3 May 1938, AJA, Hebrew Union College Records, MS-5, Box A-18, Folder 14.
252. See *LJM*, X, no.3 (June 1939), p.22.

CHAPTER TWELVE

The Second World War

Maintaining the Congregation

Soon after the outbreak of the Second World War, Leslie Edgar was invited to become a Jewish Chaplain in HM forces. This role took him away from the LJS for most of the war, leaving IIM with much reduced support;[1] Solomon Starrels had departed from the LJS in 1933 and Maurice Perlzweig had left in 1938. In the early war years, IIM only had the support of Rabbi Raphael Levine (another graduate from HUC appointed in 1938 and Rabbi Reinhart's brother-in-law).

IIM devoted a great deal of effort to keeping in touch with synagogue members serving in the Armed Forces, with the children who had been evacuated and with the many families who had moved out of London, while at the same time holding together the congregation remaining in the capital. He produced a weekly circular for the congregation and sent out a copy of his Shabbat sermon to all members unable to attend services ('Sermons for Country Members').[2] To maintain the interest of those unable to attend study and discussion groups, he developed, as a substitute, correspondence materials that reached a larger audience than the groups that had operated in peacetime.[3]

To retain the allegiance of LJS members remaining in London, in November 1939 IIM launched a study group on the religious problems that troubled synagogue members 'either in their thought or in their practical life'. He invested a large amount of time in preparing for and running this study group that met regularly throughout the war.[4] Meetings were often held in members' homes to overcome the difficulties associated with the blackout.[5] IIM encouraged those living in different parts of London to meet together to discuss religious practices, and led services himself in places where LJS members were living.

IIM also wrote a monthly (later bi-monthly) newsletter for members in the Armed Forces ('News Letter for Members in the Forces'), which ran from twenty to thirty pages and provided news on synagogue members and day-to-day life at the LJS, information on the progress of the war, prayers, poetry and readings, commentaries on current philosophical and political issues, articles on Jewish topics and thoughtful pieces on how Britain might be after the end of the war. Although they were heavily censored, the newsletters were a remarkable achievement. One of those who maintained his contact with the LJS because of IIM's efforts was John Rayner, a refugee from Germany, who was later to become the leading rabbi of the Liberal Jewish movement.[6]

In 1943 the Council for Progressive Jewish Education was founded jointly by the Liberal and Reform synagogues. During the war years the Council assumed responsibility for the religion classes held at the LJS and other Liberal synagogues, as well as at West London Synagogue. It worked closely with the Central Council for Jewish Refugees at Woburn House and the Refugee Children's Movement based at Bloomsbury House, on the religious education of refugee children. IIM was prominent in writing the religious syllabi for the Central Council.[7]

IIM worked with Miss Marjorie Moos, by now a long-standing teacher at the LJS, to produce special correspondence courses for young evacuees. From her arrival at the LJS as a young woman in the 1920s, Miss Moos had been devoted to IIM. She painstakingly transcribed in longhand many of his sermons, speeches and addresses and regularly corresponded with him on synagogue matters. During the war she redoubled her efforts, travelling far and wide to help IIM stay in touch with the dispersed congregation, and she assisted him to rewrite the Religion School curriculum for those young children learning through correspondence.

Early in 1941 the government announced a scheme for providing financial assistance to those organisations supporting German refugees and registered with the Central Committee for Refugees. Dr Mattuck's Refugee Committee was able to benefit from this provision, which meant that IIM was now freed from his intensive fund-raising activities. However, the reprieve was temporary for in August that year, Rabbi Levine decided to return to America to rejoin his family there.

IIM pursued a variety of avenues to obtain rabbinic support. He considered, but dismissed, the idea of appointing a number of the continental rabbis who had emigrated to Britain, such as Rabbi Brasch, because he felt that their English was not good enough. He also considered appointing Michael Franklin, the son of Netta Franklin, as a 'lay assistant' since he had studied for a number of years at a theological school in New York and had been judged as being unfit for military service. However, this idea did not come to fruition either.[8]

IIM eventually appointed Rabbi Jakob Kokotek as a temporary Assistant Minister, a refugee from Germany who had assisted at the synagogue on an ad hoc basis during the 1930s. Rabbi Kokotek was able to help with some of the 'outside jobs', but IIM did not feel sufficiently confident in his abilities to offer him a permanent contract. With the congregation continuing to decline notwithstanding the arrival of increasing numbers of German Jewish refugees,[9] and perhaps hoping to find someone akin to himself thirty years earlier, IIM wrote to Julian Morgenstern in Cincinnati asking if he knew of 'a young man who would like something adventurous and an opportunity to give help in this country'.[10] As he had anticipated, Morgenstern was unable to identify someone willing to leave America at that time to take up residence in war-torn Britain.[11]

Synagogue life was increasingly disrupted by the war. Part of the building was taken over by the St Marylebone Borough Council as a public air raid shelter, and part of the basement became an Air Raid Precautions (ARP) Post.[12] When the war started, IIM staggered services to limit the number of people in the building at any one time. However, normal arrangements were restored within a few months. After the first air raids, the synagogue housed for several days 300 people from West Ham, who had been bombed out of their homes and placed there temporarily by the London County Council while more permanent accommodation was found for them.[13] As well as tending to those housed temporarily at the LJS, IIM regularly toured the air raid shelters of bomb-shattered London and 'cheered many a frightened soul with his own cheerfulness.'[14]

Under IIM's unflagging leadership the synagogue became a hive of industry in support of the war effort. The Women's Society was particularly active in helping evacuated children, the Armed Forces and refugees. Towards the end of the war, the Women's Society gathered goods and supplies to be sent to the women and children liberated from the Belsen Concentration Camp as well as to displaced Jewish families.

On the night of 1 November 1940, a 1,000 lb bomb fell on the synagogue.[15] The building was seriously damaged, but seventy people sheltering in the air raid shelter in the basement were unharmed. Sir Pelham Warner, Captain of All England, now friend of IIM, insisted that he use the Oak Room at Lord's for services on a temporary basis. Despite his intense grief at the damage to the synagogue he cherished, IIM accepted the offer and led the Sabbath service at Lord's. He spoke of 'the roads we have trodden, of the obstacles we have had to climb'.[16] He reassured the congregation that only one third of the synagogue had been destroyed and it would surely be restored. Subsequently he led services in a nearby church hall and sometimes in people's homes while urgent repairs were being made to the Montefiore Hall to enable it to be used as a temporary synagogue. IIM felt that the hall was made 'a very attractive and cosy place of worship', and lamented that Sabbath services were very poorly attended.[17]

IIM's War Sermons

As he had done during the First World War, IIM frequently gave his views on the Second World War in his sermons at the LJS. However, both the tone and content of his sermons during the years 1939–45 were very different from his earlier war sermons. From the outset he had no doubts about whether the war was necessary, or about the issues that were involved. To IIM, war had become inevitable. Hitler had been offered every form of peaceful settlement and he had refused them all. The war must now be faced with courage and fortitude because it was a fight between right and wrong, between justice and injustice.[18] IIM felt no compunction about praying for victory. Four weeks after the outbreak of the war he declared:

> In the past every nation has fought wars which their religions if true to themselves could not approve, wars for territorial conquests, commercial markets, or mere national glory. These are the things for which Hitler has made the present war. But those who have been forced to take up arms against him are moved by the desire to prevent the triumph of aggression and the spirit of barbarism. Their victory will give righteousness a better chance. Their aims are fully righteous, and the nature of their cause entitles them to the full support of religion.[19]

However, he felt that the war was even more than a fight between right and wrong – the future of civilisation was at stake. He defended his view:

> If anyone is tempted to brush this statement aside as an exaggeration, let him review in his own mind the record of the Nazi rulers, first in Germany itself, and then toward other nations. There is no principle of decency, honour or justice which they have not violated – and that because these things have no value to them.[20]

He was so convinced of the righteousness of those who fought against Hitler that he was completely confident victory would be achieved and the world would be freed from the oppression of Nazism.[21] He made it clear that the enemy was not the German people per se, but Hitler, and he called for a public statement from the Allies saying that a Germany freed from Nazi rule would be allowed to take her place among nations. He hoped that the German people had not been crushed totally by Nazism to become 'mere cogs in a machine for making war', and would rise, alongside all humanity, with a stronger grip on spiritual realities.[22]

While IIM was concerned with the future of civilisation in general, he made no apologies for considering the particular fate of Jews whom he felt carried a double burden and whose suffering was aggravated simply because they were Jews. In his New Year message in September 1941 he pronounced:

> With so many Jews oppressed and persecuted wherever the Nazis rule, and threatened wherever their influence reaches, we must plead for arrangements in the settlement of the post-war world which will save these Jews from their miserable lot, and do all that is possible to avoid such calamities anywhere in the future. But the Jews have also their contribution to make to the future.[23]

He kept the LJS congregation informed of the horrors occurring in Germany, which he described as 'one large concentration camp', and also of the tragedies happening in Poland, which had been split between Russian and German rule. The Polish Jews under German domination were being treated with increased venom motivated, he said, 'by hatred for the Jews as Jews and as Poles'.[24] He pointed out that traditionally Polish-Jewry had, to a large extent, been the house of Jewish learning and had produced a number of Jewish saints. Now, however, 'the light has gone out' and there was, at least for the time being, nowhere to replace it.[25]

Looking to Palestine, as some were suggesting, was not the answer, IIM said, since the spiritual and religious strength of the Jews in Palestine was dependent on the strength of world Jewry and that was not good. As IIM saw the situation, even in those countries where Jews shared in national life without restriction, they faced problems. Nevertheless, he felt it incumbent on Anglo and American-Jewry in particular to remain strong and to provide a focus for Jewish religious life.[26]

Despite his unerring belief in the rightness of the war, IIM recognised that it raised two crucial questions for religion – did the existence of war mean that religion had failed, and how could it survive in such an antipathetic environment? In response to the first question, IIM argued that it was not the failure of religion, but the triumph of irreligion that had led to war:

> Nazism which is responsible for the war has been actually opposed to religion, although it has not always avowed it. It has denied and scorned everything religion stands for in the moral and spiritual realm. For loyalty to God it has put loyalty to the state; for the law of God, it has substituted the law of the state and of the dictator. But

> even more significant is the attitude of Russia who has shown anything but a peaceful spirit or a righteous attitude.[27]

In response to the second question, IIM contended that in wartime religion could not only provide solace, but also the vision for overcoming the failings of an imperfect world. He suggested that there were two ways in which religion could seek good out of evil: by using its spiritual and its organised power to support 'the good purposes, the righteous purposes, the pure purposes, wherever it finds them, even in war', and by keeping the spirit of the nation equal to its high purpose.[28] He recognised that the latter function was a difficult task 'when anger, resentment, bitterness and the spirit of vengeance all threaten to rise day by day. However because it was so difficult, it is all the more urgently necessary'.[29]

IIM continued to preach with undaunted optimism throughout the war. Even in the bleakest times during 1940, when the allies suffered severe losses and Britain came under heavy bombardment, he urged the nation to carry on fighting with 'undiminished zeal', to repair what had been damaged and to work for the future. Above all, it was essential for people to retain a sense of righteousness. It was the loss of this belief by the French leaders, he maintained, that had led to the collapse of France.[30] IIM even tried to find a rationale for what was happening in Germany. Nazism, he argued, was an unmitigated evil, but one that God had sent for a purpose. According to IIM, 'Jewish martyrdom had a divine purpose for good',[31] but he did not elaborate on what that good might be. His attitude to the Holocaust borders on the apologetic. IIM was not alone in taking this approach. Cecil Roth, the Jewish historian and journalist, similarly declared that the sufferings of the Jews were a test: 'it was necessary for the instrument to be put through the fire before it could be tempered into the finest steel'.[32]

IIM's repeated calls for hope and faith extended beyond the LJS to non-Jewish audiences. Increasingly his sermons regarding the war were given at Sunday services, which despite the war effort still attracted large audiences. Particularly notable were his series of addresses on 'Religion and the War', delivered during the early part of 1941. He urged his audiences to think beyond the war and about the type of world that would emerge from it, especially the type of international organisation that would be needed to assure both the freedom of nations and the freedom of individuals. Learning from the First World War, something stronger than the League of Nations was essential.[33]

However, even more crucial than an international organisation was to build a new world based on religion. He argued that the rivals to religion – materialism and humanism – had both failed to guide life in the right direction and it was therefore the responsibility of religion to purify the world and enlarge its hold on men and nations. It concerned him that, because of the major part it was playing in securing victory, Russia would have a prominent part to play in moulding the future of Europe, but Russia was an anti-religious country. He hoped earnestly that Russia would change its stance on religion. If it did not, he feared that 'the prospect for the future of Europe is very dismal'.[34] It is striking that at such an early stage in the war IIM discerned the factors that would lead to the 'Cold War'.

Although many of IIM's war sermons were intended for wider audiences, some were designed specifically for Jewish people, including a series of five sermons he delivered at the LJS during April and May 1940 on 'The Faith of a Modern Jew', in which he set out his views on the differences between Liberal and Orthodox Judaism. It is interesting that he should choose to do this in the depths of war when synagogue attendance was very low. The sermons were deeply religious in their content and highly learned. In his introduction to the series of sermons, IIM said that his intention was to 'speak directly to the intellect rather than to the emotion'.[35]

A possible reason for IIM choosing to preach in detail on the tenets of Liberal Judaism at this time might be that he was beginning to perceive that the form of Progressive Judaism which he had pursued since he was a young man, was now not only being challenged by other sections of Anglo-Jewry, but also from within the Liberal Jewish fold. He therefore felt the need to reassert Liberal Judaism's basic principles and the reasons for them. This possible explanation is supported by the fact that in a number of his later war sermons he defended Liberal Judaism against the criticism that it lacked warmth. He argued that Liberal Judaism used 'thought to create feeling, by rousing the aspirations which can create a sense of exaltation' rather than through 'elaborate or intensive ritualism'.[36] The call by LJS members for the re-adoption of traditional practices was perhaps now becoming stronger.

As the fortunes of the war allies changed and the possibilities of victory became more certain, IIM preached on the direction of peace negotiations. He chastised those who, after the failure of the peace negotiations following the First World War, were cynical about achieving a positive outcome.[37] To IIM the lessons to be learned from the last peace were obvious – the refusal of America to join the League of Nations, economic nationalism, and the policy of appeasement in the face of those who committed crimes against humanity. They now had to be heeded if civilisation were not to perish in a third world war.[38]

He applied the teachings of Judaism to consider how Germany and the Germans should be treated after the war, concluding that while

Judaism forbids revenge as evil, those who had given the orders to torture and kill old men, women and children could not 'morally and in fairness to humanity be absolved from their guilt'. To overlook their crimes he said, would be 'a crime against humanity'.[39]

He also asserted that Germany as a whole should bear the consequences of its national conduct, again not as revenge or punishment, but as a matter of 'moral law'.[40] In practice this meant that:

> Her power to make war in the future must be destroyed, so far as possible, her national independence must for a time, until she has learnt to value peace with righteousness above war as an instrument of national policy, be curtailed; and so far as her economic resources permit, she must be compelled to make some reparation for the incalculable harm her crime has done to others.[41]

It is notable that, whereas in the early stages of the war IIM had argued clemency be shown towards Germany, his views had now shifted and he was making no distinction between the Nazi rulers and the German people collectively. However, IIM did insist that individual Germans should be treated with dignity and that consideration be given to their human needs, which might ultimately help to bring about a change of heart in the German nation and show the way to world peace.[42] All of this must have been very painful for IIM personally given his veneration of all things German previously mentioned, his German relatives, and the seminal part that German Jews had played in his development.

Outside the Synagogue

Busy as he was with congregational affairs, IIM found time during the war to maintain many of his existing external activities and for new involvements. Often in tandem with Lily Montagu, IIM travelled between the various Liberal congregations that now existed, some of which were now lacking a rabbi or had become severely depleted in their membership because of the war. To help maintain the congregations he frequently preached, gave addresses and attended meetings. In spite of the war and evacuation, IIM and Lily Montagu oversaw the setting up of two new congregations – Ealing Liberal Synagogue in 1943 and Southgate Progressive Synagogue in 1944.

IIM also continued to travel around the country spreading understanding of Liberal Judaism. On a number of occasions he went to talk with students at Oxford and Cambridge universities, and in the summer of 1943 he again visited the church of St-Francis-on-the-Hill in

Barry, Glamorganshire, at which he had made several addresses in the pre-war years. He made such a strong impression there that he was invited to make a return visit two years later to speak on 'Jewish Problems and the Future of "Liberal Religion"'.[43] In January 1945 he spoke on 'Modern Developments in Judaism' at a Gravesend Clerical Luncheon.[44]

Despite the difficulties created by the war, IIM stayed in touch with members of WUPJ by 'photographically reduced air mail letters'.[45] With work in Europe at a standstill, IIM turned his attention to the developing Progressive communities in Palestine and South America.[46] From the early part of the war, he gave a lot of thought to the role that WUPJ might play in representing the claims of Jews before a peace conference and in reconstructing Jewish life in those countries where it had been destroyed.

In August 1941 IIM drafted a memorandum setting out proposals on the post-war work of WUPJ, which were largely endorsed by its leading members.[47] IIM presided at the WUPJ conference held at the LJS on 11 October 1942, which deliberated on 'The Prospect for Progressive Judaism After the War',[48] and when in 1943 WUPJ organised a series of conferences on 'The Seat of Authority in Progressive Judaism', IIM was one of the opening speakers.[49] During 1943, he led a small group of British representatives from WUPJ to develop proposals on their statements to the peace conference that followed the war. His hope was that these statements would form part of an interfaith delegation to the conference.[50] He was the author of the 'petition' that emerged from these discussions.[51]

As the war progressed, relations between Jews and Christians began to show signs of strain as a result of the hardships of the war. Although Hitler's outpourings received little sympathy in England, even amongst anti-Semites, they did raise questions as to the place of the Jews whose existence until then had been taken for granted. On the Jewish side, the relapse into barbarism of a civilised country produced an uneasiness that unsettled relations between Jews and their gentile neighbours. The evacuation of Jewish people from London and other urban areas had brought them into contact with rural communities who had never before encountered Jews. Evacuees were often seen as 'black marketeers', who aggravated housing, petrol and food shortages. German-Jewish refugees experienced both anti-Semitism and xenophobia; they were aliens as well as urban Jews, a nest of spies and potential saboteurs.[52] This anti-refugee hysteria led to the categorisation of German refugees and the internment of those considered to be a significant risk to national security, an arrangement on which, interestingly, IIM did not comment.

Under the leadership of the newly appointed Archbishop of Canterbury, Dr William Temple[53] and Chief Rabbi Hertz, the Council of Christians and Jews was set up in 1942 in an attempt to deal with the tensions and to discuss post-war reconstruction. IIM was a member of the Executive Committee of the Council, but his main efforts on interfaith dialogue were still largely directed towards the London Society of Jews and Christians. The Dean of St Paul's, W.R. Matthews, later said that the society would not have survived the difficult years of the war had it not been for IIM's faith and patience.[54]

In June 1941 IIM chaired a series of lectures on 'Co-operation between Jews and Christians' under the auspices of the London Society of Jew and Christians, and two years later presided over a number of conferences organised by the society, which brought together various religions. In 1944 he was appointed as Chairman of a joint committee of the London Society of Jews and Christians and the Council of Christians and Jews, which oversaw the production of a report drafted by Dr Charles Myers[55] on the psychology of anti-Semitism and problems of Jewish-Gentile relations.[56] These moves were more proactive than those of the Board of Deputies, which continued to be hampered by its traditional caution and the acrimonious debates between Zionists and anti-Zionists that dominated its wartime meetings. From 1942 until 1943 IIM was the personal Jewish Chaplain to Sir Samuel Joseph, an LJS member, when he was Lord Mayor of the City of London.

In May 1943 IIM made the first of a number of broadcasts on BBC radio. In 1929 the lay leadership of the JRU had approached the BBC to negotiate airtime for IIM. The suggestion was rejected after the BBC director concerned was advised by Chief Rabbi Hertz that the broadcast would be unacceptable to the Orthodox community, and would simply provide unwarranted publicity for a new subversive movement 'that has always been propagandist'.[57] Ten years later a further approach regarding a BBC broadcast, this time made by IIM himself, was also vetoed by the Chief Rabbi on the grounds that IIM represented a very small section of the Jewish community.

But in April 1943 IIM was invited by the BBC Home Service to give a talk on 'Judaism: A Religion of Conduct'[58] as part of a series on 'Great Religions of the World'. By this time he had staunch supporters at the BBC, mainly as a result of his work with the London Society of Jews and Christians. Although the Chief Rabbi was on the BBC Board, on this occasion he was not consulted because the talks were not organised by the Religious Affairs Department.[59] Prior to the broadcast, a number of people wrote to the BBC expressing their uneasiness about Judaism being represented by IIM. They felt that the broadcast should be made by someone able to speak for a larger proportion of Jewish people in the country rather than a small section of Anglo-Jewry and by someone 'of more conservative views'.[60] To allay the BBC's fears, IIM offered to send them a copy of his script in advance of the broadcast so that they could take advice from those who had objected to him speaking on the radio. He said that he was willing for any relevant amendments to be made and realised that what was wanted was 'a fair and objective presentation of Judaism'.[61]

The broadcast went ahead. IIM in conversation with Sir Frederick Whyte explained that Judaism was an attitude to the universe, a conception of man and his destiny and a way of life, all centred in the belief in the living God.[62] IIM cited the first chapter of Genesis and the Prophets to stress the optimistic nature of Judaism. He talked about the unity of the Jewish people, but hinted at different interpretations of Jewish law. He discussed the meaning of the 'Jewish mission'.

IIM's broadcast was described as 'masterly'.[63] He was lauded for having carried out his task 'in the manner in which the great bulk of the community would have desired' and with 'ability and serenity'.[64] He received letters of gratitude and appreciation from many different quarters, including a letter from the press office of the Board of Deputies saying that numerous listeners had benefitted from his 'admirable contribution'.[65] IIM admitted to being 'bowled over' by the praise of the editor of the *Jewish Chronicle*, who said that IIM was owed 'sincere thanks'.[66] IIM's talk was published in *The Listener* and later that year he made a second broadcast, 'Your Questions Answered', on the General Overseas Service of the BBC.

However, IIM's success in the media did little to ease the tensions between him and the Chief Rabbi, who had 'come out on the warpath' against United Synagogue members putting forward the suggestion that, during the war, Orthodox synagogues might cooperate with Liberal congregations. IIM commented: 'Dr Hertz need not fear for the truly Orthodox Jews. Liberal Jews are prevented by their principles from trying to impose their ideas or methods on others.'[67]

At the outbreak of the war, IIM was appointed as the sole agent of CCAR to disburse funds to refugee rabbis in England, for which he was paid $1,000 per year. In a statement (purpose unknown),[68] IIM explained that this role was an extension of that which he had played since his arrival in the country in 1912 of a 'de facto representative' of American Reform Judaism, carrying out 'missionary work' in England to spread Liberal Judaism. He said that his duties had always included administering, when the occasion arose, grants from CCAR.[69] Perhaps in an attempt to emphasise his American identity, in December 1941, IIM offered his services to the American Ambassador, the Republican John Gilbert Winant, who wrote back to him saying that he was grateful for IIM's 'thoughtfulness', but did not wish to take him up on his offer.[70]

Lay Ministers

In 1943, when helping to prepare a campaign to spread Liberal Judaism, IIM suggested that those members of Liberal synagogues who had been leading services and worship for some years should be given the status and recognition of congregational leaders. They would be given the title of 'Lay Minister', having fulfilled certain conditions and having undergone a programme of training in Jewish teachings and Hebrew to be led by IIM assisted by other rabbis. They would wear a gown and carry out all the functions of a minister except for the acceptance of converts. IIM partly devised the scheme as a means for overcoming the shortage of Liberal rabbis, but he also saw it as the continuation of the Jewish tradition of preaching being carried out by a maggid rather than by a rabbi. Lily Montagu was one of the first group of people to be trained as a lay leader, although she had by then been leading services for a number of years, as was Samuel Rich, a leading member of the South London Liberal Jewish Synagogue and one of the first teachers at the LJS Religion School.

Speaking a year later at the induction service which marked the end of the training for the first cohort of lay ministers, IIM outlined the duties expected of lay ministers, and also their spiritual requirements, which were the same as those of a fully qualified minister – they needed to be imbued with the spirit of Judaism, the spirit of faith in God and the spirit of the House of Israel.[71] However, he believed that few lay leaders would possess the skills necessary to become acceptable preachers, namely 'a knowledge of the fundamentals of Judaism, the ability to make them significant by applying them to the circumstances of our time, and the ability to express thought in appropriate words and effective speech'.[72] IIM's high expectations of those delivering sermons reflect the emphasis placed on homiletics skills at the time of his own training.

The Problem of Peace

At the end of the war, two services were held at the LJS on 13 May 1945, the Day of National Thanksgiving. A marquee was erected alongside the Montefiore Hall to accommodate the congregation. IIM preached on 'The Meaning of Victory'. On 19 August that year he led two services held to mark the end of the war with Japan.[73]

Although he described the victory of the Allies over Germany as a 'momentous event in the history of mankind' and 'a great salvation', the sermon he gave at the National Thanksgiving Service lacked the joy of his sermon that followed the ending of the First World War.[74] He was clearly weighed down by the thought of the work that now needed to be carried out to reconstruct a shattered and confused world:

> Millions of lives have been lost. The material is widespread and in many places so great as to amount to annihilation. But there is something more. The war has jeopardised valued institutions and weakened a fundamental moral concept. It has shaken our civilisation to its foundations. It was not just a horrible interlude in human history which cannot resume its course at the point at which it was interrupted. The war marked the close of an era. The world that preceded it has gone.[75]

He tried to view the destruction caused by the war as an opportunity to build a better world, but was gravely worried about the 'unimaginable catastrophe' for humanity if the unity of nations failed to prevent another war. He stressed the 'tremendous responsibility' that the United Nations established in San Francisco had for assuring the future fate of humanity.[76] IIM strongly disagreed with those who argued that the immense power of the new weapons of war, particularly the atomic bomb, would prevent nations from making war. He said that such a view was based on a 'dangerous illusion' that would offer a false sense of security and prevent 'the arduous labours and the incessant vigilance that will be needed to establish real security'.[77] He agreed with Sir Arthur Keith, President of the British Association, who had said that man's power given him by the discoveries and inventions of science had outstripped the development of his moral sense, which harboured a grave danger.[78] IIM believed that the development of the atomic bomb revealed the 'incalculable gravity of that danger'.[79]

Above all else, IIM's joy in victory was checked by the inordinate losses of Jewish life at the hands of the Nazis. While others were celebrating the end of the war, IIM was contemplating what the Holocaust meant for the future of Judaism. He was becoming acutely aware that it had opened a gap between Jews and non-Jews, a gap that over the next nine years he sought to breach despite his declining health.

NOTES

1. Between 1938 and 1941 IIM was supported by the American rabbi, Raphael Levine, and from 1941–45 by Rabbi Jakob Kokotek, a refugee, who had become involved in the LJS several years earlier.
2. See LJS newsletters for 1941. The 'Sermons for Country Members' were still being sent out for a while after the war ended.
3. Rabbi R. Levine, 'Progressive Judaism in Wartime', in *Progressive Judaism, Bulletin of the World Union for Progressive Judaism*, 1, 11 (November 1940), pp.8–9, LJS Archives, Box 100.
4. Papers for the study group, London Metropolitan Archives, ACC//3529//002/037–042.
5. See Levine, 'Progressive Judaism in Wartime'.
6. Transcript of talk by John Rayner (undated) LJS Archives, Box 139a.
7. *LJM*, XIV, no.2 (February 1943), p.13.
8. Letter from IIM to Louis Gluckstein, 18 August 1941, LJS Archives, Box 1/2.

9. Sir Louis Gluckstein, 'Sixty Years of LJS History', *LJS News*, November 1972.
10. Letter from IIM to Dr Morgenstern, 9 October 1941, American Jewish Archives (AJA), Hebrew Union College Records, MS-5, Box A-18, Folder 14.
11. Correspondence between Dr Morgenstern and IIM October 1941–March 1942, LJS Archives, Box 1/2.
12. The Younger Members' Organisation of the Liberal Jewish Synagogue, *The Years Between 1911–1951, LJS exhibition catalogue* (London: ULPS, 1951).
13. See IIM's *News Letter to Members in the Forces*, No. 1, November 1940.
14. John Rayner, 'The Legacy of Israel Mattuck', sermon given at the service in memory of Rabbi Dr Israel I. Mattuck, at South London Liberal Synagogue, 11 April 1954, LJS Archives, Box 135c.
15. The intended target was the electricity substation around the corner from the synagogue.
16. From the typed text of a talk by Lily Montagu in LJS Archives, Box 139a.
17. *Newsletter to Members in the Forces*, No. 4, February 1941, p.4.
18. 'Be Strong and of Good Courage', a message from IIM in September 1939 (day unknown), Montagu Centre Collection (MCC).
19. 'Strength in the Lord', sermon given by IIM at the LJS, date not given but starts with an introduction saying it is four weeks since the commencement of war, in ibid.
20. Ibid.
21. 'Faith and Life', sermon given by IIM at the LJS, 14 September 1939, MCC.
22. Ibid.
23. Quoted in 'A New Year Message', *The Times*, 16 September 1941, p.2.
24. 'The Present Position of Jews in Other Lands', sermon given by IIM at the LJS, 19 November 1939, MCC.
25. Ibid.
26. Ibid.
27. 'Religion in a Warring World', sermon given by IIM at the LJS, 26 November 1939, MCC.
28. Ibid.
29. Ibid.
30. 'The Moral Factor', sermon given by IIM at the LJS, 15 February 1941, MCC.
31. IIM's Rosh Hashana message, September 1943, reported in the *JC*, 1 October 1943, p.12.
32. Quoted in Geoffrey Alderman, *Modern British Jewry* (Oxford: Oxford University Press, 1992), p.301.
33. 'Religion and the War-Peace Aims', sermon given by IIM at the LJS, 23 February 1941, MCC.
34. 'The Foundations of a New World', sermon given by IIM at the LJS, 22 September 1941, in ibid.
35. 'The Faith of a Modern Jew: 1 God', notes on a sermon given by IIM at the LJS, 28 April 1940, in ibid.
36. 'Thought and Feeling in Religion', sermon given by IIM at the LJS, 5 December 1943, in ibid.
37. 'The Lesson of the Last Peace', sermon given by IIM at the LJS, 7 November 1943, in ibid.
38. Ibid.
39. 'The Treatment of Germany', sermon given by IIM at the LJS, 17 February 1945, in ibid.
40. Ibid.
41. Ibid.
42. Ibid.
43. Letter from the Reverend R. Lomas to IIM, 14 August 1945, Mattuck Family Archive kept by Robert Edgar (MFAb).
44. Outline of his address archived with his sermons, MCC.
45. The Hon. Lily H. Montagu, *The World Union For Progressive Judaism, The First Twenty-Five Years, 1926–1951*, p.13.
46. Foreword by IIM in *Progressive Judaism, Bulletin of the World Union for Progressive Judaism*, 1, 11 (November 1940), pp.1–2, LJS Archives, Box 100.
47. See copy of the draft of IIM's 'Memorandum on Post-War Work for the World Union for Progressive Judaism', together with copies of letters commenting on his proposals from leading members of the Governing Body, including Dr Julian Morgenstern, Dr Elbogen, and Dr Vogelstein, AJA, WUPJ Records, MS-16, D25/g.
48. *LJM*, XIII, no.9 (November 1942), p.68.
49. *Bulletin of the World Union for Progressive Judaism*, December 1943, p.14.

50. Summaries of the two meetings of the English members of the first and second commissions, undated MS, LJS Archives, Box 59.
51. 'Statement from the World Union to the Peace Conference', manuscript in ibid.
52. Todd M. Endelman, *The Jews of Britain 1656 to 2000* (Berkeley, Los Angeles, CA and London: University of California Press, 2002), p.224.
53. IIM welcomed Dr Temple's appointment as a force for social change. See *Newsletter to Members in the Forces*, No. 17, March 1942.
54. Leon Roth and W.A.L. Elmslie, *The Significance of Biblical Prophecy for Our Time, The Rabbi Mattuck Memorial Pamphlet No. 1* (London: London Society of Jews and Christians, 1955), Preface by The Very Reverend W.R. Matthews, Dean of St Paul's, President of the London Society of Jews and Christians, p.3.
55. It is not known who Dr Myers was.
56. Minutes of the meeting of the joint group held at Bloomsbury House, 30 March 1944, London Metropolitan Archives, ACC//3529//002/014.
57. Quoted in Meir Persoff, *Faith Against Reason – Religious Reform and the British Chief Rabbinate, 1840–1990* (London and Portland, OR: Vallentine Mitchell, 2008), p.236.
58. The talk was broadcast between 7.40 and 8.00 p.m. on 10 May 1943.
59. Letter from IIM to Rabbi Morris Lazaron, 9 July 1943, AJA, Morris Lazaron Papers, Box 5, Folder 34, MS-71.
60. Letter from Eric Fenn, Assistant Director of Religious Broadcasting at the BBC to IIM, 27 April 1943, LJS Archives, Box 1/2. The Reverend Fenn made it clear that he had no misgivings himself and alluded to the several times he had met IIM at meetings of the London Society of Jews and Christians.
61. Letter from IIM to Eric Fenn, 28 April 1943, in ibid.
62. Ibid.
63. 'Judaism and the Wireless', *JC*, 14 May 1943, p.10.
64. Ibid.
65. Letter from Sidney Salmon, Press Officer Secretary, the Board of Deputies of British Jews to IIM, 11 May 1943, London Metropolitan Archives, ACC/3529/002/013.
66. Letter from IIM to Rabbi Morris Lazaron, 9 July 1943, AJA, Box 5, Morris Lazaron Papers, Folder 34, MS-71.
67. *News Letter to Members in the Forces,* No. 7, May 1941, p.4.
68. This arrangement was made as part of IIM's bid to retain his American Citizenship. There was a clause in the citizenship legislation that enabled him to live abroad as a US Citizen providing he could demonstrate that he had been 'sent' as a representative of an American organisation.
69. Statement by IIM, undated, LJS Archives, Box 1/2.
70. Letter from Second Secretary of State, Henry Stebbins, American Embassy to IIM, 12 January 1942, London Metropolitan Archives, ACC/3529/002/012.
71. 'The Place of Lay Ministers in Judaism', sermon given by IIM at the induction service for lay ministers at the LJS, 19 November 1944, MCC.
72. Ibid.
73. Liberal Jewish Synagogue Annual Report, 1945, LJS Archives.
74. 'The Meaning of Victory', sermon given by IIM at the National Thanksgiving Service held at the LJS on 13 May 1945, MCC.
75. Ibid.
76. 'Victory and Peace', sermon given by IIM at the LJS, 19 August 1945, MCC.
77. Ibid.
78. 'Judaism and the Future', sermon given by IIM at the LJS, 5 October 1945, MCC.
79. Ibid.

The Post-war Years

Withdrawal from the LJS

Correspondence suggests that it had been IIM's intention to retire from his congregational duties at the LJS when he reached the age of 60 to allow him to do more for the Liberal Jewish movement as a whole and to give him extra time for the studying he had long wished to pursue. However, the advent of the Second World War had prevented him from doing so.[1] Towards the end of the war IIM wrote to the Jewish War Services Committee to negotiate Leslie Edgar's early release from the Armed Forces,[2] but he was not released until 18 October 1945. Edgar's eventual return came as a huge relief to IIM. It meant that he was now able to transfer some of his day-to-day congregational responsibilities to his son-in-law. To help Edgar in re-establishing his credibility in the synagogue, IIM wrote to HUC to enquire about the possibility of him being awarded an honorary degree of Doctor of Divinity.[3] Despite IIM's eloquent rationale for this, the doctorate was not conferred on Edgar until 1958.

The process of withdrawing from the LJS was not an easy one. IIM decided to stop participating in LJS council meetings, but he was eventually persuaded by the lay leadership to continue his attendance. During 1946 IIM passed over editorial responsibility for the *Liberal Jewish Monthly* to Leslie Edgar, but felt that he could not make his exit from leadership of the LJS until he had secured the rebuilding of the synagogue. Once the Religion School, the young people's groups (the Alumni Society and the Younger Members' Organisation, which had been set up in 1933 to cater for the post-Alumni age group) had been re-established, IIM turned his attention to fund-raising for the reconstruction of the synagogue. The launch of the Reconstruction Appeal in 1946 was a moving occasion, with IIM talking with great pathos about his experience of arriving at the LJS on the 1 November 1940 to find it had incurred severe bomb damage.[4]

Although it was to be several more years before works on the synagogue were completed, a special service was held in the partially completed sanctuary on the afternoon of Sunday 21 September 1947. IIM described the event as 'historic and thrilling' and one that 'will live in our memories'.[5] Later in 1947 a Commemoration Service was held at the LJS to celebrate IIM's thirty-five years at the synagogue. He was presented with an album containing photographs, addresses and other materials relating to his long ministry.[6]

The opportunity for IIM to change his 'work plan' eventually came in 1948. By then he felt that the ministry of the LJS could now be placed safely in the hands of Leslie Edgar. At the beginning of the year, he signalled his intention of resigning from his role as Senior Minister to become Minister Emeritus on 1 June 1948. IIM received many letters expressing regret at his 'semi-retirement',[7] although the announcements made in the *Liberal Jewish Monthly* stressed that IIM would maintain his strong links with the LJS congregation and contribute regularly to services.[8]

The announcement of IIM's new role was timed to coincide with his completion of thirty-six years' ministry in England. To mark the occasion he gave a sermon at the LJS that reflected on world developments during that period. The sermon contained very little of the buoyant optimism that characterised his early sermons in England; he felt that the foundations of the world were rocking as the result not only of two devastating world wars, but more especially of the rise in totalitarian movements. He said that, whereas in the first decade or so of the twentieth century he and others had been convinced that it was possible to change the world and make it a better place, there was now a widespread feeling of impotence.[9]

He went on to say that that fascism, Nazism and communism represented 'a revolt against the liberalism of the nineteenth century'. However, they were also a symptom of deeper problems: loss of spirituality and deteriorating moral standards. Men had lost faith in themselves and hankered for 'an authority in which to sink their empty souls'. He therefore saw that the task of religion in general and Judaism in particular was to help people restore their self-respect and to 'instruct men in their dignity'. His conclusion that 'humanity is sick at heart' was a very sombre one.[10]

On 26 January 1949, a reception was held at the LJS in honour of IIM and as a tribute to both him and Edna Mattuck for all that they had done for the synagogue. At the reception a portrait of IIM was unveiled in the Montefiore Hall, which was filled to capacity. 'The company of friends' present at the unveiling included many founding members of the synagogue, some of whom had travelled long distances to be present.[11] IIM's portrait was painted by the Hungarian portrait artist, Professor Arthur Pan, who had recently painted Field Marshall Smuts and Winston Churchill. The portrait replaced the one painted by J.H. Amshewitz that had been damaged during the war when the synagogue was bombed. During the reception it was revealed that Professor Pan had admitted that IIM had not been easy subject. When Pan used his usual technique of drawing his sitter into conversation so that their pose would be unstrained and their expression natural, he was almost too successful. On one occasion he was apparently moved to exclaim: 'Stop your clever talk, Dr Mattuck, and let me concentrate on my work!'[12] A specially framed reproduction of the portrait was presented to Edna Mattuck and other reproductions of the portrait were sold to raise money for the Synagogue Reconstruction Fund.

A Change of LJS President

IIM's leadership of the LJS congregation not only continued for longer than he had planned, but his final three years as Senior Minister were also uneasy ones because of his tense relationship with the lay leadership of the synagogue. After Claude Montefiore resigned shortly before he died in 1938, the role of LJS president was left vacant for several years. The natural successor was Louis Gluckstein, vice-president of the synagogue. However, Gluckstein felt unable to follow immediately in the footsteps of such an esteemed man as Montefiore. Only in 1942 did he eventually agree to take on the presidency of the synagogue. However, since he saw active service during the Second World War it was some time before he was fully established in the role.

Colonel Louis Halle Gluckstein (later Sir Louis) was prominent in public life. He was called to the Bar in 1922 and elected as Member of Parliament for Nottingham East in 1931. From 1945 onwards he devoted a large amount of time to LJS affairs and his many skills and extensive experience benefitted the synagogue. However, Gluckstein was also a very forceful character and soon found himself in disagreement with IIM, who hitherto had been given a comparatively free hand in the running of the LJS. During 1947 Gluckstein and IIM had a particularly notable disagreement, which resulted in an exchange of strongly worded letters. In March IIM wrote to Gluckstein saying that he feared that Gluckstein's recent actions were leading to 'a fundamental change from the distinctive character [the synagogue] has developed through the years of its existence'. IIM's main concerns appear to have been what he regarded as an 'excessive' consideration of financial issues and his exclusion from decisions on administrative affairs. He felt that, as the synagogue's rabbi, he had a role in applying religious principles to both financial and administrative matters.[13] IIM's concerns had been prompted by Gluckstein failing to consult him on the launch of a campaign to obtain funding for the rebuilding of the synagogue. IIM felt that his lack of participation in the planning of the appeal was 'unprecedented' and was obviously quite offended: 'when, the other night you presented to the Council the plan for the campaign it made me feel that the honorary officers were of the opinion that my help was not needed. It was not a pleasant feeling, but, to use a phrase of Montefiore's – there it is'.[14] IIM was obviously not satisfied by Gluckstein's response[15] and, in reply,[16] went on to cite a number of other concerns as well as setting out why Gluckstein's explanations had missed the point he had made. The two men subsequently met to discuss their disagreement, which appears to have resolved matters, and over the next few years they found a mutually acceptable way of working together. Gluckstein backed IIM to the hilt when he was criticised publicly and IIM supported Gluckstein staunchly in the major disagreement he had with the Board of Deputies (see below). However, IIM still objected to the way in which Gluckstein ran the council of the LJS. In an exchange of correspondence with Lily Montagu in 1950 he voiced his misgivings on how Gluckstein had handled elections to the council.

> I think that you ought to know that things have gone from bad to worse. What has happened about the Council elections is, to put it mildly, not very creditable, and certainly not appropriate for a religious institution.[17]

He felt so strongly about the way synagogue affairs were handled under Gluckstein that he started to avoid meetings at the LJS.[18] The episode reinforces how symbiotically Montefiore and IIM had worked together and, although IIM cited his role as synagogue rabbi as the reason for his displeasure, the impression given by the correspondence is that of a clash between two strong-willed men who both wanted to be in control.

Developing ULPS

Preserved from the storm of destruction that swept across mainland Europe, in the post-war years Anglo-Jewry assumed a new importance in the Jewish world. Long accustomed to feeling itself the western extremity of a large European Jewish community, it now held a prominent position without a hinterland, which caused many to reflect on the future of the community. Towards the end of the war, IIM spoke of the future of Liberal Judaism. He perceived that Liberal Judaism would have a much greater prominence in the post-war era, and a special role in promoting the revival of religion. He based this perception partly on his belief that people would now be seeking what he referred to as 'true ideas'.[19] With the emphasis that Liberal Judaism placed on freedom of thought and earnest thinking about religion, it was ideally placed to fulfil this need for truth.

IIM's second reason for believing in a growth in Liberal Judaism was that, as the 'Judaism of tradition enriched by modern thought', it could satisfy best the current religious needs of Jews. He predicted: 'It is most unlikely that many Jews will in the future hold the fundamental ideas for which Orthodox Judaism stands. I can go further. It is certain that many will not. Many, perhaps even most Jews, do not even now.'[20] IIM appears to have been convinced that whatever Judaism decided to call itself in the future, it would be essentially liberal in nature.[21]

A third factor he cited in support of his perception was the changing atmosphere of Jewish life in Western countries. Orthodox Judaism in Britain had traditionally drawn its inspiration from Polish Jewry, but now that Polish Jewry had been decimated the community leaders were expressing anxiety about its future. This led IIM to conclude that 'Left to itself, Judaism in England will develop along different lines; and there can be no question what those lines will be.'[22]

It was this utter certainty that probably hastened IIM's decision to divest himself of his congregational responsibilities and concentrate on developing new Liberal Jewish communities, plans for which he had already drawn up before the end of the war. In September 1944 he wrote to Leslie Edgar enclosing an outline of his proposals for the development of the movement, which included establishing new communities in Bethnal Green, Edgware and Ealing, obtaining new buildings for the existing communities in Southgate and North London, and various measures for publicising Liberal Judaism. Not all of his plans were to come to fruition.[23]

After the war ended, news of IIM's declining health leaked out, and suggestions were made that the Liberal Jewish movement would not endure since his fame and skills were seen as being its main source of strength.[24] This analysis proved unfounded and IIM's predictions, at least initially, appeared to have been correct. The post-war years were a time of rapid expansion for the LJS and other Liberal communities, as those who had served in the war came home and started families and as evacuees returned to London. Many people who might otherwise have left the Liberal congregations felt that after the Holocaust it was essential to maintain their Jewish affiliations. In addition, the expansion of the Liberal movement reflected the increasing Anglicisation and embourgeoisement of East European Jews, who wanted to retain their ties to Judaism but were dissatisfied with the all-Hebrew, multi-hour, sex-segregated services of the United Synagogue.[25]

The expanding Liberal Jewish movement, now called the Union of Progressive and Liberal Synagogues (ULPS), was able to employ a professional Organising Secretary and a Publications Officer. In 1947 IIM was appointed deputy-president of ULPS and made plans to spend a large amount of his time working alongside Lily Montagu, now ULPS president, to spread Liberal Judaism.[26] He wrote to a friend: 'You are quite right, I mean to do more work than ever; but I realise in advance there will be a big gap between "to do" and "done".'[27]

In the spring of 1946 IIM launched a campaign for spreading Liberal Judaism, which was inaugurated by a series of lectures on Sunday afternoons at the Friends' House in Euston Road. The lectures were mainly aimed at those not yet acquainted with the fundamental ideas of Liberal Judaism'.[28] They were subsequently published under the title of *Liberal Judaism – its Thought and Practice.*[29]

In January 1946 IIM spoke at the Mansion House, Dublin at a public meeting convened to form a new congregation. Over 600 people attended; a further 150 were unable to gain admission because the room was full. A follow-up meeting was held a few weeks later at the Shelbourne Hotel, which IIM attended in an advisory capacity, and at which the congregation was formally established.[30] However, it was not until he became Minister Emeritus that IIM was able to devote a significant amount of time to supporting the growing movement. He was then instrumental both in helping to re-establish the smaller Liberal synagogues that had languished when their membership scattered during the war and also in building new congregations in Southend, Wembley and Blackpool and a Liberal Jewish group in Leicester.

IIM's endeavours to spread Liberal Judaism included contact with students at Oxford and Cambridge universities, where, unlike Anglo-Jewish young people in general, Jewish students were very organised, and assembled for prayers on Friday nights and Saturday mornings. IIM was more successful in engaging with university students than his American rabbinic counterparts. He founded study groups and preached at the well-attended Liberal services organised by the students.[31] He invited young people to his homes in London and Long Crendon to foster their involvement in Liberal Judaism (see Chapter Fourteen),[32] and spoke at a number of youth conferences such as at the Joint (Liberal and Reform) Youth Conference held at Heacham in Norfolk in November 1948. Rabbi Reinhart was invited to speak at the conference and careful arrangements were apparently made to ensure that IIM and Reinhart were not there at the same time.[33] He was also the main speaker at several Liberal Youth Federation conferences and gave his attention to extending and strengthening religious teaching for school age children.

In 1946 IIM inaugurated a course for training teachers for Liberal Jewish religion schools. At the first session he gave a lecture on 'The Aims of a Liberal Jewish Religion School', and at the next session he gave another on 'The Syllabus of a Liberal Jewish Religion School'.[34] He subsequently assumed the role of Director of Studies for the training of lay ministers, religion schoolteachers and speakers on Liberal Judaism.

The Jewish Fellowship

In 1942 IIM had been a founding member of the Jewish Fellowship, which was largely made up of those who remained staunchly opposed to the notion of a Jewish National Home. It set out to challenge the Board of Deputies, which had become increasingly inclined towards the pro-Zionist camp when its President, Neville Laski, was replaced by the Eastern European-born Selig Brodetsky.[35] The president of the fellowship was the former MP for Cheltenham, Sir Jack Brunel Cohen, but it was largely led by Anthony de Rothschild, Leonard Montefiore and Lionel Cohen. IIM was generally regarded as the spiritual leader of the fellowship.[36] Whereas the earlier League of British Jews had been supported by most of the leading families in the Jewish establishment, not one of these families – whose hold on communal life was rapidly diminishing – joined the fellowship. IIM found the attitude of 'the Dukes' (the Anglo-Jewish establishment) 'very depressing'.[37]

The Jewish Fellowship was founded during the turmoil surrounding the Biltmore Declaration of May 1942, which was the first official call for Palestine to be established as a Jewish Commonwealth by the mainstream Zionist movement.[38] The meeting at which the declaration was made was held in at the prestigious Biltmore Hotel in New York, with 600 delegates and Zionist leaders from 18 countries attending. Prior to the Biltmore Declaration, the Zionist movement refused steadfastly to formulate the ultimate aim of the movement, preferring instead to concentrate on the practical task of building the Jewish National Home. The major shift was prompted by intense opposition to the British White Paper of 1939 and based on a realisation that, after the war, America would play a larger part in the fulfilment of Zionism.[39]

Although it was established in 1942, it was not until November 1944 that the Jewish Fellowship went public, owing to the reluctance of the fellowship's leaders, including IIM, to create controversy during the heights of the war. In addition, behind-the-scenes attempts were being made to find the body a broader platform by merging it with the Anglo-Jewish Association.[40] When the merger failed to materialise and the fellowship was formally launched, IIM found himself within a small minority even within the restricted circle that constituted the fellowship's membership. While the majority of the members of the fellowship saw it as a platform for their 'Britishness' and English patriotism, just a small number, including IIM, Basil Henriques and Joseph Leftwich (the Fellowship's Secretary), were committed to restoring the centrality of religion in a Liberal Jewish version of Jewish life. The fellowship's earliest pamphlet, *What the Fellowship Stands for*, stressed that the fellowship would: 'Uphold the principle that Jews are a religious community... stimulate Jewish life in this country... seek to revive the religious spirit among Jews and to place the Torah, the Synagogue and the ethics of Judaism at the heart of Jewish life.'[41] These words were probably penned by IIM.

The Jewish Fellowship, which has been described by writers as 'the last gasp' and 'the last stand' of opposition to Zionism in Anglo-Jewry,[42] did not last long because it was overtaken by events. IIM's correspondence with Rabbi Morris Lazaron of Baltimore[43] provides interesting insights into IIM's thoughts during the life of the fellowship. In 1942, he wrote to Lazaron encouraging action in America to provide impetus for activity in Britain.[44] He indicated that he would be doing something himself (probably referring to early moves to establish the fellowship), but it is interesting to note that he felt unable to take the lead and believed that his efforts would be limited to stimulating others to take the initiative forward.[45] This was perhaps because of his many other commitments.

However, he appears to have changed his mind, probably as a result of the proclamation by a group of Zionists of their intention to take over the Board of Deputies, which IIM regarded as a 'Crisis in Anglo-Jewry', and referred to as 'Zionist Totalitarianism'. He warned:

> The gravity of such a development lies in the ultimate issues that are involved. What those who are trying to 'capture' the Board want is to further the Jewish nationalist view, in the decisions that will have to be made in post-war reconstruction about the future position of the Jews. These decisions will affect not only the position of the Jews in some countries, but the position of the Jews in all countries.[46]

Although the Jewish Fellowship claimed that it did not engage in political activities, in fact it became the most forceful opponent of the Zionist Organisation in Britain and was therefore anti-Zionist rather than non-Zionist. IIM frequently referred to himself as a non-Zionist, but by involving himself in an organisation that opposed Zionism he had entered an anti-Zionist phase.[47]

In letters to IIM, Rabbi Lazaron mentions IIM's role in drawing up a proposed non-Zionist constitution for Palestine that sought to bridge the divide between Arabs and Jews.[48] It called for the end of the British Mandate and the setting up of an independent Palestinian state, where the different communities had control over their respective municipal institutions. It was therefore a reiteration of the proposals put forward by Alfred Hyamson and Colonel Stewart Newcombe[49] in 1937 in response to the Peel Commission. IIM's involvement in this informal group is interesting for two reasons. First, he seems to have changed his previous stance regarding the British Mandate in Palestine; whereas prior to the war he was advocating 'the British Government guarantee the political and cultural rights of the Jews of Palestine by permanently continuing the Mandate',[50] he was now party to proposals that included ending the Mandate. Second, IIM was prepared to work with Arabs and non-Jews in compiling the document published in 1945 under the names of Newcombe and the MP Ralph Beaumont.[51]

The draft constitution had little influence, perhaps because – as Lazaron commented to IIM – it failed to face squarely the most pressing issues that militated against its implementation.[52] He was probably referring to the fact that the proposed constitution omitted any reference to the 1939 White Paper's contentious call for an independent Palestinian state and the clause that gave the Arabs control of Jewish immigration. However, it is probably this lack of reference to these clauses that made it possible for IIM to endorse the document. The omission also reinforces IIM's personal objections to the 1939 White Paper previously mentioned.

IIM shared with Lazaron his concerns on the 'terrible threat that hangs over Palestine and which draws nearer every day', and outlined his belief that the only solution was for the Palestine problem to be taken out of the political arena and to be placed in a religious context, 'in other words taken out of the hands of the nationalists and put in a bi-national framework'.[53] He saw this as necessary because 'The Zionists have landed us in a terrible mess. What they want is impossible; by insisting on it they are killing the opportunity of getting what is possible.'[54]

However, IIM was not optimistic that either side in the conflict would be willing to listen to his suggestion. By this time the fellowship was under heavy attack for its failure to condemn the 1939 White Paper publicly, which was interpreted as tacit support for its content. In 1947 IIM wrote an article that appeared in the *Jewish Chronicle*, in which he conceded that the White Paper was 'a mistake', but added that it had not in practice prevented all Jewish immigration to Palestine.[55] Zionists possibly construed such a statement as an attempt by IIM to dilute his earlier criticisms of the White Paper and it did little to enhance his reputation.

The fellowship lost much of any credibility it might have had in the Anglo-Jewish community by linking Zionism to Nazism and criticising the Zionist movement in the non-Jewish press, which was seen as a threat to community solidarity.[56] It was also an anathema to Zionists that the fellowship should choose to voice its opposition at a time when crucial decisions were being made on the future of Palestine. Given the strength of his beliefs, it must have been galling to IIM that the main tactic adopted by Zionists to undermine the fellowship was to attack its religious intentions, accusing it of conducting anti-Zionist propaganda behind a religious camouflage.[57]

Some of the criticisms against the fellowship were aimed at IIM personally. Citing the pioneering work of the American social psychologist, Kurt Lewin, the Zionist commentator, Barnet Litvinoff, condemned IIM as 'an interesting example of self-hatred'.[58] As Senior Rabbi at the LJS and head of the Liberal Jewish movement, IIM was also viewed by opponents of the fellowship as a symbol of its domination by Progressive Jews. Paul Goodman, a leading Zionist publicist, described the fellowship as 'a number of Englishmen of Jewish faith inspired by the leader of a Synagogue'.[59] This was damaging to the fellowship because of the great schism that existed between Orthodox and Progressive Judaism and because the vast majority of the Anglo-Jewish community retained a deep suspicion of the Liberal Jewish movement.[60] Despite his leadership skills and his eloquence, IIM's prominence had the impact of helping to isolate the fellowship from the rest of Anglo-Jewry.

While some members of the fellowship privately acknowledged its failure to appeal to a large proportion of Anglo-Jewry,[61] IIM appears to have harboured a sincere belief that it represented the majority of British Jews. In October 1945 IIM and Louis Gluckstein met with Selig Brodetsky in a private meeting to discuss the attitude of the Board of Deputies on Zionism. The minutes of this meeting indicate that IIM warned Brodetsky that the LJS's position as a board member would be jeopardised 'if the Board's policy and attitude continued to diverge from that of the majority of the Board'. This statement, as well as adding credence to the Zionist claim that the anti-Zionist movement and Liberal Judaism were one and the same thing, seems to contain a contradiction. As one writer has asked, 'What was the Board's policy if not that decided by a majority of Board members, and as such how could Mattuck claim logically that his policy was opposed by the majority of the Board?'.[62]

Despite Zionist claims, the fellowship failed to develop a formal relationship with the non-Jewish anti-Zionist organisations that existed at the time, including the Committee for Arab Affairs chaired by Sir Edward Spears. However, IIM appears to have developed informal links with some of its members, such as Sir Ronald Storrs.[63] At the height of the battle over Palestine in 1947, IIM dined with Storrs and during the meal the two men discussed the efforts of anti-Zionist Jews in opposing Zionism. Storr's private papers include copies of IIM's letters to the press on Zionism and his articles on Palestine in the *Liberal Jewish Monthly*.[64]

The course followed by the fellowship was very different from that of its parallel in America, the American Council for Judaism (ACJ), which was established in 1942 following the CCAR conference in Cincinnati, at which a resolution was adopted in support of a Jewish army. A 'Statement of Principles' was drawn up and signed by ninety-five non-Zionist rabbis, mainly the older members of CCAR, of which IIM was one.[65] The statement included views with which IIM would have fully concurred:

> In the light of our universalistic interpretation of Jewish history and destiny, and also because of our concern for the welfare and status of the Jewish people living in other parts of the world, we are unable to subscribe to or support the political emphasis now paramount in the Zionist program. We cannot but believe that Jewish nationalism tends to confuse our fellowmen about our place and function in society and also diverts our own attention from our historic role to live as a religious community wherever we may dwell. Such a spiritual role is especially voiced by Reform Judaism in its emphasis upon the eternal prophetic principles of life and thought, principles through which alone Judaism and the Jew can hope to endure and bear witness to the universal God.[66]

The ACJ became dominated by its lay members and ever more politically radical in its opposition to Zionism, making the Jewish Fellowship appear comparatively moderate. It may have been this overt political radicalism, but also a wish to avoid a charge of their being an international anti-Zionist group, that deterred IIM from encouraging closer links and official cooperation between the ACJ and the fellowship.[67] However, he was unimpressed by what he referred to as the 'totalitarianism' of CCAR when a resolution was passed calling on the ACJ to disband.[68]

When the war ended, the European Jewry that had survived the Holocaust was in a pitiful condition. Many survivors were in poor health and did not have a home to go to or, if they did, they did not want to return there because of memories of persecution. A large number of penniless, stateless Jews were living in Displaced Persons Camps (DPCs) until a home could be found for them. As IIM knew from his correspondence with LJS members working in the camps, conditions were grim.[69] Few countries were willing to provide homes for the displaced Jews and immigration to Palestine was severely limited by the British Government under the terms of the 1939 White Paper.

In these circumstances the plight of the Holocaust survivors became more important than debates about Jewish nationalism. On 30 January 1946 IIM was part of a deputation from the Jewish Fellowship to the Anglo-American Commission of Enquiry on European Jewry and Palestine, set up to agree upon a policy regarding the admission of Jews to Palestine. The deputation submitted a memorandum stating the fellowship's view that the sufferings of Jews in Europe should be brought to an end by them being granted full equality in their countries where they chose to remain. Those who chose to leave should be given support to emigrate, including if they desired to Palestine.[70]

This message was reinforced by IIM in a sermon that he gave at the LJS in May 1946 on 'The Palestine Report'. He again stressed the need for the future of Palestine to be removed from the political arena and placed in a universal context. He called for 100,000 Jews to be admitted to Palestine on humanitarian grounds and for other countries to ease immigration for Jewish refugees. He was highly critical of the American Zionists, whose political demands he said were reducing the opportunities for suffering Jews to emigrate to Palestine.[71]

While in New York in the autumn of 1946 (see Chapter Fourteen), IIM was interviewed by the *New York Times*. In this interview he defended the British Government's policies and actions in Palestine. He suggested that criticisms of the British Government were based on 'some misconception of the problem of Palestine'. Notwithstanding official policy, immigration to Palestine had continued albeit that the numbers making their home in Palestine was 'pathetically small compared to the need', and the limitation on numbers was not due to any lack of sympathy on the part of Britain.[72] He expressed his strong concerns about the developing deadlock on Palestine and the tide of anti-Semitism that was resulting from the situation. He foresaw 'destruction and carnage' following the ending of the British presence in Palestine. He voiced his support for proposals to establish a United Nations Trusteeship over Palestine to help prevent a 'terrible war' and promote a non-political solution as 'befitting the spiritual character of the country as the Holy Land of three great religions'.[73]

Membership of the fellowship never exceeded 2,000, and during 1946 and 1947 a number of influential lay leaders such as Leonard Montefiore left the movement. IIM and Rabbi Reinhart from West London Synagogue became its main driving force. As a result, an increasing emphasis was placed on strengthening Jewish religious life rather than on fighting Zionism. IIM's and Reinhart's leadership of the fellowship was to be brief.

After several years of brutal fighting in Palestine, in 1947 Britain eventually gave up its mandate. Following the statement of British Foreign Secretary, Ernest Bevin, yielding the mandate, IIM wrote:

> Political Jewish nationalism is bankrupt. It has only succeeded in forcing the decision out of the hands of Britain, the country that has again and again proved its friendliness to the Jews, into the (realm) of international politics, and that at a time of the most confusion and the most intense conflict among the nations ... The measure of the

> bankruptcy of political Jewish nationalism is indicated by the fact that one of its prominent friends in parliament could only urge that the Jews and Arabs in Palestine should be allowed 'to fight it out even though it should involve some bloodshed'.[74]

IIM regretted deeply that the mandate had proved unworkable. However, he was even more saddened that 'a section of Jews must share the blame for its failure'.[75] The demands from Jewish nationalists that Palestine be made a Jewish state had given rise to equally extreme demands from Arab nationalists. The opposing interests of the Zionists and the Arab nationalists were irreconcilable.[76] The anger that lay behind IIM's statements is palpable.

Following Britain's relinquishment of the Palestinian mandate, the newly formed United Nations voted for Palestine to be divided into a Jewish and an Arab area. IIM made a last-minute attempt to put forward proposals that would, he hoped, avoid bloodshed. In response to a letter from Spears to *The Times*, in which he ruled out any Arab compromise on the issue of immigration, IIM wrote suggesting a plan, which he believed, would settle the Palestine problem:

> the friends of the Arabs can ... further peace by urging their leaders to agree now to a reasonable amount of Jewish immigration; sufficient, at least, to meet the sad needs of the Jews in Europe, but not so large as to threaten the numerical preponderance of the Arabs. The friends of the Zionists can, correspondingly, serve the cause of peace by urging the leaders of the Zionist Organisation to abate their political claims, which were developed to their present extent under the stress of circumstances ... The sacrifices involved are immeasurably less than the sacrifices which war would take.[77]

As just and sensible as IIM's ideas might have been, they were out of step with the drift of Jewish thinking and, put forward as they were only a month prior to the State of Israel coming into being, tended to suggest that IIM was out of touch with developments. His proposals were derided in the press as 'contradictory, meaningless and dishonest'.[78]

Once the State of Israel was established in 1948, and the AJA agreed to incorporate into its constitution the fellowship's aims regarding the religious basis of Jewish life in England, the fellowship lost its *raison d'être*, and it was agreed that it should be disbanded. The absorption of non-Zionists into the AJA did not help their cause, since the AJA had steadily declined in membership and was now seen as being reactionary in its attitudes. It also appeared aristocratic in an increasingly democratic age.

Although it was short-lived, the fellowship is considered by historians to have been more effective than its American counterpart, because of the leadership provided by IIM and others like him who had a distinguished record of public service.[79] During its brief life, the fellowship published the *Jewish Outlook* as a counter to the Zionist press. IIM was one of the main contributors to this periodical, the strong editorial line of which was that Jews had to decide if they were Jews or political Zionists, they could not be both.[80] In 1947 IIM also conceived the idea of establishing the *Journal of Jewish Studies*, a quarterly review also published by the fellowship. The aim of the journal was to allow Jewish scholars to 'give free play to their discoveries and speculations'.[81] The Executive Editor of the *Journal of Jewish Studies* was Dr C. Rabin, a lecturer at Oxford University.[82] IIM became a member of the editorial board and a regular contributor to the journal. On behalf of the editorial board, IIM wrote to Julian Morgenstern at HUC to seek his backing and to invite him to become one of its advisory editors, alongside Professor Martin Buber, Dr Leo Baeck and Dr Finkelstein, President of the Jewish Theological Seminary in New York.[83] For its first issue, IIM contributed an essay on 'The Mystery of Israel', in which he analysed a philosophy of the purpose of Jewish existence and an interpretation of Jewish suffering, held by the eminent Catholic writer, Jaques Maritain. The *Journal of Jewish Studies* appeared intermittently due to lack of finance, but gradually grew in stature.

After the founding of the State of Israel, IIM persisted with his struggle against what he regarded as the 'un-Jewish' implications of the Jewish state, seemingly refusing to regard the year 1948 as significant as far as the Jewish condition in the Western Diaspora was concerned. In May 1948 IIM was invited by the ACJ to visit America to speak at various eastern American cities on the dangers associated with the newly established State of Israel. His addresses included the lecture he gave at the fourth annual conference of the Philadelphia branch of the ACJ and an address at the annual meeting of the New York Chapter ACJ, held at the Hunter College Auditorium. The New York audience of over 1,000 members was the largest that that chapter of the ACJ had ever attracted.[84] It was in fact to be one of the ACJ's last public statements against Jewish statehood.[85]

Back in England, IIM remained in close touch with those who continued to emphasise the religious basis of Jewish life, such as Rabbi Louis Wolsey in America. IIM told Wolsey that he regretted the increasing separatism of Jewish organisations in America and deplored the fact that they were 'shouting that the Jews in America and other countries must develop their own life'. He concluded: 'I agree with you that we should let the Zionist State proceed. In any case we cannot do otherwise. But what

I feel we ought to try to do is to prevent the State from dominating Jewish life throughout the world.'[86]

However, IIM's supporters in America were becoming fewer and fewer even within anti-Zionist circles. When in 1945 his book *What Are the Jews?* was submitted to the Jewish Publication Society for publication in America, it was turned down, having been described as 'inadequate' by Rabbi Samuel Schulman, a long-time opponent of Jewish nationalism and one of IIM's long-standing friends and admirers. After finishing his lengthy critique of IIM's book, Schulman wrote, 'I feel like a father who, having thrashed his son, said that it hurt him more to give the thrashing than for the boy to take it.'[87]

On the creation of the State of Israel, even IIM's close confidant, Rabbi Wolsey, formally withdrew as a member of the ACJ. In a press statement he called for the dissolution of the ACJ and pleaded for an effort to heal all wounds in order to strengthen Israel by creating a united spiritual front of American Jews. Wolsey's recognition of the realities of the situation and his willingness to state his changed position in public won him the acclaim that was to elude IIM because of his continued non-Zionism.

IIM's personal secretary, Joe Foreman, later said that IIM was a pragmatist and would have eventually come to terms with the existence of the State of Israel, and there were some signs of this before his death. For several years before he died, IIM was a contributor to the Friends of the Hebrew University in Jerusalem, donated to Israeli charities such as the Council of the Ashkenasic Jewish Community of Jerusalem,[88] and supported the development of Progressive communities in Israel. However, he never publicly renounced his position on Israel and, until the end of his life, he criticised developments in Israel which he found unpalatable, such as the opposition of Orthodox Jews to the drafting of young women for national service.[89]

Other Activities

IIM's gradual withdrawal from the LJS and his 'semi-retirement' enabled him to concentrate on much cherished activities. He gave more time to WUPJ, of which Leo Baeck was now the revered President.[90] In 1946 IIM took a leading role in preparing for the first post-war WUPJ conference, which was held in London. It included a garden party at the Mattuck's 'Wildwood' home (see Chapter Fourteen). The theme of the conference was 'The Task of Liberal Judaism in the Post-war World'. Correspondence suggests that IIM was excited by the conference and the opportunity that it would provide for him to be reunited with colleagues from whom he had been separated during the war, despite the fact that it would be surrounded by 'sad memories and anxieties'.[91] He gave a stirring conference address on 'Religion in the Crisis', in which he spoke of the spiritual challenges confronting the world and emphasised the need to maintain faith in God as a means for overcoming that crisis.[92] IIM had clearly emerged from the war with his faith still strong, but he must have been sorely disappointed when at one of the sessions, Rabbi Weiler from South Africa called on the anti-Zionist leadership of the WUPJ, including IIM as its Chairman, to eliminate the anti-Zionist element of the movement since it prevented WUPJ from gaining the support of the masses.[93]

With other members of the Executive Committee IIM sought to rebuild Progressive Judaism in Europe, especially in Germany. In the post-war years he visited affiliated communities across Europe to assist refugees and Holocaust survivors. IIM was also very involved in dealing with post-war negotiations. WUPJ was awarded 'consultative status' with the Economic and Social Council of the United Nations, UNESCO and UNICEF, and IIM, with others, attended various conferences to discuss rehabilitation programmes in Germany and the Netherlands. He represented WUPJ at important peace conferences held in Geneva and at Lake Success, New York,[94] and was prominent in the preparation of the Bill of Human Rights.[95] He felt that Jews had a threefold interest in this declaration: because Jews had, more than any other group, suffered the denial of human rights; because, like all religions, they are concerned with freedom for religion; and because the declaration embodied principles that had their roots in Judaism.[96]

The WUPJ conference of 1946 was followed almost immediately by another international conference on 'Freedom, Justice and Responsibility', which brought together Jews and Christians from across the world.[97] The idea of holding the conference was first proposed by the National Conference of Christians and Jews in America in the late summer of 1944, when the war was entering its final stages. The Council of Christians and Jews in England decided to cooperate in the project and it was agreed that the conference would be held in Lady Margaret Hall College, Oxford between 30 July and 6 August 1946. IIM was one of the main organisers of the conference and helped to shape the agenda at preliminary meetings held during January 1946, and at residential sessions held in April. A number of commissions were set up. 'Commission 2' was co-chaired by IIM and L.W. Grensted Nolloth, Professor of Philosophy of the Christian Religion at Oxford University.[98]

The findings of Commission 2 were felt to be so important by those attending the conference that it was decided that they should be published to provide a guide to future Jewish-Christian cooperation. The work on the publication was led by IIM, Father Corbishley (Master of Campion Hall, Oxford), Rabbi Dr Isidor Epstein (Director of Studies at Jews' College), Professor T.H. Robinson (Emeritus Professor of Semitic Languages, Cardiff University), and Dr D.E.L. Allen (Lecturer in Theology and Religious Knowledge, Durham University). IIM was described as having contributed with 'a quiet but far-seeing sanity'.[99] *The Foundations of Our Civilisation, Fundamental Postulates of Christianity and Judaism in Relation to Human Order* was published in 1947 by the Council for Christians and Jews. It included a paper co-written by Dr Epstein and IIM, 'The Social and Moral Postulates of Judaism', which is remarkable for the cooperation it demonstrated between an Orthodox and a Liberal Jew.

In the early part of 1947 IIM worked with Leo Baeck and Rabbi Arthur Marmorstein (then a lecturer at Jews' College and later its Chairman) to found the Society for Jewish Study, the purpose of which was to promote Jewish scholarship with the aim of breaking down divisions in Anglo-Jewry. However, for reasons that are unknown, by 1950 IIM had withdrawn from this society.[100]

In 1947 IIM gave another BBC broadcast, this time on 'The Faith of a Jew' as part of a series on 'What I Believe'. In the broadcast IIM averred the unshakeable nature of his belief in God.[101] The broadcast was published both in *The Listener* and as part of a booklet produced to accompany the series. The following year, Lord Dowding quoted from this broadcast during a parliamentary debate on the slaughter of dogs.[102]

At the end of 1947, IIM's second book, *The Essentials of Liberal Judaism*,[103] was published dedicated to the memory of Claude Montefiore. It was a 'text-book' based on the confirmation class lessons he had given at the LJS over the years, in which he explained the basics of Liberal Judaism with the aim of dispelling some common misconceptions.[104] Via a series of logical steps, IIM led the reader to an understanding of what it means to be a Jew. The book also dealt with the intellectual, emotional and personal elements of God. While upholding his own opinions vigorously, IIM referred to 'Traditional Judaism' with deep respect and included a number of sections that explored the differences between Christian and Jewish thought. In this particular book IIM did not explicitly polemicise against Zionism, which is not even mentioned by name, but he did insist on the essentially religious character of the Jewish people. The extent of IIM's Jewish learning was displayed in the appendix to the book.

The book was described by Leo Baeck as 'instructive and inspiring'.[105] Because the material it contained had been used for teaching purposes, its language was very precise yet nevertheless adult. A liberally inclined Jewish journal, the *Jewish Outlook*, heralded the book as 'intellectual without being heavy, spiritual without being mystic, and readable without being light'.[106] Another review said that while the religious philosophy expounded was of 'a rather extreme type' of Reform Judaism, the book nevertheless made a 'useful contribution to the task of clarifying religious thinking of present-day Jews'.[107] In 1950 *The Essentials of Liberal Judaism* (together with his three lectures 'Liberal Judaism – its Thought and Practice') were translated into Italian and were published in Italy in connection with the formation there of a section of WUPJ.[108]

At the end of 1949 IIM embarked on a series of 'deeply intellectual' lectures held in the Council Room at the LJS, to which a selected group of people were invited including a trainee rabbi, Herbert Richer, who felt that he had been 'commanded' by IIM to attend the lectures.[109]

During a trip to America, IIM delivered the HUC Alumni lectures (on 'The Challenge to Judaism', 'The Way of Integration' and 'The Task of Liberal Judaism') in November 1946,[110] their first presentation since the war. Julian Morgenstern wrote to him afterwards to thank him for his lectures, and to say that his treatment of the problem of Judaism in the Western World was 'authoritative, suggestive and stimulating'. The College contributed $250 to their subsequent publication.[111] On the same trip, IIM also gave a sermon at Temple Emanu-El in New York on 'Jews and Faith'. He was disappointed that his proposed sermon on 'Britain and the Jews' had been rejected by the serving rabbi, Goldenson, but wrote to Leslie Edgar reporting with some amusement that he had managed to say 'some of the things that I wanted to say under the other heading'.[112] He went on to speak at 'Rabbi Wice's congregation in Lincoln' (not the South Street synagogue where IIM had served before his ordination). He turned down a number of other invitations to speak despite the fact that Edna Mattuck was encouraging him to 'talk a lot'.[113]

By this time, IIM appears to have had little contact with CCAR and to have held a greater allegiance to HUC. Tucked away in Ohio and isolated from the teeming mass of Eastern European Jewry in New York, the College still respected some of the 'classical' Reform values espoused by Kaufmann Kohler,[114] whereas within CCAR a clearly discernable shift of opinion had occurred. The optimistic, universalistic American Judaism, which IIM still strongly espoused, had lost much of its credibility.[115]

Further Controversy

During the Second World War the Jewish community was fairly unified in its response to hostilities and to Nazism. However, as in the aftermath of the First World War, tensions arose soon after peace was declared. In August 1945 IIM wrote to the Board of Deputies expressing a number of concerns about developments in the Jewish community, especially the lack of recognition given to Liberal Judaism. He cited as an example of his complaint an occasion on which representatives of the board met with the Minister for Education to discuss the Jewish aspects of the forthcoming Education Bill. No representatives from the Liberal or Reform sections of the Jewish community had been invited to the meeting.[116] IIM and Louis Gluckstein agreed to meet with the president of the board, Professor Brodetsky, to discuss IIM's 'difficulties'. Despite agreements reached at this meeting,[117] relations between the board and the Liberal Jewish movement deteriorated rapidly.

The main issue of contention was that of Jewish marriages. In 1946 North London, South London and Brighton Liberal synagogues all applied to the Board of Deputies to appoint marriage secretaries. Given the Chief Rabbi's previous acquiescence to the appointment of marriage secretaries at both the LJS and Liverpool Liberal Jewish Synagogue, the board not only agreed to the requests, but also considered changing its constitution so that in future the president could approve applications from all Liberal synagogues without reference to the Ecclesiastical Authorities (the Chief Rabbi and the Sephardi Haham).

However, by this time Hertz was no longer the Chief Rabbi and a new one had yet to be appointed. The interim Chief Rabbi, Rabbi Lazarus, opposed both the appointment of the three marriage secretaries and the change in the board's constitution. His objection was that Liberal synagogues were prepared to remarry women who had not received a *Get* from their former spouses, which he and the Beth Din said encouraged adultery and created *mamzerim*.[118] Protracted negotiations between the LJS and the board ensued, led by Louis Gluckstein, who was advised by IIM. Gluckstein and IIM eventually agreed to arbitration on the matter as an alternative to legal action, provided that the Orthodox Beth Din was not involved. The Beth Din objected and the board would not proceed against its wishes, thus creating a stalemate.[119]

In parallel with this dispute, the LJS, the West London Synagogue, the Sephardim and Agudists[120] were also developing concerns about the board's stance on Palestine. IIM, amongst others, felt that as a member of the Executive of the Jewish Agency, Brodetsky, the President of the board, had a clash of interests, and submitted a motion criticising his involvement. The motion was heavily defeated and the LJS and the other parties to the motion considered withdrawing from the board. However, in the end, it was the issue of marriage secretaries that caused the LJS and others to walk out. In 1949 the LJS tried once again to change the board's constitution to allow it to approve marriage secretaries without reference to the Beth Din. Rabbi Israel Brodie, who was more traditional than his predecessor, was now Chief Rabbi. He ruled that approving marriage secretaries for

Liberal synagogues would 'give the misleading impression that those synagogues conformed to authoritative Jewish Law in the performance of marriages'.[121]

Until now, IIM had worked largely behind the scenes in supporting Gluckstein in his rows with the Board of Deputies, but at this point he entered the fray publicly to defend Liberal marriage ceremonies. He preached a strongly worded sermon at the LJS, which was reproduced in the *Jewish Chronicle*, as 'The "Liberal" View of Marriage'.[122] He pointed out that some women could not receive a *Get*, either because their husbands had gone missing or refused to give a *Get* unless they were paid significant sums of money. He maintained that Liberal practice saved women from injustice and the oppression of extortion, and thereby adhered to the Jewish commandments of doing justice and protecting the weak.[123]

IIM's rebuttal launched the two sides of the argument into further confrontation on both a theological and a practical level. The fact that the *Jewish Chronicle* had chosen to print IIM's sermon also brought the newspaper into conflict with the Chief Rabbi, who objected to this display of openness and tolerance. Both Brodie and Dayan Isidor Grunfeld labelled the article 'higher anti-Semitism', and claimed that the article had 'deeply offended many conscientious Jews'.[124] Two articles by Dr Grunfeld launching a general attack on Liberal Judaism were published in the *Jewish Chronicle* in the latter part of 1949. However, IIM felt that the articles did 'more good than harm', because the orthodoxy they expounded was 'so obscurantist and anachronistic' that it was only likely to appeal to 'the most hidebound Agudists'.[125]

Under the more tolerant leadership of the Dr Cohen, the Board of Deputies agreed to a formula that allowed Liberal representatives to return to the board in 1951, but the matter of the marriage secretaries was not resolved until after IIM's death. It appears that by this time IIM had lost some of his power to bring people over to his way of thinking and that some of his arguments were losing their currency. Without the moderating influence and the backing of Claude Montefiore, IIM was losing the allegiance of some of those who might previously have supported him. Times were changing, but IIM apparently was not.

NOTES

1. Letter from IIM to Miss Marjorie Moos, 30 January 1948, LJS Archives, Box 1/2.
2. Copy of letter from IIM to Leslie Edgar, 5 May 1945, Mattuck Family Archive kept by Robert Edgar (MFAb).
3. Letter from IIM to Dr Morgenstern, President of HUC, 31 December 1946, London Metropolitan Archives, ACC/3529/002/018.
4. Rabbi Dr Leslie I. Edgar, *Some Memories of My Ministry* (London: Liberal Jewish Synagogue, 1985), p.33.
5. Letter from IIM to unknown recipient, 16 September 1947, LJS Archives, Box 1/2.

6. See The Younger Members' Organisation of the Liberal Jewish Synagogue, *The Years Between 1911–1951, LJS exhibition catalogue* (London: ULPS, 1951), p.11.
7. LJS Archives, Box 1/2.
8. *LJM*, XIX, no.3 (March 1948), pp.27–8.
9. 'Our Changed World', address given by IIM at the LJS on the completion of thirty-six years' ministry in England reported in *LJM*, XIX, no.3 (March 1948), p.26.
10. Ibid.
11. 'Memento of a Great Occasion', *LJM*, XX, no.3 (March 1949), p.29.
12. Ibid., p.30.
13. Letter from IIM to Louis Gluckstein, 21 March 1947, LJS Archives, Box 1/2.
14. Ibid.
15. Letter from Louis Gluckstein to IIM, 25 March 1947, LJS Archives, Box 1/2.
16. Letter from IIM to Louis Gluckstein, 27 March 1947, in ibid.
17. Note from IIM to Lily Montagu, 11 May 1950, London Metropolitan Archives, ACC/3529/002/018.
18. Ibid.
19. 'Liberal Judaism and the Future', sermon given by IIM at the LJS, 20 January 1945, Montagu Centre Collection (MCC).
20. Ibid.
21. Ibid.
22. Ibid.
23. Letter from IIM to Leslie Edgar, 20 September 1944, LJS Archives, Box 1/2.
24. See Edgar, *Some Memories of My Ministry*, p.31.
25. Todd M. Endelman, *The Jews of Britain 1656 to 2000* (Berkeley, Los Angeles, CA and London: University of California Press, 2002), p.220.
26. Letter from IIM to Miss Marjorie Moos, 30 January 1948, LJS Archives, Box 1/2.
27. Letter from IIM to undisclosed recipient dated 16 February 1948, in ibid.
28. *LJM*, XVII, no.2 (February 1946), p.13.
29. I.I. Mattuck, *Liberal Judaism – Its Thought and Practice* (London: ULPS, 1947).
30. *LJM*, XVII, no.2 (February 1946), p.13.
31. See ULPS Oral History Project 1994–1995, interview with Rabbi John Rayner, LJS Archives, Box 139a.
32. Ibid.
33. Interview with Herbert Richer conducted by Rosita Rosenberg, 14/15 May 2012.
34. *LJM*, XVII, no.6 (June 1946), p.43.
35. Selig Brodetsky (1888–1954) was a Professor of Mathematics, a member of the World Zionist Executive, the President of the Board of Deputies of British Jews and the second President of the Hebrew University of Jerusalem. His relationship with IIM is interesting. They were contemporaries, had a common background and a similar education (Brodetsky achieved outstanding success at Cambridge), but the two had an entirely different religious outlook. The fact that Brodetsky was brought up in London's East End rather than Reform-dominated America appears to have been the salient factor accounting for the divergence. Had IIM's family emigrated to London rather than to Boston, his career might have been totally different.
36. Peter Egill Brownfield 'The League of British Jews: Challenging Nationalism on Behalf of Jewish Universalism', The American Council for Judaism: Fall 2001: www.acjna.org/acjna/articles
37. Stephen E.C. Wendehorst, *British Jewry, Zionism, and the Jewish State, 1936–1956* (Oxford Historical Monographs) (New York: Oxford University Press, 2012), p.83.
38. See Brownfield, 'The League of British Jews'.
39. Michael Oren, *Power, Faith and Fantasy, Decision at Biltmore* (New York: W.W. Norton & Company, 2007), pp.442–5.
40. The Anglo-Jewish Association was formed in 1871 to help Jews abroad.
41. Quoted in Rory Miller, *Divided Against Zionism, Anti-Zionist Opposition in Britain to the Jewish State in Palestine 1945–1948* (London and Portland, OR: Frank Cass, 2001), p.7.
42. See Brownfield, 'The League of British Jews'.
43. Rabbi Morris Lazaron, the co-founder and vice-president of the American Council for Judaism, served from 1915 until 1946 as rabbi of the Baltimore Hebrew Congregation. Originally a supporter of what he viewed as cultural Zionism, he later altered his views, as set out in an essay, 'Why I Was A Zionist and Why Now I Am Not', excerpted from his unpublished autobiography. He was the brother-in-law of the outstanding Zionist, Abba Hillel Silver.

44. Letter from IIM to Morris Lazaron, 28 January 1942, American Jewish Archives (AJA), Morris Lazaron Papers, Box 5, Folder 34, MS-71.
45. Ibid.
46. 'The Crisis in Anglo-Jewry', *LJM*, XIV, no.7 (July 1943), p.51.
47. Gideon Shimoni argues that the fellowship was made up of a mixture of non- and anti-Zionists but that the belonging to an organisation which actively opposed Zionism made them all anti-Zionists. See Gideon Shimoni, 'The Non-Zionists in Anglo-Jewry, 1937–1948', *Jewish Journal of Sociology*, 28, 2 (1986), p.104.
48. AJA, Morris Lazaron Papers, Box 5, Folder 34, MS-71.
49. Albert Hyamson was a council member of the fellowship and Stewart Newcombe was a British Army officer who had served in India and Arabia.
50. Letter from IIM to Morris Lazaron, 5 July 1938, AJA, Morris Lazaron Papers, Box 5, Folder 34, MS-71.
51. See Newcombe and Beaumont, *A Constitution for Palestine* (London: self-published, 1945). The membership of the group included three Jews (IIM, Albert Hyamson and Emile Marmorstein, all non-Zionists), two Arabs (identity unknown) and a number of Christians including Newcombe and Beaumont.
52. Letter from Morris Lazaron to IIM, 5 June 1945, AJA, Morris Lazaron Papers, Box 5, Folder 34, MS-71.
53. Letter from IIM to Rabbi Morris Lazaron, 3 July 1945, in ibid.
54. Ibid.
55. Rabbi Israel Mattuck, 'American Jewry', *JC*, 7 February 1947, p.11.
56. See Brownfield, 'The League of British Jews'.
57. See Miller, *Divided Against Zionism*, p.85.
58. Quoted in Brownfield 'The League of British Jews'.
59. Quoted in Miller, *Divided Against Zionism*, p.89.
60. Ibid., p.89.
61. See Brownfield, 'The League of British Jews'.
62. Ibid., p.114.
63. Sir Ronald Storrs was the first governor of Jerusalem after the British conquest of Palestine in 1917.
64. See Miller, *Divided Against Zionism,* p.167.
65. See 'Statement of Principles By Non-Zionist Rabbis', AJA, American Council for Judaism Records, Box 6, Folder 1, MS-17.
66. Ibid.
67. Thomas A. Kolsky, *Jews Against Zionism*: *The American Council for Judaism, 1942–1948* (Philadelphia, PA: Temple University Press, 1990), p.187.
68. Letter from IIM to Morris Lazaron, 9 July 1943, AJA, American Council for Judaism Records, Box 5, Folder 34, MS-71.
69. See correspondence between IIM and Jane Leverson, who worked as a civilian relief worker in Poland during the immediate post-war years, LJS Archives, Box 39.
70. Memorandum produced by the Jewish Fellowship, 1 February 1946, signed by Basil Henriques, copy in LJS Archives, Box 1/2.
71. 'The Palestine Report', sermon given by IIM at the LJS, 4 May 1946, MCC.
72. 'Rabbi Defends Position of Britain on Actions in Palestine', *New York Times*, 27 November 1946.
73. 'Non-Zionist Rabbi for UN Trustees', *New York Times*, 29 April 1948.
74. 'Mr Bevin's Statement on Palestine', sermon given by IIM at the LJS, 1 March 1947, MCC.
75. Ibid.
76. Ibid.
77. *The Times*, 19 April 1948.
78. Edward Atiyah, *The Times*, 21 April 1948.
79. See Miller, *Divided Against Zionism,* p.158.
80. 'A Time for Decision', *Jewish Outlook,* 2, 7 (February 1948), pp.2–8.
81. A memorial tribute in the *Journal of Jewish Studies*, quoted in 'Israel I. Mattuck – His life and Work', *LJM*, *In Memoriam of Israel Mattuck, 1883–1954* (June 1954), p.9.
82. He was soon succeeded by Professor J.L. Teicher, Professor in Rabbinic Studies at Cambridge University.
83. Letter from IIM to Julian Morgenstern, 22 November 1945, AJA, Hebrew Union College Records, MS-5, Box A-18, Folder 14.

84. Dan Rottenberg (Foreword) (ed.) *Philadelphia Jewish Life, 1940–2000* (Philadelphia, PA: Temple University Press, 2003).
85. See Kolsky, *Jews Against Zionism*, p.176.
86. Letter from IIM to Louis Wolsey, 24 November 1948, London Metropolitan Archives, ACC//3529//002/011.
87. Quoted in Jonathan D. Sarna, JPS – *The Americanization of Jewish Culture, A Centennial History of the Jewish Publication Society* (Philadelphia, PA, New York and Jerusalem: Jewish Publication Society 1989), p.197.
88. See letter from the Council to IIM, 10 February 1953, London Metropolitan Archives, ACC/3529/002/019 (1).
89. 'The Place of Religion in Human Life', sermon given by IIM at the LJS on Yom Kippur, 18 September 1953, MCC.
90. Leo Baeck became President of WUPJ in 1938 following the death of Claude Montefiore, but given the situation that developed in Germany and his deportment to the concentration camp at Theresienstadt in 1943, he was not able to assume real leadership until after the Second World War when, following his miraculous survival he lived mostly in England.
91. See file of correspondence, London Metropolitan Archives, ACC/3529/002/003.
92. Israel Mattuck, 'Religion in the Crisis', republished by WUPJ following IIM's death, in May 1954.
93. See report on the conference, *JC*, 2 August 1946, p.15.
94. It is not known exactly when this conference was that IIM is said to have attended, but it was possibly during his 1947 trip to America.
95. See 'Israel I. Mattuck – His life and Work', p.11.
96. IIM, 'Human Rights – A Standard for Civilization', in *LJM*, XIX, no.8 (October 1948), pp.87–8.
97. See correspondence in London Metropolitan Archives, ACC/3529/002/002.
98. See *Freedom, Justice and Responsibility, Reports and Recommendations of the International Conference of Christians and Jews, Oxford, 1946* (London: Council of Christians and Jews, 1946).
99. Introduction by Professor L.W. Grensted to *The Foundations of Our Civilisation, Fundamental Postulates of Christianity and Judaism in Relation to Human Order* (London: Council for Christians and Jews, 1947), p.6.
100. The Society for Jewish Study, 1950, LJS Archives, Box 1/2.
101. Rabbi Dr Israel Mattuck, 'The Faith of a Jew', *The Listener*, 31 July 1947, pp.182–3.
102. *LJM*, XIX, no.5 (May 1948), p.54.
103. Israel I. Mattuck, *The Essentials of Liberal Judaism* (London: ULPS, 1947).
104. Ibid., p.vii.
105. '*The Essentials of Liberal Judaism* – A review by Dr Leo Baeck', in *LJM*, XVIII, no.10 (December 1947), p.85.
106. 'Essentials – Important New Book', *Jewish Outlook*, II, 6 (January 1948), p.8.
107. Bernard J. Bamberger, in *In Jewish Bookland,* p.4, undated cutting, Mattuck Family Archive kept by Jill Mattuck Tarule (MFAa).
108. *LJM*, XXI, no.9 (November 1950), p.145.
109. See Interview with Herbert Richer.
110. *American Israelite,* 31 October 1946, p.6.
111. Letter from Julian Morgenstern to IIM, 3 November 1946, AJA, Hebrew Union College Records, MS-5, Box A-18, Folder 14.
112. Letter from IIM to Leslie Edgar (undated, partly missing), London Metropolitan Archives, ACC/3529/002/018.
113. Ibid.
114. Michael A. Meyer, *Response to Modernity – A History of the Reform Movement in Judaism* (New York: Oxford University Press, 1988), p.302.
115. Jonathan Sarna, 'Converts to Zionism in the Reform Movement', in S. Almog, R. Jehuda, and A. Shapira (eds), *Zionism and Religion* (Hanover, NH: University Press of New England, 1998), p.196.
116. Letter from IIM to A. Brotman, Secretary of the Board of Deputies, 20 July 1945, and the reply from A. Brotman, 20 August, LJS Archives, Box 1/2.
117. See memorandum of the meeting dated 25 October, drafted by Louis Gluckstein in ibid.
118. A *mamzer* is a child of a union that is forbidden in the Bible. In this case, the Beth Din considered a woman who had not received a *Get* as still married to her first husband and the children of the second marriage to be the result of adultery.

119. Lawrence Rigal and Rosita Rosenberg, *Liberal Judaism: The First Hundred Years* (London: Liberal Judaism, 2002), p.132.
120. See previous note on the Agudists.
121. See Rigal and Rosenberg, *Liberal Judaism*, p.133.
122. *JC*, 30 January 1948, p.13.
123. Ibid.
124. David Cesarani, *The Jewish Chronicle and Anglo-Jewry, 1841–1991* (Cambridge: Cambridge University Press, 1994), p.200.
125. Letter from IIM to Julian Morgenstern, 24 January 1950, AJA, Hebrew Union College Records, MS-5, Box A-18, Folder 14.

CHAPTER FOURTEEN

Private and Family Life

Adjusting to Life in England

Previous chapters have concentrated on IIM's career, but it is of some interest to look at how his home and private life developed once he moved to England. It provides a useful backdrop to his public life.

When accepting the position at the LJS, IIM agreed to secure accommodation within easy reach of the synagogue. His first home in London was 15 Buckland Crescent in Swiss Cottage, where the Mattuck family lived between 1912 and 1916. In December 1914 Edna's father, Simon Mayer[1] (whom IIM referred to as 'Daddy'),[2] came from America to live with the couple following the death of Edna's brother, Alfred. Simon Mayer lived with the couple until his death in December 1935.[3] He became well known among the congregants of the LJS and was very involved in synagogue affairs.[4] Edna's brother Louis also lived with the Mattucks in Swiss Cottage until he was called up for war service, after which he stayed with them when he was on leave from the US Army.[5]

When they first came to England, IIM and his family were not always made to feel welcome socially. Several years later, IIM recounted an instance of the unfriendliness towards himself and his wife. Soon after their arrival, a woman had asked Edna if she was the wife of the new minister of the LJS and when told she was, the enquirer had replied, 'Well I hope you go back soon!'[6]

In addition to the lack of welcome, IIM sometimes found English culture uncomfortable. He expressed impatience with what he saw as the coldness of English people, whom he also felt 'talked too much about little things'.[7] For a while he retained his American accent, although he consciously attempted to alter it and to adopt English idioms. An article that appeared in the *Jewish Chronicle* shortly after he took up his post contains an anecdote of IIM using the word 'fall', but quickly correcting himself and substituting it with 'autumn'.[8]

There are a number of indications that IIM missed life in America, such as this reminiscence contained in a sermon:

> Shortly after I went to live in England I experienced the misery of nationalism in myself. While travelling one day to Oxford, I happened to look out of the window in time to see an American flag flying in shreds in the strong wind. It showed the effects of England's windy climate, but the stars and stripes remained unclouded by dirt and wind. When I saw them, – well, you have heard of lumps in your throat, and you know how one feels on nearing home after a long absence – I am not ashamed but I am grateful that a small piece of bunting can mean so much to me.[9]

Despite their somewhat inauspicious introduction to English life, within a few years of their arrival IIM and Edna had established a large circle of friends and acquaintances. They socialised with prominent members of the LJS and developed amongst the congregation friendships that they 'valued deeply'.[10] The Mattucks were close to the Joseph family, particularly Arthur and Amy Joseph (the brother and sister-in-law of the LJS architect, Ernest Joseph), with whom they regularly went on holiday, and also Ben and Vera Strauss,[11] whom IIM described as 'being amongst our most intimate friends'.[12] Amy Kirchberger, a teacher in the LJS Religion School and founding member of the Alumni Society, was also a close family friend and joined the Mattucks on family outings. On one occasion, IIM said she 'was almost like a daughter in our family'.[13] She became a poet and married the American rabbi, Sheldon Blank,[14] and emigrated to America. The Blanks were lifelong friends of the Mattucks.

As we have seen, IIM threw himself wholeheartedly into the task of developing the LJS and other congregations. Nevertheless, he found time to maintain membership of the Athenaeum, the Grecian Club,[15] the Harvard Club, the American Society and the English Speaking Union.[16] He also began to explore Europe. In the summer of 1913 he took two months leave of absence from the LJS to visit Munich and the surrounding area,[17] perhaps to visit Edna's relatives who still lived there.

At home IIM read widely, but not as much as he would have liked. He bemoaned the fact that, as a result of his rabbinic duties, he never had enough time for studying, and once said in frustration 'my ignorance grows each day'.[18] He longed to write a simple commentary of the writings of the Prophets, which he eventually did.[19] When his professional responsibilities permitted, he delved into ancient texts – which he said appealed to him more and more –[20] to extend his Jewish knowledge, and he also kept up with contemporary thought and world developments.

Family Life During the First World War

On 8 March 1914, IIM and Edna's second child, Dorothy, was born in Hampstead. Despite having a young family, the Mattucks remained in London for the first eighteen months of the war. However, they decided to leave their Hampstead home when German air raids began over the city in 1916. Their son, Robert, later recalled Zeppelins flying over the family home and he (then aged 5) and his father running to take shelter under a balcony.[21]

The Mattucks acquired a large property in the country, 'Woodlands' in Burkes Road, Beaconsfield,[22] to and from which IIM commuted unless his work commitments required him to stay in town. He found as many opportunities as possible to spend 'quiet time' with Edna, and the two enjoyed the Buckinghamshire countryside together. For one who had spent most of his life to date in urban settings, IIM came to develop an almost idyllic view of country life as illustrated by a diary extract:

> A little reading in the morning and in the garden. A walk with Edna and the children in the afternoon. Many signs of spring: violets white and purple, barely numerous in the sheltered spots, freshly green plants all along the wayside and the lark singing his carols.[23]

IIM resented 'swapping the freshness of the country for the smog of the city',[24] although Edna sometimes joined him in London, 'making lighter' his 'difficult days'.[25] The couple travelled by train to and from their home and enjoyed meeting people on their journeys.[26] The Strauss family, who sometimes stayed with the Mattucks in their Buckinghamshire home, provided accommodation for IIM when he needed to remain in London overnight.[27] Despite the wartime shortages, the couple continued to entertain at their country home. Newspaper articles attest to the fact that the Mattucks entertained many a dignitary. For example, on one occasion in 1917 the guests at 'Wildwood' included 'three ministers, a plutocrat from South Africa and an English officer'.[28]

Committing to England

At the outbreak of the First World War, IIM was urged by friends and colleagues in America to return there, and he later revealed that he had received various invitations from congregations in America to become their minister.[29] These invitations included one from his former synagogue in Far Rockaway, where his successor was not proving popular.[30] These approaches were apparently rejected, because by then the Mattucks had committed themselves to staying in Britain.[31] The combination of IIM's successes, his increasing prominence and the existence of avenues yet to be explored appears to have been seductive.

When they first decided to leave America, IIM and Edna had not seen the move as a long-term commitment, and had not been expecting to stay in England beyond the five-year duration of IIM's initial contract with the LJS, because they were 'young at the time, indeed very young' and 'did not think far into the future'.[32] However, the congregation was established more quickly than they had anticipated. Whereas IIM initially might have thought that his stay would be limited to five years, he now found himself committed to the continuing development of the congregation. Therefore, when in June 1916 the Council of the LJS passed a motion to extend IIM's contract indefinitely 'as a matter of course' and to increase his salary, IIM accepted with some alacrity.[33] A month later he was called up to join the Military Reserve and was requested to present himself to the Hampstead Recruiting Depot.[34] Either by virtue of his American Citizenship or because of his profession, he avoided enlistment.

Family Life in the Post-War Years

The Mattucks lived in Buckinghamshire until 1922, when they bought 'Wildwood', in North End, Hampstead.[35] Correspondence suggests that the move was made because Dorothy and Robert now needed access to schools not available in Buckinghamshire.[36] 'Wildwood', where IIM lived for the remainder of his life, was a substantial house with four floors. There was a large drawing room divided into two parts. Here the rugs were often rolled back for dancing, and Edna sometimes played the piano to accompany the children singing.[37] There was a separate dining room, which had windows that let in little light. IIM's study, which was originally designed to be a ballroom, led off the dining room and ran the width of the house; it was filled from floor to ceiling with books. The study was used for major family events such as *sedarim* at which IIM gave scholarly explanations of Passover and is reported to have 'chanted the service like a cantor'.[38] Because it was an old house all the floors 'sloped and humped and shook when one walked'.[39] The main rooms were furnished with antiques collected by Edna mixed with some very modern pieces.[40] The large kitchen was on the lower ground floor from which food was sent to the upper floors via a lift. There were two flights of stairs which the Mattuck children used for playing games of hide and seek.[41]

'Wildwood' was sufficiently large to accommodate the family together with a cook and two housemaids (and sometimes an au pair), who had rooms on its upper floors alongside the day and night nurseries.[42] Family photographs show that, from the time of Robert's birth, the Mattucks employed a nanny to help look after their children, including one long-standing nanny ('Nana')[43] named Miss Preece, who accompanied the family on their trips to America.[44] Neither of the Mattucks drove; initially, when necessary, they hired a chauffeur-driven car, a 'stately Daimler' driven by the same man, 'Jenkins', who was 'extremely respectful'.[45] The family later bought a car and employed their own chauffeur.[46] Because of their lifestyle, congregants saw the Mattuck family as being 'very upper class' and IIM as a 'gentleman rabbi'.[47] According to relatives, the large properties in Buckinghamshire and Hampstead were purchased with Mayer family money.[48]

We are told that IIM was 'supremely happy' in his married life and that Edna, who was 'intensely proud of him', gave him 'every support' in his role at the LJS.[49] After the move back to London, she became very involved in synagogue life. For many years she was responsible for decorating the Sukkah and has been described by people who knew her as 'fun, practical and approachable',[50] and as being 'cheerful and very good company'.[51] A diary that IIM kept briefly in the early part of 1918 reveals that he found Edna (known as 'Intie' by the family, including her children), 'dear company' and that he delighted in the 'quality of love' that his home offered.

For IIM marriage represented 'an outstanding place of religious importance' and 'a trust between two human beings so deep as to take the whole of life within its power'. As he admitted himself, he had a romantic and idealised view of marriage.[52] A sermon that he gave in 1927 on 'Marriage and Freedom' offers some insights into IIM's relationship with Edna, or at least, the kind of marriage to which he aspired.

> There is a wedding service of which we all know which admonishes the wife to obey the husband. I do not know whether to admire the naiveté or condemn the folly of a minister who asks a bride if she will obey her husband and accepts without the slightest doubt her answer 'yes', especially if such a minister be himself a married man! Marriage is a relation [sic] between equals.[53]

IIM's children are said to have given him 'great joy and courage' in his pioneering work.[54] Perhaps because of the rigours of his role and the stresses of the war years, he and Edna did not extend their family further until December 1921, when Naomi was born in Amersham, Buckinghamshire. IIM expressed regret that his long hours of work prevented him from arriving home until after his children were in bed.[55] Dorothy later recollected that her father had a card that he often hung on his study door saying 'Do Not Disturb' when he was forced to work 'to the subordination of family life'.[56]

However, Dorothy also remembered sitting on her father's knee on Saturday mornings while he told her stories from an album of Bible pictures.[57] To IIM, the religious education of children was a vital function of the Jewish home. While a religion school could help to emphasise and explain certain aspects of Judaism, it could never take the place of parents in conveying ideals 'through the channel of love'. His wish was that 'religious education will never be taken away from the home'.[58] From when they were very young, IIM also instilled in his children a love of reading and of the arts. Dorothy was later to recall that 'in all our homes there were books and more books'.[59] Similarly, Robert remembered 'the good books, the music and the theatre' and a 'life of intellect'.[60]

A great deal of family life revolved around the planning and preparation of food and meal times were very important in the Mattuck household. At meals IIM would often entertain his children:

> [M]y father was addicted to telling funny stories, and he would stand, carving knife and fork in hand waving one or both of them to emphasise the point of the story. We thought the stories were very funny, and laughed a lot, but we would have liked hot food as well.[61]

Nothing is known of Dorothy's early education other than she attended independent schools close to the family home in Buckinghamshire. Robert attended a 'conventional preparatory school', where he was apparently shouted at and bullied by the teachers.[62] In 1922 both Robert and Dorothy were enrolled at the co-educational King Alfred School, located just around the corner from 'Wildwood', in Manor Road.[63] From its inception, King Alfred School had a reputation for its progressive approach to education and 'an absence of formality and petty rules'.[64] It was run on a plan borrowed from the Dalton School in New York.[65] The rationalist and non-denominational nature of the school is likely to have appealed to IIM, but the enrolment of Robert and Dorothy there was 'something of an accident'. Throughout his life, it remained surprising to Robert that his 'intelligent and highly educated' father seemed to have no real plan for the secular education of his children.[66] IIM attempted initially to enrol Robert in the day branch of a public school, only to be told that English children were given preference for places there, perhaps because of anti-Semitism.[67] In anger, IIM went to the opposite extreme and enrolled his children in a highly unconventional school.

Notwithstanding the encouraging atmosphere of King Alfred School, Robert found it difficult to settle to academic work,[68] although he did chair the school's council of students and teachers.[69] Retrospectively, Robert believed that he would probably have fared much better at a traditional school, where there would have been less independent work and more emphasis on scholarship than on human relationships.[70]

As a teenager Robert had a somewhat tense relationship with his father, whom he regarded as being 'traditional' and 'rigid'.[71] We gain an insight into some of the tensions between IIM and his adolescent son from several sermons he delivered about this time on family life and relationships between parents and their children:

> [Adolescence] is the age when the boy or girl conscious of growing up is moved increasingly by the desire to assert himself. It is then that there is liable to begin the most tragic of conflicts, the conflict between parent and child which may extend into manhood and womanhood. It is so tragic because underneath it lies a deep love which feels pain yet cannot relieve it ... The father and son feel the power that draws them together yet they irritate each other.[72]

We can detect from such addresses that IIM was striving to be a modern parent, allowing his children the freedom to learn from their mistakes and seeking to influence their action rather than exerting his authority over them. He expressed his abhorrence of imposing on children their careers and marriage partners.[73] His liberal approach on these issues was soon to be tested by his son, and later by his younger daughter, Naomi.

Dorothy became very involved in the LJS from an early age. She attended the Religion School, where she was taught in the choir loft at the Hill Street premises of the synagogue by the former pupil, Leslie Edgar, who was to become her future husband. She was confirmed by her father in April 1930 and subsequently supported him in developing new Liberal congregations. She also became his co-worker on educational aspects of synagogue life.[74] It has been suggested that, because of her brother's tendency to rebelliousness, Dorothy felt the need to conform.[75]

Although Naomi was later to refer to herself as her parents' 'little mistake',[76] she seems to have received a great deal of attention from both of her parents, but especially from her father who she recalled regularly made up stories, 'according to my particular demand of the day', to tell her after tea in the drawing room:

> I thought they were marvellous, and much preferred them to any in the books ... The central character was a woodcutter and he had many adventures. The plots were based on the type of Hans Andersen, which were considered the acme of the fairy story.[77]

As a child, Naomi was very attached to her father. She looked up to and admired him[78] and saw him as being 'very close to God', but was somewhat afraid of him:

> He was not a harsh father, nor severe with me, indeed he was devoted and made a great deal of affectionate fuss of me. I loved to sit on his lap or be held in his thin arms. But he was a stern man, with a sense of right or wrong that knew no compromise. If I angered him, or if he believed that I had done something wrong, such as tell a lie, he could be very frightening indeed. The worst moments were if I had refused to do something which I had been asked, and he would fix me with a cold unbending look and say: 'Will you do it, or shall I help you?'[79]

Perhaps thinking back to his own childhood and the support he received from his father, IIM was very involved with the education of his children. Naomi, who attended a liberal co-ed primary school, recalled: '[H]e helped me with my arithmetic homework, using his gold pen to make accurate figures beside my incorrect smudges. With Latin too he patiently advised me. But he expected too much of me.'[80]

IIM now had many close personal friends in the LJS congregation. He is reported to have been an easy luncheon or dinner guest, willing to eat non-Kosher food and possessing an endless supply of anecdotes. Reportedly, few could surpass him in telling amusing stories.[81] One long-standing LJS member recalls that congregants would compete for IIM's company, inviting him to prestigious dining venues.[82] Some LJS members were invited to 'Wildwood', where they were treated to the sight of IIM 'supervising' the washing up, and glimpses of Mattuck the family man.[83] 'Wildwood' became known for the 'spirit of fun which prevailed'.[84] The Mattucks entertained a great deal and would employ additional staff to help prepare for and serve at large dinner parties and at the tea parties held on the 'Wildwood' lawn, which were not 'one less jot elaborate' than those held in the drawing room.[85] The 'Wildwood' garden was also the scene of many glittering evening garden parties when the garden was dotted with little fairy lights and candles that gave the events 'a magical effect'.[86]

IIM played golf and tennis although, by his own admission, quite amateurishly, testing 'my own endurance and my friends' patience'.[87] He also enjoyed mountain climbing, swimming and visiting galleries. He devoted time to helping to maintain his Buckinghamshire and then his London gardens, although he lacked the knowledge to offer anything other than 'unskilled labour', which he did not enjoy but which he felt was good for his soul.[88] The gardens were largely maintained by a gardener, who came two days a week.[89] IIM loved visiting the countryside and insisted that the family go with him. They would take a train into the country, usually from Marylebone. Favourite places they visited included South Mimms, Burnham Beeches and, at bluebell time, Hadley Woods. IIM was a devotee of ordnance survey maps and many a moment was spent with him sitting on stiles, puffing on his pipe, reading the map. In the evenings prior to these outings, he would sometimes sit in his armchair planning routes. When the family hired a car and were driven out of London, IIM was teased by his family for concentrating on his maps rather than enjoying the countryside:

> 'We should be passing through a lovely beechwood' [or] 'And on the left there should be a magnificent view of the sea'. 'Yes' said my mother 'There is, why don't you look at it?' With great surprise he would then hold his finger on the map and look at the view. 'Yes, yes' he would say excitedly 'It is exactly as I thought it would be from the map.'[90]

Much to the amusement of the chauffeur, IIM was always keen to explore cart tracks. The trips into the country were punctuated by meals, either stops in pubs or picnics.[91]

One of IIM's passions, which the family did not share, was exploring English churches. On their country walks he insisted on visiting any church they passed, and their walks were sometimes planned so he could see a particular church or its brasses. Once the family had a car, his pleasure knew no bounds; on country trips he was now able to fit in visits to several churches rather than the one or two the family were able to visit when out walking. His children were somewhat embarrassed when he struck up conversations with the vergers and gravediggers he encountered. His younger daughter, Naomi came to dread visits to cathedrals because IIM could spend a whole morning looking at just one chapel or crypt.

During the 1920s the Mattuck family took a number of holidays in English beach resorts such as Minehead, Swanage and Port Isaac. Initially, the family took lodgings before they realised that it was more in keeping with their lifestyle to rent a property and take their staff with them to look after them.[92] A favourite family event was the annual boating holiday taken with friends at Henley-on-Thames.[93] The rented summer houses on the Thames generally had tennis courts where IIM would play with his family and friends, and he would spend hours punting or poling on the river with his son.[94]

American Ties and Citizenship

Because of the intervention of the First World War, the Mattucks did not return to America until 1919, when the whole family made the long voyage. The purpose of the two-month trip was to visit relatives and to show Robert and Dorothy, now aged 8 and 5, significant places in America. During the trip, the Mattucks also visited many friends they had not been able to see for a number of years, including friends in Far Rockaway.[95] Simon Mayer accompanied them on the trip.

After the war, friends and family from America visited the Mattucks in England, some of who stayed with them in Buckinghamshire. However, most of the wealthy Mayer relatives elected to stay at Claridges Hotel in Mayfair.[96] Dorothy later recollected that during the post-war period many prominent American rabbis, such as Stephen Wise and Abba Silver, stayed in the family home.[97] It appears strange that IIM's friends included people with whose views we are later to learn he strongly disagreed professionally and whom he criticised publicly.[98] However, as he once explained:

> Some of my friends pay me the compliment of saying that they agree with me in few, if any of my ideas. The disagreement I tell them is mutual; so that we try one another's patience endlessly – but friendship should be equal to the strife.[99]

During the 1920s the Mattucks made two trips to America – in 1925 and again in 1927. The 1927 trip (also mentioned in Chapter Ten) was primarily a family holiday, the main purpose of which was to show the three children some more of the sights of America. After weeks of preparation and mounting excitement, the family set sail from Liverpool for what proved to be a very uncomfortable journey to New York.[100] Simon Mayer sailed with the Mattucks to and from America and they joined him in Lincoln later on in their trip, so the children could see the town where Edna grew up.[101] This trip was the first time IIM had visited his family in New York for eight years.[102]

The family went as far west as Colorado and Utah, travelling everywhere by trains on which the family had their own drawing room carriage[103] (very different in style from how IIM had probably travelled across America as a young man). The sights they visited included the Niagara Falls and Yellowstone Park, to see the bears and sulphur springs.[104] In Colorado, the family stayed with Rabbi Leo Franklin[105] of Temple Beth El in Detroit, who appears to have been a friend of the Mattucks.[106] During his stay in Detroit, IIM spoke at the Teachers' College at Temple Beth El on the future of Judaism.[107] Back on the east coast, the family stayed in Boston from where they made a trip to Worcester, where IIM met with some of his former teachers, which he said made him realise his debt to them.[108] While in Worcester, IIM spoke on 'New Forces Remaking an Old World' at a meeting of the Worcester Economic Club held on 4 May in the Hotel Bancroft's Ballroom.[109] Throughout the trip, the family was accompanied by a governess, Miss Grant, to help continue the children's studies and to look after them when IIM and Edna were busy.[110]

Making the 1927 trip to America had not been without its difficulties. For the first few years that he was in England, IIM had experienced no difficulty in being registered by the American Embassy as an American citizen living in Britain. However, when he tried to renew his registration in 1921, questions were asked about his plans for returning to America. The Department of State was not satisfied by his response and ordered the American Consul in London not to re-register him as an American citizen. He was advised that, according to American law, a naturalised citizen who absented him or herself from America for over five years was deemed to have relinquished his citizenship. IIM appealed against this decision and submitted a lengthy affidavit explaining how he had come to be appointed as the rabbi of the LJS and why it was not possible at that time for him to return to America. He insisted that he had every intention of doing so 'at the earliest possible moment'.[111] Despite these efforts, in January 1922 the American Consul wrote to IIM advising him that his appeal had been unsuccessful.[112]

At this point IIM called on the services of his brother, George, who made a special trip to Washington to plead IIM's case. The Department of State refused to reverse its decision.[113] Despite this, IIM was somehow able to visit America in 1925 to receive his honorary doctorate from HUC,[114] but in 1927 his application for an emergency passport was refused. Again with the help of George, IIM enlisted the support of Senator Frank B. Willis in trying to overturn the decision.

IIM drew up a detailed case[115] in which he argued that all his relatives lived in America including his parents, who owned a house in New York. He also pointed out that he had recently invited two American rabbis to take up pulpits in England because of the shortage of English rabbis and were he to be forced to return to America, his place was likely to be taken by another American. He added that both his wife and son were American citizens, he had remained registered with the American police as an American citizen and had been filing annual income tax returns to the Federal Office in Brooklyn. His submission was obviously compelling because the appeal was successful and he was able to renew both his American citizenship and his passport.[116]

It is clear from the effort he devoted to the matter that his American citizenship was very important to IIM. His loyalty and love of America was more than the result of a feeling of gratitude to a country that had enabled him to escape from the poverty and privations of Eastern Europe; it had a strong religious basis. Like many American Reform rabbis, IIM saw America as being very different from other countries in which Jews lived. With its democratic constitution based on the principle of freedom, it was congruent with Judaism and provided the perfect environment for it to flourish – America was the modern spiritual Zion. Rabbi David Philipson, one of Mattuck's mentors, went so far as to declare that Judaism was so thoroughly in accord with republicanism that it deserved 'all its adherents to become imbued as soon as possible with free republican ideas'.[117] IIM fully endorsed such a view.

With their children now old enough to make long journeys, the Mattuck family began to venture into Europe. In 1928 they travelled to Germany to visit the cities of Cologne, Nuremberg and Dresden as well as the countryside of the Black Forest. The trip was eased by the fact that IIM was able to converse in fluent German.[118] A year later, the family travelled around Holland visiting Amsterdam, The Hague and Scheveningen.[119]

Family Life Before the Second World War

With three rabbis besides himself now employed by the LJS, IIM was able to extend his travels at home and abroad, which he felt brought new experiences into his life, and which made it 'bigger, more comprehensive, more significant and richer'.[120] In 1931 he visited both France, where Edna's brother Louis lived with his French wife, and also Germany. The family also holidayed in Britain. While in Devon in June 1935, the car in which he and his family were being chauffeured was involved in an accident close to Honiton.[121] Despite the severity of the accident IIM was only slightly injured. Edna, Dorothy and Naomi, who were also in the car, were bruised and shocked.[122]

Dorothy and Naomi continued to accompany their parents on holidays during their teenage years and into early adulthood, and both went with their parents on the trip they made to America in the early months of 1936. The visit is recalled by relations still living in America. The family is reported to have been very anglicised, especially Edna Mattuck, who is said to have spoken with a 'strongly aristocratic English accent'.[123] IIM is remembered as 'very charming, witty, and overall nice'.[124] On their way to America on board the Cunard White Star ship the *Majestic*, IIM and his family had travelled alongside a number of 'Jewish celebrities', including Sir Samuel Herbert, who were bound for America to appeal on behalf of their 'sorely stricken German brethren'. During the voyage IIM gave the sermon at a service held in a temporary synagogue constructed on board the liner.[125]

The main purpose of the 1936 trip to America was to bury Simon Mayer, who had died a few weeks earlier, in the cemetery close to his former home in Lincoln. While in America IIM and Edna also visited their friends, Rabbi Sheldon and Amy Blank, who were now living in Cincinnati.[126] It is interesting to note that this trip did not appear to have been occasioned by the death of IIM's father and mother in the late summer and autumn of the previous year.[127]

In November 1937 IIM began a six-month sabbatical,[128] during which time 'Wildwood' was let out. A large proportion of the sabbatical was spent in the South of France, where IIM carried out research for his book, *What Are the Jews?* However, the couple also spent some time travelling in Egypt. When he returned to the LJS in May 1938, IIM gave a sermon on 'An Older World' and gave an address to the LJS Synagogue Society[129] on his impressions of life and religion in Egypt. One of his lasting memories of the trip was witnessing in a small town close to Cairo a joyous young Muslim child decorating a heifer for the festival of Birham.[130]

Prior to his death, Simon Mayer, who had been living with the Mattucks for two decades, was now beginning to age and find the damp English climate, to which he had never adjusted, more difficult to bear. He slept a lot in an armchair, but when he was awake his behaviour caused tensions in the household. Although he was 'a kindly man' who gave generously to the charities with which he was involved, he became increasingly difficult about what he would eat and his deafness made communication difficult.[131]

By the early 1930s the relationship between IIM and his son Robert was also becoming more strained. IIM was disappointed that Robert had failed to gain a place at Balliol College, Oxford. His brother, Bernard, wrote to him from New York reassuring him that Robert would 'knock 'em for a goal next time'.[132] After a year of tutoring under the Shakespearean scholar G.B. Harrison, Robert was offered a place at Jesus College, Cambridge assisted by the connections that IIM had made with the university.[133] During his four years at Cambridge Robert studied philosophy and the literature of Shakespearean England. Having suffered from depression in his final year,[134] he obtained a Third Class degree, but was later automatically awarded a Master of Arts from the university.[135] Although he did not excel academically at Cambridge, Robert enjoyed college life, especially the 'good talk, good reading, good studying, good company, good playing of games'.[136]

While still at Cambridge, Robert formed a relationship with Corinne Weil, a social worker from Evansville, Indiana[137] and the sister-in-law of Solomon Starrels, now a rabbi at the LJS. Corinne and Robert met when Corinne and her mother visited Corinne's sister Gertrude and Solomon Starrels in London, as part of a European tour in May 1929.[138] After Corinne returned to America, Robert and Corinne communicated regularly for almost five years, their long and somewhat overtly sexual letters often overlapping in the post.[139] Corinne seems to have been very drawn to Robert despite his self-confessed 'stuffiness' at that time.[140] They were passionately in love and their sexualised behaviour was out of keeping with the general social mores of the day. Their relationship appears to have caused major disagreements in the Mattuck household during the late summer of 1932 when Corinne visited England.[141]

We know from IIM's sermons that he strongly disapproved of premarital sex. In a very candid sermon on 'Marriage and Morals' he argued strongly for premarital chastity to safeguard the sanctity of marriage:

> Just as unfaithfulness in marriage destroys that completeness [of marriage], so unchastity before marriage destroys it in advance. If marriage does not bring to the bridegroom or bride a new experience, it must always remain the poorer for that lack.[142]

It is therefore probable that IIM regarded Corinne as being somewhat brazen.[143] Nevertheless, Robert and Corinne were married by IIM at the LJS on 28 June 1934. At Robert's insistence, the religious ceremony at the LJS lasted for just a few minutes and excluded 'all the Jewish bits'.[144] Robert and Corinne set up home in the 'Mill Shed', a converted barn in Turnville Heath in the Buckinghamshire countryside. They worked there as writers and theatre and arts reviewers for several London publications, and Robert also worked on films and documentaries.[145] They entertained as house guests many well-known actors and writers, such as Fenner Brockway the pacifist and former Labour MP, and lived a somewhat bohemian existence.[146] Robert was fascinated with the Bloomsbury Group, on whom he fashioned his lifestyle at this time. He and Corinne later said that they retired first and went out to work later.[147]

Once Robert and Corinne were married, the tensions between Robert and his family appear to have abated. IIM, whom on his insistence, Corinne referred to as 'II', Edna Mattuck, whom she called 'Mattick',[148] and Dorothy often visited Turnville Heath, where they enjoyed meeting Robert and Corinne's friends,[149] and where IIM sometimes played golf with his son. Occasionally the young couple met up with IIM and Edna in London to go to the theatre and Robert once or twice accompanied his father to the Grecian Club.[150] Corinne felt that IIM gradually accepted her and that they were 'getting to be friends'. IIM supported the young couple financially,[151] but despite all this, Robert continued to believe that his father never really understood the work he and Corinne did.[152]

From Corinne's correspondence with her mother we learn that in the mid-1930s, IIM was experiencing repeated bouts of ill health[153] ('tummy and nerves' and 'tired depressions'),[154] and that in the summer of 1937

Edna had a major operation from which she recovered quite quickly. She was well enough to travel with IIM to a conference in Holland and then to take a three-week holiday in Switzerland. Robert and Corinne were invited to join them on this holiday, but refused the invitation because they felt that IIM had already been over generous in his financial support of them.[155]

Robert and Corinne moved to America to live in 1938, ostensibly because of the widespread belief that England would be invaded by Germany in the event of war, but also because Corinne was missing her family.[156] In addition, Robert felt that he never quite belonged in England and did not want to be a foreigner at a time of war.[157] He also harboured a strong desire to free himself from his father's expectations of him.[158]

In 1939 Robert joined the faculty of Goddard College, a progressive arts college located in rural Vermont, in the second semester of its existence. In his early years there he taught philosophy, drama, literature and one of the first college film courses in America. During his career he developed a keen interest in student counselling. He remained with Goddard College for fifty years, during which time he came to be regarded as one of its 'erudite and admired elders'.[159] Nevertheless, he always felt that he was a 'good second-rate person' rather than the 'first-rate person' and faculty member at Harvard or Yale that he believed his father would have preferred him to be.[160] Corinne developed an interest in the care of young children. She ran the nursery school at Goddard College and became involved with an organisation called Head Start[161] locally and nationally. Both of Robert's daughters, Susan and Jill, attended Goddard College. Susan became a social activist, and Jill, who obtained a masters degree and a doctorate from Harvard, became a university professor.

Robert had little interest in Judaism, against which he is said to have rebelled completely.[162] His daughter, Jill Mattuck Tarule (her married name) has suggested that he would have been surprised to learn that that his father had rebelled similarly against his Orthodox background and had a reputation for radicalism. She draws some interesting parallels between Robert's career and that of his father – they both crossed the Atlantic (albeit in opposite directions) to play a leading role in the development of progressive bodies, knowingly placed themselves in marginalised positions and saw their work as a mission.[163]

IIM's disappointment that his son did not become a rabbi may explain the support and encouragement he gave to Leslie Edgar, who in 1931 was ordained as a minister at the LJS, and who three years later married Dorothy.[164] After his confirmation in 1921, Edgar was taught advanced Hebrew by IIM. During these lessons, IIM made it clear to him that he hoped he would train as a Liberal rabbi.[165] On IIM's recommendation, Edgar was sponsored by private funds to go to Christ College, Cambridge to study for a degree in preparation for more specialised training.

During this training, which partly took place at King's College, London, Edgar became very involved in LJS affairs. He chaired the young people's society and instigated early morning Sabbath services for younger members of the synagogue. He also preached at developing Liberal congregations.[166] All of this must have impressed IIM, for in 1925 he wrote to Edgar at Cambridge to tell him that he had discussed matters with Louis Gluckstein, then vice-president of the LJS, and it had been agreed that, on the completion of his training, Edgar would be offered a position at the synagogue as IIM's assistant. Edgar replied to say how honoured he felt to be invited to serve under IIM.[167]

Dorothy obtained a place to study French at Lady Margaret Hall, Oxford, but left after less than a year. She then enrolled at Bedford College, London (also to study French), but again did not complete the course having decided to devote her efforts to supporting her future husband when she became engaged to Leslie Edgar at the age of nineteen.[168] Dorothy and Leslie married[169] on 14 June 1934, just two weeks prior to the marriage of her brother, Robert. She later recollected that the only time that she saw her father nervous was when he walked her down the aisle before robing on the *bimah* to conduct the wedding.[170]

For a short time after their marriage, Dorothy and Leslie Edgar lived at 'Wildwood', before moving to Downshire Hill in Hampstead. The family subsequently moved to Reynolds Close in Hampstead Garden Suburb. Despite failing to complete her studies, Dorothy had a lifelong love of English literature, of which her knowledge was encyclopaedic. She abhorred slovenly grammar and was regarded as being 'formidable', even though she was slightly less than five feet tall.[171]

Unlike Robert and Dorothy, Naomi was not granted American citizenship. Nevertheless she went to America at the same time as Robert and Corinne because it was felt that she would be safer in America than in England. She studied Government and Economics at Radcliffe College and then attended Yale Drama School. Apparently Naomi was somewhat wayward as a student,[172] although she was described by her sister-in-law, Corinne, as being 'brilliant' and as having 'her head screwed on'.[173]

The Impact of War

Shortly before the Second World War, the Mattuck family acquired a second home – Bradden's Yard, in Long Crendon near Aylesbury. They quickly became integrated into the Long Crendon community and IIM took great delight in his country garden, where he was able to relax from his many and pressing involvements.[174] Family archives contain numerous photographs of him sitting in a deck chair in the Long Crendon garden reading a newspaper and smoking a pipe. According to his grandson, Robert Edgar, above the garage was a space that was used to store apples, which gave the building a distinctive aroma,[175] and in the garden was a building that was converted to provide a study for IIM.[176] This building, known by the family as the 'Doll's House', had a minstrel's gallery where there was a bed that IIM used on the occasions when he worked long into the night. The house had a walled kitchen garden with a peach tree and also a large garden with plum trees.[177]

During the war, IIM and his family were largely based at the house in Long Crendon. As she had dual citizenship, Dorothy Edgar could have gone to live in America. However, she chose to live with her parents at Bradden's Yard while her husband served in the army. The strain placed on IIM by the war and the additional burdens he carried were exacerbated by the fact that wartime legislation, the Aliens (Movement Restriction) Order 1944, restricted his movements. Because of his occupation, he was granted exemption from the prohibition of owning a car. However, he was required to notify the police before entering an 'Aliens Protected Area',[178] and each time he needed to stay in London overnight he was obliged to notify the Buckinghamshire police of his absence. Until he was able to acquire a generic permission to stay at 'Wildwood' as necessary,[179] IIM endured the relentless and time-consuming journey to and from London by train, since there was no petrol for car journeys. He often arrived home after 11 p.m.[180]

IIM managed to take several months' rest but, according to his son-in-law, Leslie Edgar, 'he was clearly worn out'.[181] His depression caused by the war was not helped by the unexpected death in 1941 of his brother George, at the age of 56, which was a 'hard blow' to him.[182] His was also downhearted that two of his children were now living in America, and after the death of Claude Montefiore in 1938 he had no close confidant whose opinion he respected.

To add to the pressures, the US State Department once again raised questions about IIM's American citizenship. In 1940 a US Nationality Act was passed, which meant that Americans remaining in the British Isles would lose their American citizenship. In September 1941 IIM received a letter drawing his attention to the new legislation and asking him to contact the American Consulate General in London immediately, to inform them whether or not he intended to return to America in the near future.[183] His initial application to extend his citizenship was unsuccessful despite the support he was given by HUC.[184] He made contingency plans to stay in Ireland temporarily while the matter of his citizenship was resolved.

However, when he submitted a second application in February 1942,[185] he was able to secure a temporary extension. The President of the United States then signed a number of amendments that postponed until October 1946 the implementation of the relevant sections of the new legislation.

The Family after the Second World War

During the war Naomi started working in American television. When she returned to England in 1945, she obtained a position working for *The Economist*, and in 1947 she went to work for the BBC in the North American Service before becoming a TV director in 1950. Among other accomplishments, Naomi directed the BBC series, *The Six Wives of Henry VIII*. She was also responsible for several successful programmes on ballet, for which she had a personal enthusiasm having as a girl studied ballet under Dame Peggy van Praagh.[186]

In December 1946, Naomi married Kenneth Capon, whom she had met before the war at gatherings at Robert and Corinnne's home in Buckinghamshire.[187] Kenneth Capon became a well-known architect.[188] Although IIM and Edna were disappointed that Naomi had married an older, non-Jewish man and did not attend her wedding,[189] they were eventually reconciled to the marriage. However, the relationship between Naomi and her parents remained strained.[190] The Capon couple lived for a while at 'Wildwood' and then after their son, William, was born, they moved into a house designed by Kenneth Capon built at the bottom of the garden at 'Wildwood'.[191]

Loss of American Citizenship

Although the matter of IIM's citizenship had been postponed until after the war, in 1946 he was confronted once again with the choice of either having to return to America or losing his American citizenship. With the help of an American lawyer, Nathan Gold (a cousin of Edna's)[192] practising in Lincoln, Nebraska, and the prominent US senator, Kenneth Werry,[193] IIM embarked on a lengthy battle to retain his citizenship. However, because of the fact that he was not born in America, Senator Werry eventually suggested that IIM should cease the fight to retain his American Citizenship. He advised him instead to seek entry to America as an immigrant.[194] Although IIM said that he 'saw the wisdom of the senator's advice', and was offered employment to ease his return to America,[195] he rejected this course of action. This was partly because of the length of time that it would have taken him to be accepted as an immigrant, since the quota for Russian immigrants was filled and there was a long waiting list.

He was also aware that, as an immigrant, his rights and movements would be limited.[196]

It appears from the correspondence relating to his American citizenship that in the immediate post-war years, IIM considered returning to America and setting up home in Lincoln.[197] However, he also wished to continue to meet some of his obligations in England and Europe and to be free to travel freely between America and Britain to see family and friends.[198] He was hopeful that an amendment to the Nationality Act tabled by Senator Werry would enable him to retain his citizenship. However, his hopes were to be dashed. In April 1948 Senator Werry wrote to Nathan Gold to advise him that the amendment was likely to be dropped due to intense opposition.[199]

At the same time as he was seeking the advice and support of Senator Werry, IIM was also pursuing other avenues for retaining his citizenship, helped by his lawyer brothers Maxwell and Bernard. These alternative approaches included mounting legal arguments based on the fact that IIM had been registered as a US tax payer and had maintained a home in America since his departure for England in 1912. However, the legal route did not prove any more successful than political lobbying.[200] In 1948 IIM lost his battle to retain his American Citizenship and became 'stateless'.[201] To travel outside England from then on he was forced to apply to the British Home Office for a 'certificate of identity' for use as a travel document in conjunction with the requisite immigration visas.[202] He obviously elected for this arrangement rather than face the prospect of becoming an immigrant in what he regarded as being his own country.

IIM persisted with the battle to regain his American citizenship, but without the same level of determination as previously – a letter to IIM from his brother Maxwell refers to his lack of action and his 'vacillation' on the matter.[203] On Maxwell's advice, in 1949 IIM adopted the line of argument that he was forced to remain in England because Edna was not willing to consider returning to America due to her desire to remain close to her grandchildren.[204] He also explored the possibility of a private bill to cover his individual case.[205] The matter was not to be resolved before he died.[206]

Final Trips to America

While he was dealing with the question of his citizenship, IIM continued to visit America, now travelling by air rather than by sea. In the autumn of 1946 he took a three-month 'vacation trip' to America as part of a six-month sabbatical from the LJS, leaving Leslie Edgar with responsibility for the High Holyday services. This was the first time since he had taken up his post that IIM had not been at the LJS for the High Holydays.[207] He had prepared for the trip with great excitement having been separated from his friends and family for many years because of the war. He started the American trip with a month-long visit to his son, Robert, now living in Plainfield, Vermont. This was the first time he had seen Robert since 1938 and the first occasion on which he met his two granddaughters, both of whom were born during the war.

As the result of his citizenship status, it appeared at one point that IIM might be 'marooned in the United States'.[208] He had left England on an American passport that was due to expire while he was away. His hope was that by being in America when the passport needed to be renewed, this would strengthen his case. However, despite the reassurances given him by Congressman Sol Bloom,[209] chairman of the powerful Foreign Affairs Committee, IIM's expectations proved ill judged. The State Department refused to issue him with a new passport, and he was detained in America for several weeks while the British Home Office arranged for him to be issued with an affidavit and a British visa in New York, to enable him to travel back to England as a 'returning citizen'.[210] Finally able to return to England, IIM used the remainder of his six-month sabbatical to work on three publications: 'a manuscript for another book' (either *Jewish Ethics* or *The Thought of the Prophets*, both of which were to be published in 1953), and a series of lectures.[211]

In 1947 IIM and Edna took a month-long break in America, when they again visited their son in Vermont, and also spent some time in Saratoga Springs with their New York relatives.[212] On their return in June, IIM talked to the younger members of the LJS on 'Liberal Judaism in America',[213] and also gave an address on 'Judaism in America' at The Friends' Meeting House, under the auspices of the Anglo-Jewish Association. IIM appears to have been deeply disappointed by what he had seen in America. As he perceived it 'the population of America consists of different sections. The melting pot has not fused the different elements, but only overlaid them with plating'.[214]

IIM had also been disturbed by the 'widespread feeling of apprehension' that seemingly permeated the country. Americans were worried about their economic future as well as being afraid that there would be another war. These tensions were impacting on the Jewish community, which was beginning to experience increased anti-Semitism and was suffering from 'a general state of spiritual confusion'. However, IIM was most appalled by the political prominence of the 'Palestine question', with electoral candidates vying with each other in expressing their support of Zionist aims.[215] During his visit, IIM had been confronted with anti-British feeling and had been asked again and again why Britain had not admitted into Palestine 100,000 Jews as recommended by the Anglo-American Commission of Enquiry on European Jewry and Palestine.[216] The visit had clearly not been a success.

Following his 'flying visit' to America, organised by the ACJ in the spring of 1948, IIM took a long holiday with his family in Switzerland, having first attended a meeting of the United Nations Commission on Human Rights in Geneva as a delegate from WUPJ.[217] It was his intention to return to America later in the year for a meeting of the WUPJ, but other factors intervened and the trip to America in the early part of 1948 was to be his last.

A Worrying Time at Home

IIM was affected adversely by the privations that followed the end of the Second World War, such as food rationing and the shortage of fuel, about which he complained bitterly to friends and colleagues in America.[218] His mood was not helped by the worries surrounding his citizenship status. However, he became even more stressed when his daughter, Dorothy, contracted pulmonary tuberculosis in May 1948. She had a major operation in the latter part of 1948 and was subsequently convalescent for a year in the King Edward VII Sanatorium in Midhurst, West Sussex. A nurse was engaged to assist Leslie Edgar in the care of his two children, Gillian and Robert.

The strain on IIM was evident in his professional life. During the latter part of 1949 he entered into correspondence with a firm of solicitors (George Barnett and Co., located in Uxbridge) regarding the disbursement of a legacy he had been left by a congregant (William Joel) to give to health charities. In this correspondence, the solicitor chided IIM for his provocative remarks and lack of courtesy, concluding with the comment 'If we come in contact again on such a subject, perhaps you will act differently. You will observe the word "if"'.[219]

In January 1949 Robert returned to England for his first visit since he had left in 1938. Writing to his wife Corinne in America, he conveyed his impressions of his family. He found the atmosphere in 'Wildwood' 'rather bleak' and 'absurd' in its 'bourgeois formality', and his parents 'rather remote'. He felt that they had become trapped in a life of 'jealousies' and 'a little passé in their work and position'. Edna was rushing around as she did when she was in America however, 'not for fun but to keep things going the old way'. IIM seemed 'quite old'. Naomi and Kenneth Capon living in a bedsitting room at 'Wildwood' seemed to Robert awfully 'Protestant' and like the 'outsiders upstairs'.[220] This description of life at 'Wildwood', even taking into account Robert's possibly prejudiced view of his parents, paints a somewhat poignant picture.

NOTES

1. Simon Mayer joined the couple shortly after they came to England in 1912. He then returned to Lincoln, Nebraska for a few years, possibly to put his affairs in order. See *American Israelite,* 30 October 1913, p.30. Simon Mayer returned to live in England permanently in 1914.
2. Tape recording of the diary kept by IIM between January and April 1918. The diary is read by his daughter, Dorothy Edgar née Mattuck, Mattuck Family Archive kept by Robert Edgar (MFAb).
3. National Archives and Records Administration, Reports of Deaths of American Citizens Abroad, 1835–1974, record for Simon David Mayer, available from Ancestry.com. His body was taken back to America and he was buried in Lincoln, Nebraska. *American Israelite,* 6 February 1936, p.6.
4. For example, he was one of the delegates at the conference of the WUPJ when it was held in Berlin in 1928, *LJM*, XIII, no.64 (September 1928), p.2.
5. Louis Mayer lived with the Mattucks until his move to France when he married a French woman. At some point Edna Mattuck appears to have become estranged from her brother. In correspondence between Edna Mattuck and her lawyer cousin, Nathan Gold, in Nebraska, she requested that her interest in her brother's affairs be kept secret from him, Mattuck Family Archive kept by Jill Mattuck Tarule (MFAa).
6. 'Memento of a great occasion', *LJM*, XX, no.3 (March 1949), p.29.
7. See tape recording of the diary kept by IIM.
8. *JC*, 11 May 1912, p.18.
9. 'Post War America', address by IIM, day unknown, July 1927, Montagu Centre Collection (MCC).
10. See letter from IIM to Marjorie Moos, 30 January 1948, LJS Archives, Box 1/2.
11. Ben and Vera Strauss were founding members of the LJS and involved in the LJS religion classes.
12. Letter from IIM to Rabbi Barnett Brickner in Toronto, 8 February 1923, AJA, Barnett and Rebecca Brickner Papers, MS-98, Box 1, Folder 7.
13. Letter from IIM to Miss Irene Hageman, 19 May 1952, London Metropolitan Archives, ACC/3529/002/019(1).
14. Sheldon Blank graduated from HUC in 1923. During the autumn of 1925 he spent time at the LJS assisting IIM with the High Holydays, which is probably when he met Amy Kirchberger.
15. The Grecian Club was formed in 1939 for the discussion of philosophical, ethical, scientific, aesthetic and other problems. As well as attending meetings, IIM was an occasional speaker alongside prominent people such as G.K. Chesterton and Lord Samuel. Information leaflet, LJS Archives, Box 1/2.
16. *Harvard College, Class of 1905, 25th Anniversary Report* (Norwood, MA: printed privately for the class by Plimpton Press, June 1930), p.415.
17. National Archives and Records Administration, application for passport 1915. Copy on Ancestry.com website.
18. See tape recording of the diary kept by IIM.
19. *The Thought of the Prophets* was published in 1953. See later discussion in Chapter Fifteen on the last years of IIM's life.
20. See tape recording of the diary kept by IIM.
21. 'Odd Accidents and Greater Insight: An Evening with Robert Mattuck', transcript of taped interview by Jo Chickering, January 1963, MFAa.
22. This was in a very wealthy part of Beaconsfield.
23. See tape recording of the diary kept by IIM.
24. Ibid.
25. Ibid.
26. Ibid.
27. Ibid.
28. *The Lincoln Sunday Star* [Nebraska], 29 July 1917, p.14.
29. 'Rabbi Dr Mattuck's Fortieth Anniversary Address, The Spirit of Liberal Judaism', *LJM*, XXIII, no.2 (February 1952), p.16.
30. Letter from Joseph Fried, President of Temple Israel, New York to IIM, January 29 1915, LJS Archives, Box 1/2.
31. See 'Rabbi Dr Mattuck's Fortieth Anniversary Address', p.15.

32. Ibid.
33. See letter from IIM to Mr Bethal Halford (LJS Council member), 16 July 1916, LJS Archives, Box 1/2.
34. Call up notice, 1 July 1916, MFAa.
35. 'Wildwood' is an eighteenth-century house that had previously been lived in by Mrs Craik, the novelist, by George MacDonald who wrote the 'Princess' books, and by Holman Hunt, the artist. See 'Odd Accidents and Greater Insight'.
36. Letter from David Fichman to IIM, 1 August 1923, LJS Archives, Box 1/2.
37. Naomi Capon (née Mattuck), *Snippets from the Past – A Childhood from the Twenties* (unpublished manuscript, undated, c.1975), p.32.
38. Letter from Corinne Mattuck to her family, 30 March 1937, MFAa. Corinne Mattuck described the chanting as 'so lovely' and feared that it might make her Orthodox.
39. See Capon, *Snippets from the Past*, p.10.
40. Ibid., p.67.
41. Ibid., p.66.
42. Ibid., p.7. The nurseries were later turned into bedrooms for Naomi and Dorothy.
43. Ibid., p.2.
44. Photographs in MFAb.
45. See Capon, *Snippets from the Past,* p.115.
46. Ibid., p.114.
47. Interview with Michael Nathan, 15 November 2011, conducted by Rosita Rosenberg.
48. Meeting with Robert Edgar, 4 January 2012.
49. Rabbi John Rayner, '80th Anniversary of Rabbi Mattuck's Induction', *LJS News*, January 1992, p.5.
50. Interview with Margaret Rigal, 2 November 2011, conducted by Rosita Rosenberg.
51. See interview with Michael Nathan.
52. 'The Ethics of Marriage', sermon given by IIM at the LJS, 13 February 1927, MCC.
53. 'Marriage and Freedom', sermon given by IIM at the LJS, 27 February 1927, in ibid.
54. The Hon. Lily H. Montagu, 'Rabbi Dr Israel I. Mattuck, Memorial Tribute', in LJM, *In Memoriam, Israel I. Mattuck, 1883–1954* (June 1954), p.3.
55. See tape recording of the diary kept by IIM.
56. Draft article by Dorothy M. Edgar, 'Some Recollections of Rabbi Dr Israel I. Mattuck and Rabbi Dr Leslie I. Edgar', MFAb.
57. Ibid.
58. 'The Work of Our Religious School', sermon given by IIM, undated, 1914, MCC.
59. See draft of article by Dorothy M. Edgar, 'Some Recollections'.
60. Ibid.
61. See Capon, *Snippets from the Past*, p.52.
62. See 'Odd Accidents and Greater Insight'.
63. Dorothy Mattuck attended the school from 1922–30, and Robert Mattuck from 1922–28.
64. See website for King Alfred School.
65. See 'Odd Accidents and Greater Insight'.
66. Ibid.
67. Conversation with Jill Mattuck Tarule, 13 November 2011. It is possible that the school to which IIM applied was either St Paul's or University College School, admission to which became more difficult for Jews after the First World War. See Todd M. Endelman, *The Jews of Britain 1656 to 2000* (Berkeley, Los Angeles, CA and London: University of California Press, 2002).
68. Information provided by Jill Mattuck Tarule.
69. Information provided by Robert Edgar.
70. See 'Odd Accidents and Greater Insight'.
71. Conversation with Jill Mattuck Tarule, 11 May 2012.
72. 'The Authority of Parents and Freedom of Children', sermon given by IIM at the LJS, 29 January 1928, MCC.
73. Ibid.
74. 'The Spirit of Israel Mattuck', sermon given by Rabbi John Rayner at the LJS, 25 January 1992, LJS Archives, Box 135c.
75. Conversation with Jill Mattuck Tarule, 11 May 2012.
76. See Capon, *Snippets from the Past*, p.13.
77. Ibid., p.56.

78. Ibid., p.120.
79. Ibid., p.119.
80. Ibid., p.120.
81. 'Dr Mattuck's Seventieth Birthday', *LJM*, XXV, no.2 (February 1954), p.26.
82. See interview with Michael Nathan.
83. See Rayner, '80th Anniversary of Rabbi Mattuck's Induction', p.5.
84. The Hon. Lily H. Montagu, 'Edna M. Mattuck, Memorial Tribute', *LJM*, XXVIII, no.3 (March 1957), pp.43–4.
85. See Capon, *Snippets from the Past*, p.63.
86. Ibid., p.66.
87. Entry for IIM in *Harvard College, Class of 1905, 25th Anniversary Report*, p.77.
88. See tape recording of the diary kept by IIM.
89. See Capon, *Snippets from the Past*, p.10.
90. Ibid., p.117.
91. Ibid., p.117.
92. Ibid., p.106.
93. See 'Dr Mattuck's Seventieth Birthday'.
94. See Capon, *Snippets from the Past*, p.111.
95. *American Israelite*, 10 July 1919, p.2.
96. Information provided by Robert Edgar, 5 January 2012.
97. See draft of article by Dorothy M. Edgar, 'Some Recollections'.
98. In his sermons and in editorials of the *JRU Bulletin* and the *LJM*, IIM often commented unfavourably on the statements and activities of Rabbi Stephen Wise.
99. 'The Conference of Jews and Christians – from the Jewish point of view', sermon given by IIM at the LJS, 24 October 1926, MCC.
100. See Capon, *Snippets from the Past*, p.124.
101. *New York Times*, 27 May 1927.
102. *JRU Bulletin*, III, 32 (April 1927), p.9.
103. See Capon, *Snippets from the Past*, p.125.
104. Ibid., p.126.
105. It is unclear how IIM became acquainted with Rabbi Franklin as he was a generation older than IIM. It is possible that he was a family friend of the Mayers, since between 1892 and 1899 he was the rabbi at the synagogue in Omaha, Nebraska.
106. A letter from Julian Morgenstern to IIM following IIM's lectures at HUC was sent via Dr Leo Franklin, AJA, Hebrew Union College Records, MS-5, Box A-18, Folder 14.
107. 'The Future of Judaism', outline of address, 1927, MCC. When he returned to England, IIM mentioned this event because he was very impressed by the fact that the Teachers' College was regularly attended by hundreds of Jewish men and women to study Jewish history and literature. See 'The Jew in America, Part One', address given by IIM to the North London Liberal Congregation Literary Society, July 1927, MCC.
108. *JRU Bulletin*, XII, 56 (November 1927), p.10.
109. 'Rabbi Mattuck in Worcester: Head of London Liberal Jewish Synagogue to Address Economic Club', *Jewish Advocate*, 28 April 1927, p.2.
110. See Capon, *Snippets from the Past*, p.129.
111. Copy of affidavit, MFAa.
112. Letter from John Claffey, American Vice-Consul, to IIM, 11 January 1922, in ibid.
113. Ibid.
114. How he had been able to make this trip is unclear, because an application he made for an emergency passport to visit France in November 1925 was refused by the American Consul. Letter from John Claffey, American Vice-Consul to IIM 14 November 1925, MFAa.
115. Copy of submission, MFAa.
116. See Court Order admitting IIM as an American citizen, July 1927 and letter from John Claffey, American Vice-Consul to IIM, 3 April 1928, MFAa.
117. David Philipson writing in the *American Israelite*, 29 December 1898, quoted in Jonathan D. Sarna, 'Converts to Zionism in the American Reform Movement', in Anita Shapira, Shmuel Almog and Jehuda Reinharz (eds), *Zionism and Religion (Tauber Institute for the Study of European Jewry)* (Hanover, NH : University Press of New England, 1998), pp.188–203, p.197.
118. See Capon, *Snippets from the Past*, p.129.
119. Ibid., p.131.
120. 'The Place of Religion in Human Life', sermon given by IIM at the LJS on Yom Kippur, 1953, MCC.

121. 'Remarkable Escapes in Four-Fold Collision', *Western Times*, 14 June 1935, p.7.
122. Letter from IIM to Adolph Oko, 13 June 1935, AJA, Adolph Oko Papers, MS-14, Box 3, Folder 8.
123. Email from Arthur Mattuck, 29 July 2011.
124. Email from Arthur Mattuck, 7 August 2011.
125. *JC*, 24 January 1936, p.52.
126. *The American Israelite,* February 6, 1936, p.6.
127. When the trip was mentioned in the *LJM*, it was described as a trip relating to the burial of IIM's father-in-law. See *LJM*, VI, no.9 (February 1936), p.178.
128. Rabbi David Shor from America was employed by the LJS for six months to cover IIM's absence, *LJM*, VIII, no.5 (October 1937), pp.46–7.
129. The Synagogue Society was an LJS discussion and study group.
130. 'Different Kinds of Religion', sermon given by IIM at the LJS, 11 January 1946, MCC. Birham is a monthly holiday on which Muslims exchange gifts.
131. See Capon, *Snippets from the Past*, pp.122–3.
132. Letter from Bernard Mattuck to IIM, 16 January 1929, LJS Archives, Box 1/2.
133. Conversation with Jill Mattuck Tarule, 11 May 2012.
134. Information from Jill Mattuck Tarule, 25 August 2013.
135. Conversation with Jill Mattuck Tarule, 11 May 2012.
136. See 'Odd Accidents and Greater Insight'.
137. Corinne's father, Emile, who died when she was five, and her mother came to America from Germany in the 1880s when they were both very young. Corinne went to university in Chicago where she trained in social work. She became exhausted by her work and travelled to England with her mother to see her married sister, Gertrude, by way of recuperation. This is when she met Robert Mattuck. Conversation with Jill Mattuck Tarule, 10 May 2012.
138. Their meeting is chronicled in a diary kept by Corinne Weil during the trip, MFAa.
139. Ibid.
140. See 'Odd Accidents and Greater Insight'.
141. The disagreements are covered at length in a letter from Dorothy Mattuck to her brother, Robert Mattuck, 22 October 1932, MFAa. During Corinne's visit to England in 1932 the couple stayed together in a hotel in Dorset, which would have been very outré at the time (receipt in MFAa).
142. 'Marriage and Morals – The Jewish View', sermon given by IIM at the LJS, 24 February 1935, MCC.
143. Conversation with Jill Mattuck Tarule, 3 October 2012.
144. Ibid.
145. See 'Odd Accidents and Greater Insight'.
146. Conversation with Jill Mattuck Tarule, 11 May 2012.
147. Ibid.
148. Corinne became very close to her mother-in-law. Conversation with Jill Mattuck Tarule, 3 October 2012.
149. Correspondence between Corinne Mattuck and her mother, MFAa.
150. Letter from Corinne Mattuck to her family, undated (c.1936), in ibid.
151. Ibid.
152. Conversation with Jill Mattuck Tarule, 11 May 2012.
153. Jill Mattuck Tarule recalls that it was generally understood that IIM was solicitous of his health and while not being a hypochondriac he was prone to bouts of depression and illness. Conversation with Jill Mattuck Tarule, 11 May 2012.
154. Letter from Corinne Mattuck to her family, 28 August 1937, MFAa.
155. See various letters between Corinne Mattuck and her mother in Evansville in ibid.
156. Ibid.
157. See 'Odd Accidents and Greater Insight'.
158. Conversation with Jill Mattuck Tarule, 11 May 2012.
159. Bryan Pfeiffer, staff writer, 'Goddard Puts Heads Together on its Future', *Rutland Herald*, 12 December 1997.
160. See 'Odd Accidents and Greater Insight'.
161. A federal organisation catering for disadvantaged pre-school aged children to prepare them for school by enhancing their cognitive, social, and emotional development.
162. Conversation with Jill Mattuck Tarule, 13 October 2011.
163. Conversation with Jill Mattuck Tarule, 11 May 2012.

164. In an email, 14 August 2011, Jill Mattuck Tarule, stated 'one might conclude that Dorothy married the rabbi my father, the first born and only son, was supposed to have been'.
165. Rabbi Dr Leslie I. Edgar, *Some Memories of My Ministry* (London: Liberal Jewish Synagogue, 1985), p.7.
166. Ibid., p.9.
167. Letter from Leslie Edgar to IIM, 30 November 1927, MFAb.
168. Rabbi David Goldberg, 'Obituary for Dorothy Edgar', *LJS News*, April 2005, p.7.
169. After she was married Dorothy referred to herself as Dorothy Mattuck Edgar. The register was signed by Claude Montefiore, Alfred Edgar (Leslie Edgar's father) and Simon Mayer. See *LJM*, V, no.4 (July 1934), p.31.
170. See draft article by Dorothy M. Edgar, 'Some Recollections'.
171. See Goldberg, 'Obituary for Dorothy Edgar'.
172. Conversation with Jill Mattuck Tarule, 3 October 2012.
173. Letter from Corinne Mattuck to her family, 30 March 1937, MFAa.
174. Rabbi Leslie I. Edgar, 'A Personal Appreciation', 'Rabbi Dr Israel Mattuck', in LJM, *In Memoriam, Israel I. Mattuck*, p.4.
175. Description from meeting with Robert Edgar, 1 December 2011.
176. ULPS Oral History Project 1994–5, interview with Rabbi John Rayner, LJS Archives, Box 139a.
177. Meeting with Robert Edgar, 1 December 2011.
178. Letter from Superintendent R. Read to IIM, 4 March 1944, MFAb.
179. Letter from IIM to the Police Superintendent of Buckinghamshire Constabulary, 17 June 1940, London Metropolitan Archives, ACC/3529/002/018.
180. Ibid.
181. See Edgar, *Some Memories,* p.31.
182. Letter from Israel Mattuck to Arthur Sundlun, 9 April 1941, MFAa.
183. Letter from the American Consul, Glenn A. Ashby to IIM, 9 September 1941, in ibid.
184. Letter from IIM to Julian Morgenstern, 9 October 1941, LJS Archives, Box 1/2.
185. See letter from IIM to the Irish High Commissioner, 3 October 1941, MFAa.
186. In 1956 Naomi wrote a children's book, *Dancers of Tomorrow*, based on her script for a television programme of the same name. Naomi Capon, *Dancers of Tomorrow* (Leicester: Brockhampton Press, 1956).
187. Conversation with Jill Mattuck Tarule, 11 May 2012.
188. He designed the campus for Essex University.
189. In a letter to Nathan Gold, Edna Mattuck's cousin, 17 September 1946, IIM said: 'Naomi was being married yesterday …' indicating that he was not at the wedding, MFAa.
190. Letters from Robert Mattuck to his wife Corrine, January 1949, in ibid.
191. Conversation with Jill Mattuck Tarule, 11 May 2012.
192. Nathan Gold was confirmed by IIM at the South Street Synagogue in Lincoln in May 1907. See *American Israelite*, 16 May 1907, p.3.
193. Senator Werry was the Republican representative for Lincoln, Nebraska. He held very traditional views, which must have been an anathema to IIM. He worked alongside McCarthy in seeking to eradicate homosexuals from the military forces. At one point Senator Werry was pursuing an amendment to the Nationality Act, 1940 to exempt American citizens living abroad because of their professions from its provisions. However, at some point he appears to have stopped pursuing this amendment.
194. Letter from Senator Werry to Nathan Gold, 13 January 1948, London Metropolitan Archives, ACC/3529/002/012. He advised that IIM would be given preference because his wife was born in America and his two older children held American passports.
195. Letter from IIM to Nathan Gold, 27 January 1948, in ibid.
196. Ibid.
197. See correspondence, London Metropolitan Archives, ACC/3529/002/012.
198. Letter from IIM to Nathan Gold, 27 January 1948, in ibid.
199. Letter from Senator Kenneth Werry to Nathan Gold, 14 April 1948, in ibid.
200. Letter from Nathan Gold to IIM, 22 December 1947, in which he urges IIM to advise Senator Werry of the other avenues being pursued to avoid duplication of effort, in ibid.
201. In travel records for 1948, IIM is listed as 'stateless'.
202. Letter from James Powell, American Consul at the American Embassy to IIM, 15 October 1947, London Metropolitan Archives, ACC/3529/002/012.
203. Letter from Maxwell Mattuck to IIM, 21 December 1950, MFAa.

204. Maxwell Mattuck identified an amendment to the 1940 Nationality Act which granted exemption to a man who was forced to remain abroad to be with his wife, a US citizen, who was unable to return to America due to illness. See letter from Maxwell Mattuck to IIM, 27 May 1949, MFAa.
205. Letter from Maxwell Mattuck to Rabbi A. Feldman, 7 May 1949, AJA, Abraham Feldman Papers, Box 24, Folder 4, MS-38.
206. Letter from Maxwell Mattuck to Rabbi Dr A. Feldman, 17 May 1949, in ibid.
207. Letter from IIM to LJS congregation, 28 August 1946, LJS Archives, Box 1/2.
208. Letter (undated) from W. Lyons from the Home Office Aliens' Department to E. Cooper of the London Regional Refugee Council, MFAa.
209. Telegram from Sol Bloom to IIM, 3 October 1946, in ibid.
210. Statement prepared by IIM on his return to London in support of his bid to retain his American citizenship, MFAa.
211. Letter from IIM to Julian Morgenstern, 31 December 1946, London Metropolitan Archives, ACC/3529/002/018.
212. Information from Jill Mattuck Tarule, 25 August 2013.
213. *LJM*, XVIII, no.4 (April 1947), p.31.
214. Rabbi Dr I.I. Mattuck, 'The American Scene', *LJM*, XVIII, no.1 (January 1947), p.1.
215. Ibid., p.1.
216. Ibid., p.2.
217. Letter from IIM to unknown recipient, 10 March 1948, MFAa.
218. See letter from IIM to Harold Mayer, 4 May 1947, in ibid.
219. Letter from Barnett and Co. (signature indecipherable) to IIM, 14 December 1949, LJS Archives, Box 38.
220. Letter from Robert Mattuck to Corinne Mattuck, 2 January 1949, MFAa.

CHAPTER FIFTEEN

Final Years

Failing Health

For the last few years of his life, IIM was a very sick man. In December 1950, at the age of 67, he was taken ill with coronary thrombosis, which came as 'a grievous shock' to the LJS congregation[1] as well as to his friends and family. He was ordered to take complete rest and, much to his wife's relief,[2] he scaled down both his congregational and ecumenical activities. However, when he felt able, he continued to write with 'urgency',[3] even when he was too weak to handle the heavy reference books that he consulted. His illness had made him physically incapacitated, but his mind was still very alert.[4] He produced two further books, *The Thought of the Prophets*[5] and *Jewish Ethics*,[6] which together put into writing one of his main preaching motifs: that on both an individual and collective level it is righteousness or good conduct that binds the divine and the human.

'Prophets' (as IIM referred to the book), which was dedicated to H.N. Spalding, a benefactor who sponsored the comparative study of religions, concentrated on the collective teachings of the Prophets rather than on their individual personalities and the divergences in their thoughts (hence the title 'thought' rather than 'thoughts'). His aim in writing the book was to promote hope in humanity and religious values after two global wars had devastated the world. In his other book, 'Ethics', IIM sought to provide an account of the theory and application of 'right conduct' from a Jewish perspective. He explained Jewish ethics by referring mainly to texts from the Bible and from the Talmud.

IIM thought that 'Prophets' was the better of two books,[7] the content of which is explored further in Chapter Seventeen. Both books received favourable reviews. *The Thought of the Prophets,* which was published as part of the 'Ethical and Religious Classics of East and West Series', was described by one eminent reviewer as 'penetrating', and 'well-rounded' in its analysis of the salient features of prophetic teaching, 'skilful' and 'timely' in its interweaving of quotations and explanations of their modern significance, and as 'satisfying a real need'.[8] A review in the *Jewish Chronicle* said that it was a book of distinction and deserved to be widely read.[9] The book was welcomed not only by Jewish readers but also by non-Jews. A reviewer in the *Church Times* said:

> The value of this little book is out of all proportion to its size ... Almost always he [IIM] has something fresh to say, or says something that has been said before, in a new and arresting way ... It is an intellectual pleasure and a spiritual satisfaction to read this book.[10]

On behalf of its publishers, the eminent Jewish historian, Cecil Roth commented on drafts of 'Ethics' and said how delighted he was to find IIM 'writing a book so wholly unexceptionable from the conservative angle'.[11] 'Ethics' was greeted by the *Jewish Chronicle* as 'a very useful little book that should find a warm welcome from the educated layman'.[12] Reviewing the book in the *Liberal Jewish Monthly*, Dr J.L. Teicher, Professor of Rabbinic Studies at Cambridge University said:

> Dr Mattuck displays a fine spirit of penetration into the texts and very often delights the reader with original interpretation. His freshness of approach to the texts is captivating. Even more so, his description of the Jewish ideal of ethical life. Underneath the sober and objective description, the personality of the author is clearly discernible: honest, kind, wise, modest, just and infused with the spirit of humanity.[13]

IIM was pleased with Teicher's favourable review, but wrote a letter to Dr Teicher, reproduced in the *Liberal Jewish Monthly*, in which he took issue with some of his opinions on the general subject of ethics.[14] Again, 'Ethics' was reviewed favourably in the non-Jewish press, such as in *The Times Literary Supplement* and *Common Ground*.[15] Despite IIM's illness, it was described as 'lucid'.[16]

As his health permitted, IIM worked on a revised version of the Liberal Jewish prayer book for home use (the *Home Service Book*).[17] He continued to write articles for the *Liberal Jewish Monthly* and in liaison with Lily Montagu he oversaw the putting together of a volume of essays in celebration of Leo Baeck's eightieth birthday, to which he wrote the preface and contributed an essay on 'The Missionary Idea'.[18]

Just before he was taken seriously ill, in December 1950 IIM made a notable radio broadcast on the BBC's Home Service programme. His broadcast on 'The Living God', was part of a series on *Men Without God?* and was reproduced in *The Listener*.[19] IIM maintained his contact with HUC. Although he was unable to attend, in March 1950, a paper he had prepared on 'Judaism as a Missionary Religion' was considered at a conference held at the college, organised by the Institute of Reform Jewish Theology under the auspices of CCAR. In his paper he suggested that Judaism had the potential for once again becoming a missionary religion.[20]

Due to the shortage of building materials and difficulties in obtaining building licences, it had taken many years to restore the LJS and it was not re-consecrated until 1951. A re-consecration service was planned for April 1951, but it had to be reorganised to take place on 23 September that year because of IIM's ill health. Although he had a temporary setback in June and remained unwell, he mustered the strength to deliver a stirring address at the first of the two re-consecration services. Part of his address, 'The Present Task of the Synagogue', was broadcast by the BBC, but a subsequent commentary apparently was not complimentary.[21] Louis Gluckstein was incensed by the way in which IIM had been 'slandered', noting with a degree of bitterness how regularly publicity about the LJS seemed to go wrong.[22] Also preaching at the service was IIM's long-standing friend, Rabbi Lazaron from Baltimore, who came to London to 'fulfil a ten-year-old promise' to IIM.[23]

Despite the fact that he was 'scarcely out of convalescence',[24] IIM opened an exhibition of the LJS's history, 'The Years Between 1911–1951', held at the synagogue between 1–7 October 1951. He was not well enough to attend the WUPJ Conference held in London later in the month and Leslie Edgar substituted for him as chairman. However, he did attend the service held in December to celebrate the 250th anniversary of the founding of Bevis Marks Synagogue.

IIM gradually withdrew from his remaining involvements, such as his membership of the council of the Bernhard Baron Settlement in the East End of London, which he passed on to Leslie Edgar.[25] The one exception was the London Society of Jews and Christians, the meetings of which he sometimes presided over even though, by then, his role as its co-chairman had been taken over by Edgar. When he felt sufficiently well, IIM entertained people in his Hampstead home. Those who saw him reported that he remained 'cheerful, thoughtful and helpful'.[26]

Although IIM's movements and activities were now severely restricted, he was impatient to complete the writing of his books. He devoted the limited energy he did have to this task rather than his correspondence and other paperwork which, to his chagrin, suffered badly.[27] However, he did manage to stay in touch with his closest friends and acquaintances such as the Blanks in Cincinnati, to whom he was now admitting that it was unlikely that he would ever be able to travel back to America.[28] On the occasion of Sir Pelham ('Plum') Warner's eightieth birthday, IIM wrote to his long-standing friend, with whom he had previously dined regularly, to congratulate him on being '80 not out'. Sir Pelham Warner replied saying that he had been very touched by IIM's letter.[29]

On 19 January 1952 IIM preached at a Thanksgiving Service held at the LJS to commemorate the fortieth anniversary of his induction as minister of the synagogue. In his sermon he alluded to the challenges that he had faced in establishing Liberal Judaism in England and paid tribute to the endeavours and courage of the early reformers with whom he had worked. However, the disillusionment evident in many of his sermons in the years immediately following the end of the Second World War was to the fore in this address.[30] He railed against the 'spiritual cowardice' that allowed scheming and unscrupulous dictators to take power, which they used to 'terrible effects on the life of humanity'.[31] He was also saddened by the 'artificial traditionalism to which some have reverted' even though they claimed to maintain a progressive form of Judaism.[32] His address gives the strong impression of a man who is tired and who feels at odds with the world around him. However, IIM was comforted by the evidence of the 'friendly feelings' of the council and the congregation during his address. He told Louis Gluckstein that he and his wife would long cherish the occasion.[33] Leading members of the council subsequently visited the Mattucks at their home to present them with celebratory gifts.[34]

Shortly after the service, IIM had a major operation on an oesophageal pouch. For a time after this operation he regained some of his former energy, so much so that he was urged by his friend,[35] the well-known American psychoanalyst Lawrence Kubie, not to 'take off on a jet-propelled flight, and undertake too much'.[36] By February 1952 he was well enough to chair the WUPJ Executive Committee meeting held in London. Towards the end of the year he gave the address at the service held at the LJS to celebrate the fiftieth anniversary of the founding of the Liberal Jewish movement. He sat on the *bimah* alongside fifteen ordained and lay minsters although he did not preach. At a reception held after the service, one of the speeches was given by John Rayner, a minister in training, who spoke of how he had been inspired by IIM. A decade later, John Rayner became the Senior Rabbi at the LJS.

IIM continued his membership of a number of advisory committees, such as that of Children's Social Adjustment Society, although he no longer went to their events or meetings. The only new organisations with which IIM became involved during his final years were the London School of Religion, set up in 1951 as a centre of adult education 'for the free and disciplined study of all aspects of religion' and the Religious Bodies Consultative Committee, chaired by the Dean of Chichester, which brought together representatives of different religious communities to consider moral aspects of international problems and to give advice on possible action.[37] In his dying years, IIM was perhaps feeling more comfortable with the liberal, rationalist clerics than he did with his Jewish peers.

In June 1950 IIM was one of the signatories to a statement issued by the Religious Bodies Consultative Committee warning that European civilisation was facing a total rejection of the body of beliefs and practices painfully built up through the ages and was instead in danger of adopting a new regime based on materialism and violence.[38] The statement called for urgent action to address this threat. He also made a 'remarkable contribution' to two further statements published by the consultative body, 'The Spiritual Inheritance of Europe' and 'The Need for a Law of Nations', setting out the moral principles on which international law should be based.[39]

Late in 1952 IIM underwent further surgery; he was discharged too soon after the operation and had to return to hospital for further treatment. The surgeon blamed the early discharge on IIM because he 'flattered to deceive' on his health.[40] IIM was still 'guardedly optimistic' that everything would now be all right.[41] However, during the first few months of 1953 IIM was largely confined to his home and attended very few events. In January 1953 he gave an address at a meeting of the London Society of Jews and Christians on 'Religion and Civilisation in the Modern World', in which he reflected on the connection between the growth of irreligion and the deterioration of moral standards in the Western world. The address focussed on the three issues with which IIM had become preoccupied in his declining years – the denial of individual rights by totalitarian regimes, establishing a just social order and assuring future peace between nations. In his address he argued forcefully that each of these problems called for a strengthening of the religious foundation of human life.[42]

During his convalescence IIM held a number of meetings and interviews in his home, such as the interview in February 1953 with Charles Solomon, Assistant Editor of the *Jewish Chronicle*, when he discussed the work of H.N. Spalding in Oxford.[43] He complained to his friend Amy Blank in America that he was ready to retire from the governing body of the WUPJ, but that Lily Montagu and other colleagues would not allow it.[44]

At various points in his career IIM had endeavoured to introduce systematic arrangements for training Liberal rabbis, and in his final years he was still pursuing the idea of establishing a college for rabbis, which he was discussing with John Rayner. While the ULPS Ministers' Conference favoured a separate institution, IIM was inclined towards a 'house' at Cambridge, both because he thought that it would be more affordable and because it would have the requisite academic standing.[45] While the discussions were taking place, interim arrangements were established. In his role as Deputy President of ULPS, IIM invited applications for 'young men [sic] to train as rabbis for the Liberal Jewish Ministry'.[46] To mark the commencement of the search for new rabbis, IIM wrote an article for the *Liberal Jewish Monthly* on 'The Functions of the Liberal Jewish Minister'. Clearly thinking of his own controversial career, IIM highlighted the importance of prospective Liberal Jewish ministers being resilient:

> More than in other callings a minister expresses himself in his work ... The sense of vocation will help him to face the difficulties and defy the frustrations which inevitably attend the minister's work ... For reasons rooted in a general aspect of Jewish life which history has imposed on it, the Jewish minister may have to face special difficulties and frequently meet frustration. To overcome the consequent discouragement and depression, he needs a strong faith to impart urgency to his work which will maintain undaunted and unweakened, his devotion to his high aim.[47]

Early in June 1953 IIM was unable to lead the consecration service for the new synagogue building in Ealing as planned. However, he did officiate at the ordination service for the (then) Reverend John Rayner, held on 20 June 1953. At the WUPJ conference held in London in July 1953, he gave an address on 'The Need for a Religious Renaissance',[48] which he was barely able to deliver. His mood was pessimistic. He detected in the world 'a widespread fear of a third and most destructive war', and that in a 'large section of mankind the view prevails that individual men have no inherent worth'. He called for a religious revival to address this spiritual crisis. He said that Liberal Judaism was equal to the task of returning value to the individual and helping to build a better society, but only if it could avoid 'the lure of old rites'.[49]

IIM gave a deeply spiritual address on the afternoon of Yom Kippur in September 1953. He may have been speaking of himself when he said:

> The normal human being wants to push out further and further the horizon of his existence. A man may lose that urge with advancing years and with the practical demands of living which may draw him into phlegmatic acceptance of a humdrum existence.[50]

Due to his ill health IIM was able to deliver only part of the sermon he had prepared,[51] and the following month he was again too ill to take the chair at the fourth Claude Montefiore Lecture. IIM's last public appearance was on 20 December 1953, when he gave the address at the service held at the LJS to celebrate Lily Montagu's eightieth birthday, in which he emphasised the religious message of Lily Montagu's life and work. He epitomised her life in the sentence 'She lives by faith in God'.[52] A prayer IIM had written for the occasion was read by the Reverend Philip Cohen, now Associate Minister at the LJS.

Just a few days later, on 28 December, IIM was too ill for a public celebration of his seventieth birthday. The congregation of the LJS sent their congratulations and best wishes to IIM and his wife, and a deputation from the WUPJ called upon him at his home to make a presentation. Basil Henriques (now Sir Basil), a vice-president, spoke on behalf of the WUPJ. He was accompanied by Lily Montagu, Rabbi Harold Reinhart, Rabbi Leslie Edgar, Rabbi Dr Werner van der Zyl, Bruno Woyda and the Reverend Andre Ungar. A deputation from the LJS Council also visited IIM. The LJS deputation included the president, Sir Louis Gluckstein, Lily Montagu, the Hon. Mrs Netta Franklin, Rabbi Leslie Edgar, the Revd Philip Cohen and the Reverend Vivian Simmons. He received a large number of telegrams from constituents of the WUPJ, Liberal and Progressive congregations and many leaders of the Anglo-Jewish community.[53] From America, Julian Morgenstern wrote, 'I congratulate you from the bottom of my heart and extend to you earnest wishes for many more years health and continued service, and of abundant happiness in the midst of your loved ones.'[54]

Morgenstern's wish was not to be fulfilled. During IIM's long illness, Edna Mattuck 'fought for his life',[55] and the doctors and nurses who attended to him quickly came to 'revere and love him'.[56] Edna was by then herself unwell and undergoing hospital treatment. This had prevented the couple from making a planned trip to their cottage in Buckinghamshire in the summer of 1953, where they were to have met up with David Kessler, proprietor of the *Jewish Chronicle*, who had a home in the same village.[57] IIM remained in good spirits. His personal doctor, Dr C. Berkley Way wrote:

> He bore all of his pain, discomfort and frustration of his distressing and tedious illness with exemplary patience, courage, dignity, and humour. Rarely did I leave his presence without a smile caused by either a story from his seemingly inexhaustible repertoire or by a caustic, but witty, criticism of his illness or treatment. Such fortitude made the task of looking after him appear a little lighter.[58]

As it became clear that IIM's health was deteriorating, in 1951 his son, Robert, brought his family to England for the first time to visit him. They arrived at 'Wildwood' on 30 December, too late to celebrate IIM's birthday with him, much to IIM's disappointment. However, they stayed in England until the latter part of February 1952.[59] (Robert and his family's arrival in

England had been delayed by three days because of a violent storm in the Atlantic that almost capsized the ship on which they were travelling.)[60] Soon after IIM's seventieth birthday, Robert returned to England to see his father on his own in January 1953.[61]

With characteristic meticulousness, IIM prepared for his death, ensuring that his affairs were in order and making arrangements for donating some of his books and papers to interested individuals and institutions.[62] He was in the process of writing another book on Judaism and Christianity (to be called *Christ-Jesus*)[63] when he died at 'Wildwood' on 3 April 1954,[64] having spent several days in an oxygen tent. Two days before his death, his physician suggested that he should listen to a playing of Fauré's *Requiem* on the radio:

> He had never heard it, and making the effort, for he was very weak, he found consolation in its quiet beauty. He loved music and it seems appropriate that it should have been the last work that he heard, for it hymns the Love, Mercy and Wisdom, rather than the Wrath of God.[65]

A Memorial Service was held for IIM at the LJS on 8 April 1954. The attendance was large and included his immediate family (including Robert who had come over from America), members and non-members of the synagogue, personal friends (numbered amongst them were friends of the Mattucks from Long Crendon), and representatives of many organisations, both from within and beyond the Jewish community. Lily Montagu gave the memorial tribute. The service, which was conducted by Leslie Edgar[66] and Philip Cohen, included a prayer adapted from words spoken by IIM at the memorial service for Claude Montefiore in 1938:

> God our father we turn to thee with the burden of sorrow to ask that in thy presence it may be transfigured into a guiding light. Though we worship you now in mourning for the death of our revered teacher and beloved friend, Israel Mattuck, we would thank you for the high gifts of mind and heart which he has endowed, for his wisdom and learning by which he gave instruction, for his holiness and his deep knowledge of thee, our God, by which he kindled and supported faith by others.

In another prayer Leslie Edgar said of IIM:

> Admired, respected and acknowledged for what he was even more than what he achieved, inspiring love and reverence and friendship,

> we know that greatness has been with us, and for that privilege teach us O God to be ever and deeply thankful.

Passages from IIM's writings were also read. At a private family service a poem by one of IIM's longest-standing friends, Amy Blank, was read. IIM had included this poem in the supplement to Volume 1 of the *Liberal Jewish Prayer Book*.

Memorial services were held or tributes paid to IIM from the pulpits of all of the congregations of the Union of Liberal and Progressive Synagogues, including at South London Liberal Jewish Synagogue on 11 April 1954, when Rabbi John Rayner gave an address on 'The Legacy of Israel Mattuck'. He referred to IIM as 'a heroic seeker of truth' and praised his devotion to Liberal Judaism, scholarship and commitment to the mission of the Jewish people, as well as the attributes that made him a 'loveable person'. In conclusion he said, 'We thank God for this human man, whom we have been privileged to know, and we pray that his influence may not only dwell with us, but bear fruit in us, throughout our lives.'[67] Resolutions expressing deep sorrow, recording a sense of loss and paying tribute to IIM and his outstanding services, were passed by synagogues across the world. At HUC a special tribute was paid in the College Chapel and Kaddish was recited in his memory at the daily service for a week.

At the LJS, a special council meeting was convened immediately before the Memorial Service at which the following resolution was passed:

> That this Special Meeting of the Council of the Liberal Jewish Synagogue desires to record its sense of profound sorrow and irreparable loss at the death of its revered and beloved Teacher and Spiritual Leader, Rabbi Dr Israel I. Mattuck. The Council expresses its abiding gratitude for all that Dr Mattuck has personally meant to the members of the Congregation and for all that he has given in friendship, instruction and inspiring leadership. Throughout forty-two years, he gave of himself unsparingly to our Synagogue of which he was so largely the creator and which is one of his many enduring memorials. The Council is proudly and thankfully conscious of our Congregation's privilege of having had a Minister of such exceptional distinction, profound wisdom and noble personality. He dedicated his life and his great qualities of mind, heart and character to our Synagogue and to the cause of Liberal Judaism. By his scholarship and deep spirituality, he made himself not only the exalted Teacher, Guide and Friend of our Congregation but a

> powerful influence in the religious life of this nation and in Jewry throughout the world.
>
> And to Mrs Mattuck, who so fully shared in her husband's devoted services to our Synagogue, and to all members of her family, the Council offers its heartfelt sympathy in the great loss which they, and so many others in and beyond Jewry, have suffered through his death.

Despite his many differences with them, at its next meeting the Board of Deputies observed a minute's silence as a mark of respect for IIM.[68] Such was the prominence that IIM had achieved, his death was announced in BBC news bulletins on the radio:

> The death has occurred at his home in London of the leader of the Liberal Jewish movement in England, Dr Israel I. Mattuck. He was seventy. Dr Mattuck was born in the United States [this was factually wrong as he was born in Lithuania] and was the first minister of the Liberal Jewish Synagogue in London.[69]

Obituary notices appeared in *The Times*, the *New York Herald Tribune*, the *Jewish Chronicle*, and the *South African Jewish Chronicle* as well as many other newspapers and periodicals in Britain and overseas.

IIM was cremated and his ashes scattered in a bed in the Liberal Jewish Cemetery in Willesden. After IIM's death, Edna Mattuck's health deteriorated. She refused treatment for the double breast cancer diagnosed early in 1954 and she died less than three years after her husband, on 24 January 1957, aged 68.

In Memoriam

Three months after his death, an *In Memoriam* edition of *Liberal Jewish Monthly* was published, commemorating IIM's personality, life and achievements and containing contributions from both Jews and Christians. This was circulated far and wide and requests were received for multiple copies of the special edition, including from Archibald Hillman, with whom IIM had corresponded for many years as a young man. Correspondence shows that Hillman had followed IIM's career closely, but suggests that the two men had not remained in contact.[70] IIM's brother, Jacob Mattuck came to visit his grave in July 1955 at the end of a tour of western Europe that he made that spring with his wife Rae.[71]

In his English will, IIM left an estate of around £11,000,[72] which was executed by his two daughters. Robert Mattuck was the executor for his father's estate in America, which largely consisted of stocks and shares. He worked closely with Maxwell and Bernard Mattuck in New York to establish trust funds for each of IIM's grandchildren. This apparently involved him in a great deal of complicated paperwork and schooling by his lawyer uncles.[73]

In the years that followed IIM's death, a number of arrangements were made to commemorate his life and work. The LJS erected a bronze plaque in his memory: 'This plaque is dedicated with affection and gratitude to the memory of Rabbi Dr Israel I. Mattuck wise leader and beloved minister of this synagogue 1912–1954.'[74] The plaque was erected in the entrance hall of the synagogue, alongside a plaque dedicated to Claude Montefiore, following a special service held on 3 December 1955. The ULPS Rabbi Mattuck Fund was also established to provide financial support for rabbinic students.

A number of publications appeared dedicated to his memory, some of them including IIM's writings, such as *The Significance of Biblical Prophecy For Our Time*.[75] The revised prayer book, *Services and Prayers for Jewish Homes*, on which IIM was working at the time of his death, was published in 1955, paying tribute to IIM. Some of his writings were also published posthumously, such as *Religion Can Help the World*, a symposium published in 1957 that included a contribution from IIM,[76] and *Progressive Judaism*, published by WUPJ in 1956, which contained a reproduction of the sermon on 'The Task of Liberal Judaism' that he gave at the inaugural conference of the WUPJ in 1926, and the address included in the World Union Youth Manual published in 1956, which IIM wrote in 1953.[77] In the introduction to this latter pamphlet Lily Montagu commented:

> The two issues published in this pamphlet reveal the character of the man who produced them. He was strong in his faith. Where his religion was concerned he could brook no compromise. He led a holy life in his home, in his pulpit and in his large world, for he was always in contact with his God. He had a clear intellect and could explain the reason for his religious opinions, and could give them without equivocation to the world.[78]

At HUC a short study course on 'Jewish Ethics' led by Dr Brav was set up based on IIM's book on this subject[79] and IIM's brother, Maxwell, arranged for the Israel I. Mattuck Memorial Prize to be established at the College[80] in memory of IIM. The prize continues to be awarded periodically to the author of the best original essay on an announced topic in the field of Jewish Ethics.

For two years after IIM's death, Edna Mattuck worked with IIM's secretary, organising and distributing IIM's correspondence and personal papers. A large proportion of the paperwork was given to Leslie Edgar in the hope that he would one day write IIM's biography. However, Leslie Edgar never had the time to fulfil this expectation and for many years the papers remained untouched under his study table.[81]

NOTES

1. 'Israel I. Mattuck – His Life and Work', in *LJM, In Memoriam of Israel Mattuck, 1883–1954* (June 1954), p.9.
2. The Hon. Lily H. Montagu, 'Edna M. Mattuck, A Memorial Tribute', *LJM,* XXVIII, no. 3 (March 1957), pp.43–4.
3. Letter to Leslie Edgar from IIM's physician, Dr Way, 2 May 1954, Mattuck Family Archive kept by Robert Edgar (MFAb).
4. Sheldon Blank, 'Israel I. Mattuck', in *CCAR Yearbook*, Vol. 54 (1954), p.160.
5. Israel I. Mattuck, *The Thought of the Prophets* (London: Allen and Unwin, 1953).
6. Israel I. Mattuck, *Jewish Ethics* (London: Hutchinson's University Library, 1953).
7. Letter from IIM to Amy Blank, 11 June 1953, American Jewish Archive (AJA), Sheldon and Amy Blank Papers, MS-730, Box 14, Folder 2.
8. 'Dr Mattuck's New Book on *The Thought of the Prophets*, an Appreciation by E.I.J. Rosenthal, MA, DPhil, lecturer in Hebrew, University of Cambridge', *LJM,* XXIV, no. 7 (July 1953), p.93.
9. Review by Professor S.H. Hooke, *JC*, 29 September 1953, p.14.
10. Quote from the *Church Times* in 'Reviews of Dr Mattuck's New Books', *LJM,* XXV, no. 1 (January 1954), p.11.
11. Letter from Cecil Roth to IIM, (undated) February 1952, Mattuck Family Archive kept by Jill Mattuck Tarule (MFAa).
12. Review by D. Daiches Raphael, *JC*, 22 May 1953, p.14.
13. *LJM* Vol. XXIV, no. 6 (June 1953), pp.74–6.
14. *LJM* Vol. XXIV, no. 7 (July 1953), p.103.
15. See quote from the review in *Common Ground* (the organ of the Council of Christians and Jews) in 'Reviews of Dr Mattuck's New Books', *LJM,* XXV, no. 1 (January 1954), p.11.
16. Harry Cushing, 'An Advocate Review', *Jewish Advocate*, 20 August 1953, p.8.
17. Letter from Peggy Lang, ULPS Publications Officer to IIM, 28 January 1952, London Metropolitan Archives, ACC/3529/002/019(1).The work on the new prayer book was completed by Leslie Edgar and published in 1957.
18. Aspects of Progressive Jewish Thought, with an Introduction by the late Rabbi Israel I. Mattuck (London: Victor Gollanz, 1954).
19. Rabbi Israel Mattuck, 'The Living God', *The Listener*, 7 December 1950, pp.692–3.
20. 'Suggest Reform Judaism as Missionary Religion', *The Jewish Exponent*, 31 March 1950, p.6.
21. Letter from Louis Gluckstein to IIM, 24 October 1951, LJS Archives, Box 1/2.
22. Letter from Louis Gluckstein to IIM, 24 September 1951, in ibid.
23. 'Rabbi Lazaron Will Preach in Rebuilt London Synagogue', *The Sun*, Baltimore, 28 September 1951, p.23.
24. The Younger Members' Organisation of the Liberal Jewish Synagogue, *The Years Between 1911–1951, LJS exhibition catalogue* (London: ULPS, 1951), p.5.
25. Letter from Louis Gluckstein to IIM, 9 April 1952, LJS Archives, Box 1/2.
26. John D. Rayner, 'Israel I. Mattuck', talk given at the South London Liberal Synagogue on 28 June 1957, LJS Archives, Box 135a.
27. See correspondence in London Metropolitan Archives, ACC/3529/002/019(1).
28. AJA, Sheldon and Amy Blank Papers, MS-730, Box 14, Folder 2.
29. Letter from Sir Pelham Warner to IIM, 16 November 1953, MFAb.
30. 'Rabbi Dr Mattuck's Fortieth Anniversary Address', in *LJM* Vol. XXIII, no. 2 (February 1952), p.17.
31. Ibid.
32. Ibid.
33. Letter from IIM to Louis Gluckstein, 22 January 1952, LJS Archives, Box 1/2.

34. Ibid.
35. Dr Kubie was also a close acquaintance of IIM's son Robert. The two worked together on progressive education in America. Kubie's father was one of the founding members of the Far Rockaway synagogue where IIM had his first permanent pulpit.
36. Letter from Dr Kubie to IIM, 28 May 1952, MFAb.
37. The Very Reverend A.S. Duncan Jones, Dean of Chichester, 'His Work For the Religious Bodies Consultative Committee', in *LJM, In Memoriam*, p.14.
38. 'A Challenge to Religion', *The Times,* 6 June 1950, p.2.
39. See Duncan-Jones, 'His Work for the Religious Bodies Consultative Committee', in *In Memoriam*, p.14.
40. Undated letter from IIM to Amy Blank, AJA, Sheldon and Amy Blank Papers, MS-730, Box 14, Folder 2.
41. Ibid.
42. 'Religion and Civilisation in the Modern World', address given by IIM at the London Society of Jews and Christians, 5 February 1953, Montagu Centre Collection (MCC).
43. Letter from Charles Solomon to IIM, 20 February 1953, London Metropolitan Archives, ACC/3529/002/019(2). H.N. Spalding was an Oxford don who devoted himself to cultivating better relations between the West and the East by fostering scholarly approaches to the history, art, religion and philosophy of Oriental countries.
44. Letter from IIM to Amy Blank, 27 May 1953, AJA, Sheldon and Amy Blank Papers, MS-730, Box 14, Folder 2.
45. Letter from IIM to Leslie Edgar, 21 April 1952, London Metropolitan Archives, ACC/3529/002/019(1).
46. *LJM,* XXIV, no. 4 (April 1953), p.47.
47. 'The Functions of the Liberal Jewish Minister', *LJM,* XXIV, no. 3 (March 1953), pp.29–31.
48. 'The Need for a Spiritual Renaissance', address given by IIM at the conference of the WUPJ, 5 July 1953, MCC.
49. Ibid.
50. 'The Place of Religion in Human Life', sermon given by IIM at the afternoon service on the Day of Atonement at the LJS, 18 September 1953, in ibid.
51. See note accompanying reprint of the sermon in *LJM,* XXIV, no. 10 (December 1953), p.147.
52. *LJM,* XXV, no. 2 (February 1954), p.19.
53. Annual Report of the Liberal Jewish Synagogue, 1953, LJS Archives.
54. Letter from Julian Morgenstern to IIM, 28 December 1953, AJA, Hebrew Union College Records, MS-5, Box A-18, Folder 14.
55. The Hon. Lily H. Montagu, 'Rabbi Dr Israel I. Mattuck Memorial Tribute', *LJM, In Memoriam*, p.3.
56. Rabbi Leslie I. Edgar, 'A Personal Appreciation', 'Rabbi Dr Israel Mattuck', in ibid, p.4.
57. Letter from IIM to David Kessler, 14 January 1954, London Metropolitan Archives, ACC/3529/002/019(1). In this letter Israel Mattuck stated: 'Edna has to go into hospital for treatment. She is now waiting to go into hospital again to have treatment for the result of the last treatment.'
58. Edgar, 'A Personal Appreciation', p.4.
59. Information from Jill Mattuck Tarule.
60. See *Trenton Evening Times,* 30 December 1951, p.1.
61. He returned to America by air on 7 January 1954.
62. See correspondence in the London Metropolitan Archives in which he deals with the transfer of various parts of his library, London Metropolitan Archives, ACC/3529/002/019(1).
63. See letter to Leslie Edgar from IIM's physician, Dr Way.
64. The publication was fairly well advanced. Papers found in his briefcase after his death include a detailed outline of the planned publication, London Metropolitan Archives, ACC//3529//002/067.
65. See letter to Leslie Edgar from IIM's physician, Dr Way.
66. He became 'Rabbi' in 1951.
67. John Rayner, 'The Legacy of Israel Mattuck', sermon given at the service in memory of Rabbi Dr Israel I. Mattuck, at South London Liberal Synagogue, 11 April 1954, LJS Archives, Box 135c.

68. *JC*, 16 April 1954, p.20.
69. Note of the announcement recorded by his daughter, Dorothy Edgar, MFAb.
70. Letter from Archibald Hillman to Edna Mattuck, 6 July 1954, London Metropolitan Archives, ACC/3529/002/020. IIM obviously lost contact with Archibald Hillman after his move to England although from time to time he did hear from him indirectly. For example in 1929, Rabbi Abraham Feldman wrote to IIM to say that while lecturing in Worcester, he had met Archibald Hillman, now a prominent attorney there, and Hillman asked that he be remembered to IIM. Letter from Abraham Feldman to IIM, 15 February 1929, AJA, Abraham Feldman Papers, MS-38, Box 24, Folder 4.
71. The event is recorded in the diary he kept of the tour. He was taken to the grave by Edna Mattuck. Diary in the possession of Jacob Mattuck's son, Arthur Mattuck.
72. Ancestry.com. England & Wales, National Probate Calendar (Index of Wills and Administrations), 1858–1966 [database on-line]. Provo, UT, USA: Ancestry.com Operations Inc, 2010. Original data: Principal Probate Registry. Calendar of the Grants of Probate and Letters of Administration made in the Probate Registries of the High Court of Justice in England. London, England © Crown copyright. Even allowing for inflation, this amount seems comparatively small, perhaps confirming that the Mattuck lifestyle was largely funded by Mayer family money. Alternatively, IIM may have passed most of his estate to his wife prior to his death.
73. Information from Jill Mattuck Tarule, 25 August 2013.
74. The Liberal Jewish Synagogue Religion School newsletter, 8 December 1955, LJS Archives.
75. Dr Leon Roth and W.A.L. Elmslie, *The Significance of Biblical Prophecy in Our Time*, *The Rabbi Mattuck Memorial Pamphlet No. 1* (London: London Society of Jews and Christians, 1955).
76. *Aspects of Progressive Jewish Thought* was published by the WUPJ in honour of Leo Baeck's 80th birthday in 1955. *Religion Can Help the World* was published by the World Congress of Faiths and edited by Arthur Peacock.
77. Israel Mattuck, *Progressive Judaism* (London: World Union for Progressive Judaism, c.1956).
78. Ibid., p.2.
79. *The American Israelite*, 29 May 1954, p.2.
80. *LJS Weekly Newsletter*, 2, 34 (18 April 1955).
81. Notes made by Dorothy Edgar, née Mattuck, dated 31 May 1999, MFAa. After Leslie Edgar's death in 1984, IIM's papers that had been held by him were distributed in various directions: some went to the LJS and from there a proportion were given to the London Metropolitan Archives; some were given to Rabbi John Rayner, who succeeded Leslie Edgar as Senior Rabbi at the LJS in the hope that he might write IIM's biography. Since this didn't happen, when John Rayner died, further papers relating to IIM were sent to the LJS Archives.

CHAPTER SIXTEEN

Mattuck the Man

This chapter explores IIM's character and his personal attributes. It draws on information from disparate sources: the memories of those who knew him, including those of family members that offer glimpses of IIM's personality not available to those who knew only his public persona; newspaper articles and letters; obituaries, tributes and eulogies. It aims to shed light on the way in which he went about his work, his relationships with others, his actions and his achievements. It also seeks to explain some of the difficulties he encountered and the ways in which he was less successful.

Perhaps the first thing to say about IIM is that he was an enormously powerful character. Most people who met him were struck by the sheer force of his personality, which, as we have seen, was evident from a very early age – in the way he negotiated with HUC, or in his assertive letters to Claude Montefiore before he took up his post at the LJS, for example. Almost without fail, IIM evoked respect and sometimes awe, even amongst family members.[1] Many of those who disagreed with his views and whom he challenged attested to his charisma and gravitas. People were always aware that they were in the presence of an outstanding and great man.[2] In a crowded room, IIM was not someone who would have been easily overlooked, despite his small stature.

As one of his early contemporaries during IIM's HUC years commented, he was destined to 'be somebody'. While it would be a mistake to suggest that IIM went out of his way to seek the limelight, he liked having an audience, was very comfortable in a public arena and was not fazed by the wide coverage his activities and pronouncements received. He may not have deliberately courted popularity, but nor did he shun fame.

Although he sometimes gave assurances to the contrary, IIM does seem to have been sensitive to the criticism of others to a greater extent than might have been anticipated of a man of his eminence and ability. IIM's private papers record the disappointment he sometimes felt when he did not receive the positive attention and reactions he believed he merited or were relevant. He appears to have needed regular reassurance from those whose opinion he respected, such as Claude Montefiore. We have learned of bouts of depression and of minor ailments that seem to have been engendered by criticism and feedback that took him by surprise. It is interesting to reflect on the fact that, despite his sensitivities, IIM chose to place himself in a marginal position and associate himself with an iconic movement, which meant that he was almost certain to come under fire and to face hostility. That he was willing to expose himself to uncomfortable criticism is testament to how passionately he felt about his beliefs.

Notwithstanding the episodes of angst, self-doubt and depression, particularly in his later years, IIM was generally regarded as being a cheerful person and as having a very attractive personality. Rabbi John Rayner, who knew him well, portrayed IIM as 'lovable and admirable'.[3] Other people have commented that, of the 'Three Ms', IIM was possibly the most engaging. It is reported that he applied his humour to encourage others and to prevent them from becoming weary when they met with disappointments.[4] He has been described as being 'good company' and reputedly was in great demand socially because of his wit and endless fund of anecdotes. IIM's passage into the higher echelons of British society may well have been eased by Claude Montefiore. However, once he was established, it was IIM's own charisma that enabled him to network and form friendships with prominent personalities both in the Jewish community and non-Jewish circles.

IIM adapted well to the peculiarities of English life and was comfortable with being in the company of the rich and famous. However, he also had 'the common touch', being able to establish a rapport with the immigrants that he met in the East End of London, the less wealthy members of the LJS, and the villagers where he had his country home. IIM had a wide circle of very close friends from many different walks of life, in Britain and across the world, including many non-Jews.

Although he was able to relate to all manner of people, IIM rarely mentioned his humble origins or his early life in Eastern Europe. There is some evidence to suggest that he may have been embarrassed by, or at least ambivalent towards those who had a similar background to his own, and that he wanted to distance himself from his roots. Throughout the ten years of his correspondence with his school friend Archie, IIM made no mention of the vast wave of immigration then occurring. When he gave addresses and sermons on immigration issues while still in America, he spoke passionately against immigration restriction and painted a graphic picture of the conditions from which Eastern European refugees were fleeing, but he did not allude to his own personal circumstances. Later on IIM referred to Britain as his 'second home' and to Worcester, Massachusetts as his 'home town', apparently holding no allegiance to the land of his birth, and fought continuously to retain his American citizenship. While he did not neglect to highlight the appalling hardships of Eastern Europeans during and after the First World War, he did not express any personal empathy with their plight. Indeed his close association with the English 'Cousinhood' seems to have caused him to downplay his background even more so than previously.

It might be posited from this discussion that IIM was somewhat snobbish: he spoke with admiration of the social circumstances of the German Jews he encountered in Cincinnati, Louisville and Lincoln; and when he came to England he speedily adopted the mores, lifestyle and manners of the well-to-do members of the LJS congregation (the country home, membership of the Athenaeum Club, patronage of numerous charitable bodies). However, a more generous interpretation of IIM's love of refinement may lie in another aspect of his personality – his ambition.

IIM was definitely driven. From a very young age he knew he wanted to be successful both socially and professionally. He had major ambitions and was seemingly fearless in seeking to achieve them: he did not just want to go to university, he wanted to enrol at the best; he did not just want to be a rabbi, he wanted to be a prominent one; he was not satisfied with leading a growing congregation in a suburb of New York, he set his sights on a pulpit in one of the most prestigious synagogues in Manhattan. After his arrival in London, we see IIM moving from one challenging goal to another. Initially his focus was on the LJS. He was not content with consolidating the congregation, he wanted it to be one of the largest in the land and to be housed in a magnificent building extensive enough to accommodate all aspects of congregational life. Once that was achieved, he set himself aims on wider and wider stages – developing the Liberal Jewish movement, gaining the respect of other faiths, working internationally.

Not only was IIM willing to acknowledge the extent of his ambition, he was positively proud of it and saw it as something others should seek to emulate. In an address he gave to young people shortly after his move to London, he shared with them his 'good start in life'. He spoke of the necessity of having 'powerful hopes' to achieve 'some modicum of success'. He warned that those who did not set goals ran the risk of being 'wrecked on the rocks of failure' and doomed to a future in which they 'drifted around aimlessly on the vast sea of life'. He opined that the greatest promise of success came to those who said to themselves 'I know what I want to do' and 'I know what I want to be'. Ambition was not something to be embarrassed about, it should be 'the first word in our lexicon'.[5]

IIM possessed many assets that enabled him to achieve his ambitions, not least of which was his boundless energy and propensity for hard work.

At the height of his career he led the largest congregation in Britain, travelled around the country delivering sermons and addresses, headed a growing religion school, taught and ran discussion groups, edited and wrote most of a substantial monthly journal, authored numerous pamphlets, helped to found new congregations, studied long into the night, chaired conferences and meetings, participated in the activities of numerous charities and societies, and still found time for leisure activities and for his family. He was willing to deal with strategic matters such as Liberal Jewish policy on topical issues, but also to attend to detailed organisational and administrative tasks. IIM emerged from the Second World War a tired and ailing man and was forced to slow down, but his tenacity kept him going and, even when he became very ill, he continued to study and write with fervour.

IIM was not just exacting of himself, but had high expectations of those with whom he worked. He was universally loved by his colleagues, but he sometimes left them exhausted. What was the source of this drive and energy? The answer to this question might lie in IIM's immigrant background. Unlike his close colleague, friend and mentor Claude Montefiore, who was born to wealth and status and whose life ran its course in an untroubled manner, IIM made seismic shifts both in lifestyle and belief. Within a few years of arriving in America, IIM seems to have developed a keen appreciation of the opportunities for education, advancement, material comfort and quality of life now open to him. His boundless energy enabled him to take advantage of the opportunities that came his way.

Although he was undeniably ambitious, IIM was never coldly calculating in seeking to achieve his ends. Nor does his success appear to have been obtained at the expense of others, and there is no doubting the sincerity of his pursuit of more lofty goals relating to service to God and the spreading of prophetic values. He is remembered as having been a kind man who willingly gave his time to support and advise others. There are many references to his wise counselling and practical sympathy; Lily Montagu for one regularly turned to him for spiritual and practical guidance and as a result of consulting him always felt 'stimulated and refreshed'.[6]

Notwithstanding his concern for others, IIM does seem to have been somewhat self-centred and self-indulgent. According to his family, he was very solicitous of his own health and well-being and was a 'fussy eater'.[7] However, it is easy to overlook such human frailties given his many gifts and talents, and he does deserve recognition for his outstanding attributes. IIM was highly intelligent and his educational achievements were quite remarkable given the fact that he is unlikely to have had any secular schooling prior to his emigration to America. He appears to have been proud of his attainments, often commenting that educational attainment was a particular characteristic of Jews from Eastern Europe.[8]

IIM is often lauded for his scholarship, which combined traditional Jewish learning with modern writings, and for his way of thinking along 'rational and logical lines'.[9] Throughout his career he yearned to spend more time on scholarly pursuits than he was able to due to the demands of his rabbinic role. While he appears to have derived immense satisfaction from studying and reading, he viewed it as being more than an enjoyable pastime – it was also a religious duty.[10] However, IIM's love of scholarship and learning was also a product of background. In the Eastern European Jewish community in which he was raised, male status was closely bound up with religious scholarship.

IIM was no distant and theoretical scholar; he used scholarship to further his various leadership roles and to solve concrete and topical problems and issues. He read widely to provide material for his sermons, lectures and addresses, which as a result covered an astounding variety of topics. He was a true polymath. No problem was too complex or too technical to receive his detailed attention. His son-in-law, Leslie Edgar, commented:

> It was an unforgettable experience to see Dr Mattuck grappling with a problem; the more worrying and perplexing, the more remarkable was it to see him grappling with it. Invariably, he found a solution, with imagination, originality and penetrating insight.[11]

Not one person who remembers IIM or gives an appraisal of his life fails to mention his extraordinary eloquence. IIM's ability to express himself orally, and perhaps to a lesser extent in writing, was definitely his genius. His sermons were 'in a class by themselves',[12] characterised by their intellectual penetration and infused with 'spiritual profundity'.[13] He had a skill for selecting the right words and stating things succinctly. He could disentangle the most complicated of matters so that they could be understood by everybody. His repeated use of metaphors and climaxes gave his sermons great power and even some of his strongest critics praised his ability to hold and sway an audience. He delivered his messages with passion, sincerity and drama, mesmerising young and old alike. Claude Montefiore was in awe of what he referred to as IIM's 'lucidity'. His preaching was at its finest when it was at its most risky – when he was applying Prophetic values to topical events and spoke of the Jewish obligation to right social wrongs.

Also noteworthy were IIM's leadership skills, especially in moulding the congregation of the LJS and providing the Liberal Jewish movement with a firm direction and vision. He was a consummate chairman of meetings, determined to deal with big issues, allowing those with differing views to put their point across and able to sum up complicated discussions in a few words. He was a fine and loved teacher of both young people and adults, and had great respect for those whom he taught, skilfully drawing out their views and revealing their abilities.

Dating back to his school days, IIM was a spirited and polished debater, and his debating skills proved invaluable in enabling him to convert detractors into disciples. IIM did not enter a debate with the aim of arguing for victory. He was no sitter on the fence, but showed that he understood the position of those who did not agree with him and that he desired nothing but a reasonable decision. He was not unkind or discourteous to those holding opposing views to his. However, he did condemn people he believed relegated truth to second place, who refused to face facts, or who appeared to be swayed unduly by emotional considerations or the opinions of others.

IIM was a first-class organiser and administrator, and although he heartily disliked fund-raising, he is often remembered as having been 'not a bad beggar'.[14] The first synagogue in St John's Wood Road was testament to his skills in attracting financial support. It was said of IIM that with his remarkable array of talents he could have been outstanding in any role he chose to pursue.[15] Was IIM aware of the extent of his skills and abilities? It seems that not only was he aware of his gifts, but he consciously used them to achieve his ends. Indeed, his awareness of and confidence in his talents sometimes made him appear, if not vain, perhaps a little arrogant, especially as a young man.

Although IIM was a rationalist and did not allow his feelings to cloud his judgement or to deflect him from what he saw as his mission, he was not lacking in emotion and sentiment. Despite the ocean that separated him, IIM seems to have retained a close relationship with at least one of his brothers (George), and he was undoubtedly deeply attached to his wife and children. He had an image of himself as a good family man and lived up to that image. He was deeply moved by the plight of his co-religionists in Eastern Europe, the victims of Nazism, and the sufferings of non-Jews. His distinctive liturgy and sermons were designed to appeal to the heart as well as the intellect. He was a man of many enthusiasms – the theatre, poetry, museums, playing golf, boating on the river – and a great lover of the country, flowers and art.

IIM appears to have been totally fearless in saying what he believed and adhering to his beliefs in the face of strong contrary opinions, criticism and resistance. He was also prepared to fight and make sacrifices for his convictions, the largest of which was possibly his decision to stay in Britain to serve the cause of Liberal Judaism when his heart and family were in America. The doggedness of IIM's beliefs was remarked upon from the time of his days at HUC and was an attribute admired by many of his followers. Rabbi John Rayner saw of IIM's perseverance and his determination to convey what he believed as 'nothing short of heroic'.[16] During the 1920s and 1930s IIM ventured again and again to challenge prejudice, even daring to take on the Chief Rabbi in various disagreements from which he did not emerge unscathed.

In many instances IIM was able to say what he felt without alienating his audience (witness the continued support of Kaufmann Kohler despite the extraordinarily forthright letters IIM wrote to him). However, his frankness sometimes upset people unnecessarily and placed obstacles in his path that made it more difficult for him to achieve his aims. Perhaps the difficulty was not in IIM's laudable commitment to speaking out, but his lack of sensitivity to timing and context. Using his own phraseology, he was a better missionary than diplomat. He was certainly intelligent and brave, but not always wise.

IIM was proud of being Jewish and found it difficult to comprehend the self-effacing nature of Anglo-Jewry and the reluctance of British Jews to proclaim their Jewish identity. However, he appeared to feel no pressing need to live in an exclusively Jewish area. While studying at Harvard, he was very keen to avoid the areas of Boston inhabited by recent immigrants from Russia. He did live in Jewish neighbourhoods in Cincinnati, Lincoln and New York, but these neighbourhoods were dominated by middle-class German Jews and were therefore a world apart from the Lithuanian *shtetl* where he was born and the semi-ghetto of Worcester where he grew up. When he came to England, the areas in London and Buckinghamshire where he made his home were areas where few Jews lived at that time. It may be surmised that living in non-Jewish areas perhaps gave him a feeling of alienation and made him more acutely aware of his Jewishness.

Mention must be made of IIM's private life. There are many references to IIM opening his home to colleagues and congregants. 'Wildwood' was the setting for many garden parties and 'at homes'. His wife and his daughter Dorothy were very involved in synagogue life and IIM made several close friends from the LJS congregation. However, he does seem to have been at the same time a very private man; he rarely spoke about himself, even in correspondence with close family members and long-standing friends. In his sermons and his addresses he discussed freely ideas and theories, philosophy and social science, ethics and aesthetics. However, it is almost impossible to extract from them anything meaningful about IIM personally.

Throughout his life IIM sought to maintain a certain distance between his domestic and professional life. During his early years in Britain, he placed a high value on the time that he was able to spend with his wife and children at his home in the countryside and sometimes resented leaving his family and having to travel to town for professional reasons.[17] Even when his commitments became immense, he ensured that he was able to take time off from his duties for holidays and to relax. He was outgoing, sociable and hospitable, but he also needed private space.

From all of this we can conclude that IIM was very human; whereas both Claude Montefiore and Lily Montagu were pious, bordering on the saintly, IIM lived very much in the real world – although, as we are about to discuss, he was a man of deep spirituality and unconquerable faith. He had vision and insight, he was given to elevated thoughts and his gaze was sometimes fixed on the eternal, but he was no paragon. He was fallible and he had his foibles, his ideas were limited by the thinking of the age in which he lived, his standards were exacting and he was sometimes tenacious to the point of obstinacy. Nevertheless, he was a highly gifted man who excelled in many different ways and had some superlative qualities of both mind and spirit, and who therefore deserves to be remembered with veneration.

NOTES

1. Conversation with Robert Edgar, 30 April 2012.
2. Rabbi Leslie I. Edgar, 'A Personal Appreciation', 'Rabbi Dr Israel Mattuck', *LJM, In Memoriam, Israel I. Mattuck, 1883–1954* (June 1954), p.4.
3. John Rayner, 'The Legacy of Israel Mattuck', sermon given at the service in memory of Rabbi Dr Israel I. Mattuck, at South London Liberal Synagogue, 11 April 1954, LJS Archives, Box 135c.
4. The Hon. Lily H. Montagu, 'Rabbi Dr Israel I. Mattuck, Memorial Tribute', *LJM, In Memoriam*, p.2.
5. 'Starts in Life', sermon given by IIM at the LJS, 7 April 1912, Montagu Centre Collection (MCC).
6. See Montagu, 'Rabbi Dr Israel I. Mattuck, Memorial Tribute', p.2.
7. Conversation with Jill Mattuck Tarule, 7 October 2012.
8. For example see 'The Jew To-day: Discussion of a Friendly Christian View (with reference to "The Jew Today" by Sidney Dark)', sermon given by IIM at the LJS, 4 March 1934, MCC.
9. Draft of article by Dorothy M. Edgar, 'Some Recollections of Rabbi Dr Israel I. Mattuck and Rabbi Dr Leslie I. Edgar', Mattuck Family Archive kept by Robert Edgar (MFAb).
10. Israel I. Mattuck, *The Essentials of Liberal Judaism* (London: Routledge and Keegan Paul, Ltd, 1953), p.11.
11. See Edgar, 'A Personal Appreciation', p.5.
12. See Montagu, 'Rabbi Dr Israel I. Mattuck, Memorial Tribute', p.2.
13. See Edgar, 'A Personal Appreciation', p.3.
14. 'Dr Mattuck's Seventieth Birthday', *LJM*, XXV, no.2 (February 1954), p.25.
15. See Edgar, 'A Personal Appreciation', p.5.
16. See Rayner, 'The Legacy of Israel Mattuck'.
17. Tape recording of the diary kept by IIM between January and April 1918 read by IIM's daughter, Dorothy Edgar, née Mattuck, MFAb.

CHAPTER SEVENTEEN

Mattuck's Religious Outlook

To all his endeavours IIM brought a religious outlook that combined a personal piety and simple theology with a radical view of the purpose of Jewish existence and the future of Progressive Judaism. Some of IIM's religious beliefs have been touched upon in the course of telling his life story, but here they are explored in greater detail.

Belief in God

IIM said that religion was not just a communal affair; it was also a matter of personal belief and 'the good Jew is a religious Jew'.[1] He saw personal faith as enlarging life and giving it meaning; to be without it would be to miss 'glory and honour'.[2] IIM was 'God intoxicated' and the commandment 'Thou shall love the Lord thy God with all thy heart and soul and might' was of paramount importance to him.[3] Jews might disagree about certain aspects of their faith, but the existence of God was incontrovertible.[4] Central to IIM's belief in God was avowal of the single, omnipresent, ethical God. In keeping with Jewish tradition, God was non-physical and concerned alike with the fate of the Jewish people and humanity in general.

God's existence did not require great definition; God guided and ruled the universe without a comparable opponent, and any description of God's attributes was but 'an attempt to put into words our limited human apprehension'.[5] God's qualities included love and justice – including the threat of punishment for sin – perfection, power that arises from nature and eternity in time and space.[6] To IIM, belief in God involved the whole person with intellectual and emotional beliefs combining to create a relationship with God.[7] However, he acknowledged that this relationship might be hard to attain since God was revealed fragmentarily and God's essence remained a mystery.[8]

Prayer, both individual and collective, was important to IIM as a means for 'feeling in the presence of God.[9] In his first Shabbat sermon at the LJS he declared that prayer was 'the soul's expression of its longing for the divine', which both vitalised and strengthened faith. There was not only 'a prayer of words', but also 'a prayer in deeds'.[10] However, although prayer was as important to IIM as food and drink, it was only a starting point leading to the love of humankind.[11] He was critical of excessive personal piety and abhorred the concept of reward and punishment.[12] Public worship was of the utmost importance; it was the 'chief act' of a religious community, which could not exist without it, just as an army could not function with only scattered soldiers.[13] However, it was also essential that prayer should be practised in the Jewish home as 'an exercise of faith in God'.[14]

To IIM, faith was not only a source of comfort; love of God also meant 'obedience to His Law', which he said had a special meaning to Liberal Jews. It meant obedience to 'all of the revelations of righteousness and truths that have come from God', but while some ideas transcended temporal contexts, such as those set down in the *Shema,* others were no longer relevant to modern life, such as those on polygamy and slavery.[15] His view was that God 'reveals his law progressively to mankind, teaching men more of truth and righteousness as they develop and can learn more',[16] that is the belief in 'progressive revelation', which is what rendered Progressive Judaism fundamentally different from Orthodox Judaism. On some matters, such as the dietary laws, Progressive Judaism allowed individuals to come to their own decisions 'with an instructed Jewish Conscience'.[17]

At various times IIM cited nature and its creation, the advance of human society and the guidance of Jewish history as reasons for his faith in God. However, he believed that the ultimate reason for faith was 'something in ourselves which finds intellectual and emotional satisfaction in that faith'.[18]

From IIM's belief in the supreme importance of faith, it followed that religion must not only be practised, but practised on a consistent basis. Faith was not merely a statement of intent and occasional doses of religion would not do; faith was not 'a medicine which is needed sometimes, it is like food and air which are needed constantly'.[19] The practise of religion also involved sacrifice, pursuing a mode of life that 'forgoes physical pleasures for the sake of a better life of the spirit'.[20]

Rationalism

The 'classical' Reform Judaism to which IIM adhered was heavily influenced by nineteenth-century rationalism. In IIM's words this 'imposed a desire for logical consistency in religious thought and religious life'.[21] For IIM, belief in God was compatible with both scientific endeavour and with Biblical criticism. He affirmed God's creative power and its compatibility with Darwin's theory of evolution – evolution is God's method of creation.[22] However, IIM's belief was not sustained alone by 'scientific method'; it was also evidenced by the nature of man and the universe.[23] He once said that while some people found it sufficient to 'feel God', others like him 'have to think Him'.[24]

By the 1920s the pendulum was beginning to swing in the other direction, and IIM, in parallel with his American peers, started to give more credence to the emotional aspects of religion. He continued to reject belief in miracles, divine interventions or breaches of natural law, but he was now willing to accord them a certain psychological value.[25] He also reconsidered the role of mysticism in religion, conceding that 'a certain amount of mysticism is indispensable to religious life',[26] albeit that mysticism alone was inadequate for union with God.[27]

However, IIM remained unconvinced of the religious value of spiritualism. He was aware that spiritualism had increased in prominence during the First World War, offering as it did 'a tangible consolation against immeasurable sorrow',[28] yet he could find no concrete evidence to support it and particularly disliked modern forms of spiritualism, denying as they did the value of human reason as a guide to reality and truth. As an example of modern spiritualism, IIM pointed to the fatalism in Thomas Hardy's novels, which depicted life under the domination of irrational forces.[29] He felt that such beliefs degraded God and derogated from God's moral character.[30]

Prophetic Values

Although IIM was the product of a rationalist era in religious history, underneath his somewhat austere logicality there burnt a spiritual passion not dissimilar to that of the Prophets to whose teachings he was devoted, and who were the source of his many addresses on social issues. The Liberal Judaism he promulgated for over forty years, apart from providing strength and guidance for life and rousing the spirit to approach God, impelled Jewish people to work for a social order that showed respect for the human personality and respected the equal rights of all members of society, especially the right to live life with dignity.[31] To IIM, social salvation was more important than individual salvation.[32] While Liberal Judaism rejected the concept of the coming of the personal Messiah, it did affirm the hope of a messianic age, progress towards which Jews must contribute by seeking to improve the world and freeing it from evil.[33] It was this messianic perspective that accounted for what IIM called his 'persistent optimism'.

IIM saw the Prophets as holding 'a supremely important place in the history of Judaism'.[34] He credited them with differentiating Judaism from other religions of antiquity, and also with enabling 'the ancient Hebrews to survive a national destruction like that which ended completely the history of many other small ancient nations'.[35] Since the Prophets were characterised by 'a mighty faith and an urgent moral zeal',[36] their ideals transcended the ages. The Prophets had an intense awareness of God that enabled them to attain spiritual and moral heights whilst 'remaining in the framework of human life'.[37] They did not claim a divine quality for themselves, but divine inspiration and therefore divine authority for what they said.[38]

The substance of the prophetic messages was that 'ethical conduct establishes the bond between the individual and God so a community is brought into relation with God by the ethical quality of its corporate life.'[39] IIM perceived that there should be no disparity between the ethical life required of an individual and the conditions necessary for an ethical society. He pointed out that the Prophets 'never thought of the community apart from its individuals and never thought of its individuals except in community'[40] And for 'society to fulfil its obligations, individuals must fulfil their duties'.[41]

Just as the Hebrew Prophets lambasted the religious institutions of the society in which they lived, so IIM called for 'an effective alliance between the working man and the institutions of religion', noting that their current separateness meant the 'loss to the cause of social betterment.'[42] He believed that acting in concert they could 'raise the estate of all men to obliterate the strife which divides men from men' and 'lead society some steps nearer toward the goal of perfection for which it is destined.'[43]

The Jewish 'Mission'

The teachings of the Prophets were not only the source of the emphasis that IIM placed on ethical conduct, they were also the source of his belief in Jewish universalism, combining as they did love for the people of Israel with concern for mankind in general. The so-called 'mission of Israel' was a cardinal dogma among American Reform rabbis at the time of IIM's rabbinic training, and was a prominent theme in his sermons and addresses, from his early days at the LJS until long after it had ceased to be discussed by his American colleagues. According to IIM, the doctrine held that the Jewish Diaspora was a providential act of God that made it possible for Jews to bring their religious and moral messages to the rest of the world.[44] Israel's dispersion was not a misfortune; it was a means for the performance of Israel's divine task.[45] The universalism of Liberal Judaism also obliged it 'to accept gladly sincere proselytes'.[46]

When explaining the concept of the 'mission impulse' to the LJS congregation, IIM was at pains to point out that Jews were the 'chosen people' not because they had been granted special privileges; they had been allocated the special task of communicating the spiritual legacy transmitted to them by God.[47] However, this 'chosen-ness' was tempered by the 'liberalism of the modern age', which meant that Judaism could not proclaim the superiority of its message over other religions.[48] It was simply the case that Jews had been 'entrusted with something of the truth' and felt 'impelled to share that truth with others'.[49]

IIM was committed to interfaith dialogue, respectful of other monotheistic faiths and preached tolerance of differing viewpoints. Nevertheless, there was a messianic flavour to IIM's belief in the irreplaceable purpose of Jews to lead the nations of the world to a more Godly existence. On one occasion he averred that 'Judaism was the first [faith] that dared utter for itself the hope of a universal acceptance',[50] and on another observed that 'as the genius of Rome [was] for jurisprudence, of Greece for art, of the Anglo-Saxons for government', so Israel's was for religion.[51]

IIM believed that, on account of their 'special' role, it was vital that Jews retain their separate identity, however universal the message of Judaism might be. He argued that it was through their distinctive organised religion and their particularistic institutions that Jews were able to demonstrate 'the eternal and universally applicable message in the Jewish religion'[52] and participate actively in the universal task of ushering in a better age. He emphasised the role of synagogues in disseminating the universal appeal of Judaism, but only if they divested themselves of outmoded observances.[53] Liberal Judaism had a particularly important role to play in disseminating the universal value of Judaism by 'giving the eternal principles of the Jewish religion a modern framework'.[54]

Attitude to Tradition

It was 'the mission of Israel' that informed IIM's attitude to traditional practices and customs in Judaism. He had little time for the 'romanticism that drew delight from the contemplation of the familiar and old usages'.[55] Jewish ethics were of a far higher order than Jewish traditions, which as 'oriental trappings' could obscure both the truth and beauty of Judaism.[56] In his inaugural address at the LJS he articulated his vision for Liberal Judaism, stressing that Liberalism meant complete freedom of thought and practice. Fully evident in IIM's sermon was his passionate belief in Judaism – not any particular formulation of it but the spirit of Judaism: 'which is deeper than the words in books, subtler than the commands of codes, loftier than the rites of priests, but it has in a measure inspired them all ... as the soul is greater than the body; the form perishes, but the spirit endures for ever'.[57] The aim of Liberal Judaism, he said, was to:

> interpret the spirit of Judaism in the light of the age and to fix the attention upon the spirit and away from the letter. [We] accept only that of tradition which [we] can honestly and sincerely accept as valid. [We] study it as a fact of history and eliminate it from religion when it has no significance for life. What we cannot accept on present day evidence we cannot accept on the dictum of tradition.[58]

Unlike his more radical American Reform Colleagues, such as Emil G. Hirsch, who promulgated a break with traditional Judaism, IIM saw Liberal Judaism as being firmly grafted to the old trunk of traditional Judaism: 'The past is our inspiration. The engine that drives the boat is at its rear but the pilot stands on the forward parts; so religion inspired by the past must be directed and guided forward.'[59]

Although he was later to state that he had been brought up in Orthodox Judaism and therefore had no inclination 'to criticise it, to throw stones, so to speak, at the rock whence I was hewn, to assault with arguments the belief that basically influenced my personal development',[60] in the early years of his career at the LJS he did launch a number of strong challenges against traditional Judaism. Just a few months after his arrival he noted the growth in the number of indifferent Jews, including the 'two days per year' ones,[61] and expressed his concern about the absence of real, spiritual piety that might influence conduct in a way that mere observances would not. He condemned religion which took 'no cognisance of the facts of life and ignored the challenge of science', which considered 'life in general altogether below its sphere and unworthy of consideration', and which made its business with 'higher and greater things than the incidents in the struggling and striving and working life of mere men'.[62] He further castigated dishonesty and hypocrisy, and reminded his listeners that it was the duty of religion 'to accept the facts which science, history and life present and to interpret them'.[63]

IIM had high expectations on the role of Liberal Judaism. At his first Rosh Hashana service at the LJS, he told his new congregation: 'Ye are not worthy Jews if ye strive not to be above the common. The effectiveness of Judaism in the history or the movements of the world is being weakened by the indifference of those who are in name its adherents.'[64] Indifference could be displayed by disassociation or could be concealed 'under a cloak of piety'.[65] He deplored those Jews who joined synagogues without giving a 'thought to the inner interests of the Jewish faith'[66] and staunchly defended Liberal Judaism against its critics, who seemingly, he said, never wearied in pointing to what they called 'the easiness of Liberal Judaism'.[67] He perceived that the critics thought only in terms of ceremonies and overlooked the fact that Liberal Jews were required to study the history and the literature of Judaism.[68] He also reminded opponents that 'the price of liberty is eternal vigilance', that freedom meant responsibility, and making rational choices was more demanding than simply accepting tradition.[69] Liberal Judaism was not simply 'Orthodox Judaism minus something'; it was Judaism 'enlarged and enriched with the knowledge of the present'.[70]

IIM had little patience with the full gamut of traditional rites and ceremonies that were often adhered to with 'a spirit of artificiality and hollow sham'.[71] He rejected the view that ceremonies were commanded and sacramental, pointing out that the Prophets had taught that they were unimportant and transitory in nature.[72] He sought to impress upon the LJS congregation 'a clearer understanding of the exact place which these elements occupy in religious life'.[73] Although it was 'the right and duty of the individual to decide for himself', he said that he personally objected to those 'rites and ceremonies that were 'ugly and out of date, repulsive or meaningless'. However, he admitted to enjoying those 'that have an element of beauty, and those whose meaning is not objectionable'.[74]

He preached that any observances followed by Liberal Jews should have an elevating character and 'be in perfect harmony with their own mode of life, or else they would lead to superstition or idolatry'.[75] He counselled that a ritual's significance should be clear and not require detailed explanation and that care should be taken to avoid the 'elaborate frills with which many rites are trimmed ...; weighting them down with tinsel destroys their life and cannot touch the heart because the heart loves the language of simplicity'.[76]

On other occasions, IIM spoke less critically of rites and ceremonies, saying they were a visible sign of historic continuity, could enhance the spiritual life of the individual and stimulate loyalty to Judaism and to God.[77] While acknowledging a lack of unanimity amongst Liberal Jews on which ceremonies should be retained, he expected the Sabbath, the main Jewish festivals and the Holydays to be observed.[78] When Liberal Judaism was criticised by the novelist Israel Zangwill in his book, *Voice of Jerusalem*, for the retention of some characteristics that seemed to the author to be narrowly Jewish, IIM defended his position saying that a religion without institutions risked the 'loss of influence, partly through vagueness, partly too through crudeness'.[79]

The Jewish People

We have seen that opposition to Zionism was a consistent theme in IIM's career. To IIM Jewish nationalism negated the historic character of the Jews as a people of religion and destroyed the uniqueness of Judaism. This belief was explored in detail in *What are the Jews?*, which was published at a time when Zionism was becoming increasingly prominent in Anglo-Jewry, leading IIM to fear it would undermine other views of Jewish life. In the book, IIM rejected the idea of the Jews as either a race or a nation. He concluded that 'if there ever was a Jewish race, it must long ago have lost its racial homogeneity through intermarriage and conversion'.[80] Although he accepted that the Jews had initially existed as a nation, he pointed out that for 2,500 years Jews had been dispersed to many lands and that if any national unity remained, it was merely 'the memory of an ancient life in a common land'.[81]

The main tenet of IIM's view of the Jews was that, despite the Diaspora, they had remained united by their faith, and divided only by the language and mores of the countries in which they lived. He argued that any discrimination that Jews experienced, including anti-Semitism, arose from their religious distinctiveness and their minority status rather than any national or racial differences.[82] IIM perceived that, while a Jewish homeland might solve 'the Jewish Problem' for the Jews living in it, to the Jews in other lands it would bring no political gain, and might even create dangers for them.[83]

IIM accepted that the religious conception of Jewish life 'did not necessarily exclude the promotion of Jewish nationalism.'[84] There were, nevertheless, certain principles that prevented Liberal Jews from becoming Zionists. Liberal Judaism emphasised the universal character of Judaism and strove to give it full expression; it had consciously abandoned the connection between Judaism and Palestine, aiming instead to make 'Judaism at home in every land'. [85] In addition, IIM noted that, in common with many Orthodox Jews, Liberal Judaism was opposed to the growing secularisation of the Zionist movement,[86] which detracted from the religious function and value of Jewish life. He was adamant that the world would be the spiritually poorer if the Jewish religion were to die.[87]

IIM was sympathetic to the philanthropic aims of Zioism, although he perceived that these efforts would always have a limited impact.[88] He expressed some support for the Zionist claim that, in a Jewish national homeland, the social teachings of Judaism might find their full and clear expression and provide a model to be followed by humanity in general.[89] He also acknowledged that an accommodation between Liberal Judaism and Zionism might theoretically be possible if Zionism were to recognise 'the primacy of the Jewish religion in Jewish life'.[90]

The Problem of Evil and Enduring Faith

One of the most striking aspects of IIM's personal faith was his uncompromising commitment to seeking out, speaking and putting into action what he saw as being 'the truth'. His favourite quotation was the rabbinic dictum 'truth is God's seal'.[91] Truth was not something aside from faith that might either corroborate or refute it; it was the very essence of religion, the use of God's gift in the service of God.[92] To him, Liberal Judaism, more than any other religion, combined religion with truth because it opened Judaism to growing knowledge. Liberal Judaism sought to make Judaism synonymous with truth.[93]

Nevertheless, IIM admitted that there would always be limitations to human knowledge and some problems might always remain unsolved; man could never presume to know everything.[94] The limitations to human knowledge particularly applied to what he called 'the problem of evil': if God represented perfect goodness and was the creator of the world, why did evil exist, why did men suffer and why did they sin?

IIM found a partial explanation for the problem of evil in the Book of Job, where Job was instructed to accept the 'no knowing' and to retain his trust in God.[95] IIM also referred to the purposeful agony of Isaiah's Suffering Servant.[96] For IIM, the history of the Jews provided an outstanding example of the concept of suffering in the service of God.[97] However, ultimately IIM relied upon the argument of free will.[98] He pointed out that there was also much to be thankful for in the world and that it was not only evil that needed explanation; goodness too must be explained.[99] Despite the fact that most men succumbed to sin, as the child of God, man was 'naturally imbued with the knowledge of the Law of God'.[100] IIM's high valuation of the human personality pervades his sermons and writings.

To IIM, the existence of evil challenged faith but could not destroy it.[101] Notwithstanding the cruelty he lived through, IIM's essentially simple faith remained unshakeable. Even when life was hard, the hardships could not conceal God's goodness to those who, like IIM, revered him. Until his dying day, IIM's faith still gave him, 'A constant feeling that there is something to live for, that life always has meaning and value, with all the strength courage and joy that come from it.'[102] He retained his belief in spiritual, human and moral progress and adhered to the 'daring affirmation' central to Judaism that 'this is a good world'.[103] He drew attention to the abolition of slavery and child labour and many other examples of advances in society, which he saw as resulting from the influence and guidance of God.[104] In a broadcast on the BBC's Home Service in 1950 he reflected:

> In the last analysis all our knowledge has in it an element of faith. We can never be sure that we know anything but we live by convictions to which faith gives the power of certainty. For life demands positive affirmation. We cannot live with an eternal

> question mark. And faith in God makes an affirmation about the universe which makes sense of human life.[105]

From his final public addresses it is possible to detect that, by the end of his life, IIM had accepted that Liberal Judaism had not achieved its potential as 'the religion of the future' because of the eclipse of liberalism by authoritarianism. He may also have sensed that progress in the 1950s did not mean the same as it did when he arrived in England. However, in one of his final sermons he reaffirmed his commitment to the essence of Liberal Judaism and spoke movingly about how presenting Judaism as a universal religion had been 'an adventure of faith' and how 'only through such adventures can religion attain to its full power and perhaps maintain an effective life'.[106]

Reflection on IIM's Religious Beliefs

We have seen that IIM's faith was relatively simple yet profound, and striking for its consistency, rationality and endurance. He articulated it with passion and precision. However, what is distinctive about IIM's religious outlook is the gifted and radical way in which he brought his beliefs to bear on social, economic and political issues of his day and the sheer determination with which he sought to establish a revolutionary religious outlook in an alien environment. His theology was totally in keeping with the 'classical' Reform Judaism he espoused as a young man and in his sermons, addresses and writings there were few discernible points of departure from the tenets of the Pittsburgh Platform. But while IIM's religious outlook per se may not have been particularly original, what he chose to do with it and the genius he had for expressing it made him an important and outstanding historical figure.

NOTES

1. 'The Place of Religion in Human Life', sermon given by IIM on Yom Kippur 1953 at the LJS, Montagu Centre Collection (MCC).
2. Ibid. Here he is quoting from the author of Psalm 8.
3. Israel I. Mattuck, *The Essentials of Judaism from the Liberal Jewish Point of View* (London: ULPS, 1946), p.1.
4. Israel I. Mattuck, *The Essentials of Liberal Judaism* (London: ULPS, 1947) p.1.
5. Ibid., p.9.
6. Ibid., pp.10–16.
7. 'The Faith of a Modern Jew: 1 God', notes on a sermon given by IIM at the LJS, 28 April 1940, MCC.
8. Ibid.
9. See Mattuck, *The Essentials of Liberal Judaism*, p.83.
10. 'The Place of the Synagogue in Modern Life', sermon given by IIM at the LJS, 26 January 1912, MCC.
11. Ibid.
12. Ibid.

13. See Mattuck, *The Essentials of Judaism from the Liberal Jewish Point of View*, p.6.
14. Ibid., p.6.
15. Ibid., p.3.
16. Ibid., p.3.
17. 'The Fundamentals of Progressive Judaism', address written by IIM for the World Union Youth Manual written in 1953 and published in Israel I. Mattuck, *Progressive Judaism* (London: World Union for Progressive Judaism, 1956), p.14.
18. See Mattuck, *The Essentials of Liberal Judaism*, p.28.
19. See 'The Place of Religion in Human Life'.
20. Ibid.
21. 'Liberal Judaism in the United States', sermon given by IIM at the LJS, 27 January 1923, MCC.
22. See 'The Fundamentals of Progressive Judaism', p.12.
23. 'The Faith of a Jew', broadcast by IIM on the BBC Overseas Services, in *LJM,* XVIII, no. 8 (October 1947), pp.57–9.
24. See 'The Faith of a Modern Jew: 1 God'.
25. See Mattuck, *The Essentials of Liberal Judaism,* pp.34–9.
26. See 'Liberal Judaism in the United States'.
27. Ibid.
28. 'What should be our attitude to spiritualism?', sermon given by IIM at the LJS, 17 March 1929, MCC.
29. Ibid.
30. Ibid.
31. See Mattuck, *The Essentials of Judaism from the Liberal Jewish Point of View,* p.10.
32. 'The Social Teaching of Liberal Judaism', sermon given by IIM at the LJS, 12 May 1912, MCC.
33. See Mattuck, *The Essentials of Judaism from the Liberal Jewish Point of View,* p.10.
34. Israel I. Mattuck, *The Thought of the Prophets* (London: Allen and Unwin, 1953), p.15.
35. Ibid., p.15.
36. Ibid., p.16.
37. Ibid., p.27.
38. Ibid., pp.36–7.
39. Israel I. Mattuck, *Jewish Ethics* (London: Hutchinson's University Library, 1953), p.28.
40. Ibid., p.30.
41. Ibid., p.83.
42. 'The Ideals of Labour', sermon given by IIM at the LJS on 11 March 1913, MCC.
43. Ibid.
44. 'Liberal Judaism and the Future of the Jews', sermon given by IIM at the LJS, 28 October 1916, MCC.
45. Ibid.
46. See 'The Fundamentals of Progressive Judaism', p.18.
47. 'Liberal Judaism and the Mission of the Jews', sermon given by IIM at the LJS, 30 May 1914, MCC.
48. Ibid.
49. Ibid.
50. 'Judaism as a Universal Religion', sermon given by IIM at the LJS, 15 March 1912, MCC.
51. See 'Liberal Judaism and the Mission of the Jews'.
52. Ibid.
53. Ibid.
54. See Mattuck, *The Essentials of Judaism from the Liberal Jewish Point of View,* p.11.
55. See 'Liberal Judaism in the United States'.
56. Ibid.
57. 'What is Liberal Judaism?', inaugural sermon given by IIM at the LJS, 20 January 1912, MCC.
58. Ibid.
59. Ibid.
60. 'Judaism', address given by IIM in Dublin, January 1946 at the consecration of the synagogue, MCC.
61. 'Freedom in Religion', sermon given by IIM at the LJS, on Passover, 1 April 1912, in ibid.
62. 'The Need for a Liberal Interpretation of Judaism', sermon given by IIM at the LJS, 31 January 1913, in ibid.

63. Ibid.
64. Ibid.
65. Ibid.
66. Ibid.
67. 'Liberal Judaism and the Jewish Tradition', sermon given by IIM at the LJS, 3 March 1917, MCC.
68. Ibid.
69. Ibid.
70. 'The Task of Liberal Judaism', sermon given by IIM at the International Conference of Liberal Jews, at the LJS, 10 July 1926, in Israel I. Mattuck, *Progressive Judaism*, p.8.
71. 'Our Attitude to Ceremonies', sermon given by IIM at the LJS, 11 April 1913, MCC.
72. Ibid.
73. Ibid.
74. 'The Religion of the Future', sermon given by IIM at the LJS, 27 June 1925, MCC.
75. 'Essentials and Non Essentials in Judaism', sermon given by IIM at the LJS, 9 May 1910, in ibid.
76. See 'Our Attitude to Ceremonies'.
77. 'The Place of Tradition in Liberal Judaism', sermon given by IIM at the LJS, 14 February 1920, MCC.
78. See 'Essentials and Non Essentials in Judaism'.
79. 'Liberal Judaism as a Universal Religion', sermon given by IIM at the LJS, 12 November 1921, MCC.
80. I.I. Mattuck, *What are the Jews? Their Significance and Position in the Modern World* (London: Hodder and Stoughton, 1939), p.34.
81. Ibid., p.50.
82. Ibid., p.121.
83. Ibid., pp.131–2.
84. Ibid., pp.131–2.
85. Ibid., p.214.
86. Ibid., p.215.
87. Ibid., p.252.
88. Ibid., p.127.
89. Ibid., p.227.
90. Ibid., p.215.
91. John Rayner 'The Legacy of Israel Mattuck', sermon given at the service in memory of Rabbi Dr Israel I. Mattuck, at South London Liberal Synagogue, 11 April 1954, LJS Archives, Box 135c.
92. John Rayner, 'The Spirit of Israel Mattuck', sermon given by Rabbi John Rayner at the LJS, 25 January 1992, LJS Archives, Box 135c.
93. See 'The Task of Liberal Judaism', p.6.
94. See Mattuck, *The Essentials of Liberal Judaism*, p.40.
95. Ibid., pp.41–2.
96. Ibid., p.45.
97. Ibid., p.46.
98. Ibid., pp.43–7.
99. Ibid., p.47.
100. See 'The Fundamentals of Progressive Judaism', p.19.
101. See 'The Faith of a Jew'.
102. See Mattuck, *The Essentials of Judaism from the Liberal Jewish Point of View*, p.2.
103. 'This is a Good World', sermon given by IIM at the LJS, 8 February 1912, MCC.
104. See Mattuck, *The Essentials of Liberal Judaism*, p.67.
105. 'The Living God', transcript of IIM's interview for the BBC for the series, *Man Without God*, 26 October 1950, MCC.
106. 'Judaism and the Future', sermon given by IIM at the Diamond Jubilee service at the LJS, 19 October 1952, in ibid.

CHAPTER EIGHTEEN

Mattuck's Legacy and Place in History

IIM came of age at a time when Jewish religious orthodoxy was beginning to be questioned amongst Eastern European Jews in America. It had worked in the segregated, closed environment of the virulently anti-Semitic Russian Empire, but was less suited to the New World. Many of the children of Jewish immigrants from Eastern Europe felt alienated by the traditionalism of their parents and were drifting into a secular mode of life. The trend was reinforced by the fact that an increasing proportion of the Eastern European Jewish people emigrating to America had by now distanced themselves from Judaism. A large proportion of the second generation of Eastern European Jews who retained their faith adopted the emerging branch of American Judaism that became known as Conservative Judaism. According to Michael A. Meyer, a much smaller number, like IIM, opted for Reform Judaism.[1] In making the transition when he did, he was something of a pioneer and there would have been few role models to support him in making the dramatic shift.

We have seen that IIM embraced the culture of the German Jews with whom he socialised at Harvard and took a relatively low-key approach to his Jewish identity. The sons of Eastern European immigrants entering Harvard as students a year or so after IIM were less willing to do so. Only a year after IIM left Harvard these students, who formed a small but noticeable presence there, founded what was to become known as the Harvard Menorah Society, the aim of which was to 'foster the study of Jewish History and Culture'.[2] In contrast to the informal Jewish group in which IIM had participated, the Menorah Society, championed by Horace Kallen and Henry Hurwitz,[3] sought to celebrate Hebraic culture publicly and to encourage Jewish students to take pride in being Jewish.

Although the founding members of the Menorah Society wore their Jewish identity openly at a time of increasing discrimination at Harvard, the group explicitly eschewed establishing a religious organisation as this might have threatened their quest to belong to the main student body.[4] Instead the Menorah Society likened itself to other organisations on campus that promoted particular cultures – the society rejected the use of Yiddish language in its proceedings and aligned itself with the European intellectual traditions originating among German Jews in the nineteenth century.[5] Class aspirations remained paramount. While perhaps understanding the social status concerns of the early members of the Menorah Society, IIM would have been uncomfortable both with their Zionist tendencies and their downplaying of religious belief.

IIM studied at HUC during a troubled period in the college's history, as Kaufmann Kohler sought to impose on the faculty his vision of a universal Jewish culture. By the time Kohler had achieved his aim, his outlook was already beginning to lose its appeal and to become outdated. IIM entered HUC just a few years too early to form part of the cohort of Eastern European students who were transformed by their experience at the college into 'classical' Reform Jews, but who as rabbis went on to transform the Reform movement during the 1930s.[6] This cohort, which included amongst its numbers Abba Hillel Silver and Solomon Freehof, 'sent the movement heading back toward a greater identification with Jewish tradition and the rest of the Jewish community'.[7] In contrast to those who followed him, IIM continued to espouse the theology and spirit that Kohler propounded for the remainder of his career.[8] IIM's position in the history of HUC is therefore very similar to his position in the history of Jewish students at Harvard – he was on the cusp of change. It is perhaps symbolic that when he was ordained in 1910, he was in a class of his own: his ordination marked the division between one generation of rabbis and another.

In America IIM was one of the last, if not *the* last, in a line of Jewish religious radicals. When he came to England his ideas and views were regarded as highly controversial, since the reform of traditional Judaism had barely begun and was being resisted to the utmost degree by most of Anglo-Jewry. Whereas in America IIM was in the rearguard of developments, in England he was a pioneer, a stranger in a strange land upholding an unpopular cause. He was widely regarded as an oddity not only for his American accent and mannerisms, but also because of the novelty of his religious outlook. Judging by press coverage following his arrival, Anglo-Jewry was perplexed by IIM and he in turn was equally perplexed by the criticism and hostility he encountered.

When IIM accepted the 'call' to England, America was at the crest of a wave of optimism and this spirit, reinforced by his Judaism, accompanied IIM across the Atlantic Ocean. He could not possibly have predicted the turbulent times and world-changing events that he was to live through over the four decades of his career in Britain's – two world wars, the Holocaust and the foundation of the State of Israel. History was to betray the Jews and IIM's belief in universal humanity.

IIM also lived through colossal social and intellectual change. He was 'catapulted into a maelstrom of political passions and ideological storms'[9] as nineteenth-century liberalism became eclipsed by the totalitarian movements of fascism and communism, the rivalry between which led to human suffering – especially Jewish suffering – beyond anything that IIM might have imagined when he set foot on English soil. In addition, he witnessed the transformation of Anglo-Jewry. When he arrived in London, Jewish affairs were dominated by 'native', highly assimilated, aristocratic Jews, but by the time of his death, the families that had made up the 'Cousinhood' had almost completely retreated and all the main Jewish communal bodies were dominated by people with Eastern European backgrounds.

It is something of a paradox that IIM, with his firm and unwavering views on Zionism, found himself in a country where Zionism was to become more prominent than in any other Diaspora country. Due to historical factors going back to the nineteenth century, notably the philanthropic activities of Sir Moses Montefiore, the strong strain of Christian religious advocacy of Jewish restoration of Palestine, and the impact of British diplomatic interests in the Middle East, Anglo-Jewish communal organisations had an interest in Palestine even before Britain became the Mandatory power there.[10] IIM became embroiled in the issues arising from the Britain Mandate in Palestine and the chronic ideological controversy about the Zionist idea that spanned his career in England.

The seismic shifts that formed the backcloth to IIM's ministry had opposite impacts on his career; they served both to enhance his prominence and to limit his achievements. IIM's short-term influence was immense. All the signs were that, prior to his arrival, the nascent Liberal Jewish movement was fragile and its chances of survival were very low. Without underestimating the contribution of Claude Montefiore and Lily Montagu, who both played a seminal role in establishing Liberal Judaism, the endurance of the Liberal Jewish movement can be attributed almost exclusively to IIM. It was IIM who shaped the ideas, practices, liturgies, organisational structures and procedures of English Liberal Judaism. IIM was generous in paying tribute to those who worked alongside him in the early days of the movement, but there can be no doubt that he was the inspiration and, above all the communicator, of Liberal Judaism. Claude Montefiore and Lily Montagu laid the foundation stones of Liberal Judaism in England, but IIM built the edifice.

Many of the first members of the LJS joined the new synagogue because they wanted a form of religion that was comparable to English church services confirming their status in English society; they wanted to be 'more English than the English'. Once IIM arrived they joined because of his persuasive arguments, his charisma, his scholarship and his organisational abilities. Although some found his statements too controversial, most were proud to be associated with a man who quickly gained a national profile and a high standing in Anglo-Jewry. Social workers were attracted by the emphasis he placed on social responsibility, and families came who wanted a high quality Jewish education for their children. IIM was particularly successful in drawing in those who had either left Judaism or were on the verge of doing so – the unaffiliated, the indifferent and the remiss.

Having first focussed his attention on consolidating the congregation of the LJS, IIM turned his attention to spreading understanding of Liberal Judaism and to developing new congregations. He was sufficiently liberal in his outlook to enable communities to be formed in a way that best suited the needs of congregants. It was no small achievement that during the forty years of his ministry, IIM was one of the prime movers in founding sixteen Liberal congregations, despite tremendous opposition and the trials of two world wars.

Not only was IIM pivotal in building the congregation of the LJS and several other communities, his leadership of the LJS Religion School, his engagement with young LJS members and his links with university students were vital in ensuring the sustainability of the Liberal Jewish movement. He recruited a new generation of synagogue members and also identified and developed future lay and religious leaders including Leslie Edgar, who became his son-in-law and succeeded him as Senior Rabbi at the LJS, and John Rayner who served as the rabbi at South London Liberal Synagogue before taking over from Leslie Edgar at the LJS.

IIM's skills and energy were critical in developing the Liberal Jewish movement in Britain but, more importantly, he was responsible for the character of the movement – he gave it a distinctive theology. This theology was a very radical one, almost a replica of the American Reform movement at the time of its widest swing in the pendulum away from tradition, which he preached frequently and with great clarity. He did make some concessions to the conservative culture of Anglo-Jewry, but they were largely limited to what he referred to as 'outward practices'; the core beliefs of English Liberal Judaism as IIM developed it remained truly radical.

Speaking out on political, economic and social issues was undoubtedly IIM's hallmark. He was an independent thinker and, at no time during the four decades of his time in England, did he fail to throw down the challenge of independent thought. He insisted on equal rights for men and women long before such an idea was dreamt of elsewhere in Anglo-Jewry and repeatedly took a high profile on controversial issues such as money lending, gambling, conscientious objection, birth control and euthanasia. Over time, IIM's views began to shape practices across the Jewish community. Although he was somewhat coy about saying so, it is nevertheless clear that West London Synagogue, adopted more progressive practices because of IIM's pioneering initiatives and, when it was officially formed, the British Reform movement benefitted from the many battles he had fought and won.

IIM's influence became more and more extensive. As Chairman of the Executive Committee of WUPJ, he helped to spread Liberal Judaism in Europe and elsewhere. He guided it skilfully through several crises, he was largely responsible for the breadth of its programmes, and his counsel often determined its policy.[11] Working in tandem with Lily Montagu, his radical brand of Judaism was replicated in English-speaking countries such as South Africa, New Zealand and Australia. However, his influence extended beyond Progressive Judaism. Before his arrival in England, organised dialogue and joint working between Christians and Jews would have been unimaginable. However, like many American Reform rabbis of his generation, IIM excelled in representing Judaism to the Christian community, and one of his most impressive achievements was in shaping the views of non-Jews on both Judaism and on current social issues.

Through the London Society of Jews and Christians, IIM came into contact with leading Christian theologians such as Canon Raven, Dean Matthews and Archbishop William Temple, who were influenced by him to no small degree. They knew that he was a man who respected their point of view, and who could be relied upon to state the facts about the Jewish religion objectively and without hidden motives, polemic or defensiveness.[12] They frequently turned to him when they needed a reliable explanation of a Talmudic passage. It is interesting to note that whereas IIM was often criticised by Jewish communal leaders for detracting from the cohesiveness of Anglo-Jewry, he was described by a prominent Christian leader as 'a peace maker' and 'one of the reconciling spirits of our time'.[13]

IIM's Sunday services attracted audiences of over 1,000 people, including a large proportion of non-Jews, putting them on a par with the audiences attracted by Stephen Wise at his Sunday services at Carnegie Hall, New York and Emil G. Hirsch at Temple Sinai in Chicago. IIM's polemic lecture-sermons had a major impact on shaping public opinion on matters that some others did not have the courage or inclination to discuss. The non-Jews attending his Sunday services were deeply impressed by a Judaism they could understand and by the relevance of its teachings, as expounded by IIM, to general human problems.

IIM came to England with a Jewish and rabbinic education that few in Anglo-Jewry could match, including Jewish scholars, with the obvious exception of Israel Abrahams. His learning enabled him to speak with authority on religious matters, and his extraordinary knowledge of Jewish sources, which he added to throughout his life, allowed him to challenge and work as a peer with some of the great Jewish scholars of his later years, such as Isidore Epstein. Some scholars who devoted themselves full time to Jewish studies expressed admiration at the range of his Jewish knowledge. Since his demise, there have been few Jewish scholars who have been able to speak with an authority equal to IIM's.

In his later years IIM published a number of books written in his eloquent but concise style: he said in a single sentence what others made less clear in many.[14] The books were praised by reviewers from across the Jewish community for their scholarliness and their accessibility, and although they may not have made a major impact on Jewish learning in general, they became highly influential in Progressive Jewish circles both in England and elsewhere. Several generations of Liberal Jews were brought up on his deceptively slim *Essentials of Liberal Judaism*. Equally impressive and influential were his wartime newsletters to LJS members of the Armed Forces, and the journal he edited (initially entitled the *Jewish Religious Union Bulletin* and subsequently renamed the *Liberal Jewish Monthly*), which served as 'an invaluable medium of instruction and propaganda'[15] and which, because of its penetrating analysis of world events, gained the respect of many opponents of Liberal Judaism.

The character that Liberal Judaism developed as the result of IIM's leadership can largely be traced to the 'classical' Reform Judaism of his formative years, but it can also be attributed to several facets of his personality and the duration of his tenure during which he exercised them. Liberal Judaism owes much to his courage, his tenacity, his razor-sharp intelligence, his incisive mind, his oratorical skills, and the coherence of his religious beliefs. However, there were also a number of ways in which IIM's personality limited his success.

While IIM certainly ensured the survival of Liberal Judaism in England, the radical course that he steered for the movement meant that it was only ever going to appeal to a limited number of people. The form of Liberal Judaism that he promulgated was one that had taken root in America in the favourable and particular conditions that existed there. IIM sought to transplant 'classical' Reform Judaism into a largely hostile environment, where it was out of kilter with the general conservatism of Anglo-Jewry. It was a bold experiment and his commitment to intellectual purity meant that he was willing to make few concessions. His determination, articulacy and charisma enabled his views to prevail in a congregation where the members generally had little Jewish education or regarded religion merely as an ornament of their respectability. The limited appeal of 'classical'

Reform Judaism was reinforced by IIM's candidness: his controversial and sometimes provocative statements served to alienate some of those who might otherwise have been sympathetic to his viewpoint, and even some of those within the Liberal Jewish movement itself.

As IIM himself identified, the conditions that existed after the Second World War were conducive to modern religions. However, his unwavering commitment to a form of Judaism that grew out of Victorian liberalism and optimism meant that British Liberal Judaism was poorly placed to take advantage of the new opportunities. To a diminishing number of those who knew him well, IIM was unforgettable and without equal, but to others his form of Judaism was increasingly passé. There were even some murmurings of discontent at the LJS.[16] In his *Essentials of Liberal Judaism*, IIM stated that the aim of Liberal Judaism was 'to develop as life changes in social outlook and human thought grows'.[17] It is therefore ironic that, under his leadership, Liberal Judaism failed to respond to new needs, fresh currents of opinion and changed conditions.

During the 1930s and 1940s there was a sea change in American Reform Judaism, but due to IIM's resistance to change, English Liberal Judaism remained radical and was at risk of becoming another form of orthodoxy. IIM was aware that 'classical' Reform Judaism was increasingly under attack for its negativity, its rejection of what were perceived to be indispensable aspects of Judaism and for creating damaging dichotomies between reason and emotion, universalism and nationalism, ethics and ritual, and Jewish religion and Jewish peoplehood.[18] However, what others saw as continuing evolution, IIM saw as 'a crisis'.[19] One admiring reviewer of this time summed up IIM's position as:

> that of a brave soldier who was left behind in a lonely outpost of a great battle, to defend a crucial position. He held that position stubbornly, defended courageously, and won a lone victory, while the rest of the army was defeated and surrendered to the enemy.[20]

This situation was compounded when IIM's role as Senior Rabbi at the LJS, and then as religious leader of the Liberal Jewish movement, was taken over by his son-in-law, Leslie Edgar. Having been personally nurtured and prepared for the role by IIM,[21] and because of his close family relationship, Leslie Edgar felt unable to reinvent Liberal Judaism to suit the circumstances of post-war Britain. He continued four-square IIM's insistence on the best of modern scholarship, inclusiveness, intellectual honesty, the free discussion of religious problems presented by the modern age and an overriding universalism and ethics-led view of what it means to be Jewish. However, he injected little that was new. IIM's impact on post-war Liberal Judaism was therefore profound in that Leslie Edgar replicated his views and outlook, but as a result it started to become a religion of the past rather than a religion of the future.[22] In particular, although the congregation of the LJS grew and continued to attract a core of earnest believers searching for the religious satisfaction that the conventions of the majority did not give them, it lost its attraction for many young people, whose involvement in the movement was largely secular.

Leslie Edgar was a man of outstanding intellect – he obtained a double first from Cambridge – and a man of strong principles. However, he was a stabilising link between the pre- and post-war generations[23] rather than the forerunner of a new era in Liberal Judaism. Several of his contemporaries and those who knew him well recognised what a massive undertaking it was for him to follow such a charismatic and outstanding leader as IIM.[24] In spite of the understandings he gained while serving as a Jewish Chaplain in the Armed Forces during the Second World War, Leslie Edgar found it difficult to sustain the inspiration that IIM gave the Liberal Jewish movement. As Senior Rabbi at the LJS, Leslie Edgar was de facto religious head of the Liberal Jewish movement. As a result, during his tenure, many of IIM's views remained official policy, but within individual Liberal synagogues changes started to be made by rabbis who came from a different background from that of radical Reform. Tensions started to build up in the movement and it began to lose some of the spiritual vitality that had characterised it under IIM's early leadership.

Leslie Edgar worked long and hard for what he believed. Due to ill health brought about by his unremitting labours,[25] his leadership of the Liberal Jewish movement was comparatively short. He retired at the age of 56 in 1962 and was followed as Senior Rabbi at the LJS by John Rayner. It was at this point that the 'second phase' of Liberal Judaism began.[26] Although IIM had been his iconoclastic mentor and still exercised an immeasurable influence on him, John Rayner questioned IIM's lack of attention to rabbinic Judaism and believed that he had underestimated the emotion and the difficulties of self-discipline.[27] In placing the emphasis on attracting those who had left Judaism IIM had, John Rayner felt, rendered the movement too restricted in its appeal:

> Liberal Judaism created for itself an unfortunate image, as a form of Judaism for those more or less alienated from traditional Jewish life and learning, for those who want to be Jewish but not overmuch, as a rescue operation for the victims of assimilation.[28]

John Rayner argued that the cataclysmic events that had occurred since the founding of Liberal Judaism required two things: to restate what

Liberal Judaism stood for and to bring the movement more forcefully to the attention of the wider Anglo-Jewish community 'as a serious alternative to orthodoxy, and ultimately perhaps as the norm of Jewish life in this country'.[29] Furthermore, the revised message must now be expressed in the 'idiom of our own day' and 'even better' than it had been propounded by the founders of Liberal Judaism, including by IIM.

Under John Rayner's spiritual leadership, Liberal synagogues readopted (or in the case of the newer ones, simply adopted) some traditional elements in services. There was more use of Hebrew, increased wearing of *tallitot* and (practices that IIM had declared optional and personally disliked), more enjoyment of and other minor festivals such as *Tisha B'Av*. There was also more discussion of Jewish observance outside the synagogue. While IIM was willing to countenance only one form of Jewish identity, a religious one, John Rayner recognised that many Jews now had a composite Jewish identity; they wished to be connected to the history of the Jewish people as well as to the Jewish religion and so *Yom ha-Atz-ma'ut* (Israel Independence Day) and *Yom ha-Sho'ah* (commemorating the Holocaust) were introduced.

However, John Rayner's debt to IIM remained abundantly evident. IIM had established the principal of 'freedom of the pulpit' and John Rayner, along with some other Liberal rabbis, continued to criticise Israeli government policy and some Israeli and Zionist attitudes, whenever they felt them to be falling short of the particular ethical standards expected of Jews. Rituals and observances may have become more traditional, but the theology of Liberal Judaism had not.

John Rayner was not the only person responsible for changing Liberal Judaism. Under the leadership of Rabbi Sidney Brichto, the first full-time executive director of the Liberal Jewish movement, it detached itself from the LJS. It moved to the refurbished West Central Synagogue, renamed the Montagu Centre, and introduced a new funding regime that made it financially independent from the LJS. Although it remained the oldest, largest and most influential of the Liberal synagogues, the LJS no longer dominated ULPS, and greater diversity in practice and belief began to characterise the movement. This trend towards increased pluralism was reinforced when in 1964 ULPS joined in the running of the Leo Baeck College set up by the Reform movement in 1956. From 1965, rabbinic students trained together for both Liberal and Reform synagogues. The rabbinic leadership of the Liberal Jewish movement now included rabbis from a multiplicity of backgrounds and with varying views on the balance between tradition and modernity.

Over the last four decades Liberal Judaism has continued to evolve, reflecting changes in society and the religious needs of successive generations. It is now markedly different from the radical form of Judaism shaped by IIM. However, the legacy of IIM remains strong and suffuses the movement. The emphasis on inclusivity, the importance placed on ethical values, the insistence on equal rights for women, and the prominence of inter-faith dialogue can all be traced back to IIM. While the philanthropic work of the type IIM advocated has not been such a necessity since the coming of the welfare state, Liberal Judaism still stresses the paramount importance of *mitzvah* (doing good) and *tikkun olam* (healing the world), some would say at the expense of the movement's spiritual agenda.[30]

This biography of IIM has brought attention to a number of other ways in which the spirit of IIM lives on. His prayer books, which he compiled single-handedly, have been described as being 'idiosyncratic' by some, but also praised for being 'bold, imaginative, creative, universalistic, visionary, and almost completely emancipated from any subservience to traditional norms'.[31] They display his keen eye for the apt in unlikely places and breathe of broad learning and genuine inward piety. As David Einhorn did in the nineteenth century, IIM stands out above all other compilers of Progressive Jewish liturgies in the twentieth century.

After the Second World War some newer members of the Liberal Jewish movement found IIM's prayer books overly severe, yet his prophetic ethical zeal and spiritual, literary and prayerful inspiration permeate John Rayner's subsequent liturgical efforts with Rabbi Chaim Stern (*Service of the Heart* and *Gates of Repentance*).[32] IIM clearly impressed on John Rayner the necessity of composing new prayers in the vernacular that speak to the heart and mind of the inquiring modern Jew. His influence is also still very much in evidence in the current Liberal Jewish prayer books (*Siddur Lev Chadash*, edited by John Rayner and Chaim Stern, and *Machzor Ruach Chadasha*, edited by rabbis Andrew Goldstein and Charles Middleburgh), [33] which continue IIM's practice of drawing on a wide range of Jewish and non-Jewish sources.

IIM's 'text-books' are still read with appreciation within the movement. However, the process of writing this biography has also brought to light his exceptional sermons and addresses, which not only provide a fascinating insight into his religious and ethical beliefs, but which are also an invaluable commentary on topical events from a Liberal Jewish point of view. The prophetic values that he espoused with fervour in his sermons and addresses (and his other writings) remain as valid and topical today as they were sixty or seventy years ago. They constitute an important component of the telling of IIM's life story but they are also an invaluable resource for current and future generations.

Once the 'maverick outsider',[34] Liberal Judaism is now more in the mainstream of *k'lal Yisrael* (shared sense of community amongst Jews) than it was in IIM's time and has, in some ways, become part of the Jewish establishment. As Rabbi David Goldberg has pointed out 'It is no longer daring and slightly scandalous to join a Liberal synagogue.'[35] Non-conformity is more acceptable than it was and certainly in terms of religious practices, Liberal Judaism has moved from being extremely radical to a left of centre position, which has broadened its appeal. Although the overall size of the movement has only grown slightly during the past two decades, and there has been a shifting of the membership from the metropolitan to newer suburban and provincial synagogues, Liberal Judaism now attracts people from all walks of life, from other branches of the Anglo-Jewish community as well as a significant number of converts. Although comparatively small, the Liberal Jewish movement is just as vibrant and more self-confident in its relationship with tradition than it was in IIM's day. To use John Rayner's parlance, it is no longer just a 'rescue operation'.

Some of the movement's longer-standing members regret what they see as the loss of the pioneering and proselytising spirit that imbued its early years, and are uncomfortable with the reintroduction of some traditional practices, such as *tashlich*.[36] However, the movement continues to place itself at the 'cutting edge' of Jewish affairs. This has meant that it has not captured the hearts and minds of the majority of the Anglo-Jewish community, but it has retained the commitment of a number of families who were amongst the founders of the JRU and the LJS.

At the same time as the Liberal Jewish movement has become less radical, the Reform movement has also evolved. The vast majority of Reform synagogues have now adopted, in some form or another, the once controversial initiatives introduced by IIM. As the two movements have become closer in their principles and practices, the possibility of a merger between the Liberal and the Reform movements has at times been broached, but never achieved. Ostensibly one of the sticking points to merger has been the question of Jewish identity, with Liberal Judaism more readily without conversion the child of a Jewish father and a non-Jewish mother, provided the child has had a Jewish upbringing.

In the second decade of the twenty-first century, a move towards a closer relationship between the two Progressive movements is again being discussed and is seen by some as being inevitable, and as a necessity for survival in an era of a rising tide of ultra-orthodoxy, particularly since the two movements have now trained their rabbis together for fifty years. Others maintain that such a move will only be achieved at the expense of the dilution of the principles that IIM stood for and which the movement still holds dear. These people call instead for 'urgent reconstruction' and a refreshed 'theology credible in today's world'.[37]

In many respects the legacy of IIM is invisible; this is partly due to the mere passage of time. People now take for granted many of the values that he promulgated and they are no longer novel in the way that they were 100 years ago. However, it is also the result of a changed social climate: while many of IIM's messages are no less potent than they were, they are now more acceptable. However, some aspects of IIM's legacy are still clearly recognisable in the movement. IIM's belief in speaking the truth, his insistence on intellectual integrity and willingness to say what he believed in have an abiding presence. Although perceptions of what constitutes truth may have changed from one generation to the next, Liberal Jews today still take great pride in belonging to a movement that speaks out candidly on issues of the day and see it as an effective counterbalance to the desire for conformity that still exists within Anglo-Jewry.

Finally, in this assessment of IIM's legacy, we might ponder on what IIM himself might have made of Liberal Judaism today. He would have been delighted by the continued growth of religion schools in Liberal communities and of religious education in general, but critical about the establishment of Progressive and cross-community Jewish day schools – he disapproved of faith schools because he wanted Jews to be integrated into wider society, not be separated from it, and because of their tendency to reduce religion school attendance.[38]

IIM may have been pleased about the emphasis on dialogue with a range of faith groups and interaction with other cultures, conversions from many different religions and the introduction of the membership category of 'Friends' to encourage the participation of those with an interest in Judaism, all of which are in keeping with his belief in the universalism of Judaism. However he may have looked askance at the growth of mixed marriages, and the number of non-Jewish partners who chose not to convert, as a step too far along the path to assimilation. A marriage blessing for a mixed faith couple would have been unimaginable to him, and the recognition of homosexual unions as out of the question, although he might have admired the spirit that has led the movement to be in the vanguard of the issue of same-sex marriages and endorsed the emphasis placed on the values of honesty and fidelity in such marriages.

Many of the rituals and observances that have been reintroduced would have been anathema to IIM. He would not have condoned the rationale of those congregations that choose to process the scroll or of those people who bow for the *Aleynu*. He would have been horrified that Torah services now sometimes include readings dealing with subjects such as animal sacrifice, which would have been taboo in IIM's day. He would have questioned the greater use of Hebrew and the return to the traditional structure of the liturgy in the Liberal Jewish prayer books. He may have been surprised by the affection with which many young people now regard Israel, albeit that they do so at the same time as having enormous concerns about the infringement of human rights. He would also have had misgivings about the more recent practice of both boys and girls *leyning* (reading) from the Torah, the voluntary undertaking of *mikveh* (ritual bath) for converts and *bedecken* (veiling) for brides.

On the other hand, IIM would have taken some consolation in the fact that Liberal Jews continue to reject fundamentalism and to resist the reintroduction of practices that risk marginalising members of the Jewish community or subject individuals to what are regarded by most Liberal Jews as being humiliating rituals, such as *mamzerut*, *chalitzah* and the giving of a non-reciprocal *Get*. These practices are seen as contradicting the ethical principles that lie at the heart of the prophetic Judaism in which IIM believed so fervently: justice, equality, human dignity and human rights.[39]

IIM would also have applauded the high profile roles that are now assumed by women as both lay leaders and rabbis, and although he may also have been disappointed that Liberal Judaism has failed to become a mass movement, he is likely to have been delighted that there are now forty Liberal congregations in various parts of Britain. As he pronounced himself, religious intensity, congregational commitment and integrity of principle, are more important than numerical growth.[40] Taking a wider view, he is likely to have been gratified that many of the ideas for which he stood now have currency across the Anglo-Jewish community and that the Liberal Jewish movement continues to show leadership on controversial issues, 'punching above its weight' in commenting on ethical questions.

As IIM would have wished, Liberal Judaism is thoroughly in keeping with 'the spirit of the age', remains faithful to many of the principles he pioneered, and the movement looks like it is here to stay. Many younger members of the movement may have a hazy knowledge of who Israel Isidor Mattuck was, but his ongoing presence is indisputable and, because of him, Liberal Judaism has stood the test of time and is enrolling the great-great-grandchildren of its founders in its religion schools. There has been change, but there has also been continuity and much of that continuity can be attributed to the legacy of IIM.

NOTES

1. Michael A. Meyer, *Response to Modernity – A History of the Reform Movement in Judaism* (New York: Oxford University Press, 1988), p.296.
2. Daniel Greene, *The Jewish Origins of Cultural Pluralism: The Menorah Association and American Diversity* (Bloomington, IN: University Press, 2011), p.22.
3. Henry Hurwitz became the editor of the *Menorah Journal* to which IIM was a regular contributor.
4. See Greene, *The Jewish Origins of Cultural Pluralism*, p.22.
5. Israel I. Mattuck, *The Essentials of Liberal Judaism* (London, ULPS, 1947), p.26.
6. Joan S. Friedman, 'The Making of a Reform Rabbi: Solomon B. Freehof from Childhood to HUC', *American Jewish Archives Journal* Vol. 58, no. 1–2 (2006), p.2.
7. Ibid., p.13.
8. Yaakov Ariel, 'Kaufmann Kohler and His Attitude Towards Zionism: A Re-examination', *American Jewish Archives Journal* Vol. 43, no. 2 (1991), p.216.
9. *Kol Nidre Sermon*, given by Rabbi David Goldberg at the LJS, 13 September 2013.
10. Gideon Shimoni, *From Anti-Zionism to Non-Zionism in Anglo-Jewry, 1917–1937*, *Jewish Journal of Sociology* Vol. 28, no.1 (1986), pp.19–48.
11. Sheldon Blank, 'Israel I. Mattuck', *CCAR Yearbook* 54 (1954), p.160.
12. John Rayner, 'The Legacy of Israel Mattuck', sermon given at the service in memory of Rabbi Dr Israel I. Mattuck, at South London Liberal Synagogue, 11 April 1954, LJS Archives, Box 135c.
13. Leon Roth and W.A.L. Elmslie, *The Significance of Biblical Prophecy for Our Time*, *The Rabbi Mattuck Memorial Pamphlet No. 1* (London: London Society of Jews and Christians, 1955), Preface by The Very Reverend W.R. Matthews, Dean of St Paul's, President of the London Society of Jews and Christians, p.3.
14. John D. Rayner, 'Israel Mattuck, A Man of the Past – and the Future', *Manna* (Winter 1993), p.15.
15. John D. Rayner, 'Israel I. Mattuck', slightly abridged version of a talk given at the South London Liberal Synagogue, 38 June 1957, LJS Archives, Box 135a.
16. 'Dr Mattuck's Retirement', *JC*, 13 February 1948, p.12.
17. See Mattuck, *Essentials of Liberal Judaism*, p.140.
18. See review of IIM's *Progressive Jewish Thought*, by David Polish, *Journal of Jewish Studies* Vol. 19, no. 1/2 (January–April 1957), p.71.
19. Dr Israel Mattuck, 'Judaism and the Future', *The Hibbert Journal* Vol. LII, no.1 (October 1953), pp.23–30.
20. 'WZ' [William Zuckerman, the editor], 'Rabbi Israel I. Mattuck, Liberal Judaism in England', *Jewish Newsletter Independent Thinking on Jewish Problems* Vol. X, no. 9 (26 April 1954) (New York), Mattuck Family Archive kept by Jill Mattuck Tarule (MFAa).
21. Rabbi Dr Leslie I. Edgar, *Some Memories of My Ministry* (London: Liberal Jewish Synagogue, 1985), p.7.
22. Rabbi David Goldberg, 'Rabbi Leslie Edgar', *LJS News*, July/August 2011, pp.4–6. In this article Rabbi Goldberg suggests that, under Leslie Edgar's leadership, Liberal Judaism became 'pickled in aspic'.
23. ULPS Oral History Project 1994–5, interview with Dorothy Edgar, LJS Archives, Box 139a.
24. See section on Leslie Edgar in Pam Fox, *A Place to Call My Jewish Home, Memories of the Liberal Jewish Synagogue 1911–2011* (London: Liberal Jewish Synagogue, 2011), pp.173–5.
25. Email from Robert Edgar 15 September 2013.
26. It is interesting to note that John Rayner's early addresses, such as his ordination address, 'The Task of Liberal Judaism' given in June 1953 are closely akin to IIM's own pronouncements. It is only as he established his position in the Liberal Jewish movement that John Rayner apparently felt free to question the views of his mentor.
27. John Rayner, 'The Next Chapter', in *A Jewish Understanding of the World* (Providence, RI and Oxford: Berghahn Books, 1998), pp.40–1.
28. Ibid., p.40.
29. Ibid., pp.40–1.
30. See *Kol Nidre Sermon*, given by Rabbi David Goldberg.
31. Rabbi John Rayner, 'The Liturgy of Liberal Judaism', unpublished paper dated 2002, LJS Archives, Box 135a.

32. Rabbi John D. Rayner and Rabbi Chaim Stern (eds), *Service of the Heart* (London: ULPS, 1967), and Rabbi John D. Rayner and Rabbi Chaim Stern (eds), *Gate of Repentance* (London: ULPS, 1973).
33. Rabbi John D. Rayner and Rabbi Chaim Stern (eds), *Siddur Lev Chadash* (London: ULPS, 1995) and Rabbi Andrew Goldstein and Rabbi Charles Middleburgh (eds), *Machzor Ruach Chadasha* (London: Liberal Judaism, 2003).
34. See *Kol Nidre Sermon*, given by Rabbi David Goldberg.
35. Ibid.
36. *Tashlik* (casting off) is a long-standing Jewish practice usually performed on the afternoon of Rosh Hashana.
37. See *Kol Nidre Sermon*, given by Rabbi David Goldberg.
38. See 'Should Jews Have Separate Schools?', sermon given by IIM at the LJS, 19 May 1923 and 'Denominational Schools', sermon given by IIM at the LJS, 1930 (undated), Montagu Centre Collection (MCC).
39. Rabbi Alexandra Wright, 'Why Liberals Brought Back Bar Mitzvahs', *JC*, 4 February 2011, p.23.
40. 'Liberal Judaism and the Future – Our Congregation', sermon given by IIM at the LJS, 11 January 1919, MCC.

Selected Bibliography

Primary Sources

American Jewish Archives (AJA), Cincinnati, Ohio

Abraham Feldman papers
American Council for Judaism papers
Central Conference of American Rabbis (CCAR) yearbooks
Collection of letters to Archibald Hillman
Hebrew Union College records
Henry Hurwitz papers
Julian Morgenstern papers
Morris Lazaron papers
Sheldon and Amy Blank papers
World Union for Progressive Judaism (WUPJ) records

Harvard University Archives, Cambridge, MA

Harvard University biographical files
Harvard University yearbooks and class albums

Liberal Jewish Synagogue Archives (LJS Archives), St John's Wood, London

Correspondence between Israel Mattuck and friends, family and colleagues in America
Correspondence relating to the appointment of IIM to the Liberal Jewish Synagogue
Liberal Jewish Synagogue Annual Reports
ULPS Oral History Project 1994 – five interviews
Various sermons and addresses given by Rabbi John Rayner

London Metropolitan Archives, London

Correspondence and other papers relating to the London Society of Jews and Christians
Correspondence between Claude Montefiore and IIM
Correspondence between IIM and family, friends and colleagues in America
Correspondence between IIM and friends and colleagues in England
Correspondence between Lily Montagu and IIM
Correspondence relating to IIM's citizenship
Obituary notices and articles following the death of IIM
Papers concerning IIM's proposed book on Judaism and Christianity
Reports and other documents relating to the World Union for Progressive Judaism, the Jewish Religious Union and liberal congregations

Mattuck Family Archive kept by Jill Mattuck Tarule (MFAa)

Capon, Naomi (née Mattuck), *Snippets from the Past – A Childhood from the Twenties* (unpublished manuscript, undated, c.1975)
Correspondence between IIM and Hebrew Union College

Letters from Corinne Mattuck to her family in America
Notes made by Dorothy Edgar, née Mattuck, dated 31 May 1999
'Odd Accidents and Greater Insight: An Evening with Robert Mattuck', taped interview by Jo Chickering, January 1963
Various documents and correspondence relating to IIM's citizenship
Various newspaper cuttings
Various photographs

Mattuck Family Archive kept by Robert Edgar (MFAb)

Correspondence between IIM and friends and colleagues in America and Britain
Draft of article by Dorothy Edgar, 'Some Recollections of Rabbi Israel I. Mattuck and Rabbi Doctor Leslie I. Edgar'
Letters relating to the invitation of Harry Pollitt to speak at the Liberal Jewish Synagogue
Originals of ordination and doctoral certificates and other papers relating to both
Tape recording of the diary kept by IIM between January and April 1918, read by IIM's daughter, Dorothy Edgar, née Mattuck
Various newspaper cuttings
Various obituary notices
Various photographs

Montagu Centre Collection (MCC)

Collection of sermons, articles and addresses dated 1906–53

Worcester Historical Museum, Worcester, Massachusetts

City and street directories for Worcester
Documents relating to the history of the Water Street area of Worcester
Journal of the *Chevra Gemara*

Secondary Sources

Behrman, S.N., *The Worcester Account* (Worcester, MA: Chandler House Press, 1996).

Birmingham, Stephen, *The Rest of Us: The Rise of America's Eastern European Jews* (New York: Syracuse University Press, 1999).

Brownfield, Peter Egill, 'The League of British Jews: Challenging Nationalism on Behalf of Jewish Universalism', American Council for Judaism, Fall 2001: www.acjna.org/acjna/articles.

Cohen, Lucy, *Some Recollections of Claude Montefiore, 1858–1938* (London: Faber and Faber, 1940).

Conrad, Eric V., *Lily H. Montagu: Prophet of a Living Judaism* (New York: self published, 1953).

Diner, Hasia. *A New Promised Land: A History of Jews in America* (New York: Oxford University Press, 2003).

Edgar, Leslie I., *Some Memories of My Ministry* (London: Liberal Jewish Synagogue, 1985).

Eliach, Yaffa, 'The Shtetl Household', www.rtrfoundation.org.

Endelman, Todd M., *The Jews of Britain 1656 to 2000* (Berkeley and Los Angeles, CA and London: University of California Press, 2002).

Feingold, Norma and Sadick, Nancy, *Water Street: World Within a World* (Worcester, MA: Worcester Historical Museum, 1984).

Greenbaum, Masha, *The Jews of Lithuania: a History of a Remarkable Community, 1316–1945* (Jerusalem: Gefen Publishing House, 1999).

Greene, Daniel, *The Jewish Origins of Cultural Pluralism: The Menorah Association and American Diversity* (Bloomington, IN: Indiana University Press, 2011).
Fox, Pam, *A Place to Call My Jewish Home: Memories of The Liberal Jewish Synagogue, 1911–2011* (London: Liberal Jewish Synagogue, 2011).
Friedman, Joan S., 'The Making of a Reform Rabbi: Solomon B. Freehof from Childhood to HUC', *American Jewish Archives Journal* 58, no.1–2 (2006), pp.1–49.
Joselit, Jenna Weissman, 'Without Ghettoism: A History of the Intercollegiate Menorah Association, 1906–1930', *American Jewish Archives Journal* 30, no.2 (1978), pp.133–54.
Karabel, Jerome, *The Chosen: The Hidden History of Admission and Exclusion at Harvard, Yale and Princeton* (Boston, MA and New York: Houghton Mifflin Company, 2005).
Kershen, Anne J. and Romain, Jonathan A., *Tradition and Change: a History of Reform Judaism in Britain, 1840–1995* (London and Portland, OR: Vallentine Mitchell, 1995).
Kessler, Edward, *An English Jew: The Life and Writings of Claude Montefiore* (London and Portland OR: Vallentine Mitchell, 2002).
Kolsky, Thomas A., *Jews Against Zionism: The American Council for Judaism, 1942–1948* (Philadelphia, PA: Temple University Press, 1990).
Kupovetsky, M., 'Population and Migration: Population and Migration before World War 1', YIVO Encyclopedia of Jews in Eastern Europe, 12 October 2010: www.yivoencyclopedia.org.
Langton, Daniel R., *Claude Montefiore: His Life and Thought* (London and Portland, OR: Vallentine Mitchell, 2002).
Levin, Dov, *The Litvaks: A Short History of the Jews of Lithuania*, trans. Adam Teller (New York: Berghahn Books, 2001).
Liberal Jewish Synagogue, *The First Fifty Years – A Record of Liberal Judaism in England, 1900–1950* (London: Liberal Jewish Synagogue, 1950).
Lipman, V.D., *A History of the Jews in Britain Since 1858* (Leicester: Leicester University Press, 1990).
Mattuck, Israel I., 'A Liberal Attitude to Tradition', *Emanu-El* (New York Edition), 30 September 1910.
Mattuck, Israel I., 'The Levirate Marriage in Jewish Law', in Julian Morgenstern, David Neumark and David Philipson (eds), *Studies in Jewish Literature: Issued in Honor of Professor Kaufmann Kohler, Ph.D, on the Occasion of his Seventieth Birthday, May the Tenth, Nineteen Hundred and Thirteen* (Berlin: Georg Reimar, 1913).
Mattuck, Israel I., 'The War and Reality'. Sermon preached at the Liberal Jewish Synagogue, 18 Hill Street, on New Year (London: Jewish Religious Union, 1914).
Mattuck, Israel I., *Our Aims* (London: Liberal Jewish Synagogue, 1916a).
Mattuck, Israel I., 'Religion and Society'. Sermon preached at the Liberal Jewish Synagogue, Morning Service, Pentecost, 27 May (Papers for Jewish People, No. XIV) (London: Jewish Religious Union, 1916b).
Mattuck, Israel I., 'Repentance and Hope'. Sermon preached at the Bechstein Hall on the Eve of the Day of Atonement (London: Jewish Religious Union, 1916c).
Mattuck, Israel I., *Judaism and the War* (London: Jewish Religious Union for the Advancement of Liberal Judaism, 1917).
Mattuck, Israel I. (ed.), *Services and Prayers for Jewish Homes* (London: Jewish Religious Union, 1918).
Mattuck, Israel I., 'Emil Gustav Hirsch', *Jewish Guardian*, 2 February 1923.
Mattuck, Israel I., *Liberal Jewish Prayer Book*: Vols. I, II and III (London Jewish Religious Union, 1926a, 1923, 1926b).

Mattuck, Israel I., *Bericht über das 'Liberale Judentum in England'* (Berlin: Weltverband für Religiös-Liberales Judentum, 1928a).

Mattuck, Israel I., *Liberal Judaism in England, Address given at the World Union for Progressive Judaism Conference in Berlin* (London: World Union for Progressive Judaism, 1928b).

Mattuck, Israel I., *The Trial of Jesus, A Jewish View* (London: Jewish Religious Union, 1929).

Mattuck, Israel I., 'The Conception of Man or Human Personality in Judaism', in *Transactions of the Society for Promoting the Study of Religions*, 1931a.

Mattuck, Israel I., *The Use of Armistice Day, From address given by Rabbi Mattuck at Armistice Commemoration Service, Liberal Jewish Synagogue* (London: privately published, 1931b).

Mattuck, Israel I., *The Jewish Approach to God* (published with *The Christian Approach to God* by Reverend A. Garvie) (London: London Society of Jews and Christians, 1934).

Mattuck, Israel I., *Immortality in Judaism* (Jewish Tract No. 21) (Cincinnati, OH: Tract Commission/Union of American Hebrew Congregations, 1935).

Mattuck, Israel I., *Faith and the Modern World* (London: Jewish Religious Union, 1937).

Mattuck, Israel I., *A Crisis in Civilization* (London: Jewish Religious Union, 1938a).

Mattuck, Israel I., *Our Debt to Claude Montefiore* (London: Liberal Jewish Synagogue, 1938b).

Mattuck, Israel I., *What Are The Jews? Their Significance and Position in the Modern World* (London: Hodder and Stoughton, 1939).

Mattuck, Israel I., *The Essentials of Judaism, from the Liberal Jewish Point of View* (London: Union of Liberal & Progressive Synagogues, 1946a).

Mattuck, Israel I., *Liberal Judaism, a Statement, in Brief, of its Teachings and Practices: Its Thought and Practice* (London: Union of Liberal Progressive Synagogues, 1946b).

Mattuck, Israel I., *The Essentials of Liberal Judaism* (London: George Routledge & Sons, 1947a).

Mattuck, Israel I., *Liberal Judaism: Its Thought and Practice* (London: Union of Liberal Progressive Synagogues, 1947b).

Mattuck, Israel I., *L'ebraismo liberale, il suo pensiero, le sue pratiche* (Firenze: Rinascimento del libro, 1950a).

Mattuck, Israel I., *Marriage – Doctrine and Practice of Liberal Judaism* (London: Union of Liberal and Progressive Synagogues, 1950b).

Mattuck, Israel I., *L'essenza dell'ebraismo liberale* (Modena: Guanda, 1951).

Mattuck, Israel I., 'Judaism and the Future', *Hibbert Journal* Vol. LII (October 1953), pp.23–30.

Mattuck, Israel I., *Jewish Ethics* (London and New York: Hutchinson's University Library, 1953a).

Mattuck, Israel I., *The Thought of the Prophets* (London: Allen and Unwin, 1953b).

Mattuck, Israel I., *Progressive Judaism* (London: World Union for Progressive Judaism, 1956).

Mattuck, Israel I., *El pensamiento de los profetas* (México: Fondo de Cultura Económica, 1962).

Mattuck, Israel I. and Coit, Stanton, *Spinoza Tercentenary Address* (London: Ethical Union, 1932).

Meyer, Michael A., *Response to Modernity – A History of the Reform Movement in Judaism* (New York: Oxford University Press, 1988).

Meyer, Michael A., *Hebrew Union College Jewish Institute of Religion: A Centennial History: 1875–1975* (Cincinnati, OH: Hebrew Union College, 1992).

Miller, Rory, *Divided Against Zionism, Anti-Zionist Opposition in Britain to the Jewish State in Palestine 1945–1948* (London and Portland, OR: Frank Cass, 2001).

Montagu, Lilian Helen and Mattuck, Israel I., *The Jewish Religious Union and Its Beginnings* (London: Jewish Religious Union, 1927).

Montefiore, Claude Goldsmid and Mattuck, Israel I., *Religion and Politics* (London: Jewish Religious Union, 1931).

Montefiore, Claude Goldsmid and Mattuck, Israel I., *Jewish Views on Jewish Missions* (London: Jewish Religious Union, 1933).

Montefiore, Claude Goldsmid, Mattuck, Israel I. and Montague, Lilian Helen, *Articles and Speeches on Various Topics* (London: Jewish Religious Union, 1913).

Nutt, Charles, *History of Worcester and Its People, Vol. 1* (New York: Lewis Historical Publishing Company, 1919).

Persoff, Meir, *Faith Against Reason – Religious Reform and the British Chief Rabbinate, 1840–1990* (London and Portland, OR: Vallentine Mitchell, 2008).

Rayner, John D., 'The Legacy of Israel Mattuck', in *The LJM, In Memoriam of Israel Mattuck 1883–1954* (June 1954).

Rayner, John D., 'Mattuck – The Boss', *LJS News* (January 1992).

Rayner, John D., 'Israel Mattuck, A Man of the Past – and the Future', *Manna* (Winter 1993), pp.14–16.

Rayner, John D., 'The Next Chapter', in *A Jewish Understanding of the World* (Providence, RI and Oxford: Berghahn Books 1998), pp.40–4.

Rigal, Lawrence and Rosenberg, Rosita, *Liberal Judaism: The First Hundred Years* (London: Liberal Judaism, 2002).

Rosenstein, Neil, *The Unbroken Chain: Biographical Sketches and Genealogy of Illustrious Jewish Families from the 15th–20th Century, Vols 1 and 2* (New York: Computer Centre for Jewish Genealogy, Second Edition, 1990).

Saperstein, Marc, '"Normative Judaism" in the Crisis of the War: Sermons by Abraham Cohen and Israel Mattuck', in Daniel R. Langton and Philip S Alexander (eds), *Melilah: Manchester Journal of Jewish Studies, Normative Judaism, Jews, Judaism, and Jewish Identity*, Proceedings of the British Association for Jewish Studies (BAJS) Conference 208, Supplementary no. 1 (2012), pp.52–65.

Sarna, Jonathan D. and Golden, Jonathan, 'The American Jewish Experience through the Nineteenth Century: Immigration and Acculturation', Brandeis University, National Humanities Centre: nationalhumanitiescenter.org.

Sarna, Jonathan D., Smith, Ellen and Kosofsky, Scott-Martin (eds), *The Jews of Boston, Essays on the Occasion of the Centenary of the Combined Jewish Philanthropies of Greater Boston* (New Haven, CT: Yale University Press in collaboration with the Combined Jewish Philanthropies of Boston, 2005).

Sharot, Stephen. 'Reform and Liberal Judaism in London: 1840–1940', *Jewish Social Studies* 41, no.3/4 (Summer–Autumn, 1979), pp.211–28.

Shimoni, G., 'From Anti-Zionism to Non-Zionism in Anglo-Jewry, 1917–1937', *Jewish Journal of Sociology* 28, no.1 (1986), pp.19–47.

Shimoni, G., 'The Non-Zionists in Anglo-Jewry, 1937–1948', *Jewish Journal of Sociology* 28, no.2 (1986), pp.89–115.

Silverstein, Alan, *Alternatives to Assimilation: The Response of Reform Judaism to American Culture, 1840–1930* (Boston, MA: Brandeis University Press, 1994).

Sorin, Gerald, *A Time for Building: The Third Migration, 1880–1920 (Vol. 3: The Jewish People in America)* (Baltimore, MD and London: Johns Hopkins University Press, New Edition, 1995).

Synnott, Marcia Graham, *The Half-Opened Door: Discrimination and Admissions at Harvard, Yale and Princeton, 1900–1970* (New Brunswick, NJ: Transaction Publishers, 2010).

Umansky, Ellen M., *Lily Montagu and the Advancement of Liberal Judaism: From Vision to Vocation* (New York: Edwin Mellen, 1984).

Wendehorst, Stephen E.C., *British Jewry, Zionism, and the Jewish State, 1936–1956* (Oxford Historical Monographs) (New York: Oxford University Press, 2012).

Younger Members' Organisation of the Liberal Jewish Synagogue, *The Years Between 1911–1951, LJS exhibition catalogue* (London: ULPS, 1951).

Unpublished Theses and Other Papers

Mattuck, Israel I., 'An Account of the Jewish Eschatology in the Sibylline Oracles' (unpublished rabbinic thesis, Hebrew Union College, 1909).

Neusner, Jacob, 'The Rise of the Jewish Community in Boston, 1880–1914' (unpublished BA thesis, Harvard University, 1953).

The Reminiscences of Maurice L. Perlzweig. Oral History Research Office, Columbia University, 1993.

Somers, William Harold, 'A Socio-Historical Study of the Jewish Community of Worcester Massachusetts' (unpublished MA thesis, Clark University, Worcester, MA, 1933).

Talamo, Joseph, 'A Preliminary Social Survey of the Jewish Population of Worcester: A Local Study of Immigration' (unpublished MA thesis, Clark University, Worcester, MA, 1915).

Index

Please note that page numbers relating to Notes will have the letter 'n' following the page number. 'IIM' stands for 'Israel Isidor Mattuck'.